The
Encyclopedia
of
Palmistry

THE

THE
ENCYCLOPEDIA
OF PALMISTRY

EDWARD D. CAMPBELL

A PERIGEE BOOK

A Perigee Book
Published by The Berkley Publishing Group
200 Madison Avenue
New York, NY 10016

First edition: January 1996

Published simultaneously in Canada.

Library of Congress Cataloging-in-Publication Data
Campbell, Edward D.
    The encyclopedia of palmistry / Edward D. Campbell. — 1st ed.
        p.   cm.
    "A Perigee book."
    Includes bibliographical references and index.
    ISBN 0-399-51977-7
    1. Palmistry.   I. Title.
BF921.C198   1996
133.6 — dc20   95-21732
                                                               CIP

Printed in the United States of America

10 9 8 7 6 5 4 3 2 1

CONTENTS

ACKNOWLEDGMENTS

I have many people to thank for this book. Monday Jones read my hand and said I could read palms. Robin Gile has shared many insights with me as we met and shared workshops and travel to fairs. So Mak offered his friendship and his comments, along with those of Hongyi on Chinese palmistry. Lori Aletha opened the door to my practice. The Experimental College of the students of the University of Washington has allowed me to learn through teaching the subject for many years. Gillian Spencer introduced me to my agent, Sandra Martin, who connected me with Perigee Books and The Berkley Publishing Group. Without Sandra I would not have known where to go with the work. Irene C. Prokop, senior editor for The Berkley Publishing Group, guided me to completion of the book with her suggestions. I would like to thank other palmists who have shared their insights with me over the years. Most of all, I would like to thank the thousands of clients who have shared with me their hands and many intimate details of their life. This book could never have been written without their input.

While others have made kind contributions, I must accept any of the faults the reader finds, for I have had the final word on what goes into this book. I hope each reader may find the subject as rewarding as I have.

INTRODUCTION

PURPOSE

The primary object of this book is to present a comprehensive survey of the major methods and developments in Western palmistry with more than an occasional reference to Eastern systems. We need to firmly recognize the entire body of knowledge we already claim, so that it can be tested and used in the expansion of our understanding of humankind. This book is written for the serious student of Western palmistry who would like to examine the various techniques available in analyzing the hand but cannot afford the money, time, effort, and/or library space that is necessary to acquire the many current and older treatises on the subject. For those who do wish to study further, the text has copious endnotes directing the serious student and practitioner to appropriate publications. To satisfy our publisher, I have included my own observations.

The secondary purpose of this publication is to gather the various observations and techniques used in hand analysis into one volume to begin the arduous task of comparative study of these techniques. I believe that when the serious student, researcher, and practitioner can see the competing applications side by side, he or she may make better choices for his or her own work and perhaps make greater strides in advancing the entire art and science of hand analysis.

The third purpose of this book is to be a helpful guide for the prospective student of palmistry and hand analysis, whether that student is a skeptic (as the author was) or is already a firm believer.

The fourth purpose of this book is to be a handy reference resource to the terminology used in the hand analysis literature and profession, whether that terminology is from the medical fields or the psychic arts.

While there are many excellent publications that pursue one or more of these plans and some that achieve some of these goals, I must confess I have found no complete guideline for this work. I admit that this book may appear to good practitioners as having many inadequacies. I hope they will share their observations with me. If the book is otherwise well received, I would like to use it as a model for further textual survey, perhaps in an expanded second edition or one that can include the works of several authors.

Because I believe that hand analysis deserves serious investigation and practitioners should have a professional role in modern society, I hope this work will encourage writing and publishing of survey texts in the field. In turn, I would hope that such publications will encourage specialized work in various fields of hand analysis.

Although this book's object is to survey the critical observations and methods of analysis associated with modern Western palmistry and hand analysis, to some extent, Western palmistry has been influenced by Eastern methods of analysis and some of these influences will also be included. Based upon that survey, my own observations, and some previously unpublished observations, I offer a critical guide and handy reference tool for the practice and further research of the serious palmist and hand analyst.

WHY STUDY THE HAND?

Part of examining the hand involves examination of the fingerprints and similar ridge lines throughout the insides of the hands. These are called dermal ridges and the field of dermal ridge examination is called dermatoglyphics.

Professional researchers Murray H. Seltzer, Chris C. Plato, and Kathleen M. Fox repeated public demand and the imperative need to develop cost-efficient methods to identify subjects either at risk for or already suffering from any given illness, without sacrificing quality of care. This appeared in a recent article on the dermatological identification of women with or at risk of breast cancer, appearing in a recent issue of the *American Journal of Medical Genetics*.[1] They pointed out that using dermatoglyphics is a rather unique and low-cost approach. I can add that because it is not invasive, it is also safe and generally painless.

In his foreword to Julius Spier's book on palmistry, *The Hands of Children*,[2] the noted psychiatrist Carl Jung observed that Spier's findings and knowledge would be of *essential* importance to psychologists, doctors and educators. Doctors are beginning to take the subject seriously. In discussions with educators, I have been able to show

them how they could avoid much trouble with children and design far more effective individual educational curriculums if only they would recognize certain traits that are clearly written in the formations of the hands.

I recall early in my practice advising a young lady on career choices. It was a short, fifteen-minute reading and I think she paid $8.00 or $10.00 for it. When I completed the reading she said that I had just told her what she had recently paid $350.00 to an employment career counselor to learn. Such feedback as that has eased my skeptical acceptance of the benefits of hand analysis. I frequently look at the hand and pinpoint areas of pain or distress in the body, from stomachaches, respiratory problems, sore shoulders, slipped disks, problems with the lower back, knee problems and a wide variety of problems all the way to grinding of teeth and temporomandibular joint dysfunction. If medicine and psychiatry were to look a little more favorably on our lore, there could be mighty strides in medical and psychological low-cost prediagnostic techniques.

I believe there are future careers for well-trained palmists in medicine, psychology, education, career development counseling, employment and health risk management, and even in sports medicine. Many a potential employer, about to spend large sums on a new employee, might well consider the report of a hand analyst before making the final choice. Simple observations that a palmist could make to distinguish the competitor from the person who is more inclined to smooth ruffled feathers could be of great benefit. A few observations on potential anger, illness, and even truthfulness might well be worth far more than any modest charges that would be made for the service.

I believe that it is time to recognize the painstaking work of palmists and researchers over the last century and a half and to raise the profession of hand analysis from its public image of charlatanism and fortune-telling to its true position as a scientific study that is well established in the halls of business, medicine, and education along with other forecasting professions such as economics, psychology, and medicine.

Let us for a moment consider fortune-telling. Palmists laugh when they are referred to as fortune-tellers. That puts them in good company with lawyers, stockbrokers, economic analysts, doctors, and, in fact, most professions, including even engineers. All of the success in our professions are based upon our abilities to see and plan for the future. Indeed, fortune-telling is the very frontier of science. Humanity's advancements have been dependent upon fortune-telling. Our failures can be laid to our blindness when it comes to future fortunes, because few, if any of us, start out to deliberately fail.

We could speak of credulous and incredulous fortune-telling, but a brief history of science would show the futility of such prejudice. Quantum physics, the basis for modern physics, even today is considered quite incredible by many. But what may be incredible with our present mental attitudes, when I try to fit it within a framework of comfortable logic and philosophy, becomes quite credible when I ask the practical question, "Does it work?" In my case, that is how I came to accept palmistry. So much of it does work that I can no longer deny it as a valuable human study.

THE PLAN OF THE BOOK

This book developed out of my students' course curriculum, which is designed to take the student, by phases, through an examination of the hand and to teach both how to examine the hand and the results of keen observations. Where such observations have been made in the past, reported interpretations as well as occasional, previously unpublished commentaries are shared.

A good palmist will start reading the subjects from the moment they come into view. The overall demeanor is observed. The reader will note the gait, the carriage of the person, the face and its expression, the odor if there is any, and how the hands are held. Much of that knowledge is beyond the bounds of this text.

The subject will often thrust a hand at the palmist, or ask which hand the reader wants to see, and the good palmist will take both hands gently as he or she reassures the subject that there is nothing to fear. The good reader communicates both to and from the subject with his or her hands.

We begin the examination with the hand forms. I look at both the front and back of the hands. The examination is both visual and by touch. I palpate various parts of the hand. I look at the fingers, the nails, the length of the various segments of the fingers, and the width, depth, and breadth of the palm. I observe the hand's shape, color, whether it has hair or not, even how well manicured are the nails.

Having made such a classification as a whole, I proceed to examine the fingers, their shape, their size in comparison to the palm, and their flexibility. I observe more closely the fingernails, long a subject of normal medical diagnostics.

From there, the examination and the book goes to patterns and shapes. One learns more of the geography of the palm and fingers. One looks at the generally unchanging dermal lines, both in the palm and fingers where they finally become fingerprints. One observes how certain parts of the hand are larger or more prominent than other areas. One learns the traditional names of all of these areas as one also studies the significance of each of these observations.

Finally, I come to the lines and marks so long associated with palmistry. They are divided into chapters dealing with the major and minor lines as well as a chapter dealing with specific marks. The chapters are all endnoted and these are gathered at the end of the book. The book also contains an extensive glossary, an appendix on several methods for taking palm prints, and a bibliography for further study.

The serious student should now read the appendix on printmaking and take at least five good sets of prints of friends before embarking on his or her own course in palmistry. A good, high-intensity light, a large magnifying glass, and a small hem marking ruler are all useful tools for the practitioner and student. Anyone who does not enjoy holding hands should not take the subject too seriously. To become proficient, think not of holding a few hands or even a hundred. Think of examining a thousand pairs of hands just to develop an eye and a feel for the subject.

The
Encyclopedia
of
Palmistry

CHAPTER ONE

WHERE WE ARE AND HOW WE GOT THERE

᭙᭙᭙᭙᭙᭙᭙᭙᭙᭙᭙᭙᭙᭙᭙᭙᭙᭙᭙᭙᭙᭙᭙᭙᭙᭙᭙᭙᭙᭙᭙᭙

Most of the ancient history of palmistry is sketchy. Tradition generally concludes that the true art of palmistry developed in India and from there traveled west through Persia and the Near East to Europe, and east into China, Korea, and Japan. The origin is shrouded in mystery and believed to date at least three thousand years ago. Fred Gettings, a historian and palmist of great repute, reports that other candidates for origination of palmistry include ancient Egyptians, Chaldeans, Sumerians, and Babylonians. He concludes that by the time Aristotle commented on it, the art was ancient.

In India there is said to be a system of palmistry that enables the palmist to tell the time and date of one's birth, how many brothers and sisters one has, and lay out the horoscope of each person read.

Certain modern palmists claim this ability. The Indian palmist V. A. K. Ayer claims that the skill is possessed by those who find references in old manuscripts where this information is written in verse. He admits that modern palmists know little of this work. Another palmist, Cyrus Abayakoon, claims to have studied it on ancient palm leaf manuscripts and he claims to practice it. He even wrote a book on it, but the book does not make any sense. Until there is proof that such a system does exist and can actually be used, I will place it in the same category as the stories of the advanced society of Atlantis.

The Indians used various systems for reading the hand that included interpreting signs found in the hand, which is a major feature of Hindu palmistry, the identification of rare lines in the hand,

and interpreting skin ridges on the palm and particularly on the thumb. We are told by Fitzherbert that the last system is not to be confused with the modern scientific study of skin ridges called dermatoglyphics. I will be looking at some of the Indian signs in this book.

V. A. K. Ayer translated one of the Sanskrit tests of an Indian system that interpreted rare signs called the Kartikeyan system. A sense of the interpretations that can be found by this method is the number nineteen found on the right hand of men. The drawing shows what I today commonly call a ring of Saturn, which is a crease line in the form of an arc like a bowl below the middle finger. It is not a favorable sign in modern palmistry, but under the Kartikeyan system it is called Hara and defined as:

> Hara is found beneath the middle finger shining like the crescent moon. In proportion to the strength of the line, it makes men beloved of their kings. In the case of women it makes them become royal consorts or equally powerful persons wearing valuable jewels. The suggestion of splendor is the cause of its name.[1]

Fred Gettings quotes a marvelous line of early Indian text as the earliest reference to palmistry. This is found in the Vasishtha Rule 21: It is forbidden for the aesthetic to earn a living "by explaining prodigies and omens, or by skill in astrology and palmistry." Vasishtha is referred to as a priest who consecrated Rama as the king of Ayodhya, and also as a family of priests. The texts are of Vedic origin.

Depending on whose translation one uses, references to information that can be read from the hand can be found in the Bible. In the King James Version of the Bible, Job chapter 37 verse 7 states: "He sealeth up the hand of every man; that all men may know his work." In seventeenth-century England, the seal was more than a mere signature. It identified the owner by his rank and position in society. Some read this as a statement that God put the marks into the hand so that those who know how to decipher this holy writing can determine the place and divine purpose of each person.

I mentioned this in a lecture in Calgary only to receive a letter of protest. The protestor had a slightly different translation that said, "He seals the hand of every man, that all men may know His work." This appears to be a quote from the American Standard Bible Reference Edition, published for the Lockman Foundation in 1973. The lady assured me that this made reference to the weather and referred to surrounding verses for support. She quoted another source as saying the translation should be "He seals *up* the hand of every man." She concluded that this verse referred to a time of year when man should withdraw from his work, should seal his hand, and contemplate his work.

This started me on the trail of the real meaning of Job chapter 37 verse 7. I found four sources that supported our antagonist. The New English Bible with the Apocrypha, Oxford University Press, 1970, states, "He shuts every man fast indoors, and all men whom he has made stand idle." The translation in The Way, The Living Bible, illustrated, Catholic edition, Campus Life Publications, 1983 (11th printing) states, "Man's work stops at such a time, so that all men everywhere may recognize his power." The New International Version, by the International Bible Society, 1984, translated the verse as "So that all men he has made may know his work, he stops every man from his labor." Finally, the Good News Bible of the American Bible Society, 1976, translates the verse as "He brings the work of men to a stop; he shows them what he can do."

My antagonist seemed to have the better of it. Yet there was some doubt still. The Oxford University Press New Revised Standard Version of the Bible seemed to be confusing. Verses 6 and 7 read together say, "For to the snow he says, 'Fall on the earth;' and the shower of rain, serves as a sign on everyone's hand, so that all whom he has made may know it." There was a note after the translation that says that the meaning of verse 7 is uncertain. Does the book of Job say that the hand is a weather barometer? Robert Young's Literal Translation of the Holy Bible, 1989, revised edition, helped add to the confusion. This translation says, "Into the hand of everyman he sealeth, [power]. For the knowledge by all men of His work."

I returned to comfort when I read the New World Translation of the Holy Scriptures rendered from original languages by the New World Bible Translation Committee, revised 1984: "On the hand of every earthling man he puts a seal for every mortal man to know his work." I believe there is a seal on both hands of all people who have hands. It is tied in with genetics and this book will help the reader understand ways to read that seal. But I admit that I have little concrete historical support from the conflicting translations of the Bible.

The English palmist, Terence Dukes, attributes the development of Chinese hand analysis to the Indian Vedic schools modified by Buddhist beliefs.[2] He acknowledges that there was also a native form of physiognomy, which he calls Jen Hsiang, that includes a primitive form of hand analysis. Another form that developed was called Shou Hsiang. *Shou* indicates *hand*. This was used by monks largely in a medical setting.

Fitzherbert traces Chinese palmistry back to at least 1000 B.C.E. in some form. It seemed to be mixed with the art of reading faces. He reports that according to his sources, Chinese palmistry is extinct among Chinese palmists today, and they all use the Western system, but I know of one Chi-

nese palmist who practices in Canada and returns periodically to China for refreshers. Parts of the traditional Chinese dating systems are included in this book.

Hachiro Asano traces the art of Japanese palmistry back to India. He traces the art through the history of sculpture, showing how the creases of the hand can be found in the ancient statues of Buddha.[3] He noted the absence of such lines in Grecian statues and concluded that this was evidence of the Greeks' lack of interest in palmistry. I have noted a considerable absence of hands and arms from surviving Greek statues but am not ready to attribute that to some lost art of Greek palm reading. Two of our books on ancient art reflect stylized lines on ancient Grecian bowls, one from about 480 B.C.E.[4] and several from various times.[5] The lack of lines in any except early Buddhist art led Asano to conclude that reading fate and personality from the palms originated in India in the first millennium B.C.E.

Asano points out that the Buddhist art used hand positions to express psychological and spiritual meanings. The form is called *mudras* and when found on Buddhas, divinities, and bodhisattvas, mudras indicate vows or attitudes. He points out similar customs in Christian art. He also notes that the Japanese *ninja* used hand positions to control their mental conditioning. This book discusses how the involuntary positions of the hands indicate mental conditioning and how certain changes of the hand positions can increase self-assurance and control.

Asano agrees with Dukes that the early history of palm reading in China was tied to face reading. He cites the existence of a text on these subjects from 1122 B.C.E. during the Zhou dynasty. The Japanese, great aficionados of fortune-telling, were a fertile land for the future growth of palm reading. Physiognomy and related hand divination was popular with the higher classes in Japan during the Heian period (794 to 1185 C.E.). It came to popularity with the merchants later, during the Edo period (1603 to 1867) and this is the time of the father of modern Japanese palmistry and physiognomy, Mizuno Namboku.

The Namboku or Japanese system uses the study of fate to give each subject the opportunity to do something about it. Fate is not to be feared so much as altered or improved. Thus, Asano describes Japanese palmistry as having "strong elements of deliverance" in it. The reader who finds misfortune then looks to other areas of the hand to find deliverance. Palmistry is described as the most popular form of fortune-telling in Japan.

I have read for a number of Japanese and have found their questions fascinating. One young lady asked me what was the best course of action for her clan, an ancient noble clan that had largely been dispossessed by MacArthur's new constitution at the end of World War II. Of particular interest to her was the recent investment directed by the head of the family in a leisure complex. Did that not violate their honor? I was presented two eighteen-year-old hands to study. These questions and questions about her future mate were central to the hour-long reading. All of her questions revolved around the family and honor. Family honor is not a typical question I have encountered in reading Western hands. Another of my most fascinating clients was a young Japanese woman born with only one hand, and that almost without fingers, having barely a rudimentary thumb and a limp single bump in the area of the little finger. For such a client to come to a palmist seems to show a remarkable cultural acceptance of the art of palmistry.

There are two fairly reliable historians of the art of palmistry in the twentieth century, Fred Gettings and Andrew Fitzherbert. Fred Gettings is a modern English palmist of great repute. Gettings's historical work appears in a wonderful coffee table book entitled *The Book of the Hand: An Illustrated History of Palmistry*, first published in 1965.[6] Fitzherbert is another modern palmist whose work is highly valued by professional palmists. Andrew Fitzherbert's more extensive treatise and valuable bibliography, *The Palmist's Companion: A History and Bibliography of Palmistry*,[7] appeared in 1992. I encourage every serious student to acquire copies of these important books for a more detailed history of the art. Most of the following material relies heavily upon these works.

There is no evidence of the actual Western origin of reading hands and not much evidence of it in the West prior to the Middle Ages. Early reference is found in Aristotle's *De Historia Animalium*. Pliny mentioned it in his *Natural History*, and there is a mention of a lost treatise on the subject dating from about 240 B.C.E. Fred Gettings refers to a quote from Juvenal, the Roman poet and satirist, who referred to it as "the cheap chiromancer's art."[8]

Today, palmistry strives to be a coherent system, but ancient palmistry was probably a matter of fortune-telling and far more an art than a science. Ancient manuscripts are adorned with fantastic signs most probably never seen in the hand. If they were seen, their very rarity would baffle the current palmist. The ancient Japanese and Chinese statutes do show lines and their systems have been known for several thousand years.

The palmistry that began to flourish in the late Middle Ages and at the beginning of the Renaissance may have come to Europe from the Arabs. Arabian palmistry was integrated into the Islamic religion. It was a legitimate part of the Islamic sciences, since the hand was a religious symbol. Apparently, the name of Allah is formed by the fingers. The planets and the prophets rule sections of the hands. Adam presides over the moon, Aissa over Mercury, Joseph over Venus, Idris over the Sun, David over Mars, Jupiter is ruled by Moses, and Saturn is ruled by Abraham. Fitzherbert finds this feature of Arabic palmistry indicative of its influence on European palmistry. Otherwise, one cannot explain how European palmists came to identify the mounts of the hand with the planets.

Thirteenth-century Europe bequeaths us several manuscripts. They are simple, covering some principal lines. The geography of the hand is left to a later time. Gettings describes the manuscripts as containing a medieval reverence for symbols. Toward the end of the fourteenth century, all of the principal lines in the hand, mounts, planets, and other markings including triangles, sister lines, quadrangles, and general proportions of the hand can be found in the literature then published. Gettings describes this as the sort of content we may find in any modern fortune-teller's palmistry. This is the period when treatises supposedly attributed to Aristotle or reliant on his work were being presented, in Gettings's view, with an eye to protecting the art of palmistry by showing that respected ancient scholars utilized it. These manuscripts were in Latin.

The first surviving manuscript on the subject in English seems to date from before 1440 and is written in Middle English. Noted medieval scholars are referred to in the ancient texts, probably to bolster acceptance of the subject. Palmistry books rode the burgeoning waves of literature upon the invention of movable type in the fifteenth century. The sixteenth century saw many a Renaissance man take up the art of palmistry, including Robert Fludd; Paracelus; Antiochus Tibertus; Andreas, who was also known as Bartholomew Cocles; Alexander Achillinus; John Indagine or John Hagen of Indagine; Joannes Rothmann; and Rudolf Gloclenius. The writings of these men added

grace and scholarship to the subject, even if they did not offer any new scientific insight into the art.

Paracelsus regarded the palm in two ways that foretold the true future of palmistry. He looked at it as a medical diagnostic tool and as a means for learning the arts. This went beyond mere soothsaying. He deserves Gettings's appraisal as the first modern palmist by considering the palm as a diagnostic tool for signs of diseases.

Rothmann was one of the early palmists to notice the similarities of readings between the astrologers and the palmists. Alexander Achillinus was a famous anatomist and was considered another Aristotle. Indagine was a Catholic priest and dean of St. Leonard's bishopric in Frankfurt-am-main and even acted as an ambassador to the pope. Each of our Renaissance men seems noted for various interests and abilities.

Rudolph Goclenius carries us from the sixteenth to the seventeenth century. He was a scholar who systematized and recorded the teachings of Paracelsus. Joannes Praetorius, once a professor of philosophy at Leipzig University, published a collection of treatises on palmistry. It contains a bibliography of over seventy books or treatises on the subject. During this century, the first accounts of Far Eastern palmistry have been published that Gettings considers both definite and reliable. In England, palmistry was beginning to fall into disrepute. The was no study of the subject in the universities as there was in Europe. The art became related to the Gypsies, who pervaded the continent and England. Since being a Gypsy could mean banishment and a possible death sentence in England, this may have had something to do with the decline of palmistry's popularity among the lower classes. The art was officially defined as "a crafty means to deceive people" from the language of a statute from the time of Henry VIII in 1530.

In Henry VIII's time the Gypsies were known as Egyptians. In 1530 a law was passed outlawing the "Egyptians" and giving them fifteen days to leave the realm upon pain of loss of their goods and estates. The law stated that these Egyptians "by palmistry could tell men's and women's fortunes, and so many times by craft and subtilty have deceived people of their money, and have committed many heinous felonies and robberies, to the great hurt and deceipt of the people they have come among."[9] Palmists continued to be frowned upon in England and their activities were outlawed in 1824.[10]

The new winds of the scientific revolution were blowing by the middle of the sixteenth century. The Royal Academy was founded, and the desire to remove the mysticism and mystery from many subjects flowed through the intellectual world. Palmistry was in for a rude shakedown. Researchers were not interested in an art that had become tainted with dishonesty and deception. Torreblanca, writing during these times, is quoted by Fred Gettings as saying that "chiromancy is not only reprobated by theologians, but by men of law and physics as foolish, false, vain, scandalous, futile, superstitious practice, smelling much of divinery and pact with the devil."[11] Alchemy could evolve into chemistry, and astrology into astronomy, but palmistry, which should have grown into medicine and anatomy, failed to make the seventeenth-century cut. It was relegated to superstition until the nineteenth century.

Palmistry died more slowly on the continent, especially in Germany, but there, too, it slipped into the obscure reaches of intellectual interest over the eighteenth century. Toward the end of the century, Kaspar Lavater, in the new scientific spirit, encouraged future students not to allow even the insignificant to go unobserved for it might be found useful. He revived physiognomy and almost revised palmistry writing on the latter 1770s. He observed that the hand could not lie as could the face, an observation accredited to Aristotle two thousand years before. His suggestions remained unheeded until we come to d'Arpentigny in the nineteenth century.

Most of the world today practices systems that developed in Europe in the nineteenth century. Two Frenchmen born just at the turn of that century laid down the path of modern palmistry. Casimir Stanilas d'Arpentigny was born in 1798 and trained for a military career. His pranks almost cut his military career short as he was expelled from military college. But he enlisted and earned his commission through the ranks, showing considerable bravery. Later in life he adopted a literary career. He was regularly invited to parties with distinctly different guests, and he began to observe that these different guests also had distinctly different hands. Over time, he identified six types of hands: the elementary, spatulate, psychic, square, knotty or philosophic, the conic and then, in a catch-all form, the mixed hand. He published his findings in *La Chirognomie* in 1839. What he established was the application of systems to the art of palmistry. He began the process of making the observations of palmists repeatable. This is the first step necessary to any scientific study of the subject. That is far more important than whether he was right or wrong in his classifications.

Adrien Adolphe Desbarrolles was born in 1801 in Paris, France. In 1859 he published *Les Mystéres de la Main*. Ten years later he published the *Journal de Chiromancie*, and later he published two other works, *Révélations Complètes*, and *Les Mystéres de l'Ecriture*. Desbarrolles was an occultist interested in the Cabala. Through this interest he brought the idea of planetary influences to palmistry. These ideas would form the fertile ground for the later works of William Benham in

America and the English Chirological Society founded by Katherine St. Hill in the late 1880s. Until recently, most of the practices of modern palmistry have been built upon the teachings of d'Arpentigny and Desbarrolles.

A son of Leipzig was also to influence the nineteenth-century growth of palmistry. Carl Gustav Carus was born in 1789, and early in his career he was made a professor at the Medical Surgical Academy of Dresden and the director of a midwifery institute. Later, in 1827, he became the royal physician to the King of Saxony. In 1848 he published *Uber Grund und Bedeutung der Verschiedenen Formen der Hand*, in which he presented his own hand clarification system based upon physiological characteristics. His clarification system is distinguished from d'Arpentigny's system by his viewpoint. Carus was looking at function. D'Arpentigny was looking at form. The Polish psychologist, Dr. Charlotte Wolff, and some others followed Carus, but most of the subsequent palmists and the modern scientists studying dermatoglyphics have concentrated on form.

Victorian England was opened to the works of d'Arpentigny by the translation of Edward Heron-Allen, who was more famous for the first accurate translation of *The Rubaiyat of Omar Khyyam*. He also wrote a book on violins that is still valued today.

As the world approached the twentieth century, three palmists appeared whose fame still survives them. Two were American, Edgar de Valcourt-Vermont, alias Le Comte C. de Saint-Germain, and William Benham. The third was Irish, though he spent considerable time in the United States. Cheiro was a handsome Irishman, who also went under other names. As a young stagehand in England he used the name Louis Warner and later called himself Count Leigh de Hamong. This he later changed to Count Louis Hamon during the

anti-German feeling in England before the First World War. The names of these three palmists will be repeated frequently in this book as their works are still being published today. Their continual publication is indicative of how little overall growth, discipline, and cohesion have touched the field of palmistry for the last century.

Cheiro wrote a number of books on palmistry. His best-known book was probably *The Language of the Hand*, copyrighted in 1897. He also wrote on other subjects, including astrology and a number of personal stories. He had some to tell as he had a varied career as a stagehand, a venter, a chemical manufacturer, head of the Russian czarist postal service for a short time, and as a British secret agent. He was a famous clairvoyant. He was even a popular reader for film stars in Hollywood for a time. He died in his home of a lung complaint and not in poverty as is sometimes rumored.

Benham was an American who published his monumental work, *The Laws of Scientific Palmistry*, in December 1900. His is still one of the least dated books of the time and and one of the most comprehensive works on the subject of palmistry. Fitzherbert still gives Benham credit for the most complete section on thumbs of any book written, but he gives him no credit for anything new. Benham was one of the first to publish that the center of the mount is found by the touching of three skin ridge patterns on the palm called the triradius, although Saint-Germain beat him by three years on this point. Benham's[12] book is still in print and is considered the bible by many practicing palmists, even today.

Fitzherbert accuses Saint-Germain of plagiarism, stealing from the works of Katherine St. Hill and Ina Oxenford. Unfortunately, in my hundred plus volumes on the subject, I lack the works of those writers to compare with Saint-Germain. The charge is serious and modern booksellers should take note of it, because Saint-Germain's work is still out there.

Saint-Germain treats each hand feature as symbolic of a particular point, and this makes it difficult or impossible to integrate a reading based upon his conclusions. His book falsely claims an introduction written by Desbarrolles, which Saint-Germain seems to disavow. One wonders why it is still reproduced. His work, *The Practice of Palmistry*, published in 1897, is a confusing piece and very difficult to follow.

In an attempt to raise the study of the hand to the level worthy of scientific research, to promote palmistry, and to protect the public from imposters and charlatans, Katherine St. Hill, Mrs. Luther Maundy, Miss Richardson, the Hon. Howard Spensley, and Julian King formed the London Cheirological Society (LCS) about 1890. They were joined a year later by Ina Oxenford, who with Ms. St. Hill, became the driving energy behind the society. The society was active until the 1930s and the last members died of old age during World War II. The modern Cheirological Society headed by Terence Dukes apparently has no direct link to the old society.

The LCS published a magazine, *The Palmist*, which was available around England and sent to members to read at fairs, thereby hoping to raise the standard of reading in the country. Fitzherbert credits the work of the society with universal influence upon later palmists. St. Hills's *The Book of the Hand* is still reportedly available.

After World War II, two well-known palmists wanted to reestablish a society to assist palmistry. Beryl Hutchinson and Noel Jaquin decided to include other occult studies in the new society including astrology, graphology (handwriting analysis), and phrenology (a study of the form of the body, particularly the head). They formed the Society for the Study of Physiological Patterns

(SSPP), which Fitzherbert reports is now the "oldest and best-established organization of its kind."[13] It now has worldwide membership.

I have met these and other palmists named in this book through their works. I invite you, the reader, to do likewise. Besides the English societies that are still active, Richard Unger has formed a group in San Rafael, California, called the International Institute of Hand Analysis. That organization publishes the *Hand Analysis Journal* and other papers and offers courses in the study of hand analysis.

In the last few decades, an entirely separate group of students have been studying hand form, and they are from the scientific community. The disciplines of their work are more likely to influence the future of the work than the continual rehashing of nineteenth-century observations by palmists. However, palmistry still has not released its burden of charlatans and so these modern researchers have not discovered the wealth of material for future study from this source. Scientific analysis of the hand through statistical inquiry started in 1920, probably with the work of Ms. Elizabeth Wilson on her M.A. thesis at Columbia University. She examined handprints of three groups of people: institutionalized schizophrenics, institutionalized retarded (very low IQ) individuals, and as controls, college graduates presumed to be psychologically normal. She made some statistically relevant findings, including the difference in the length of headlines between the subnormals and schizophrenics as a group and the normals. She also reported other investigations of the 1920s.

Dr. Charlotte Wolff became heavily involved in statistical analysis of the palm prints of groups of subjects and published summaries of her work in the 1940s and '50s. In studying institutionalized delinquent boys she observed a preponderance of defective hand features, especially with the little finger.[14] This brings to mind the palmistry-wives tale that if one wants a good crook, look for a crooked little finger. In addition, Wolff found "abnormalities" in the fate line, although considering the variety of fate lines I have seen, I find it hard to describe a normal fate line. Wolff apparently confirmed some of Wilson's findings. She submitted her skills to a blind test and scored, according to Fitzherbert, "astonishing correspondence" between the conclusions of the two types of analysis. Wolff is also responsible for bringing certain European studies to the attention of English readers.

British psychologist Rowan Bayne addressed the question of whether a fate line that ties into the life line indicates a subject suffers from early life restrictions. He compared prints of students with tied and free fate lines and after administering a series of questions to the two groups, he found confirmation of the early life restrictions. He did another test measuring the index finger, which is the ego finger, to determine if it could be a measure of self-confidence and assertiveness. Both long and short fingers scored higher than normal-length fingers. Fitzherbert pointed out that the short-fingered subject would score higher as they would be overcompensating for their inferiority feelings.

An Australian student, Andrew Symantz, publishing in 1981, conducted experiments to determine if and how the number of lines on the palm relate to anxiety. He found they did and that fewer lines indicated higher anxiety. At first this would seem contrary to the wisdom of traditional palmistry. It may be that we should somehow differentiate anxiety tests from tests of general nervousness. Perhaps they are different Down Under. One would hope for a follow-up on this test.

Ms. Yael Haft-Pomrock,[15] in collaboration with Dr. Yigal Ginath of Ben-Gurion University, published a study in 1982[16] of another comparison of the hands of schizophrenics with controls and found distinct differences in the hands. One of her students presented further evidence of hand distinctions in her Ph.D. thesis at Haifa University in 1985. Each researcher found some distinguishing marks that were statistically significant.

It is popular today to include some medical information in palmistry books. The practice was popular in Victorian times but fell off considerably between 1900 and 1960. Writing on the medical aspects of palmistry has been traced back to the earliest palmistry books in the English language.[17] In the second half of the seventeenth century, a palmistry book devoted to medicine was produced on the European continent in both French and German.[18] Current serious attention to the connections between what the hand shows and what medicine tries to detect is traced to the work of the London Cheirological Society (LCS), with early results reported in the magazine, *The Palmist*. Katherine St. Hill is credited with presenting most of the conclusions from this work in her 1929 book *Medical Palmistry*.[19] Fitzherbert encourages the reprint of this work. Other members of the LCS covered some material on medical palmistry in their books.[20] The French through Henri Mangin and the Germans through Ernest Issberner-Haldane have also contributed twentieth-century books on medical palmistry.[21] We have referred to reported findings in some of the more recent texts in later pages of this book.

Noel Jaquin covered the subject in several books, the best being reserved for his later work.[22] Beryl Hutchinson is also credited with important medical findings in her chapters on metabolic mineral imbalances and general medical signs.[23] Walter Sorrel made some interesting observations on cancer in his *Story of the Human Hand* that

Fitzherbert reports have been confirmed by several later writers.[24] Dennis B. Jackson is also credited with some original observations in his 1953 book, *The Modern Palmist.*[25]

There is a genuine medical textbook on diagnostic clues found in the hand published in 1963 and written by Dr. Theodore J. Berry, M.D., F.A.C.P., while he was an instructor at the University of Pennsylvania School of Medicine.[26] It is of more value to the specialist dealing with rare diseases. Fortunately for palmists, Dr. Eugene Scheimann also took time as a physician to examine the hands for telltale predictive signs and wrote of his observations in *A Doctor's Guide to Better Health Through Palmistry*, published in 1969. It may not have had much impact upon the medical profession, but it has been of considerable assistance to palmists. Dr. Scheimann recently collaborated with Nathaniel Altman to bring out an updated reissue of this work in 1989.[27]

Academic scientific studies of the hand in medicine, anatomy, and anthropology made advances through the century. The medical work is commonly traced back to the work of H. Cummings, who wrote in 1936 of his discovery of statistically significant dermatoglyphic patterns on those born with Down's syndrome.[28] After this work, the study of dermatoglyphics began to play an important role in the study of human genetics. Fitzherbert reported some six hundred papers had been published in the field and we counted some three hundred published between 1987 and 1993. We do not agree with Fitzherbert that the field reached its zenith in about 1982 and that new research dramatically declined after that.

Fitzherbert reported the decline of new research in dermatoglyphics after the great DNA mapping advances in the 1980s. Most of the American public is familiar with this method of identification of people from the O. J. Simpson

trial. Fitzherbert concluded that there was no longer any need to study dermatoglyphic markers to learn about genetic makeup. Certainly Amrita Bagga, publishing in India in 1989, does not agree.

Bagga published his work, *Dermatoglyphics of Schizophrenics*, in 1989.[29] He observed that so far, dermatoglyphics can not be used as a substitute for careful physical examinations and other means of diagnostic analysis, but it can help confirm the existence of some disorders.[30] We believe that further studies that couple dermatoglyphic and psychological testing analysis can increase the value of independent dermatoglyphic examinations in comparison with present DNA studies.

There are drawbacks to the use of DNA studies. We are a long way from using these studies to determine any psychological traits. The studies depend upon costly laboratory apparatus, and they are physically invasive. In a word, they are inconvenient and expensive and thus not readily available to most of the world where dermatoglyphics can be used: schools, human employment resources, psychologists, and counselors. In any event, the study of dermatoglyphics is alive and well in the 1980s and '90s, throughout the world.

The published dermatoglyphic studies in respectable, peer reviewed, professional journals from 1992 to 1994 cover a host of medical preoccupations including sudden infant death syndrome (SIDS), male testosterone levels, genital endometriosis, Alzheimer's disease, nasobronchial disorders, pulmonary tuberculosis, Down's syndrome, rheumatoid arthritis, fetal alcohol syndrome, comparisons of genetic and prenatal environmental influences, immunological disorders, congenital hearing losses, diabetes mellitus, and Minnesota Multiphasic Personality Inventory (MMPI) studies of monozygotic (identical) twins.[31]

A. C. Bogle, T. Reed, and R. J. Rose have been

conducting some research that should be of interest to all scientific palmists. In 1994[32] they published a further study that confirmed the results of an earlier study first published in 1987, which combined observations and testing of the subjects according to the scales of the Minnesota Multiphasic Personality Inventory. The tests indicated that identical twin subjects with asymmetric (dissimilar) patterns on their left and right hands were more likely to suffer from environmental distresses (as opposed to genetic distresses) than identical twins who had symmetric patterns. Those with the asymmetrical patterns exhibited "heightened developmental sensitivity to extraneous environmental stress." Viewed as a medical/psychiatric population, the asymmetric subjects would reflect more depression or anxiety and be more sensitive to environmental influences that manifest in the clinically interrelated behaviors of bodily complaints, anxiety, or depression. The conclusions of the Bogle group were based upon the comparative counting of the dermal ridge lines just between the point below the middle and index fingers on the palm on the right and left hands. We believe the joint use of the MMPI and dermatoglyphics shows great promise for future understanding of behavior and disease and a new understanding of what may be considered normal and abnormal.

The modern methods for the serious study of the hand are set forth in two books from the 1970s, Blanka Schaumann and Milton Alter's 1976 work, *Dermatoglyphics in Medical Disorders*,[33] and the 1978 text edited by Jamshed Mavalwala, *Dermatoglyphics: An International Perspective*.[34] The methods proposed in these studies will be presented in chapter 7 and in detail in the appendix of this book.

CHAPTER TWO

HAND GEOGRAPHY

Some of this chapter will be familiar to the palmist and some to the student of anatomy. I hope that in the future, all of it will be familiar to students of both disciplines. Then our storehouses of information can provide nutrition to cross-fertilize both areas. I have saved references to endnotes for later chapters because this chapter is designed merely to acquaint the reader with the language used.

Every specialized subject develops its own language. Those who wish to study any subject must develop a familiarity with its special language. Neither the palmist nor the anatomist calls the index finger that thingamajig that sticks out of the grabber at the end of the upper flappers that pinches with the whopper below it and is generally used to point. Palmists generally identify it as the Jupiter finger. In medicine it is called the second digit, because medical anatomy numbers the fingers one through five, starting with the thumb. Like anatomy, much of the language of palmistry is very old and each word is a shorthand identification for a wealth of other information and lore behind it.

This chapter familiarizes the student with the most useful terms in palmistry and medicine. Both medical and traditional palmistry terms are used in this book. The significance of these terms will be dealt with in subsequent chapters.

MEDICAL AREAS

The hand is divided by directions. In anatomy, the hand is seen as lying with the palm facing the same way as the face and the nails facing the same way as the back. Thus the palm is located on the

12

anterior, coronal, frontal, or ventral surface of the hand because all of these anatomical terms are used to describe location can relate to that side of the hand. The nails can be said to be on the posterior or dorsal side of the hand. The thumb side of the hand is known as the radial side of the hand, a term used to describe major blood vessels and nerves that travel to and from that side of the hand and arm. It is also known as the lateral side of the hand because, when it is seen lying with the palm faceup, it is more distant from the midline of the body than the little finger side of the hand. A large part of the palm on that side is known as the thenar area. The opposite side of the hand with the little finger is known as the ulnar side of the hand and is where the major blood vessels and nerves of the same name terminate. It is also known as the medial side of the hand. The fleshy portion of the hand on that little finger side is known as the hypothenar area and referred to in palmistry as the percussion. In this book I will be more concerned with the use of the terms radial and ulnar with reference to fingerprints.

The fingers are referred to as digits one through five. They are divided into phalanges, the name of the bones in the fingers. Each finger has three phalanges. The third phalange of the thumb forms part of the heel of the hand called the thenar prominence or in palmistry, the mount of Venus. I identify the different sections of the finger, the phalanges, by their distance from the root of the arm. The closer the phalange is to the root of the arm, the shoulder area, the more proximal it is. So the phalanges that start at the hand, the base of the fingers, are called the proximal phalanges. The phalanges at the other end of the fingers where the nails are found are called the distal phalanges. The ones in the middle are called the medial phalanges. Some may consider the thumb to have no medial phalange. Now you have learned two more anatomical terms for the hand: proximal for the wrist end of the hand and distal for the nail end of the hand. These terms will be used in this book.

MEDICAL MARKINGS

The main markings on the hand presently of interest in both medicine and palmistry are the patterns found in the papillary ridges and flexure lines. The papillary ridges are those fine, raised skin markings found on the palm side of the hand and the soles of the feet. Fingerprints are examples of papillary ridges. They are also called epidermal ridges, which has given rise to the use of the term dermal ridges and the use of the term dermatoglyphics for the study of the patterns of those ridges. These patterns are studied to correlate their relationship to a variety of medical, psychological, and anthropological conditions.

MAJOR MEDICAL CREASES

The major creases of the hand are called flexion creases. There are six major creases. All are known by their location. The distal crease is farthest while the proximal crease is nearest to the shoulder. The phalangeal creases relate to their position on the fingers. The metacarpophalangeal crease refers to the crease between the palm and the fingers. The bones in the palm are known as the metacarpals. The metacarpophalangeal crease lies between these two structures. The interphalangeal creases lie between the phalanges.

In palmistry more attention is directed toward the creases found on the palm. The two lines that generally lie horizontally across the hand are known in anatomy as the distal and proximal transverse creases. They correspond to the heart line (distal) and head line (proximal) in palmistry. The thenar crease corresponds to the life line in palmistry. This crease gets its name from the thenar prominence that surrounds the true distal phalange of the thumb. The wrist crease is easy to remember and in palmistry it would refer to one of the rascettes.

SIMIAN AND SYDNEY CREASES

If one of the lines completely crosses the palm, it is know as a Sydney line. If it takes the place, partially or wholly, of both the proximal and distal transverse creases, it is known as a Simian line. These terms are used in palmistry.

MINOR CREASES

There are a number of creases that tend to follow a path toward a particular finger. The creases that move toward the third, middle, or Saturn finger are called the middle finger creases and correspond to the fate, destiny, or personality lines in palmistry. The creases that follow a path to the ring or fourth finger are called the ring finger creases and correspond to the sun, Apollo, which are creativity or career lines in palmistry. The creases that end below the little finger are called the little finger creases and are known as the Mercury line, communication line, health line, hepatica line, line of Uranus, or liver line in palmistry.

The crease that describes an arc around the hypothenar area of the hand, the percussion in palmistry, is known as the hypothenar crease in dermatoglyphics and the line or crescent of intuition in palmistry. There are also lines found on the ulnar side of the hand, the percussion below the little finger and above the distal transverse crease, the heart line, are called E lines. They are called E lines in dermatoglyphics because there are usually three of them in parallel so that they form the letter E when observed on the palm on the right hand and a reverse E on the left hand if one views one's own hand. In palmistry they are known as the marriage, relationship, or nesting lines.

There are other lines crossing under the ring and middle finger above the distal transverse crease known in dermatoglyphics as the accessory distal creases. In palmistry these lines are known as girdles of Venus or lines of empathy. There may be several of any of these minor creases.

In addition to these, dermatoglyphics refers to secondary creases, which include the other lines and markings studied in palmistry. In my experience, all creases, major, minor, and secondary, are subject to change, but I have never seen the basic dermal patterns change, although they can become very hard to see for a variety of reasons, which will be discussed later.

Palmistry Geography

Traditionally, the fingers have been known by four names, and the areas of the palm by seven names all relating to the names of the first seven planets discovered, counting the sun as a planet. The thumb has no name other than the thumb. The index finger is Jupiter. Saturn lends his name to the middle finger, also called the medicus finger. Apollo, who drove the sun's chariot across the sky, alternates with the sun itself to describe the ring finger. The Apollo finger is sometimes known as the annularis finger. Annular means ring or forming a ring. Mercury describes the little or auric ularis finger, the pinky. Auricular is a term pertaining to the ear, so the little finger is considered the ear cleaning finger. The portions of the palm immediately below these fingers are called mounts, whether they protrude or not. They are identified by the same names as the fingers above them.

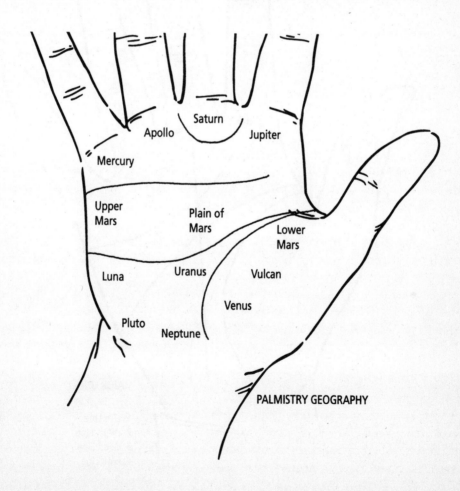

PALMISTRY GEOGRAPHY

The other areas of the traditional hand are the two mounts of upper and lower and plane of Mars, and the mounts of Venus and the Moon or Luna. These areas have been further divided by modern palmists. The upper part of Venus is sometimes referred to as Vulcan. He was the smith of the gods who forged metals in his furnace. To the extent that the thumb and the index finger form the hammer and anvil of the palm, the name is appropriate. The area between Venus and Luna toward the wrist has been assigned to Pluto and Neptune. Pluto is often also described as the lower part of Luna. Just above Neptune is an area sometimes related to Uranus.

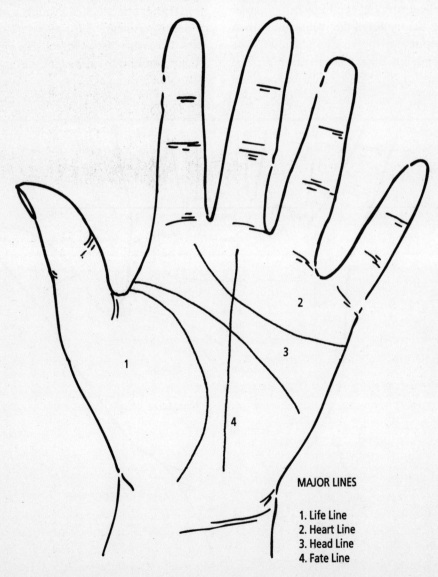

MAJOR LINES

1. Life Line
2. Heart Line
3. Head Line
4. Fate Line

Major Palmistry Lines

There are four major palmistry lines traditionally known as the head, heart, life, and fate lines. The head line is also referred to as the line of mentality. The heart line may be called the emotional line. The life line is also referred to as the line of vitality. Fate, destiny and personality all are used to describe the line that moves up the hand toward the middle, Saturn finger. It is also called the Saturn line, and sometimes is referred to as the career line, although I would reserve that name as an alternate for the Sun or Apollo line. If the heart and the head line combine, the combination is called a Simian line. It may be one line completely. However, it may also show branches that indicate the separation of the head from the heart line at the point of the branch. The head line may or may not be attached to the life line. The head line usually has one terminus near the radial side of the palm or on the life line. The heart line usually has one terminus on the ulnar, percussion side of the palm.

Minor Lines

The girdle of Venus rides like a swing beneath the outside of the Saturn and Apollo fingers. Similar swings under the Saturn, Apollo, or Mercury fingers are known as rings named by the mounts they are on, such as the ring of Apollo, etc. Such a ring on the mount of Jupiter is known as the ring of Solomon. The girdle of Venus may also be known as the line of empathy.

Lines that cross the mount of Venus from the thumb area toward the life line are known as worry lines or lines of influence in the form of new ideas or situations. Lines going up and down are referred to as influence lines in the form of people or kindred spirits. A line close and parallel to the life line on the thumb side is known as a Mars line or sister line.

Other lines that approach each of the fingers are known by the names of those fingers: Jupiter, Apollo or Sun, and Mercury. The Mercury line is also called the health line, the liver line, the hepatica line, the communication line, and even the Uranus line. The Sun line is sometimes referred to as the career line or creative line. A Jupiter line may also be referred to as a line of ambition. As we study each line, other names may be used in connection with them.

The arc that forms a crescent around the percussion from the mount of Mercury to the mount of the Moon is called the line, crescent, or curve of intuition. It, like all lines, may be broken or unbroken. There are several groups of lines along the percussion. Just below the little finger and above the heart line on the mount of Mercury are located horizontal lines called relationship lines or, more traditionally, marriage lines. I call them nesting lines. Vertical lines crossing the relationship lines are one of five areas considered to be children lines. Below these lines on the mount of upper Mars are located the enmity lines. Below that on the mount of the Moon (and Pluto) are the travel or restlessness lines. The travel lines also make up the health lines described in this book. In this same area is a line called the via lascivia or line of poison. The lines that cross the wrist are called the rascettes. Lines may often have more than one name and one function in hand analysis.

APICES

There are numerous special dermatoglyphic formations and numerous other minor lines and markings in the hand. There may be some ten thousand markings in Hindu palmistry. While I do

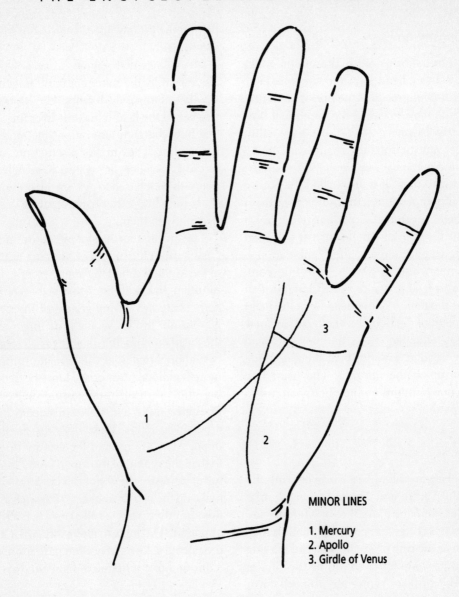

MINOR LINES

1. Mercury
2. Apollo
3. Girdle of Venus

not cover ten thousand signs, I do cover many signs in chapters 10 and 11, which describe stars and signs.

The apex is important, as it locates certain key features of the hand, such as the center of the mounts under the finger. The number of apices found on the fingers will determine the type of fingerprint being observed in cases where it is a close call. The apex is formed by the intersection of three palmar epidermal patterns. There may be no actual ridge connection between them or the ridge connection may form a variety of marks.

Unless the reader has a photographic memory, he or she will only become familiar with each of the terms above through study of the materials in this book and constant reference to real hands. Our illustrations can only be guidelines. Each hand has its own individual characteristics and subtleties. One of the first rules is to learn to love to hold and observe hands.

PSYCHOSOCIAL AREAS

Some palmists view the general shape of the hand as a guide to the importance of the worlds in the subject's life. They compare the relative sizes of the fingers as a whole to the middle and lower parts of the palm. The fingers are said to represent the mind, spirit, and aspirations of the subject. The upper part of the palm represents the practical ability of the subject in handling day-to-day matters. The lower area of the palm represents the basic drives of a person, the emotions. I find little use in this division.

Others divide both the fingers and the palm into three groups. The distal phalanges represent the spiritual and mental attitudes and aspirations of the person, the middle phalanges represent the practical and social attributes of the subject, while the proximal phalanges represent the basic needs for comfort and love. The palm is sometimes laid out in the same way, and sometimes the emotional zone is set above the heart line while the mental zone is set roughly along the mounts and plain of Mars and the bottom zone may be known as the physical zone.

The hand may also be divided into two or four

sections. The thumb side of the hand reaches out to the world and is considered the outer part of the hand. The little finger side is the inner side. In some balancing evaluations, such as personality seen through the fate line, when the line is more on the little finger side of the mount of Saturn, the person tends to be introspective. If it is more on the other side, the subject is more outgoing, even exhibitionist in some cases.

The upper and lower areas of the palm are also contrasted. The upper part is considered to show the active area of the hand. The lower part shows the passive influences of the hand. I feel this division is of little use. If the head line reaches deeply into the lower area of the mount of the Moon, the client could either have a very active psychic or spiritual life, perhaps even including trance journeys and/or out-of-body experiences, or, alternatively, the client may suffer from depression. These will be actively manifested in that client's life.

The palm has also been divided into two sets of three zones. Horizontally, the top zone below the fingers reflects the zone of consciousness and emotions and the active link to the world. The middle zone is the zone of balance, reflecting the use of common sense and the blending of imagination and reason. The lower zone next to the wrist represents primary motivations. From the thumb to the little finger, the palm may also be divided into three zones. The thumb, Jupiter, and predominant finger zone become the zone of activity where I deal with the outer world and I consciously activate this contact. The middle zone is again the zone of balance and takes in Saturn. The passive zone relates to our introspective side and takes in the areas of Apollo, Mercury, and Luna. Here I deal with the areas of instinct and creativity. I suggest that these zones be placed in the back of the mind until one has read a few hundred hands.

CHAPTER THREE

WHICH HAND TO STUDY? THE RIGHT AND LEFT HANDS

I no longer follow any traditional method of looking at the right and left hands. I believe that those Eastern methods that look only to the right hand for male clients and the left hand for females are totally inadequate and sexist, and often are value-based against the left hand. This bias against the left hand has crept into Western palmistry just as the Latin word for left, sinister, has colored our thoughts concerning left-handed persons as conniving, bad people.

For a while it even crept into the scientific study of palmistry. Charlotte Wolff, for example, relying on earlier neurobiological theories, speculated that left-handedness and ambidextrousness were atavistic attributes. She believed they were signs of human degeneration, even though she readily admitted that many successful people had these traits. She was then under the impression that right-handedness was related to the development of intelligence. Science does not accept such categorical statements today.

Wolff wrote that the left hemisphere of the brain registers "the highest human faculties—intelligence, judgement—and their transition through writing, reading, speech, and artistic performance." Even those who today would locate the speech center of the brain more on the left side of the brain would probably not agree with her remarks on art. Anyway, Wolff concluded that the right hand was the practical, active, and intelligent hand. The left hand was considered the "supporting, passive, and imaginative hand, of the primary emotions."[1]

It is inadequate to look at the hands separately to

indicate active or passive traits, to show what one came into the world with and what one is using, or even as a flat indication of one's life path. Both hands are dynamic, changing molds, constantly furnishing new information concerning the subject that affect both the active and passive life and personalities. Also, both hands present permanent characteristics in the form of dermal ridges, and these ridges are not necessarily mirror imaged on each hand.

To the extent that I use hand analysis in my healing work, I make positive suggestions on how to use the hands to bring out subtleties of character and traits that may be available to the subject but have not been used to date. I gravitate toward encouraging ambidextrousness in many of my clients.

I do tend to use right brain–left brain analogy, so long as it is considered analogy and not fact. This analogy holds that the right brain addresses spatial concepts and the left brain addresses verbal concepts. Within this parameter, left-brained individuals have been accused of being more rational while right-brained people have been considered more intuitive. However, that may be largely incorrect, although the left brain does largely control the right hand, while the right brain largely controls the left hand.

I also use the concepts of yin (female) and yang (male) to describe traits, but I am still struggling with a proper use of these terms because many of the traits — probably most — are hardly confined to either males or females but bear those colorations because of various cultural expectations. Still, for rough, descriptive purposes, these terms can be useful in counseling and teaching. In dealing with survival issues as contrasted with sensitive issues (if one can make such a contrast) I have found some success in categorizing the right hand as more reflective of survival issues and the left hand as

more of a signature of sensitive issues, especially from childhood and in reflecting traits learned from experiences with parental types.

Both of the concepts above are useful but questionable. For example, the primary emotions, those that are preorganized, do not depend upon the limbic system circuitry with the amygdala and anterior cingulate described as the key participants.[2] This finding does not relate the primary emotions to the left or right side of the brain. Dr. Damasio informs us that the secondary emotions, experienced through the feelings formed by mental connections between "categories of objects and situations, on the one hand and primary emotions on the other, require the assistance of the prefrontal and somatosensory cortices."[3] We are dealing with both sides of the brain, but present scientific evidence indicates the motor control for emotional movement is not located in the same area of the brain as the control for the voluntary act.[4] This is a very important point and I will return to it when discussing the dermatoglyphic marks on the hand, especially the loop of humor. As I distinguish the voluntary and emotional control areas of the brain, I may better understand many of the practical uses of the dermatoglyphic features of the hand in science, medicine, and psychology.

Before we jump to the conclusion, as accepted in many palmistry books and implied, even in other sections of this book, that there is some brain map that represents the actual location of current body representations, we should be aware of Damasio's conclusion that there is no such map. The current activities of the body represent dynamic activity of the neural system including the brain and the spinal column and the chemical activities of the rest of the body.[5]

This may excuse the occasional error I have had in recognizing the right-handed person. About eighty-five to ninety percent of the subjects are right-handed. I tend to think it may be as low as eighty-five percent, as the term may be commonly understood, giving weight to cultural and family influences that may cause switching. In a recent international study of the data available on human handedness, Ira B. Perelle and Lee Ehrman[6] found a range of left-handedness based upon writing from 12.2% in the USA to 2.5% in Mexico, and a self-perceived left-handedness including both strong and moderate left-handedness from 15.8% in the Netherlands to 3.9% in Mexico. Those who reported attempts at switching their handedness ranged from 12.5% in Belgium to 4.3% in Italy. There is difficulty in determining what criteria to use to determine whether a person is left- or right-handed.[7] Eating seems to be a cultural criteria. Writing was used by Perelle and Ehrman on the basis that it was the only indicator they studied that operated from "a special lateralized section of the brain." I have used a similar but physically observable mechanism but have found it to be subject to problems in about twenty to thirty percent of those I would call left-handed and something under one percent of those I would conclude were right-handed.

The mechanism I observe is the angle of the spread of the index finger and the thumb under very gentle pressure with the hand held extended. It is most easily observed with the hand resting relaxed on a flat surface. In palmistry this is called the angle of generosity. The palmist concludes that the wider the angle the more generous the person is. Actually, this is generosity reflected to close "loved" ones and not necessarily generosity to the world. Those with angles on both hands of ninety degrees and over tend to fall into that category that is now popularly called "co-dependents." They have problems forming personal boundaries between themselves and loved ones and have a very difficult or impossible time in saying no to loved ones. However, as we observe the reduction of this angle on one hand to under ninety degrees, we also usually observe a change in that person's reaction to loved ones. The word "no" enters their vocabulary. They establish their own boundaries and firmly reject unacceptable behavior of loved ones. They stop being "enablers." They end abusive relationships.

This narrow angle has indicated to me the side of the brain that is more active in handling current cognitive emotional affairs. So if I find the left hand with this reduced angle, I have usually assumed that the right brain is the dominant side of the brain in cognitive emotional thinking. I used to also conclude that the person would be a left-hander. My observation has proved wrong in up to three cases in ten that I would have called left-handers. In less than one case in a hundred it also proves wrong subjects with smaller angles on the right hand.

A very recent subject indicates the subtleties we face. A college professor who described himself as having easily learned to read came to me (some hand switching appears to be related to reading dyslexia — difficulty in learning to read). I observed that the angle on his right hand was considerably smaller than that on his left hand, and there were no obvious signs of physical trauma, past or present, nor were there any signs of congenital defects in the formation of the hands. The left hand showed an angle of generosity of over ninety degrees while the right hand was closer to eighty-five degrees. He confirmed the change in his conscious reaction to demands of loved ones. He was now more guarded and prone to say no at appropriate moments to protect himself and his own boundaries. However, he was very clear that he was left-handed, and that he wrote with his left hand. He did indicate that he could easily transpose material he was reading in his mind (a trait

WHICH HAND TO STUDY? THE RIGHT AND LEFT HANDS   23

that is common is dyslexia) but that it had never given him any problem in learning. He made no claim to being ambidextrous.

This college professor emphasized to me the importance of reading both hands to achieve an in-depth, full understanding of what may be reflected as effecting the subject's past, present and future. Handedness may help us from time to time, but because it is subject to so many variable interpretations, we may need to look for additional markers concerning what might be considered dominant behavioral and physical characteristics.

I read both hands whenever possible, but I have to admit I have often given a good reading in complete disregard to which hand I used. Sometimes I have discovered the latent left-hander in the right-handed person and been able to describe and give a reason for a certain lack of coordination or timing in that person's lifetime as well as physical activity, because of some handed changes made in early life. There is much to be said for Jung's observation that a good palmist should be intuitively gifted, although I personally do not consider myself as particularly clairvoyant.

I strongly urge the use of both hands in readings, counseling, and deeper study into the significance of the hands in the entire neuromuscular makeup of the subject as well as in various questions of personality and psychic configuration of the subject. A full reading should pay close attention to both hands.

Many readers, however, follow other conventions, so herewith follow some more traditional observations from my earlier writings on the subject. Some concepts are useful as long as they do not become the controlling guide for the student.

In looking at the hands, I try to determine which is the presently active and which is the presently passive hand. I ask the person if they are right- or left-handed, as the active hand on a right-

handed person is the right hand, and the left hand is the active hand of a left-handed person. If the subject is ambidextrous, then I determine which hand is more prominently used for fine work, such as writing.

The passive hand represents the root of the subject's drives, aspirations, temperament, and purpose. Terence Dukes refers to it as the family hand. The active hand displays the discernible qualities that one is growing from that root. Both the root and the rest of the person continues to grow, the root reaching into the unseen sources of power while the rest of the person becomes visible to and interacts directly with the social world in his or her day-to-day actions, emotions, and health.

There is a school of thought that considers the presently passive hand as covering life after the age of thirty-five. That hand is supposed to contain the Karma we create in this lifetime. The other hand is said to cover life before thirty-five and shows the Karmas we brought into this world. It is interesting to note which is the larger hand. If the person is over thirty-five and the passive hand is the larger hand, chances are that person tends to live in his or her past glories.

Terence Dukes in his book, *Chinese Hand Analysis*,[8] usefully contrasts the hands in the following way:

Passive hand digits describe conceptual structures potentially accessible to the subject.

Passive hand palmar features describe inherited physiological factors from which the subject has developed.

Active hand digits describe the present patterns and objects of the subject's consciousness.

Active hand palms describe the present condition of the subject's physiological homeostasis.

Everything connected to, or stemming from, a subject's physical patterns, psychological patterns, habits, tastes, and individual preferences manifests in a symbolic representative form in the active hand. Every inherited source of such traits, at all levels, is found within the passive hand.

However, it goes further than this implies, as the passive hand changes. (Of course, there is one field of esoterica that contends that when we heal ourselves we tend to heal the members of our families.)

Many traditional Chinese and Indian readers, and perhaps others, would look at the woman's left hand and the man's right hand for readings. Julius Spier[9] would look at the left hand of all subjects, believing that it represents life goals, while the right hand is more a reflection of what the client has done with his or her life and thus more of a reflection of the past. Where one hand only was available to draw conclusions, Charlotte Wolff would have regarded the left hand as "more revealing of the deeper-seated emotions and therefore the subject's difficulties and conflicts."[10] All of these people could be considered excellent palm readers, and the foreword to Spier's book, *The Hands of Children*, was written by Carl Jung.

Let us emphasize that change is possible. Even the sign of death in the hand may mean nothing more than transformation. Miraculous cures are possible, and death itself is not so dreaded a moment when it comes at an appropriate time. Life can be the bigger challenge. We should look to palmistry, as Hachiro Asano[11] describes Japanese palmistry, for its element of deliverance. There can be both fortune and misfortune in the hand and the good palmist should address both. The one may counter the other and the mediated experience of both can provide the worthwhile life experience that becomes one of those memorable stepping-stones on the path to personal growth and the higher consciousness or spirituality each of us may ultimately seek.

Finally, I strongly urge all to approach reading for another human humbly. The reader steps into the most private rooms of the subject's home. Do not be a trespasser or a coarse, unthinking guest. I encourage readers to be respectful of their subjects and to honor their secrets. Recognize that we can be wrong and each subject has the perfect right to challenge the reader and the reader's findings and refuse to be bound by our own views of fate.

I like to recall the remarks toward the close of a particularly insightful reading when the subject asked me when I was going to impart the bad news. My answer was simply, "But I have been doing that for the last hour." Much of reading is in the way you present it and in the way it is heard. No matter how scientific we make it, the practice will still be an art.

CHAPTER FOUR

FROM FORM TO CHARACTER ANALYSIS

Basic character traits that identify the person are found in the hand, the face, and even the figure of the client. The client's movement, poise, and balance betray him or her. Even tactile sensations, sounds, colorations, and odor are part of the assessment. In this chapter I discuss those grosser observations that have been used to describe the broader aspects of character.

In palmistry, I begin by looking at the structure and movement of the subject studied. It is as though I were trying to fathom the person's basic life form and vibrations. I look at the form of the hand and learn the person's basic approach to life. Is it passionate, intellectually curious, steady and dependable, intuitive, whimsical, sensitive, or even secretive? Here I give name to the person's basic character.

The study of the size, shape, and outward appearance of the hand is known as chirognomy (also spelled cheirognomy). Palmists have looked at shape, size, color, and have felt through touch and movement the texture, hardness, resiliency, and stiffness of the hands, trying to relate them to character. Examinations may depend upon considerable subjective analysis. Analyzing the feel of the hand is not easy to duplicate with any more accuracy than a doctor palpating a patient. I must rely upon practical experience to describe many of our conclusions and the practical experience of others similarly trained to duplicate our findings. We have not developed the tools to standardize much of our physical testing.

Each reader should try to use easily verifiable observations by means of simple methods that are easy to describe and duplicate. This practice will allow critical analysis. It will enhance acceptance of verifiable observations by the scientific community.

Many sensual images are collected in evaluating each client. Shapes may be compared to mental images of shapes. A thin, crooked hand with clawlike fingers may bring up the image of the person enfeebled by arthritis and full of pain and longing. Some palmists may also compare size to mental images. The thin hand as long as the face with an elongated middle finger may conjure up a spiritually devoted image. Size is a feature that depends upon comparative analysis. The comparisons will be to other portions of the subject's body. Color and shading also do not have independent value. They relate to the natural tones of the rest of the body. Color and shading also are subject to the variants of the weather, emotions, and time of day. One grows darker as the day progresses, for example. We can add to these three subjects the sense of touch. This includes how the hand feels at rest (hard, soft, weak, strong), the resiliency of the tissues, and the flexibility of the palms and the fingers.

Next to the fingerprints and palmar dermal ridges, form is the least likely of the appearances of the gross hand to change in an adult. I have seen change in form; deliberate, accidental, and through unknown causes. No one can say the hand form will not change, but because change is so rare, the form still appears an excellent guide to finding the basic persona of the subject. Where I have seen decided change in form, it has been accompanied by definite shifts in basic personality. Those personality changes often are traceable to the same period as the form change. In one case I recall a young man whose ego became greatly subdued after losing part of his index finger

in a logging mill accident. The index finger shows ego.

Many theories of hand analysis have developed. Each school designs a system of observations and deductions. The designs should enable the student and practitioner to compare, discuss, and pass along common observations. Based upon those observations, others should probably reach similar conclusions. Several schools of palmistry, some from ancient times, have attempted to establish standardized procedures for observations. In this book I will describe some of them and share my own present practices.

Palmists have classified the shape of the hand based upon many observational characteristics. The hand type has been divided into as many as forty-eight categories. The predominant categories today are the seven categories established by d'Arpentigny,[1] the Eastern four categories typical of the Wu-Hsing method practiced within Chen Yen Esoteric Buddhism but also attributed to Fred Gettings, the four categories of the Carl Carus clarifications,[2] and the five categories of Chinese traditional physiognomy and palmistry.[3] I will also discuss the Muchery system, Benham's character types, Asano's use of forty-eight categories of hands, and Fenton and Wright's fifteen hand forms.

While I use a slightly modified Gettings/Wu-Hsing method, I encourage the student to compare several methods. Occasionally, I have observed a hand that will fit exactly one of those described by another school of analysis. Then I wished I had that text immediately available to recall the appropriate character descriptions.

I have personally found the Gettings/Wu-Hsing method, as modified below, most useful. It most accurately describes the hands I have seen. I also like it because it is the easiest to learn and teach. This division of hand types into four categories is presently in ascendance. The Gettings/Wu-Hsing method is well represented in English in the work of Terence Dukes.[4] Nathaniel Altman relied upon five types derived from the d'Arpentigny method in his earlier works.[5] Now he has joined with Andrew Fitzherbert[6] in using the four types basic to the Gettings/Wu-Hsing method. Rodney Davies,[7] Fred Gettings,[8] Jemma Powell,[9] Lori Reid,[10] Richard Webster,[11] Dennis Fairchild,[12] and Dylan Warren-Davis[13] also use these four types known as earth, air, fire, and water. Gettings also calls them practical for earth, intuitive for fire, sensitive for water, and intellectual for air. I find the term passionate is more appropriate for fire, and intuitive could well reflect water.

Because Dukes claims great age for his ideas of palmistry, I started to give him credit for the four hand method. However, Andrew Fitzherbert, who has made an extensive study into the history of palmistry, credits Fred Gettings with the method.[14]

GETTINGS/WU-HSING FOUR TYPES

The Gettings/Wu-Hsing method is the simplest, as it involves only four types of hands. These portray alternate combinations of two traits: finger length and palm shape. There are long and short fingers and square and rectangular palms. In my own readings, I also observe three other features that overlay the basic shape. I observe whether the hand is broader or narrower at the base than where the fingers meet the palm. I also observe whether it bulges on the side of the little finger.

For many years I used a mathematical formula to decide if a hand was fire, water, earth, or air. I did this because the finger length is so important to the observation. I chose to follow the seven-eighths formula. Fingers can be considered long when the middle finger (the Saturn finger) is at least seven-eighths as long as the length of the palm. Make this measurement across the palm from the center of the wrist at the base of the hand to the base of the middle finger. I now modify the seven-eighths rule because it is too rigid and probably results in some inaccuracies. This is especially true of potential water types whose Saturn finger does not reach seven-eighths of the length of the palm. Nevertheless, one will still occasionally see me with a ruler, checking out close calls and falling back on this formula in case of doubt.

The palm itself is considered either square or rectangular. I measure width at the upper thumb level from where the thumb joins the hand to the opposite side. Length is measured from the center of the wrist at the base of the hand to the base of the middle (Saturn) finger. Here I believe measurement is important because until one develops a practiced eye, many large fire hands may pass for earth hands.

The four shapes commonly are called earth, air, fire, and water. These terms also describe characteristics found in similar terms used in astrology. Sometimes the palms do reflect the major astrological signs, though not always. Unlike the claims of certain Eastern schools of palmistry,[15] none of the current systems used in the West have so far developed the accuracy necessary to chart the moment of birth and the resulting influence of the stars.

Gettings/Wu-Hsing Earth Type

The earth hand has a square palm and short fingers. The person's characteristic is order as reflected in the word *routine*. Earth types can be dependable, timely, tolerant, and constructive. They can also be blind, materialistic, over-cautious, and overbearing. They lean toward traditions and conservatism, and rely upon experience. They may dislike change and adapting to the new. Earthen spirits can be loners, though they often have a strong love of animals and need pets. These people aspire for success in careers, justice, and continuity through traditions. They generally are self-starters and complete what they start. However, they may lack careful planning. They can be wasteful and misuse their environment.

Earth persons are the natural husbanders, the agricultural workers, the skilled craftspeople. They need to be encouraged to care for the environment. Each may need training for that.

While the earthlings may have very strong sexual appetites, they are not emotionally passionate. They should find mates through symbiosis and friendship rather than romantic, passionate love. The passionate fire person scorches them and burns them out. Generally, the earth types quickly bore passionate fire spirits. They dull the rapid intellect of air people, making them impatient or sleepy. Therefore, they do not match well with air and fire types.

The earth person does well with earth and water types, though they will never really understand the latter. Earth forms the basic stability needed by water types, the basin for that sea. Water types add the life-giving fluidity and carry the nutrition and movement that seem sorely lacking at times in the earth types.

Gettings/Wu-Hsing Water Type

The water hand has a long palm and long fingers. Also observe whether the hand has many fine lines. Pay attention to the general feel of the hand.

A hand that appears weak, with many lines, one that is fairly narrow or may have a hollow palm, is likely to be a water hand, even if the fingers may be no longer than those often seen on a fire hand. I encourage my students to ask their subjects whether the described traits really apply to the subject. This helps the student recognize what characteristics are more predominant. Sometimes the hand mirrors a potentially serious internal conflict if the subject shows both strong water and fire qualities.

Water is deep, secretive, and sensitive. He or she appears secretive because the face does not furnish a clear picture of the mind. One cannot rely on facial expressions to really tell what water people feel or think. They can be calm on the outside while churning on the inside. They can show great anger while being entirely calm within. These undines are often considered deep and mysterious by the rational populace since they may speak metaphorically, in images, rather than directly.

Water spirits have a definite need of security formed by sound borders. Without those borders, they would run wild and fragment. I would find them scattering their talents and displacing their energies. To understand this, observe water poured on a flat surface. They need a basin to rest in. These undines, when safe in their borders, thrive and are a home for the wide variety of life they nourish.

When the water spirits feel safe, they display sensitive, compassionate, intuitive, and self-effacing personalities. Without that support they can be vindictive, depressive, unbalanced, erratic, demanding, and even immoral and can run off at the mouth. For their own well-being, water spirits would do well to guard against hypersensitivity or appearing cold or intolerant. These bad qualities are probably signs of their own insecurity. They aspire for home with its security, peace, and close family.

Without security, in extreme stress, I have seen them babble on in what is considered word lettuce. They may at first seem to say something profound. Yet as one listens, none of their word combinations make sense or respond to issues clearly confronting them. When they are like this, they may show other extremes of what currently is called bipolarity, and formerly recognized as manic-depression or a form of schizophrenia. This type, possibly more than all others, needs safety and security and a strong measure of privacy for good mental health. They may not do well in the modern, urban world.

Water persons thrive through beautifying work in a safe environment. They do well at enhancing and adorning their surroundings and will work well in occupations that allow them this opportunity. While they may often seem confused, this is seldom the case in safe environs when they are engaged in creative work.

Water seen from within is not linear. It surrounds and thus does not have to depend upon linear communication. In the human body, the fluid carries a variety of messages chemically by way of hormones, neurotransmitters, and neuromodulators. These do not reach their targets following a strictly linear path. The vision of reality thus formed may vary from clarity of form to chaos and back in sometimes random, quite unpredictable fashion.

Modern, urban society relies upon a linear communication system of straight paths through otherwise unknown territory. Paths become the means to understanding the message. The mysterious territory of the body, mind, and outer world can neither be reached nor understood by simple logic except through clearly defined paths. Simple logic is a tool of linear communication. This forms

the basis of the rationalization that the fire and air types use for survival and growth and the earth type finds helpful for survival. Because of its dominant use, the simple logic of rationalization at times grows from being the medium of the message to the message.

Water represents a compound or composite logic. This logic describes a process understanding that requires compound analysis and deduction. This analysis is conducted in a soup of competing messages. The water person can process many of these messages simultaneously. Water people process information directly from the unknown territory of life without particular reference to specific paths. However, the answer the water person gives may have surprising validity, even to a person immersed in linear logic.

The water spirits smother fire as their thought processes engulf a subject rather than process it by linear analysis and deduction. Their mental processes as well as their visage is unfathomable. The direct interaction the fire person needs can be lacking. The fire person must be sparked. Fire's quick mind depends upon direct, logical paths to follow, and confusion soon brings boredom or depression. The water person's lack of linear logic confounds the air person and denies that person the recognition he or she needs for the workings of that able mind.

Whenever the strong elements of water combine with fire or air, self-discipline is vital. Fire and water can coexist and be a powerful force. Witness the steam engine, still one of the most powerful engines ever devised. To obtain useful power, it is necessary to contain each element in its own environment while providing a disciplined medium for the transmission of energies between the elements. When I see these elements together, I encourage such practices as yoga, strong meditation, exercise, and other methods of self-discipline.

Gettings/Wu-Hsing Air Type

The air hand has a square palm and long fingers. In some ways, this person is a refined earthling. They do better in an ordered environment. However, their quick minds are open and intelligent and will lead them into many new endeavors. They have the earth quality of being self-starters and finishing what they start. Being studious, they may also be intense. They are seekers of knowledge and truth, and they have open, exploring minds. They are skilled in debate, using dialectic to fathom the depths of a subject. Thus, they may also be good teachers.

Air persons need mental challenges and opportunities for public recognition. They desire recognition, fame, and want to achieve their own ideals. These idealists may have a strong romantic streak. They will dislike confinement. That, along with their use and respect of rationality, does not make them good mates for the water type. They may take political extremes and be very independent. These qualities, along with their quick minds, do not make them good mates for the slower, more traditionally bound earth types. If not burned out by the experience, air hands can do well with fire types. Air types complement other air types.

Air types may appear cool and can be deceptive, fickle, and even engage in dissipative or dull behavior.

Gettings/Wu-Hsing Fire Type

The fire hand has short fingers and a rectangular (long) palm. Fire handed people are ruled by passion. They are quick and embrace novelty with gusto. Boredom may as quickly follow. They probably start far more than they ever finish. Fire types need driving purpose to get started. Their emotions can ride the roller coaster. They can display great initial energy. Without external stimuli, they can be very lethargic. Physically and even emotionally they may crash when the energy wears out. They like to be active and expansive and thus may be impatient. This can lead to being destructive, unfeeling, blind, and even cruel.

I tell fire people that they are peak experience addicts. They work best against deadlines. In school they would cram for exams. They do best working on short-term goals as their energy plays out over time. Their life routine is anything but routine. These salamander spirits tend to ignore sleep and even meals. They may be seen eating on the run.

Fire people are found among the leadership in the advanced societies. Their hands predominate in urban environments. They take unkindly to criticism and can be argumentative and thus totally dislike being dominated. They fear restriction, yet they are constrained within the very exhaustible fuel of their surroundings. Knowing this, they are apprehensive of the future and at times may be weak-willed. They like positions of power, yet seek freedom from responsibility. While relating themselves to a rational world, their head line will often reveal that decision making is based upon gut reactions. They are another interesting study in contrasts and contradictions.

Fire persons need to seek work with constant new challenges and short deadlines. They do well at occupations related to people's needs. Those occupations frequently involve new demands. Fire spirits expire under routine tasks.

The fire person may do well with other fire

persons or air persons. In all things they seek and need change, so affairs with fire persons, even if totally monogamous, will have their ups and downs. They like the air person because he or she is the fountain of new ideas. However, they must take care not to burn the air person out with their high energy. Caution them to remember the air person needs a health routine common to the earth person (regular sleep and regular meals). Water and earth persons do not make good long-term mates for fire types. Although the fire woman is often drawn to the virile earth male for short interludes, the quick boredom gives dissatisfaction to both. The fire person may find it difficult to fully disengage the interest of the earth person. The earth person believes his or her actions are quite acceptable. This basic person does not understand that he or she is boring the fire person. Earth persons do not realize their steady, predictable character is oppressing to the fire spirit. They often are left in confusion after an affair with a fire person. They feel burned by such passion and its sudden, unpredictable changes. These grounded spirits cannot understand what has happened or the apparent abandonment.

A or V Subtypes

Type A hands, though square or rectangular, may show a decided tendency to be much broader at the base (wrist) than the fingers. I call these hands the constipated types. Those whose hands seem far broader at the base have great trouble releasing all of their energy. They have tremendous powers but only the smallest gate to release them. If one thinks of an overstuffed subject with an anal sphincter in spasm, one will never forget this type. Hence I use the term constipated. They are constipated in all of their energetic endeavors.

In order to encourage the smoother flow of their energy, suggest that they spread their fingers. As they do this, observe whether their eyes soften. This will indicate that they are diffusing their energy. They have widened and relaxed their release gate. They have tremendous powers that they concentrate on small areas.

Those with the V type of hand, wider where the fingers meet the palm than at the base of the hand, may be working on nervous energy. They will constantly court exhaustion in their endeavors. They need to learn how to conserve and focus their energies. I call these diarrhea types.

PERCUSSION

Opposite the thumb, along the ulnar (little finger) side of the hand, is the percussion. On some hands this forms a bulge, while on others it is quite flat. The larger the bulge, the more one finds a person with a natural affinity for water. They live better when they live close to water. A few fear the water. In most of those I have questioned, this fear results from a bad childhood experience with water. They may have quite literally gotten in over their heads, feeling that this needed thing could not hurt

them. They never quite got over their own self-deception. Some reflect a fear their parents had of the water. If the hand is flat on the ulnar side, the subject may feel quite content inland, in the desert and in the mountains.

Finding the water tendency on a fire or air hand, which is not unusual, indicates some possible character conflicts. Such persons often have to be encouraged to develop strong self-discipline. An explanation of the steam engine is helpful.

Water and fire can work together if the power of each is contained and used in a disciplined manner. Pointing out the basis of conflicts may help the subject come to understand some of his or her own behavior and reactions that have long been a personal puzzle.

D'ARPENTIGNY TYPES

During the last half of the nineteenth century and the first two-thirds of this century, d'Arpentigny's system formed the basis of most Western systems of hand recognition. D'Arpentigny's seven types of hands are elementary, square, spatulate, philosophic, conic, psychic, and mixed. Brenner,[16] Cheiro,[17] Frith,[18] Gardini,[19] Laffan,[20] Martini,[21] Morgan,[22] Niblo,[23] Squire,[24] Eckhardt,[25] Renald,[26] West,[27] and Yaschpaule[28] make use of this method. Richard Webster supports both this and the Wu-Hsing method in his 1994 work.[29] Several other palmist authors appear to use parts of it or at least the language and some of the descriptions. These include Altman mentioned above, Costavile,[30] Gibson,[31] Luxon and Goolden,[32] Hoffman,[33] Lawrence,[34] Lehman,[35] Levine,[36] Merton,[37] Raymond,[38] Rem,[39] Rita Robinson,[40] Spier,[41] and Wilson.[42] Yale Haft-Pomrock presents a simple, four-part hand classification that uses three terms from the d'Arpentigny system.[43]

I do not favor d'Arpentigny's system because so many hands end up classified as the mixed type. This really begs clear classification. It is presented here because it still forms the basic hand classification system found in most of the palmistry books currently available to students. According to Cyrus D. F. Abayakoon, the Egyptian palmist M. M. Gaafar had no use for it. He believed that there were no such shapes as these and it was a waste of time to accumulate information on them.[44] Cyrus D. F. Abayakoon, a noted Ceylonese (Sri Lanka) astrologer and palmist, appears to share this view.[45]

Elementary Hand

The elementary hand is described as clumsy, large-palmed, with short fingers. That distinguishes it from the square or practical hand. The elementary hand is equated with the "lowest form of humanity," one whose short-tempered, unbounded passions are destructive. People with this type of hand would eat, drink, and sleep, thinking nothing of tomorrow. This follows the abundant class-based literature found in palmistry that makes it unacceptable to certain current academic inquiries. Peter West is kinder. He notes that people with this hand type tend to be slow and do not usually engage in "advanced thinking."[46] However, their knowledge and instinctual understanding of nature can be quite gifted. They will tend to leave alone what they do not know or understand.

Square Hand

The square hand is distinguished by square palms and the ends of the fingers appear square at the distal end. This hand is found upon the realistic, practical, well-grounded person, noted for order and stability. People with this hand type may appear methodical and lack spontaneity. While they find difficulty in adapting to new conditions, they flourish in stable, predictable environments.

Spatulate Hand

One description of the spatulate hand says that it is somewhat crooked and the ends of the fingers would appear to be roundly blunt, being somewhat wider at the more distal portion just below the ends so that a vague resemblance of a spatula may be discerned. There are also two types of spatulate hands, looking at the hand areas at the base of the fingertips and at the wrist. In general, the spatulate hand will indicate a realistic, practical, and well-grounded person who is energetic, tenacious, creative, innovative, and self-confident. This person may be impulsive and extroverted while also being dynamic and exciting. Flexibility shows an increase in sensual interests at the expense of work and other responsibilities. I have found that hands that are wider at the fingers than at the wrist often indicate people who tend to exhaust themselves. Those whose hands are larger at the wrists have great trouble expressing themselves and finding outlets for all of their energy.

Philosophic Hand

The philosophic hand is sometimes known as the knotty hand because the knuckles tend to be swollen or enlarged in comparison to the rest of the fingers. Here we are supposed to find the analytical, deductive thinker. If the knots are on the first joint from the ends of the fingers, these people may be argumentative, tending to hold on to ideas. If the knots are on the next joints, these people are more likely to collect material things.

Conic Hand

The conic hand, also sometimes known as the artistic hand, is recognized by the roundness of the nail ends of the fingers. These hands are subdivided into three groups. (1) Those with small thumbs and medium-sized palms are said to represent those always drawn to artistic beauty. (2) Those that are thick, short, and that have a large thumb represent those drawn to wealth, fortune, and fame. (3) Those with very large hands with well-developed, strong palms may be highly sensual.

Psychic Hand

The psychic hand is distinguished by frequently long and always pointed fingers. These people are described as idealistic dreamers who may be quite neurotic.

Mixed Hand

The mixed hand seems to fit most of the human race. That subject will be described according to the perception of each individual palmist. The description will depend on the weight each palmist gives to the competing features of the hand. This system should appeal to the psychic or intuitive reader. That reader will find answers from other realms no matter what he or she sees in the actual hand form.

Realistically, it would be better to avoid systems that classify a mixed form as a specific type of hand. It would be easier to describe specific hands and then give the hands overlays. The mixing would come from the overlays on the basic types of hands. For example, we could have an earth hand with the overlays of an A (constipated) shape and pointed or spatulate fingers. On top of this we would consider the lines. Furthermore, the finger-prints and other dermatoglyphics of the hand will have tremendous impact upon our interpretation

of the basic type and how they best seek and attain their goals. The overlay system is an easier teaching method and provides clearer classifications.

CARL CARUS TYPES WITH FOLLOWERS' REFINEMENTS

Carl Carus divided the hand into four types: elementary, motoric, sensitive, and psychic. Both Sorell,[47] and Wolff[48] have used this approach. A description of the Carus system is also found in the books of Fred Gettings and by Francis King.[49] Both authors also describe the d'Arpentigny system. Asano[50] also describes this system but does not mention Carl Carus. Instead, he calls this the system used to point out personality differences in Charlotte Wolff's study. He further notes that when he met Dr. Wolff, she refused to discuss palmistry, saying that she had given up on it entirely. He said that in Wolff's late years she shifted from the scientific study of palmistry to a mystical approach to palmistry.

Asano related the Carus method to that developed by Ernest Kretschmer[51] and W. Sheldon. That method provides for the correlation of personality to physical types and biological conditions. The system is referred to as morpho-psychology and was used in France and Switzerland for psychological diagnosis. Asano correlated the names of types from the two systems: Wolff's simple fleshy to Kretschmer's pyknic, Wolff's motor bony to Kretschmer's athletic, and Wolff's long sensitive to Kretschmer's leptosomatic.

Asano concluded that shape alone is inadequate to explain personality. He concludes that it is essential to study the creases of the palms in order to classify them. We will discuss Asano's method after we summarize the Carus system.

Carus Elementary Type

The Carus elementary hand is large, heavy, and thick in appearance and corresponds in physical description to the d'Arpentigny elementary hand. It is coarse and not very flexible. The fingers are short. The hand usually has very few palmar lines. These are generally limited to the main flexure lines. Carus would see it as relating back to the prehensile characteristic of all anthropoidal species and would look for degenerate qualities. The dermatoglyphics are clearly defined and the lines have a thick, earthy, turgid quality.

Wolff describes two elementary types of hands, the simple type and the irregular type, and adds that it is difficult to distinguish the two types. They resemble each other and the lines are few and horizontal. The skin on the irregular hand is often finer than on the simple one. She says that the invariable distinguishing feature is the "presence of atavistic stigmata." These atavistic stigmata could include a simian line that virtually cuts off any lower transverse line or reduces it to a mere appendage; and/or an abnormal fifth (little) finger that is too small or deformed; and/or the presence of some atypical dermatoglyphic patterns on the palm and fingertips and especially on the sides of the first three fingers. She found such hands on many athletes such as boxers and wrestlers examined in Paris and detected disproportionately large mounts of Venus, abnormally protruding percussions, and short, stout brutish type thumbs.

Wolff describes the subject with the simple ele-

mentary hands are usually good-tempered, simple, and quiet, with a generally steady equilibrium
and benevolent character. However, these pleasant character traits can all be shaken under strong
emotion. Yet, even under sadness and depression,
this subject remains approachable. She feels that
he or she lives a "life of primary instinct" and thus
is slow and not very sensitive. They are gifted for
the simpler types of work.

Dr. Wolff's irregular elementary subjects include social misfits and outcasts such as habitual
criminals, idiots, and the insane. But her category
is broader than that. She also found lethargic and
docile characters with a good stout heart, who
possessed much courage and a charitable disposition. She felt that these people were dull and had
an infantile mentality. However, she also found
that a gifted neurotic who could be excitable,
unstable, and hypersensitive was at the opposite
end of the same spectrum. Both reaction types she
felt could be included in the same "schizoid group
of temperament."

Carus Motoric Type

The Carus motoric hand is also a prehensile type,
but on a more refined level. The fingers are longer
and more flexible. Even with more flexibility, the
fingers still are not very pliant. The palm shows
more lines, suggesting a richer emotional life.

Wolff would describe these hands as motoric
fleshy and motoric bony types. The motoric bony
type would possess the philosopher's fingers; that
is, the joints of the fingers would stand out and
make the fingers look bony. In the fleshy hand, the
joints and the fingers would be smooth. The bony
hand would be relatively flat, lack fat, and the
muscles would feel firm. While they do vary
widely, the nails tend to be long and have well-
developed moons.

By contrast, the fleshy motoric hand is broad
and fleshy. In contrast to the long, slender thumb
and index fingers of the bony hand, those with
fleshy hands lean toward being broad and stocky.
While both hands are muscular, it has a fleshy
appearance and is softer. The nails are generally
short and broad with small moons if they have any.
The mount of Venus tends to be fuller.

Wolff refers to the leptosome type described by
Kretschmer in describing the bony motoric personality as shy, introspective, nervous, and excitable. She labels this type as the aesthetic aristocrat
and says of this schizoid character that he loves
country peace and craves urban excitements. The
possession of ebullience, charisma, strength of
purpose, and impressionable nature render him
usually popular with many admirers and generally
he enjoys success. He is in danger of becoming
very egotistical and may take on more than he can
handle. He can be witty and is more rational and
perceptive than theoretical or abstract in his thinking processes. He is a man of action.

The fleshy motoric individual is more the extrovert. This subject is attracted to the comforts of the
good life. He or she is easily roused in a discussion.
Generally this subject is kind-hearted. Overall, this
person is secure, tolerant, and patient. While he or
she may not be brilliant, each has a good depth of
understanding often accompanied by a good sense
of humor. These are rational and objective subjects
whose judgments are balanced.

Carus Sensitive Type

The sensitive hand falls into Carus's second classification, the touch classification. Both the sensitive
and psychic hands are part of this group. The sensitive hand is also flexible, but neither so large nor as
strong as the motoric hand. Many lines can usually
be found upon the palm that are of a fine quality.

Wolff divides the sensitive type of hand into the small and long types. The small type has a small, narrow hand. The palm is relatively long, the fingers are proportionately short, and the thumb is small. It is a flexible hand; the ends of the fingers can be bent back and the thumb may be double-jointed. The fingers may have a teardrop formation and the mounts at the base of the fingers are conspicuous, displaying accentuated prominence. The nails vary widely, but they tend more often to be broad, of average length, with well-developed moons if any are present.

Wolff compares the sensitive long hand to the long hand illustrated in paintings by the old masters. It is a long, slender, and flexible hand with tapering fingertips shown with a supple dorsal inclination, i.e., the fingers bend backward. It could be called aristocratic or feminine. Wolff examined many such hands in both England and France, and she wrote in 1943 that she had never seen this type on a member of the working class. She noted that Carus called this type the physic type of hand and related it to the perfect qualities of character. She had a different notion of what constituted good character and disagreed.

Wolff felt that subjects with small, sensitive hands were hypersensitive, and this excitable nature placed them in the schizoid group. While the subjects' emotions arouse easily, they have little endurance or resistance to pressure. He or she is an easy victim. Yet, in rare moments of real danger, something within galvanizes this subject to unexpected strength and responsible action. All in all, the subjects retain childish characteristics and they are romantic escapists to the end. The subjects have vivid intelligence and are very original. Their intuition and imagination enable them to understand others.

Wolff says that this hand often belongs to schizophrenics, and when it is found on normal people, they are likely to be "the most introverted schizoid type." They are introspective, reserved loners. They are saturnine, with a prevailing mood of depression. These subjects are extravagant, yet emotionally weak and exhibit no normal emotional response to human affection. They will display lethargy or spirituality, and may delight in mysticism. These subjects are intuitive, fanciful, and imaginative rather than rational and logical subjects. They may have a great feeling for words, symbols, and the hidden meaning of things. They may be off the wall rather than methodical. Yet their love for language can lead them to become stylized and supercilious.

Carus Psychic Type

The psychic hand is soft to the touch, sometimes flabby. The lines form a challenge to any reader from sheer abundance. Look for a small thumb and watch for tapering fingers. The hand itself may be quite slender. Wolff does not describe a separate psychic hand, but relies on her description of the long, sensitive hand.

Walter Sorell was not satisfied with the Carus hand types as further refined by Dr. Wolff and reworked the classifications. He divided the hands into two general groups, the receptive hands and the realistic hands. The sensitive type went into the receptive group and the elementary type went into the realistic group. The motoric types divide into the sensitive-motoric and realistic-motoric with each in their own respectively named group. He then added the aesthetic type to the sensitive group and the spatulate type to the realistic group.

Sorell Receptive and Realistic Hands

The receptive hand appears fragile, delicate, and is long and conic in shape. These are the introspective-meditative types. They show schizophrenic tendencies and tend never to get fat.

The realistic hand is more square and broad, with a wide grip. These are the earthy, robust, energetic yet easygoing types and may display the manic-depressive personality. They may grow fat.

ASANO TYPES

Hachiro Asano, while coming from a Japanese background, has developed his own typing of hands. He has developed some forty-eight types of hands, all dependent upon location, shape, and length of the life, head, and heart lines. Space does not allow me to detail all forty-eight types that he describes. Mr. Asano makes some excellent observations of the heart and head lines and I will consider them under discussion of those major lines. He brings to us an Oriental fascination and respect for the simian line that one does not find in Western palmistry. I will discuss that further when I discuss the simian line.

The greatest problem with the forty-eight types of hands that are described by Asano is its complexity. Perhaps Mr. Asano's categories may be useful where a print of the entire hand can be viewed prior to consultation with the client. I do not believe his system can possibly cover all combinations of hand types. Besides this practical consideration, there are some technical difficulties that I find with Mr. Asano's categories.

Let me illustrate my problems with Mr. Asano's method by first sharing his detailed description of the characteristics of two of his forty-eight types of hands. Mr. Asano describes his CL III and CO II types as found once in ten thousand hands. He goes on to describe the CL III type as either a fool or a genius and as a person who is relatively unaware of women and interested in only lofty love affairs. CL III types prefer arranged marriages and their married lives center on work and bear fruit in the later years. This is more judgment on charac-ter rather than a description. He says that the CO II types are aggravated by physical weakness, tend to give up easily, are irritable, and fret. They need to educate their abilities and some have succeeded in music by "correctly cultivating their inner beings." They tend to put others on pedestals and romance proves difficult for them. They do best in arranged marriages.

Think for a moment of how many people Mr. Asano would have to interview before he could come to these conclusions. Would he have had to speak to at least twenty of each type to be sure he was correctly describing that type? Would he have needed to speak to a hundred? Say only twenty were needed. Given his figures, he would have had to have interviewed two hundred thousand subjects if only one in ten thousand CL III or CO II types may be found.

I could not begin to double-check his work. Even in a fast reading, I find it difficult to sustain 20 readings a day (I have done 109 in a four-day period). If Mr. Asano interviewed 20 subjects a day for 5½ days a week (the work week we in America are told that the Japanese maintain) he would only see 110 subjects a week and it would take him 1,818 weeks to interview two hundred thousand people or approximately thirty-five years to compile his statistics on these two hands.

In any event, Mr. Asano has many fascinating "statistics" in his work, *Hands: The Complete Book of Palmistry*, and many useful observations. I do not recall reading when he started his profession. He was born in 1931, according to his biography.

His book, *Hands: The Complete Book of Palmistry*, was published in 1985. I must presume he began compiling his statistics when he was eighteen. This displays remarkable dedication, fortitude, and application for a man who took his bacca-laureate in literature from Waseda University and, after doing graduate work there, went on to study at the Sorbonne in 1955, where he developed his interest in "personalism."

TRADITIONAL CHINESE FIVE TYPES

The five shapes of palm found under traditional Chinese palmistry are called fire, water, earth, wood, and gold (or metal). Physiognomy is also a part of the Chinese study as it is in Benham's methods, covered below.

Traditional Chinese Water Hand

The water hand should be thick, soft, tender, and the fingers conic and smooth (the knuckles will not protrude to the sides). This round-bodied person with smooth, healthy-colored skin, while perhaps not fat, will not show bones. He or she is considered wise and will become wealthy as he or she is intelligent. Gettings relates this hand to the sensitive hand, *i.e.*, that described by Wolff as the small, sensitive hand.

Traditional Chinese Fire Type

The fire hand fits well with a red, shiny face, domed brow, long head, and wide chin. The hands will show the bones and sinews and the knuckles will be bony. The hands will be sharp and strong. Although the fire person may be polite and generally well-mannered, he or she also has a quick temper. Note how a person with a bony motoric hand might also be described as the Chinese traditional fire type.

Traditional Chinese Wood Type

The wood hand fits a person who is strong, thin, straight, and tall, with hard sinews and joints. Fingers will be thin and there is a knotted appearance to the skin over the knuckles while the hands are flat and long. Gettings relates this hand to the motoric hand, most probably Wolff's bony motoric hand, though either type might fit. The wood suggests some resilience and perseverance and Gettings relates the subject's characteristics to those of the Jupiterian hand (below), which is typefied by largeness of outlook and expansiveness. The subject would be a physically active, practical, self-confident person with good common sense.

Traditional Chinese Gold Type

The gold hand has well-balanced features, is strong-boned, and has hard muscles. He or she is light in color; the Chinese would say white. The hand, as the person's general build, should be square and it should be elastic. While strong-minded, patient, sensible, and steadfast, he or she will worry over work and spend much time on business to the expense of hobbies and leisure activities. These subjects are not daydreamers. This subject seems more related to the fleshy motoric person.

Chinese Metal Type Hand

Gettings describes another Chinese type, the metal type, which reflects the description given to the psychic or long, sensitive hand.

Traditional Chinese Earth Type

The large, thickset person will typify the earth person. Look for a large nose, wide mouth, round chin, thick lips, hard muscles, and sturdy bones. The hands are thick and rounded. They sound somewhat like the elementary hands of both the Carus and d'Arpentigny systems. These hands are found on honest, frugal persons who display modesty, loyalty, and enjoy hard work. They may be opinionated and speak their own mind but are truthful and reliable. Gettings relates this type to the elementary handed persons.

MUCHERY SYSTEM WITH BENHAM OVERLAYS

Fred Gettings describes another system developed by the French astrologer, Georges Muchery. Eight hand forms are named after planets and are portrayed with traditional characteristics linked to the astrological sign associated with those planets.[52] Gettings describes eight very distinctive types associated with definite characteristics and temperaments. He notes that the difficulty with the system is that not all hands are covered. We have found this in almost all systems except the fourfold earth, fire, water, and air system with the overlays of the A and V types and consideration of the size and shape of the percussion.

William Benham also describes planetary types found through his analysis of dominance of types of mounts. Each of seven geographic areas of the palm are represented by one of the six planets plus the Sun (Apollo) known before the discovery of Neptune, Uranus, and Pluto. In his case, Benham finds which mount tends to be the strongest and then says that the hand takes on the basic characteristics of that mount.[53] Benham, like the traditional Chinese palmist, describes the appearance of the entire subject, not merely the hand.

Besides shape, in the Muchery system each hand type has distinctive marks or other qualities or peculiarities that will distinguish it. To some extent, even the water type of hand in the Wu-Hsing relies more on palmar evidence than merely shape. Mr. Asano's system certainly does.

One major objection to using characteristics that are ascribed to the planetary influences is that they are so general that they could apply to everyone. After thousands of clinical uses, I no longer will concede this as true. I might admit that each of us has some qualities represented by each of the planetary forces, but this does not account for the predominance of certain characteristics over others that I have confirmed by using that analysis. I cannot confirm that the particular planet's force has anything to do with the characteristics observed, but I can clinically confirm the repeated correlation between common traits that relate predominantly to specific planetary characteristics and the subjects whose hands and features represent those planetary influences.

Because the Muchery system also covers the Earth as a planetary hand type and Benham does not, we will cover that hand first.

Earthy Hand

The earthy hand may or may not show dirty finger-nails, but it will be firm and thick, the lines will be deep, and the head line, with a show of extreme practicality, almost a Midas touch, ends up toward or on the mount of Mercury. The life and head lines should also be closely joined, showing the cautious natural conservatism found in the earth-handed subject.

The description of the earth type in the four types of hands already given applies here. Gettings notes that Earth is traditionally related to Saturn as the governor of the physical form and the weight of materialism, the load-bearing efforts that can lead to melancholia. He notes that some saturnine personality may be found in possessors of Earth hands, though this is not entirely the case. Both Muchery's and the fourfold earth types have a certain serious, or lugubrious outlook precluding spontaneous exhibition of emotions. However, this Earth type, we are assured by Gettings, is neither as austere nor miserable as textbooks might describe the saturnine. Look elsewhere to the positive characteristics found in the stable, practical, and dependable, even if a little boring, citizen.

THE BENHAM TYPES

No serious student of palmistry today would overlook the observations of Benham, the American giant of the field at the turn of the last century. One will see his name repeatedly and his works are classic. The Benham types are more than just hand types. They describe the entire physical appearances of the subjects, their mental attitudes, and moral persuasions. Many competent palmists still look to *The Laws of Scientific Hand Reading* by William G. Benham, first published in 1900, as their bible on the subject. Benham divides his subjects into seven types: Jupiterian, Saturnian, Apollonian, Mercurian, Martian, Lunarian, and Venusian.

Jupiterian Hand and Type

The Jupiterian will have a large hand with large proximal phalanges, so that these thick and heavy parts might be inscribed in a circle. This large, thick hand is relatively soft. The Jupiterian will have a large mount of Jupiter, that fleshy mound under the index finger. It will be full and strong and its center as shown by the dermal triradius will be centrally located.

The subject should be of medium height, but large, strongly built, and inclined to be fleshy. He has the large, strong bones to support his weight. His skin is smooth and his complexion is clear. The color will appear healthy. It would be pink in those where pink shows health. This subject should have large, expressive eyes that are generally clear but may dilate under emotional pressure. This subject appears as an affable and honest spirit. The lips are full, the nose well-formed and straight, and the mouth large. The cheekbones may not be seen and the upper eyelids are thick. The eyebrows are even and may be arched. Long lashes form a graceful curl. The chin may be dimpled and is strong, showing a firm jaw. The ears will be close to the head and regularly formed. The subject may perspire freely. A female may have an abundance of fine, curly hair. Yet the male often finds baldness to be his lot. The subject has a good chest supporting a big heart and a melodious voice. Our subject appears as a natural leader.

In palmistry, the index fingers are on the active, outreaching side of the hand. We call it Jupiter. The mount relates to ego. The planet Jupiter relates to the magnanimous side of character. It governs the gentle, compassionate, and humane qualities of personality. Moral character is bolstered by a strong Jupiter, though not at the expense of being charitable, loyal, helpful, well-grounded, and having a broad outlook. Too strong a Jupiter influence could lead to self-indulgence, wide speculation, and arrogance. These qualities also are linked with the air hand, more common in the male. The index finger is also linked with these forces, though on a more spiritual level, according to Gettings.

Gettings comments that attempts have been made to associate the Jupiter of Pisces with the index finger and the Jupiter of Sagittarius with the head line.

Jupiter relates to strength, and Benham finds self-confidence in these people, the ego recognizing its own strength. They may be bombastic and vain. They are natural Leos, seeking places of leadership or at least recognition of their own leadership. This is likely to cover an easily bruised ego. They have a kind nature born out of a deep desire to be loved. They wish to give and receive love openly. Jupiterians want to be respected and not feared. They may have an innate desire not only to be loved by the masses but to mingle with them to attain this love, even while remaining true, dignified aristocrats. Thus pride and ambition are also driving forces behind this person. All in all, Benham finds little fault in these qualities. They produce one of the most invincible of all personages with many desirable characteristics, attracting both sexes.

Saturnian Hand and Type

The fingers of the Saturn hand bend toward the middle (Saturn) finger and there is a Saturn line running from the life line to the mount of Saturn. The mount of Saturn will be strongly marked with lines, and the middle finger will be long. The triradius apex on the mount of Saturn will be centrally located. The other upper mount apices will lean toward Saturn.

The Saturnian will be the tallest of the seven Benham types, appearing gaunt and thin. His pale skin will be yellowish and dry. It may be wrinkled, rough, and even hanging in folds or it may be drawn tightly over the bones. Benham describes the subject as bilious with thick, dark, and often straight black hair cut in a harsh manner. The male may lose this hair when he is quite young. He may remind one of a hatchet man. His ears may be large and his deep-set eyes generally subdued or sad, except when flashes of other emotions quickly cross them. The nose is sharp and thin and probably too long to be attractive. It is a tight nose, not dilating with breathing. His pale, thin lips seal a large mouth atop a firm and prominent jaw. Decay of the teeth and gums sets in early. Ichabod Crane could pose for this figure.

Judgment and balance come to mind as predominant forces of Saturn, and these can evidence limitations, restrictions, and fear. Strong Saturn influence can display itself in practicality and materialism. This is the counting house in which debts must be paid, so it is not surprising that we see a hard worker, one who perseveres and has great concentration. Check for the narrow angle of the thumb and see if we do not also find parsimony. However, ultimate success may always elude such a person, being just out of the grasp, despite the long reach of the middle finger. The

Saturnian's caution, conservatism, and stinginess might lead to melancholia.

With all of that, Benham notes that he or she may write well, producing fine histories and scientific treatises. But, especially if the top (distal) phalange of the thumb cannot be bent back, he or she is opinionated, does not like contradiction, and will not be restrained. This subject insists on his or her own independence.

Apollonian Hand and Type

Apollo marks the solar hand, with a ring finger longer than the index finger and a distinctive Apollo line gracing the palm. The Apollo mount will be raised and may have few or no lines. The mount may also show some development toward the little finger. Like the fire hand, the fingers are short. They are also knotty, and the first phalange of the thumb is long.

The Apollonian visage is healthy and attractive. The hair is thick and wavy and dark in color, having a fine, silky quality. The almond-shaped eyes lie below a broad, full forehead. The body is graceful, athletic, and well defined. This person is neither thin like the Saturnian nor fleshy like the Jupiterian. The eyes convey an open, honest look. A fine, straight nose adorns a full face with clear skin. The fine, white teeth are set in healthy gums. Apollo is a figure of balance, taller than the Jupiterian but not so tall as the Saturnian. The cheeks are high and firm with no hollows below them. Above his muscular long neck, sitting close to the head, are medium-sized ears. The graceful mouth rests above a rounded and shapely chin that neither protrudes nor retreats.

While the Jupiter finger may relate to ego, Gettings notes that the sun is the "planet" that reigns over self. Apollo stands for the masculine principle of command through willpower. The strong Apollonian will possess self-confidence and display a dignified, decorous appearance. Apollo is also related to creativity. The possessor of this type of hand may be creative and perhaps even brilliant. Whether creative or not, Apollonians will be lovers of beauty. They are spontaneous. The long first phalange could suggest an outreaching person, so the giving of this person's gift of creativity would appear to be magnanimous. However, a long Apollo finger can also show the gambler, the high risk taker. Gettings notes the excesses of this character could appear as bombastic behavior, egocentricity, and even incompetence. Here we find a link of the Sun hand with the fire hand. The fire sign Leo, ruled by the Sun, is also linked with the heart line and is reflected in the generous nature of these subjects.

Benham picks up on the characteristic of the Sun type being highly intuitive. Perhaps this is related to the myth of Apollo being able to see farther over the horizon from the vantage point of his chariot in the sky. This lofty person does not have to labor to learn or to be profound. This driver of the Sun appears brilliant to all who look upon him. He or she has the eye of an eagle, making the most of what others would see only as a speck on the land. The Apollonian is highly adaptable, as mythically he must travel across all lands. So Apollo may be credited with more intelligence than he really has. He or she has the artist passion, if not the talent, and can make a brilliant performer. His cheerful character may be interspersed with fits of violent temper. These angry bursts are momentary, and Apollo holds no grudge, but can convert the worst enemy. Our client tends to conquer and shackle, so this attraction may only be temporary. Benham says the Apollonian neither is nor makes a lasting friend.

The creative index is measured by the presence

of a fine and deeply cut Sun line, a well-developed mount with a centrally located apex, and perhaps the existence of stars on the mount. Squares, circles, triangles, and tridents also strengthen the Apollonian hand when found on the mount of the Sun (Apollo).

Mercurian Hand and Type

Is there a well-marked line on the percussion side of the hand that appears to follow a crescent with its middle moving toward the middle of the palm? Here we can see a well-marked line of intuition that may appear on the Mercurial hand with a long little finger and a protruding, strongly lined mount of Mercury. The lower (proximal) phalanges of the fingers, while not necessarily thick, will be long and the fingers will appear to lean outward, toward the thumb.

Identify the Mercurial hand through the prominence of the little finger and mount below it. Look for the apex centered on a well-developed mount. Observe a long and large little finger.

The Mercurial stature will be small and compact. He or she will be neat, with a strong or convincing demeanor and expression. The oval face will have balanced features and display a quickly changing intellect. There may be a transparency to the clear, smooth skin, and it may have an olive cast. Yet the blush will show through in response to emotional changes. A lofty and protruding forehead could support black or chestnut curly hair. In men the beard will be full and perhaps darker than the hair. The dark eyes, under moderate brows, show a piercing restlessness. Pale lips that are somewhat thin appear below a thin nose that may be a little more fleshy at the end. Small white teeth are evenly set in healthy gums. The whites of the Mercurian eyes reflect that the subject is nervous and a bit bilious with a little yellow shading. Sometimes an upturned chin will be long and sharp, and the strong neck will be sinewy, with a graceful appearance. He may look somewhat like the pictures of leprechauns, with a chest large for his size. The body supports graceful limbs that supply quick movement. One could be viewing an agile gymnast.

Mercury carried the messages of the gods and his planet links with communication and expression. Communication may be by means of speech. In cases where the throat chakra is blocked (see health lines) that communication may be in the form of music or the visual arts.

The strong Mercurian may be very persuasive. His or her mind is quick and may even be volatile as it works ingeniously and in a perpetually inquiring manner. But excess can lead to opportunistic and exaggerated discourse. In the zodiac, the little finger is associated with Virgo, which some say is ruled by Mercury. Gettings notes that attempts have been made to find Mercury the ruler over the life line, connected with the air sign of Gemini. Perhaps the curves of the life line around the mount of Venus, so related to earth energies and the mutability of the planet itself, links its Virgonian character to the life line.

Quicksilver symbolizes this fleetest and most active of all types. Rapid insight, grace, and skill with the head and the hands are noted by Benham. So we may find the keen mind and good athlete where dexterity and skill are required. The Mercurian is a keen judge of human character and could make an excellent palmist or face reader. However, this adroit human may also be a constant schemer. He or she might be a consummate con artist, excellent businessperson, or clever advocate and is not above taking another's ideas and plagiarizing them.

Martian Hand and Type

Is there a cross in the center of the palm, the plain of Mars? Is the distal phalanx of the thumb thick and strong? Does the palm display fairly short but deeply graven lines? Here, then, is displayed the Martian hand.

The Martians divide into the aggressors, showing a prominent lower Mars, and the resisters, showing a prominent upper Mars. Often both mounts are well developed, and then we have a clear Martian. If the center plain is also well developed with fine, red lines, we can have a volatile temper that can lead to dangerous confrontations.

The Martian appears as erect, muscular, and of medium height. His head seems to show greater development of the lower areas of the brain in its bullet shape and small size. Small, closely set ears and a Roman or long, straight nose adorn the head. The eyes may be bloodshot, but the dark irises and pupils will convey a bold, bright expression. The neck may be broad and thick. A strong voice will find support from a powerful chest. The short legs are stout and he may have flat feet. The large mouth is set over a strong chin, yet the lips are thin, with the upper lip being thinner. The yellowish teeth are small and regularly set and strong. The skin is reddish and flush at times.

Mars stands for aggression and endurance, and it is directly linked to the heroic, masculine ideal of sexuality. Strong Mars makes the subject vigorous, bold, impetuous at times, aggressive, undaunted in opinion, impassioned, and restless. Excess can be displayed in blind anger and brashness. Normally we think of the sun as the finger indicative of these energies. Gettings notes that the ring finger, Apollo, has also been suggested as the reservoir of Martian energies rather than those of the sun. In that case, those fingers that are associated with the zodiacal sign of Scorpio would

be the reservoir of the negative energies of the sun. Others find that the Martian energies are reflected through the center of the palm. This appears like the three phalanges of a finger stretching from upper Mars on the percussion across the plain of Mars and into the aggressive mount of lower Mars above the thumb and the mount of Venus (or Vulcan).

Benham would also put this hand on the good side of the ledger. He finds the Martian extremely generous with the use of his money, because wealth is only a tool to gain ends. He loves to have and generally finds friends or admirers. To these he is devoted. If upper Mars is highly formed, he will defend them. He may be tactless. While he cannot be driven, he is mutable. He can be coaxed. He is very passionate. The Martian is robust and expansive.

Lunarian Hand and Type

The mount of the Moon is the key to this type. The size of the palmar pad and the outward curve on the percussion must both be considered. When we find a spiral mark set low on the lunar mount, and it is strongly rayed on a very soft hand, we may have a lunar hand. This hand will also have many finely meshed, superficial, weak lines and the fate line will originate from the mount of the Moon. The hand's general appearance is puffy and feels flabby. The short, smooth, conic or pointed fingers, small thumb, and flaccid palm will be covered with pale flesh.

Our subject is tall and perhaps a bit flabby or even corpulent. The lower limbs appear thick, and the muscles lack tone. There is a pallor over the spongy flesh suggesting a weak heart, persistent anemia, kidney problems, or even dropsy. The eyes bulge from below a low forehead. They are accompanied by thick temples in the round head. Straggly, straight, fine hair grows from the scalp, complemented by scant, uneven eyebrows that may form a single feature as they grow together. Below the starry round eyes sits a short nose, small and upturned at the end. The eyes may water adding to their luminous appearance under swollen lids. The lips purse in the little mouth over a double chin. The yellow teeth are long and large, growing from anemic gums. Small, close-set ears lie aside the head. Flat feet may aptly complete this less-than-healthy appearing specimen. Even the voice lacks depth, being high-pitched and reedy.

Gettings describes the Moon as the "feminine vehicle or mask through which selfhood of the sun mediates with the world." Energies of these people will follow the cycles of the moon and can change with the tides. They may appear impressionable, but beware; remember the lasting impression of a fist withdrawn from a bucket of water. Lunarians have problems adjusting to the sharp edges and flat surfaces of the rational world. The hand may be associated with the sign of Cancer, the zodiac house ruler of the Moon. This person can be dreamy and idealistic, building castles in the air or on the sandy beach. The soft hand suggests laziness. The Saturnian cannot reach success because of his yearning for balance and safety. Our Lunarian wishes for success by constantly yearning for what is beyond his or her reach. Our subject is one of those persons, like the water-handed person, who needs a measure of security and support. These people often have vivid imaginations and spectacular dreams. With stars on the mount of the Moon, we find those who have constant revelations and precognition. Because they feel their difference, they may seek the safety of seclusion and retirement. The beauties of nature are found appealing. These people probably lack self-confidence, energy, and perseverance.

Venusian Hand and Type

There is an arc that runs from between the little and ring finger to the space under the middle or between the middle and index fingers. This is called the girdle of Venus and this is one sign of the Venusian hand. The mount of Venus (below the thumb), is bowl-shaped, raised, and its center is strongly rayed. The Saturn line originates on this mount. Our subject's hand appears small in relation to the general structure of the body and has a thick, short thumb. We look to the size of the development of the mount of Venus to decide how much of the Venusian qualities our subject may bear. Gauge size from both the pads on the palm and the geographic area covered. It is bounded by the life line on the inside of the palm and lies below the lower mount of Mars.

Our subject should be attractive, even beautiful. Grace, shapely appearance, and balance should greet us. Benham finds that while the Juperterian and Apollonian types represent manly beauty, the male Venusian is softly voluptuous, partaking of the feminine beauty. Transparent, soft, fine skin, velvet to touch, will display a pink cast as the healthy cardiovascular system displays itself. Tender, dark, almond-shaped eyes under healthy, well-marked eyebrows gaze from a finely proportioned, oval or round face. The faces lack signs of angularity such as high cheekbones or a jutting chin. The abundant brows are crowned by a high forehead overlayed by unwrinkled, tightly drawn skin. Dimples may adorn the cheeks in a smile. Long, silky, fine, wavy hair abundantly grows from the scalp. The subject has a long and shapely nose. The young females will have a Venusian mark on the bridge between the eyes consisting of three vertical lines. Below the nose is a beautiful mouth with full red lips covering white, evenly set, medium-sized teeth in healthy gums.

The fully rounded chin may support a dimple of its own. A long, full, and graceful neck growing from sloping shoulders carries the head. The chest gives full play to the lungs, being expansive. Shapely would be the term for the rest of the body, like a ballet dancer with fine muscle tone yet lacking severe definition. The melodious voice is quite appealing. There is a spring in the walk as the small, highly arched feet carry the subject gracefully.

Gettings described the traits of the strong Venusian as warm, well-balanced, agreeable, refined yet expressive, and idealistic. Venus expresses, often through feminine sexual energies, the ability to be receptive to emotional and artistic impressions. Excess Venusian energy may lead to lethargy, showing persons who lack self-confidence or enterprise. Benham puts the Venusian hand on the good side of his hand ledger because of its standing for love, generosity of spirit, and sympathy. However, while a strong Venusian hand in a woman could be good, such a hand in a man may spell either profligacy or suggest an effeminate personality, especially if one finds the conic fingertips and a hand with a soft consistency. A woman, Benham believes, will restrain these fiery and heated passions. A Venusian is a social animal, seeking the company of others.

FENTON AND WRIGHT SYSTEM

Sasha Fenton and Malcom Wright gave up on the "old hand-shape terminology." They observed that no one could be expected to pick out the psychic hand based upon the descriptions in the average palm book. They have sought to give more graphic descriptions and have named the following types of hands: square hand; short, wide hand; rounded, elegant hand; soft, squashy hand; clawlike hand; A-shaped hand; V-shaped hand; knotty or knobby hand; long, narrow hand; long, delicate hand; monkeylike hand; short, plump hand; square, slim hand; short, wide hand; and mixed hand.

While the descriptions are perhaps somewhat more accurate, they still beg any complete description because Fenton and Wright have not done away with the category of the mixed hand. Sometimes their description is about as problematical as the use of the term *philosophic*. What, pray tell, is universally accepted as elegant, and how do the terms *long and narrow* differ from *long and delicate* except through reference to a drawing? Their drawing of a monkey hand looks to this writer like a small air hand. Because the little finger is straight, we might not agree that the subject with that hand is slippery or untrustworthy. But our biggest problem with these descriptions is that there are too many of them. Furthermore, the characteristics they represent overlap types.

Some of the Fenton and Wright hand names merely rename those types of the d'Arpentigny system. The short, wide hand is the elementary hand. The rounded, elegant hand is the conic hand. Two spatulate hands are described, the A-shaped (my V-shaped "diarrhea" hand overlay) and the V-shaped hand (my A-shaped "constipated" hand overlay). The philosophic hand is described as the knotty or knobby hand. The psychic hand is identified as the long, delicate hand, and the drawing shows the hallmarks of a psychic hand, with the pointed fingers. So why not call it the long, pointed-finger hand? The mixed hand continues to be the mixed hand minus a few more descriptions. Presumably the square hand is the square hand. The square, slim hand is either a refined variant of the square (earth type) hand or is an air hand. The short, wide hand is a different variant as is the clawlike hand and the soft, squashy hand. The clawlike hand may resemble the Saturnian type of hand.

The soft, squashy hand reflects a subject who is a taker, not a giver. This person may display wide-eyed innocence but be very clever in business. Our subject can induce others to do any necessary physical work. These are the manipulative, selfish types. It looks somewhat like an overfed conic hand, but one that could have pointed fingertips. If it has the pointed fingers, Fenton and Wright consider it as a sign of the love of beauty. The lines are thin, often broken (especially the heart line), but rather straight.

The long, narrow handed subject is introspective and shy or uncomfortable around others. These subjects lack practicality, balance, and common sense. They may be terribly clever, artistically. They sound quite like the water personality of the Gettings/Wu-Hsing types.

The monkey hand is described as having slim, graspy fingers, useful for a quick, clever, and talented subject who is slippery and untrustworthy.

The short, wide hand is described as one that has fingers that taper toward the distal ends. The thumb appears to curve laterally and can bend far backward. These subjects are described as having great senses of humor, and being creative, generous, and helpful in their practical and realistic way. They tend to be sociable people.

CHAPTER FIVE

THE FINGERS

FINGER NAMES

The fingers traditionally have names. On the ulna side of the hand, the little finger, sometimes called the pinkie, is the Mercury finger, and it is above the mount of Mercury. The next finger, the ring finger, is known as the finger of Apollo or the Sun finger. It has also been called Uranus for reasons better explained in the next chapter. The middle finger, which is the one between the index finger and the ring finger, is known as the Saturn finger. The index finger is named after the chief of Roman gods, Jupiter. The thumb, that appendage on the radial side of the hand, generally remains the thumb. Medical terminology is more prosaic. The thumb is the first digit and we number toward the little finger with that finger being the fifth digit.

THE OBJECTS OF EXAMINATION

When we look at the fingers, we examine a variety of points. We do count them. We observe to see if the nails are clean and well manicured or dirty, chewed, or misshapen. We look at the size of the fingers, and we use special procedures to determine their sizes. Notice if the fingers are straight or crooked, and if they are bent, the direction of the bend. We notice whether the fingers are curled or relaxed, and if they are pliable or stiff. We detect whether the nails are bluish, pink, red, or pale. Do the nails have half moons or not? Notice if there is hair on the fingers, and if so, what kind of hair. We look at the fingers when relaxed and observe whether the fingers spread easily or if they are held tightly together. Are the knuckles bony, prominent, or smooth? We want to know what the ends of the fingers look like: are they pointed, rounded, square, or shaped like spatulas? We notice whether the fingers evenly align at their bases or if one or more is lower than the others. Compare their lengths both with each other and with the palm. Examine their lengths and widths from phalange to phalange and compare each digit. Then compare the fingers of one hand with those of the other.

A good palmist will look into all these matters in a matter of moments.

FINGER DEFORMITY OR LOSS

Some metaphysical schools contend that accidents do not happen. Therefore, the palmist of these schools will read significance into every deformity. If one were missing a portion of a finger, the palmist might inquire when it was lost, then would try to correlate the loss with the significance attributed to that finger. I had a client who had suffered the loss of the end of his index (Jupiter) finger in a mill accident. Before the accident he had been very arrogant. He appeared to his friends and family much restrained after the accident. Jupiter has to do with the presence and size of ego.

OBSERVE THE WHOLE HAND

Eager clients will often tender their hands, palm side up, with the question, "What hand do you want to look at?" I gently take their hands, turn them over, and rest them softly on a table or other flat surface. I start looking at the back of the hand first. The back of the hand displays the general shape of the hand. However, the palm must be examined before identifying the hand type. Here one can notice the general shape of the fingers, individually and together. One observes their color, the condition of the nails, skin, cuticles, warts, and other growths. I find out if there is any hair on the hands or fingers and of what quality.

I then have my clients move their hands. I ask them to hold up their hands so that I can compare the size of their hand (measured from the wrist to the fingertips) to the face (measured from the chin to the hairline or where the hairline would be if baldness were no problem). This tells me if the hand is long, short, or medium. By the way they hold their fingers (curled, spread, crooked, or straight), I begin to see something of their character and present concerns. After that, I tell them to relax and pretend to be concerned with equipment or something else while I surreptitiously watch them replace their hands on the table. The way they replace their hands tells me more of their present concerns. Are they truly at ease and self-confident, or cautious and insecure?

I notice whether the subjects rest their hands with fingers gently spread and comfortably apart. This displays confidence. Do they place their hands closely together with the thumbs touching or overlapping? Caution and insecurity are shown by such action. Of course, if there is only a small, flat area to rest the palms, this observation can have little meaning.

OBSERVE GESTURE

Elizabeth Brenner[1] has us begin to look for a variety of gesturing patterns: businessperson's syndrome; non-Socratic syndrome; hidden critic's syndrome; Milquetoast syndrome; pseudocommunicator's syndrome; and the withholder's syndrome. Each of these represent a personality overlay, not the basic personality. The overlay may change.

The businessperson's syndrome is recognized through bent Apollo and Mercury fingers on the dominant hand. The non-Socratic Syndrome is found on the other hand. Both syndromes probably indicate fear. They represent closing the energies of the Apollo and Mercury fingers dealing with communication, self-expression, and intuition. According to Brenner, the businessperson's syndrome results in a person focusing primarily on the external world and losing touch with his or her own drives, needs, and desires. The non-Socratic loses touch with the inner self and ends up living off his or her surface energy with no real grounding. These people may, when challenged, deny their problem and be quite convincing.

Fenton and Wright[2] note that if the Mercury and Apollo fingers tend to curl into a slight fist, the emotional life is difficult. This could show up in personal relations or home life, while the subject may do well at work.

In poker, if I saw this, I might push the bet to pressure the person out of the game. It would be a time to consider a bluff. However, consider another observation: Fenton and Wright point out that curled fingers may also be a sign of hot or dry skin.

In the Milquetoast syndrome we look for the closet meek. I compare the dominant and non-dominant thumb. I also observe whether the non-dominant thumb is tense compared to a relaxed, flexible dominant thumb. Brenner believes these Milquetoast syndrome people hold their spirits together by continual self-suppression instead of self-actualization.

The Milquetoast syndrome should not be confused with the person recovering from codependency. The codependent gives too much and will give anything rather than risk losing the love or affection of another. They are perfect subjects for abusive relationships. They may be spotted through the angle of generosity that forms between the thumb and the hand when we articulate the thumb at right angles with the index finger. When the angle is ninety degrees or greater, the person is a candidate for codependency. However, we see recovery in the dominant hand when one discovers that this thumb cannot comfortably be moved by the reader to greater than a ninety degree angle. Feeling this, along with writer's bumps, are two ways the reader's senses can check which is the predominant hand. It is more accurate than a writer's bump. Curiously, one often finds little flexibility in the distal phalange of the thumb. This shows stubbornness with the world while the codependent gives way to the family and loved ones.

The hidden critic's syndrome is unhealthy for all who meet it. Ms. Brenner observes that those with this syndrome display discrepancies in the tension levels of the Saturn fingers. Saturn is the judgment finger, representing the criticism (and discipline) that the subject can use. Here, the dominant Saturn finger is relaxed while the non-dominant is taut. This betrays that the person is far more critical than he or she may admit. The same thing may be observed through fingerprints, where the dominant Saturn finger is graced by a loop while the nondominant finger has a whorl. The difference is that the tone of the fingers can change. The syndrome shown only by the finger may change. Both the whorl and the rigid Saturn finger on the nondominant hand suggest a really strong moral code that is probably hidden in most daily activities. But transgression may bring retribution as an explosion, sudden frost, or long-term resentment. The explosion is more likely with the "killer" thumb.

Brenner names two other syndromes, the pseudocommunicator and the withholder. The first apparently has little real intention of communication, no matter what he or she may be saying. The withholder stands in silence, although he or she may know what to say.

The pseudocommunicator will have a bent Apollo finger and a straight little finger. Self-expression is displayed through Apollo, while verbal skills are reflected in Mercury. Here the tongue is not coordinated with the real interests of the subject. Thus the communication will lack sincerity.

Our withholder displays a bent little (Mercury) finger on the dominant hand. The little finger on the nondominant hand will be straight. This disparity shows that the desire to communicate is strong but is blocked, so one may receive sighs or looks of helplessness.

Fenton and Wright contend that in gesture, the dominant hand displays the current situation, and the nondominant hand shows underlying influ-ences. Self-assured persons are recognized by the fingers held loosely and straight. A slight curl in the top phalange will display caution. When both the distal and middle phalanges are bent, then caution is increased. If fingers are tightly held together, look for introspection and self-absorption or introversion.

When all of the fingers are held closely together, I find caution. David Brandon-Jones[3] also sees more than introspection. He sees a timid subject who is quite fearful.

Looking at the opposite hand with all of the fingers spread, Brandon-Jones finds antisocial tendencies. This person may shun others, probably in response to his hatred of restriction.

Clenched fists with thumbs held inside the fists display the hopeless or desperate situation. Fenton and Wright contend that the person may be next to a nervous breakdown. Brandon-Jones believes this shows temerity of one who wishes to pass the responsibility for making decisions on to another. However, we caution, check the temperature as the client may just be warming her thumbs.

Fenton and Wright find that the person who holds the little finger away from the other fingers is stubborn and self-contained. They report such a person has little desire to exchange ideas. Brandon-Jones believes this shows an almost pathological fear of any confinement, physical or mental. This would be doubly so if there were a ring of Saturn. We have observed that if such people are not married, they are unlikely to seek a traditional marriage relationship, though they might cohabit. We have noticed that the married ones are going through a period of independence when they display this posture. Do not confuse this with the subject scratching his ear.

Fenton and Wright note that in the relaxed hand, the spacing between the fingers is usually uneven. Some are close and others are held at different distances. They describe the space between Jupiter and Saturn fingers as showing the subject's ability to think for himself. They reason that because the radial side of the hand is the outgoing, active side, this suggests subjects may listen to advice but must act on their own decisions.

When the two middle fingers are held closely together, Fenton and Wright contend it shows lack of sufficient security and understanding. It may show a lack of financial security, or as Fenton and Wright contend, a conflict between the demands of career and kin or money and personal goals.

Spaces between Apollo and Saturn indicate the loner, according to Fenton and Wright. The person dislikes planning, and the V shape between the upper phalanges shows rebelliousness. This can be aggravated by whorls on these fingertips. Brandon-Jones finds these finger separations on long-haul truck drivers, long-distance runners, lighthouse keepers, gardeners, and gamekeepers. He finds that they are not only loners but usually outdoor people needing their space.

Wide spacing of any fingers can show a need for this freedom and space. Brandon-Jones points out that the gap between the Jupiter and Saturn fingers suggests an unorthodox, freethinking nonconformist such as Churchill. He observes that the wide space between the ring and little finger displays a need for freedom of action.

Spaces between Apollo and Mercury indicate the ability of independent action, according to Fenton and Wright. They point to the conductor of the orchestra as an example, and note that these people need R and R time to themselves. Watch for a sense of loneliness, they advise.

Placement of the hands on the table is important. Fenton and Wright believe that widely placed hands are signs of an active nature, of a mover. To them, the closer the hands, the more reflective the person. We have observed that the closer the hands, the more cautious the person or the smaller the table. Fenton and Wright contend that if the hands are aligned symmetrically with the two thumbs extended and touching, such a person is subliminally "aware of everything in his surroundings, all movement in the immediate environs, and may overreact to immaterial details."

Literature has pictured hand washing: Lady Macbeth with her "out damned spot" and Dickens's Uriah Heep washing his hands. Pilot is pictured washing his hands. Fenton and Wright report this is a sign of manipulative people and also a sign of severe distress. It can be seen on terrified or miserable children. Even in adults this may suggest the victim of dire stress or physical abuse. The rocking motion also shows this despair.

Hidden hands, clasped behind the back or kept in pockets, suggest a hidden agenda, according to William G. Benham[4] and David Brandon-Jones. Such a person is not "ready to show his hand." When folded in front of his chest and hidden, such a subject is defending himself against unjustified attack or intrusion.

Of course, we all know the pointed, wagged Jupiter finger belongs to the controller. The hand over the mouth signifies uncertainty or queasiness. Chins resting on fists can indicate inquisitiveness. We have heard that if the right hand holds the chin, then the person is ready to interpose his own point. That same theory holds that if the left hand holds the chin, the subject is more receptive. Our personal experience may be the opposite, and we are led to believe that the reaction will depend upon which hand is determined to be the dominant hand.

Brandon-Jones contends that if the left hand is palm down on the right when at rest, the person is receptive to what he hears. If the hands are reversed, the person is ready to jump into the discussion or activity with his own point or action. This may also depend upon which is the dominant hand. The jumper is also identified by whorls on the prints of the little finger.

Brandon-Jones cautions us to separate the outgoing, gregarious type who may freely use the hand to emphasize a point from the nervous, perhaps neurotic individual characterized by jerky, staccato movements while talking.

Brandon-Jones describes an excellent learning exercise for those who wish to understand gesture. Hit the mute button on the television set and observe the picture in silence. The student will soon follow the plot through understanding the gestures.

Let us now return to the shape of the hand.

HOW LONG IS THE HAND?

We measure the hand in relation to the face. A long hand will be as long from its connection to the wrist to the end of the middle (Saturn) finger as the face is from the chin to the natural youthful hairline. A short hand will reach about halfway or less up the forehead. Medium hands will range in between. The long hand shows ability to see detail. It may be said of this person that they may not see the forest for the trees.

The short-handed person, by comparison, wants the worldview, the big picture. If energetic, he or she can dig out the detail needed, but would rather handle the whole picture and leave the detail to others.

HAIR OR NO HAIR?

Hair is an indicator of energy. The coarser and darker the hair, the more energy the subject has. Some believe the hair exhibits the base sexual forces in humankind. Others are not so impressed. They find the hairier ones more physically aggressive, and the hairless ones show more diplomacy.

VARIOUS NAIL SHAPES

First observe the color of the fingernails. This measures the intensity of the energy as reflected by the nails. Carmine red reveals a hot, energetic blood supply. White or pale nails betoken cool subjects with restricted emotional reactions. Pink colored nails show health, warmth, and a relaxed disposition. The red-nailed person often does not know how to handle excesses of energy and may become irritable and act in a hasty manner. White nails can also be a sign of anemia, especially if the palm is also pale. Blue nails may show a circulatory problem, a lack of oxygen in the blood supply.

The ideal nail would be slightly curved from side to side and tip to base, as opposed to flattened. People with long nails may be drawn to artistic pursuits and may be good analyzers. They may be slower to act. The narrow nail is said to mirror a similar mind, the dogmatic view of life with little room for innovation or new ideas. Broad nails reveal the opposite. Short nails (not the result of biting off the ends) can show an impatient, critical turn of personality. We have often seen hands with generally average length nails yet short ones on the little finger. These people may talk too fast. They tend to speak before their thoughts are complete.

Square; Wide, Long; and Large, Square Nails: These nails indicate slower reactions. The subject appears to be slow to anger and react. When anger is expressed, it would be of the righteous type rather than impulsive. According to some Oriental doctrines, men possessing such nails are persevering and very positive and vigorous, women with these nails loathe to lose and may have stronger personalities than men. These nails are considered highly yang, or masculine. Darlene Hansen[5] says of the square nail that it shows good rational thinking, aggressiveness, and need for order in one's environment. Those who possess that nail tend to be linear thinkers with excellent organizational skills.

Short and Short, Wide Nails: These show high energy levels that are quickly released, often by anger, but also in forgiveness. Their owners are impulsive, have fast reactions, and sharp wit. The nails can be signs that sexual and emotional aggressiveness and passion rule rather than reason. Those who possess these short nails may seem to be callous, jealous, and possessive people. They do not take criticism kindly. They do not like to lose, and they show it. If the nails are extremely small, their outlook may be meager, bigoted, and narrow.

Short nails on good, strong, well-lined hands can mark a dynamic personality in all things, well suiting inherent aggressiveness. Given bad hand signs, badly formed and badly lined, particularly from the emotional standpoint, these nails will further strengthen the presumption of unpleasant qualities of personality.

Cheiro (Count Leigh de Hamong) contends that short nails run in whole families where there is a tendency toward heart disease.[6] Persons with these nails have a greater incidence of heart problems and diseases affecting the lower limbs and abdominal area of the body. He contends that where the short nail is also thin and flat, with little or no moons, it is a sure sign of weak action of the heart and, generally speaking, heart disease. However, persons with short nails do not generally have moons, anyway.

Very Short Nails: Some say that people with this type of nail use so much energy complaining that they never accomplish much of anything. They display poor resistance to disease and may seem weak and self-centered. Another quality that Dr. Eugene Scheimann[7] describes is the contrary urge to contradict everyone and argue, even when they know they are wrong. Because they like to analyze and criticize, they would make excellent quality control inspectors.

Short Fan-shaped Nails: Fenton and Wright[8] describe two types of persons who have these nails. One, found in small, soft hands, may be placid, lack vitality, and endure a long, drawn-out kind of illness. When that subject becomes angry, it is probably explained as due to illness. If the nails lie on top of the fingers as though not securely attached, the subject can have a sniveling, grumbling manner. Although these people may be competitive, they will be too lazy to engage in any competitive sport.

The second type will be found on firm, hard-packed hands with deeply embedded white or bluish nails. These people can have explosive tempers. They combine high ambitions with desire for popularity. They alternate between being bigoted, moody, and unpleasant, to charming, depending on their desires. These clients need vigorous, perhaps competitive, exercise to burn off their tensions.

Spatulate Nail: Darlene Hansen finds these on spatulate or philosophical hands. She says it is the nail of the critic, the skeptic, and the questioner. The person has lots of energy to release but has difficulty keeping up with it and may scatter it.

Long Nails: Cheiro says that long nails never show great physical strength and that persons who have them are more prone to suffer from chest and lung trouble, which is accentuated if the nails are very curved both vertically and horizontally.

The possessors of these nails can show, according to Cheiro, a resignation and calmness in all activities. This results from being less critical and more impressionable than persons with short nails. These nails can betoken idealism and artistic natures, fondness of the arts, poetry, painting, and music. People with long nails are inclined to be visionaries rather than face facts, particularly distasteful ones. Look for confirmation of this in long, straight heart lines. Hansen believes this nail shows a gentle person who loves balance and harmony. She believes this is the nail of a perfectionist.

Long, Narrow Nails and Filbert Nails: Long, narrow nails are usually found among the ladies. Here the nail shows much flesh on both sides, allowing the energy to flow rapidly past the nail. Fenton and Wright say that while these people can be "superficially charming," coy, "even babyish at times," they are materialistic, possessive, and ambitious. They want the good things in life to be provided without much effort. The narrower the nail, the touchier is the client.

Beryl B. Hutchinson[9] describes a filbert nail as a long, narrow, filbert-shaped nail. Those with this nail show lack of energy at the root. Their temper is gentle. They do not like to waste vitality on emotions that bring no pleasure. If there is no adverse mark on the nails, the health is not affected. They have the instinct to conserve energies because otherwise they will live off their nerves. Hutchinson reports that filbert nails on "overlong" little fingers signal a tendency to sulk.

Hansen says the filbert nail is an exaggeration of spatulate nails and shows an overabundance of curiosity and emotion. The subject may be very intense in short bursts of concentration. She or he also can be very loving, often possessing tremendous warmth. This is at odds with the lack of energy reported by Hutchinson.

The Date Stone: This is another nail distinguished by Hutchinson. She believes that this nail shows a starvation from all good contributions of the glandular system. It often reflects a poor arterial system and the possibility of the subject becoming neurotic because of ill health. If only found on one finger, then it may be the result of a youthful accident or hereditary peculiarity. The Date Stone nail is oval in shape, particularly at the base.

The Almond and the Pointed Nail: Hutchinson places this nail shape between the filbert and the date stone. It appears to be much admired by writers and painters and is a convention in royal portraiture. She quotes Mangin, saying that these nails show "a sensitive nature, devoted, generous, courteous, naturally distinguished and refined, with a gentleness of character in harmony with aesthetic tendencies." Hutchinson's description of the almond nail sounds much like Darlene Hansen's description of the pointed nail. Hansen finds these people nervous, artistic, idealistic, dreamers, or psychic.

The Talon, Curved, Clawlike Nail: The superficial charm displayed in people with the long narrow nail can hide ruthless ambition to grab and hold. They can display the full range of temperament to gain their desire. However, they may actually feel little or no emotion except that accompanying the calculated determination to succeed. They will claw their way to the top.

Wide, Rounded; Rounded; and Conic Nails: Rather than being square at the base, this nail is rounded. The hand energy theory maintains that energy flows smoothly around these nails, making these people more placid and even-tempered, preferring discussion to argument. Although they may worry, they seldom feel tense and angry. They do not carry grudges or like to hurt other people. The energy flow reflects a gentle, sensible person who may become detached and dreamy. The Oriental believes here one finds a warm and accommodating personality. This subject may be weak-willed and a follower of others.

In the rounded nails, the subject displays an evenness of disposition. This client is fairly well-ordered in his or her approach to life. Fond of detail, he or she can use patience to gain results. These people demonstrate genuine friendliness, a good sense of humor and, quite commonly, initiative and creative ability.

What some call rounded nails, others may refer to as conic nails.

SHAPES ON THE DISTAL END

Distal and proximal are anatomical terms. Distal means more distant and proximal means closer to the heart or center of the body. The fingertip is distal to the wrist, and the wrist is proximal to the finger. The tips of the fingers have particular meanings to palmists that the student should understand.

The length of the distal phalange has importance to the palmist. According to Fenton and Wright, the first phalange shows how we think, the second shows how we apply our thought, and the third shows how we act. Others view the first phalange as showing the state of our spiritual or higher intellectual self, the second phalange shows our needs and actions at the mundane, socially conscious level of life, and the third phalange reflects our creature comfort level of existence: home, food, sex, and physical satisfaction.

To Fenton and Wright, a long first phalange (as measured in comparison with the other phalanges) suggests an intuitive, studious, orderly, philosophical, and religious mind. The short first phalange shows materialism and possibly a suspicious nature in persons who understand only the tangibles of life and have little faith or inspiration. Others would reach similar conclusions by comparing the other two phalanges and seeing which seems to predominate, if any. Weight is given according to their predominance.

Judith Hipskind,[10] for example, finds the distal section of the phalange reflects intellect and intuition. The second or middle phalange marks the ability to organize and relate facts, and appreciation for structure. The proximal section of the phalange is, much as we have said before, concerned with earthy things.

On the thumb the distal phalange shows will, the middle phalange logic, and the proximal phalange desire.

The Western palmist looks to four types of fingertip shapes: square, pointed, spatulate, and conic.

Conic or Rounded Tips: Those possessing round or conic tips seek beauty, are clever, and are artistic in temperament. They can be shrewd and honest in business but do not like friction and are cautious. They desire truth and may be too trusting. These subjects tend to be open-minded. Liking beauty and harmony, they also prefer tranquillity to flourish. They enjoy activities in and among people.

Pointed Tips: When the hand or the fingertip comes to a point, this emphasizes focus of mind. While people with pointed fingertips can quickly see the point, they may miss the complete picture. They appear to act through inspiration or intuition and may not even be conscious of how quickly they absorb impressions. Forming quick opinions, they may become uncompromising and undiplomatic. They can also appear eccentric or whimsical. These clients may seem to need to be different. Being creative dreamers, they have a real need for self-expression.

The very pointed finger, the psychic finger, belongs to the fanciful, the dreamer, the psychic. These people may be quite attractive and personally fastidious, yet they lack energy to do much for themselves. Being so low on energy, they cannot be depended on to do anything for others.

Spatulate Tips: These people like to work with their hands. They may fidget. They can be independent people with restless minds. These clients can wear out less active people and may need adventure and the unusual. They are capable of seeing the broad picture and can be quite inventive craftspeople and engineers. These endings are also called flared tips and their owners may seem to thrive under stress and challenge. Their inquiring minds will not accept conventional answers.

Square Tips: These are careful, systematic, and balanced persons with an appreciation for the total appearance. They are down-to-earth types of people. Their minds may be slow but grind exceedingly fine. They are conformists and can be dogmatic. They love to see justice done, and they appreciate attention to detail, even if they do not do it themselves.

Side Views of Fingertips

Tapering Tip: These people may lack staying power and stamina, although they can put their minds to good use. They have imagination, are affectionate, and are typically spiritual or religious rather than materialistic.

The tapering tip can be associated with the thin finger of persons interested in lofty ideals. We may find the aesthetics whose life displays possession of a strong sense of economy.

Coarse Tip: Here we meet the more down-to-earth type, who is material, self-indulgent, and the kind of person who can enjoy coarse behavior and jokes. If it is on a short phalange, the person could be a quite unimaginative plodder. If the phalange is long, the subject could be very sharp in business. He or she could be capable and hard to beat in disputes and debates.

The coarse tip can be associated with the thick finger, signaling a lust for life and sensual pleasures.

Bulgy Tip: Tips with these bulges, also known as droplets, are found on people with a very strong kinesthetic sense. They have a very highly developed sense of touch and good manual dexterity. These subjects rarely drop anything. They can be sensitive, creative, and intellectual. They should make good musicians and great jugglers. This will add to any intensity found in the hand.

MEASURING THE FINGERS

Like many other measurements in palmistry, the finger measurement involves comparisons with other parts of the anatomy. The fingers are measured against one another and the middle finger is measured against the palm. Judith Hipskind believes that an average length middle (Saturn) finger should be seven-eighths of the length of the palm. I disagree; the average length in my experience is shorter. That is one serious reason I no longer use this length as gospel in distinguishing fire and water hands. Other hand features must be relied upon to make those decisions.

Short Fingers

People with short fingers have enthusiasm for the new, but lack patience for any tedious or lengthy working out of ideas, involved detail, or analysis. They want to go immediately to the heart of the problem and can be direct and blunt. When enthusiastic, they can be charming, warm, outreaching, energetic, and generous. They can be dynamic.

Long Fingers

These people may get lost in details, straying from the central issue as they become wrapped up in minutiae. They evidence sensitivity, caution in response, but a more thorough and complete comprehension of the subject once the response is made. Idealism and loyalty go hand-in-fingers with them. Spirituality and high aspirations may be their goals. Very long fingers belong to the contemplative person who is not fond of activity for its own sake.

Comparative Finger Measurement

Some believe that as an ideal average, the Jupiter (index) and the Apollo (ring) fingers should be of the same length and should reach halfway up the distal phalange of the Saturn (middle) finger. Others believe that the Jupiter finger should be just a little longer than the Apollo finger. Another belief is that an ideal average height for the Mercury (little) finger should extend to the distal-phalangeal crease of the ring finger. That does not confirm the ideal length, because little fingers can start from different levels. Others might say that such a Mercury finger is a bit short unless it is set lower on the palm side than the Apollo finger.

THE JUPITER FINGER

You can probably make the point with this finger, commonly called the index finger. It reflects personally perceived authority and the client's own self-appreciation, power, and ego. Here we find traces of leadership and protective paternal and maternal feelings. The fingerprint will show us evidence of powers of concentration. This finger is for guidance and direction. This is the first finger we use to explore objects, to claim them for our own world. Jupiter is the hammer finger of our grip. The thumb is the anvil. Here we reach for a grip on life, on our surroundings, on rewards, and on ourselves.

With an unbent and uncurved Jupiter finger, our perception can be straightforward. Bend it, curve it with any unusual shape, and we discover that the subject's view warps. The view is distorted from the objects of the world directly before him or her by attention to other matters of more concern such as the needs of others.

A curve in the Jupiter finger toward the Saturn (middle) finger shows the paternal or maternal or more generally the nurturing qualities coloring the client's perspective. The view is inward, toward those close by, the family, the group, the patients. The self will be sacrificed for the good of these other people. Even the most ambitious people with this sign appear ambitious for others in their family or group to succeed and will be great nurturers and pushers. These people will live vicariously through the accomplishments of others. Curve the same finger outward toward the thumb (radial) side of the hand, and they can become overbearingly egotistical and push their own merit.

When the Jupiter finger is straight and of average length, the subject can probably work well with others and be successful in interpersonal relationships. If the finger is long, then so is the desire to be a great leader. A short finger can be a sign of withdrawal by a person who cannot really exert the control he or she needs over the external world and his or her place in it. The person with a long Jupiter finger has a superabundant ego, and a short finger exhibits a lack of ego. To compliment this short-fingered person, one can note their consideration of others since they do not like to intrude and are modest. It is helpful to build up this person's self-esteem. A similar problem faces those with incomplete or inverted whorls on their Jupiter fingertips.

If the Jupiter finger is extremely long, as long as the middle finger of normal length, the person may be overbearing or unyielding.

The sign of Jupiter is $2\!\!\!\downarrow$. In the Vedic lore, Jupiter is known as Brihaspati and Brahamanspati, derived from the same root as the word Brahma, the god of creation. The source of the words means to grow and expand. It reflects the wisdom needed for growth and expansion. This gives Jupiter the power of arousing what is latent in our subjects. Another reference is to the guru, the teacher. This energy does not withdraw, but reaches out in the direction the finger points. Other signs related to Jupiter are the chariot, the begging bowl, the water lily, and the eye of Shiva, a berry used for religious and medicinal purposes.

THE SATURN FINGER

Saturn, the middle finger, lies on the division between the conscious and unconscious zones of the hand, the public and private zones of the hand, and the outer and inner self. Saturn is the personal balance, the personal judge, the measure of sobriety, and the dispenser of personal discipline in the hand.

When it is too long, then the character may tend to be morose, gloomy, grave, taciturn, in a word, saturnine. These people are too serious and need to be livened up.

This finger symbolizes the direction of judgment and critical evaluation. When the Saturn finger curves over Apollo (the ring finger), the subject is his or her own worst critic and can never do anything up to his or her own standards. An ulnar loop in the fingerprint can have the same effect. Curving the other way (which is rare) would suggest a dire view of the world at large.

If the Saturn finger is too short, the person may lack good judgment. He or she lacks the perception needed to provide clear impressions that his or her critical faculties might understand. These subjects may be good actors, depending on others to define their characters, write their scripts, and direct their actions.

The Saturn finger, along with its corresponding mount and line, are the keys to discovering whether the subject is introverted or extroverted.

The line may show breaks indicating the age when the subject changes his or her personality. This either results in or from a change in life's circumstances. That may be why so many have called the Saturn line the fate line.

The sign of Saturn is ♄. Saturn is a dreaded planet. It imposes limits on the urges to freedom. This sign shows man carrying a cross, with the cross symbolizing the world. The wisdom that may be drawn from the weight of Saturn arises from meeting the challenges of everyday life. Saturn acts slowly and rewards struggle, but often ever so slowly. Saturn can be symbolized by the arrow, the javelin, the bow, and the vulture. We will study signs later in the book.

THE APOLLO FINGER

The ring finger is named after the sun god Apollo, god of the muses and known for his fine musicianship. It rises above the mount of creativity. The creativity represented here is what we create out of love to share either with others or ourselves. Mercury deals with the inward reflections of love in close personal relations and familial-parental matters; Apollo, still in the realm of the heart and the soul, reaches toward the conscious mind, the external world, to share its gifts. Sometimes we find this sharing outward, sometimes inward, but always through a sense of love. Apollo can be a seat of outward emotions.

Long Apollo fingers may be a sign of the optimist with boundless enthusiasm and high expectations, for it is also the sign of a risk taker. The subject may be a gambler, adventurer, or Don Quixote. She or he is pulled by the excitement and challenge of life. Worldly wisdom may weigh little with these persons unless such sobriety is found in other parts of the hand.

Traditionally, the Apollo finger is associated with self-expression, which may include art, music, an ability to make things pleasing to the eye or the ear, or even the palate and nose.

If the finger is misshapen, thin beside the other fingers, then the subject may feel that his or her creative endeavors have been thwarted by life.

A short Apollo finger will allow Jupterian objectives to dominate and the person may be a doer and achiever. He or she may have little interest in the cultural enrichment, erudition, and beauty unless these are means to an end.

Hutchinson believes that if the Apollo finger leans toward Saturn, it indicates that the weight of mundane responsibilities has been too strong. Others might say there has been a real desire to reach out with one's gifts. Another thought is that the subject may be drawn to religious art. Most believe that the straight finger, as with all fingers, is the best indication of the ability to fully use the gifts shown.

The sign for Apollo is the sign of the sun, ☉. Harmony between the other planets depends upon the gravitational pull of the sun. Among the sun signs are the solar wheel, the solar horses and chariot, and the invincible weapons of Shiva's trident, Vishnu's disc, Yama's rod, Skandra's spear, and Kubera's mace.

THE MERCURY FINGER ☿

How does one decide the length of the Mercury finger? Most who consider this say that one looks to where the tip of the little finger marks the ring finger. But what if the little finger is set lower than the ring finger in the hand? Then one must estimate the length as it would be if the base were set evenly with the base of Apollo.

When the little finger reaches to the first (distal) phalange of the Apollo (ring) finger, it is considered of normal length. However, as Hutchinson points out, when measured from its base, it should be compared to the ring finger when measured from its base and thus extend to about halfway up the distal (nail) phalange. One wag palmist said that long little fingers are better for twisting people around. Hutchinson noted that though this may be true, if the person will not twist, the subject will go away and sulk, feeling unwanted and hurt.

Long little fingers are supposed to be signs of intelligence. These subjects may be good at science or math, eloquent, and could imitate and be negotiators. It may often be found on the hands of professionals.

Traditionally, a short little finger is associated with bluntness, lack of tact, perhaps short temper, and feelings of inferiority. It can also suggest shyness and lack of self-confidence in relationships, communications, business, and sexuality.

The little finger deals with close personal relations, including parental relationships, intimate love, and sex. To these areas add possible gifts with music, speech, language, and other communications, and traditionally, as Mercury was the god of thieves, business.

Julius Spier, whose work, *The Hands of Children*,[11] is introduced by Dr. Carl Jung, noted that low-set, deeply rooted, little fingers can show a parental, mother-father fixation that unconsciously controls and influences partnership relations. In my own study, I have found a curious correlation with the low-set placement of the finger and what lends it to being called a Karmic type of parental relationship. Therein the subject's parents, for good or for ill, just by their very existence, created one of the great life lessons facing the subject. This lesson, I quickly add in readings, does not imply any debt to the parent, but involves a deep realization by the subject.

Spier believed the parental lesson involved the subject unconsciously comparing all partners with the unattainable image of the parent. This would obviously result in difficulties with relationships, with the opposite sex, and/or in difficulties of sexual adaptability.

My own readings are from an age of broken homes and disturbed childhoods. The sex observation may still be relevant. However, the inference that the parent is some higher, unattainable vision that unconsciously controls has certainly lost its luster. I find it is very important to review the parental influence or lack of influence as shown at the start of the life line. This is necessary in order to understand what really may be involved. This is discussed later in the book.

I once discussed the little finger fixation with a concert pianist who had a long-standing parental problem with his mother. He reported that he had resolved that problem by coming to learn his life lesson from it in his adult life. This released the problem's hold. Upon releasing its hold, he found he could reach two more keys on the keyboard with his hand fully stretched.

Another client increased her reach on her left hand after resolving her own issues with her mother. However, at the time we read her, she had neither resolved the issues concerning her father nor increased her reach with her right hand.

When the little finger juts out, that is, away from the hand laterally, a strong desire for independence is revealed. That independence could join with an urge toward separation and fear of duty. Spier notes that the position may also suggest that the subject can maintain a platonic partnership relationship without physical demands or vice versa.

When the index finger stands apart, there is a problem relating to the environment, the external world. When the little finger stands apart, the problem is adapting to the relationship, the intimate, internal world.

A closely held little finger may show a longing to be loved, to receive affection, to cling to a partner. This can be accompanied with a show of shyness. If the clinging little finger curls toward the palm, it may be a sign of prudishness, or at least concern or worries in matters of sexuality.

Spier noted that when the upper phalange of the little finger bends outward, which is backward from the palm, the person can be extremely sensitive to noise.

Straight Mercury fingers traditionally show straight, honest dealings. They are found on the hands of those who are truthful. If the finger seems to wilt toward Apollo, it may be a sign of self-sacrifice. A kink in the little finger, especially toward the palm, when not the result of an accident, traditionally suggests a kink in the character. As Hutchinson says, "A clear, strong kink seems most helpful for anyone contemplating a life of crime."

KNOTS

When knots appear on the fingers, they are said to be philosophical fingers or philosophical hands. This is jumping to conclusions. Knots seem to slow or stop the flow of energy. When the knots occur between the distal and medial phalanges, the person tends to hold on to old ideas or to block new concepts, and can be argumentative. This discursive activity may have gotten the subject the reputation for being a philosopher.

When the knots appear between the medial and proximal phalanges of the fingers, the subject may be a collector. Here we have the energy being stopped between the social-mundane level and the creature comfort level. The person can either be a saver or be the opposite, one who refuses to accept or save anything. Most I have read are savers, collectors.

THE THUMB

The thumb also has three phalanges. The proximal phalange is the mount of Venus and it will be discussed in detail subsequently. In simplicity, the thumb's proximal phalange, the mount of Venus, can be considered desire, and its size will signify the intensity of the power behind subjects' desires. In the second, medial, phalange, we find the logic to carry out that desire. In the third phalange, we find the actual force that can be applied to carry out that desire and how it may be applied.

The thumb can be a subject all to itself and some Oriental readers limit their readings to the thumb.

The thumb rules almost half the hand. It is the anvil upon which much of the rest of the hand operates. Hutchinson suggests there are two methods of measurement of the thumb, neither fully satisfactory. One, looking at the length of the thumb from the base of its second phalange to the tip, finds that it should be as long as the little finger to be of normal length. The other says that its tip should measure halfway up the first phalange of the Jupiter (index) finger. Hutchinson finds a good thumb to contain a distal (nail) phalange that is 25 percent longer than the longest phalange of any of the other fingers.

The middle phalange reflects how desire is molded for the will to execute. If short, the desire acts through intuition. If long, desire acts through intellect. The ideal length for the medial phalange is as long as the distal phalange. Beware of rational debate over differences with a subject having a short middle phalange. You may be dismissed as stupid because the subject has arrived at his or her opinions from intuition. Long phalanges could suggest many hours of enjoyable discussion.

The middle phalange is often withered, that is, smaller in width than the distal phalange. This suggests a tactful person. It suggests one who is unsure of how to carry out his or her immediate desires, and one who suppresses his or her emotions. When the subject finally releases these pent-up emotions, the release will likely be with a bang. Therefore, the name of the more formida-ble examples of this type of thumb is the killer thumb.

These "withered logic" subjects need to be encouraged to partake in regular emotion releasing activities. We counsel sports involving the use of the upper body, particularly the shoulders and arms. Some martial arts and even counseling may also help. We have seen an actual physical change over a period of about a year. It was in a young lady who did engage in marital counseling and martial arts after our advice. Her middle phalange fleshed out and her marriage and whole life improved. That information is an added benefit of follow-up readings, something that today's palmists seldom get an opportunity to do. Tell this client to go to the golf driving range, pick up a bucket of balls, put names and faces on the balls, and whack the hell out of them at least once a week. Chopping wood, beating carpets, and skeet shooting also help.

A stiff upper phalange of the thumb shows obstinacy. The supple upper phalange, which bends slightly back suggesting flexibility, indicates a supple mind, a capacity for appreciating feelings and points of view of others, and strong emotions. The more it bends back, the more it shows susceptibility to influence from the outside. When it bends back significantly, I advise the subject not to open the door for the traveling salesperson.

Spier feels that when the nail phalange bends back so that it almost touches the middle phalange, we have subjects who adopt the identity or idea of others and believe it is their own. When they do this with objects, they may become kleptomaniacs, taking without any necessity but merely from the belief that the object, by their identification, belongs to them.

Some thumbs start deep on the mount of Venus, others higher up. Those that start higher up generally have less lateral flexion, bending to the side. Lateral flexion is the angle between the thumb and the index finger when the thumb is gently stretched to the side. It is an indicator of the liberality, tolerance, and self-confidence of the subject. In general, the wider the angle, the more liberal, tolerant, and self-confident the person.

Tolerance often changes with age and the angle of generosity also changes with age. It has been suggested that the change can be measured by comparing the writing hand with the opposite hand. If the subject is right-handed and the left hand shows a smaller angle, then the subject has become more tolerant with age. But some show the opposite, having started out very open and tolerant, only to learn through life to be more guarded.

We believe it is a little more complex than that. Sometimes, in about 6 to 8 percent of the cases, the hand used for writing does not reflect the dominant side of the brain that would normally be related to that hand. Usually this is the case of the person who was switched as a child from using the left hand. We read the left hand as dominant. Yet the right hand may show the wider angle. Here it

is important to explore with the client whether he or she actually has become more or less generous or guarded with age.

To those who have the narrower angle of generosity on their left hands, we say that they have tightened their standards of permissible behavior. They have learned to clearly establish borders between themselves and loved ones if the angle is now less than ninety degrees. They have, in that case, recovered from the problems of codependency. These subjects will no longer tolerate abuse by loved ones. Frequent relieved smiles accompany their agreements with these observations.

According to Benham, the strength of character can be measured by the size of the thumb, with larger thumbs rating higher on character strength. The height of the thumb is also important, The nearer the thumb to the wrist, the more generous the person and the more he or she shows independence and love of liberty. Benham's image of the murderer's thumb has the short, clubbed distal phalanx but does not necessarily possess the withered middle phalanx.

HOW DO THE FINGERS SIT?

Ideally, the fingers should be evenly set, rooted, at their base. This is rare. When found, the subject is likely to be a confident and proud person, and if other signs on the hand concur, he or she will be a success.

A low-set Jupiter finger could show a self-conscious person. Here again, we have the problem of measuring the actual length of the finger.

FLEXIBILITY

Just a word on flexibility. We tell our subjects as we bend their fingers back that we are testing their gullibility gauge. The fingers tell us what areas of the subject's mind are open and what areas house

already-formed strong opinions. Too much bending back suggests an undependable person who will change positions on any subject at the next suggestion.

THE KNUCKLES

Judith Hipskind has just published a new work on the knuckles that promises much.[12] It is far too early to judge the impact of this work.

MEDICAL NAIL DEFORMITIES

Most of the following is rather technical. It will generally be of interest only to the advanced student and practitioner who has learned to hold his or her medical counsel unless he or she is licensed to practice.

The deformed nail is observed in many severe systemic disorders largely through the mechanism of interference with its normal nutritional and growth properties. As pointed out by Theodore J. Berry, M.D., F.A.C.P.: "Alterations in the appearance and structure of the nail attend a variety of generalized disorders such as anemic states, dietary deficiencies, dysendocrinisms, drug or chemical toxicity, circulatory disorders, infectious diseases, and certain degenerative conditions." They can also suggest physical and emotional trauma. The nails may display splitting, shedding, or separation of the nail plate, ridging, thinning, striation or any other type of surface irregularity.

Though widely variable, the average adult nail grows about 0.1 millimeters a day. Thus it completely grows out in five to six months (160 days) on average. Apparently in pregnancy, warmer climates and with nail-biters, there is an increased rate of nail growth.

HORIZONTAL LINES

Beau's Lines

Acute infections, such as measles, common colds, scarlet fever, influenza, typhus and septicemia, are capable of interrupting normal nail growth as can nutritional deficiencies, accidental traumas and nervous shock. Those affected with malnutrition, nephrosis and many systemic chronic disorders are believed by some in the medical community to frequently have retarded rates of nail growth. When this arrest or retardation occurs in nail growth, either as a result of local or systemic nutritional effects, transverse bands or ridges appear in the surface of the plate. Such lines are known as Beau's lines, named after Dr. Beau who is credited with discovering them in the mid 19th century. Since the nail takes about 160 days to grow out, one can often date the time of the illness or trauma.

Where merely a white line appears, without any ridge or dent in the nail, they are called Mee's lines. They may occur in cases of high fever, arsenical poisoning and coronary heart disease.

Both Beau's lines and Mee's lines are related in all instances to localized nutritional derangement. This is brought about because the germinal portion of the nail (where it grows) is supersensitive to stress, such as infection, fever, trauma, toxicities (arsenic and thallium), deficiency states and in our experience, even emotional upsets. Often, when this area feels such insults, a groove, indentation, ridge, or transverse light or dark line forms, and as the nail grows the groove, etc. travels with it.

There is another condition that can be detected by paired narrow white bands in the fingernails. The condition is called hypoalbuminemia, a condition indicating low levels of serum albumin where persons can be affected with a variety of disease states where the serum albumin (a plasma protein found in the blood along with globulin and fibrinogen and also in the urine and other body tissues) is found to be persistently low. This protein affects blood pressure in the capilaries and the transport of thyroid hormones, for example. Narrow white bands parallel with the half moons (lunula) and separated from each other by normal looking nails may be present in any client with a condition of low serum albumin. It might be accompanied by edema. The bands are neither raised nor indented and sometimes the distal band is slightly wider than the proximal band.

Complete loss of the nails can suggest certain systemic diseases such as scarlet fever, syphilis, leprosy, alopecia, areata, and exfoliative dermatitis. A systemic disease is one that pertains to the whole body rather than to a localized area or regional portion of the body.

Eggshell nails are characterized by a thin nail plate, semi-transparent, bluish white, with a tendency to curve upward at the finger tip edge. They can also be a sign of syphilis.

Where the nails are very soft and easily split, there can have been contact with strong alkalis, endocrine disturbances, malnutrition, syphilis or chronic arthritis.

One will often see white spots, or striations, and rarely a whole nail may turn white. This can be an indication of local trauma, hepatic cirrhosis, nutritional deficiencies and many systemic diseases. Typically these show up after holidays, suggesting recent stress and getting off one's diet.

Hippocratic Nail

These "Watch glass nails" typically associated with "drumstick fingers" can suggest chronic respiratory and circulatory diseases, especially pulmonary tuberculosis, and can indicate hepatic cirrhosis.

Spoon Nails

When the nails are concave on the surface, the condition is called Koilonychia and can indicate dysendocrinisms (acromegaly), trauma, dermatoses, syphilis, nutritional deficiencies, hypochromic anemias or hypothyroidism.

One may find an infection of the nails, usually paronychia, caused by yeast forms (Candida albicans) that frequently affects food-handlers, dentists, dishwashers and gardeners.

The atrophy or failure of development of the nails can be the result of trauma, infection, dysendocrinism, gonadal aplasia and many other systemic diseases.

Where the nail plate is greatly thickened, it may reflect mild persistent trauma. Or it may suggest such systemic diseases as peripheral stasis, peripheral neuritis, syphilis, leprosy, hemiplegia. Sometimes it is merely congenital. Sometimes one may run across extreme thickening of all of the nails and this is usually congenital and associated with keratosis of the palms and soles. Keratosis is a skin condition characterized by an overgrowth and thickening of the cornified skin.

If an inflammation of the nail matrix causing a deformity of the nail plate is observed, it may be caused by trauma, infection, and many systemic diseases.

Any deformity of the nail plate, nail bed, or nail matrix could be caused by many diseases, traumas, or could even be caused by chemical agents (poisoning, allergy).

Some claw nails show an extreme degree of hypertrophy, sometimes with horny projections arising from the nail surface. These may be signs of congenital abnormalities. They may relate to chronic diseases such as described above concerning the greatly thickened nail plate.

A loosening of the nail plate at the finger end (distal) or free edge can indicate trauma, injury by chemical agents, hyperthyroidism and many systemic diseases.

The shedding of all nails can indicate dermatoses such as exfoliative dermatitis, alopecia areata, psoriasis, eczema, nail infection, severe systemic diseases and arsenic poisoning.

Longitudinal ridging and splitting of the nails may be a sign of dermatoses, nail infections, many systemic diseases, senility, injury by chemical agents and hyperthyroidism.

Sometimes one may see lamination and sealing away of the nails in thin layers that could be signs of dermatoses, syphilis or injury by chemical agents.

Where there is a thinning of the nail fold and spreading of the cuticle over the nail plate, it can be associated with vasospastic conditions such as Raynaud's phenomenon and occasionally with hypothyroidism.

Nail-biting (onychophagia) is not unusual for children and is not known to have harmful effects. The practice usually ceases about the age of puberty. Nail-biting in adults usually shows elevated states of tension and worry. Nail-biting and cuticle-picking are well-known nervous habits.

Superficial pitting of the nail plate, thinning or splitting and in some instances separation of the nail plate from the its bed (neuroychia) may be the marks of acute or long endured emotional disturbances.

Half Moons

We look for half moons on the bases of all fingers. Where the nails are small, they are seldom seen. If they are on all five fingers, they are said to be a sign of good health and strong metabolism. People with large half moons are said to have great stamina. One Oriental palmist, Hachiro Asano, maintains that people missing half moons on the little and ring fingers are usually weak in the lower body. From personal experience running marathons, we disagree with that assessment. Some maintain that the disappearance of half moons shows the reduction of the capacity or output of the endocrine system.

Vertical Striations

These may be related to the aging process. Very deep and clear striations can suggest diabetes. They may also be related to malabsorption of the nutrients we eat.

Clubbing

Clubbing is associated with a variety of respiratory and cardiovascular diseases, cirrhosis, colitis, and thyroid disease.

SOME OTHER MEDICAL/COLOR CONSIDERATIONS

Cyanosis, which is a bluish discoloration, is caused by an excess deoxygenated hemoglobin in the blood or a structural defect in the hemoglobin molecule. Basically, there is a lack of oxygen being transported in the arterial blood flow to feed the needs of the tissues.

Whenever the blood flow to the hands is reduced, either as a systemic or local effect, then cyanosis usually occurs. If the hand is warm, then a systemic (whole body) cause rather than a local cause is suspected. Such cause could be acute or chronic pulmonary disorders or errors in pulmonary diffusion. A severe anemic person, because of absolute diminished hemoglobin available, may not display cyanosis. A variety of drugs and even some patent medicines can cause deep blue discoloration in the fingers.

Clubbed fingers, cyanosis and polycythemia in a very young child suggests a cardiac etiology while clubbing without cyanosis may prompt a search for an extra-cardiac cause.

Yellow nails may be due to Addison's disease and white nails may be related to cirrhosis. Before you panic about yellow nails or especially yellow palms, check to see if the subject is a heavy carrot juice drinker.

According to Ayurveda, the yellow nail is a sign of a delicate liver, while the blue nail is a sign of delicate lungs and/or heart. Pale nails can indicate anemia. If the half moon is blue, the Ayurvedic practitioner would suspect a disturbed liver while if it were red, he would consider cardiac failure.

AYURVEDIC DIAGNOSIS

According to the teachings of Ayurveda from India nails are cast in three general types. If the nails are dry, crooked, rough and break easily, it is said that *vata* predominates in the body. If the nails are soft, pink, tender, easily bent and glistening, these features would then be a sign of a *pitta* personality. Strong, thick, soft and very shiny nails with uniform contours will signal the predomination of a *kapfa* personality.

ASPECTS OF THE AYURVEDIC PERSONALITY

The *vata* person's frame appears thin, body weight will be low, the skin may be rough, dry, cool and dark. The teeth may protrude (buck teeth) and be large and crooked and their gums may be emaciated. Their eyes may be small, dull, dry and black or brown.

The *vata* personality will have a variable, scant appetite. His or her thirst will be variable and they may tend to be constipated, with hard and dry eliminations. They usually are very active and their minds can be restless and active. Emotionally they would appear fearful, insecure and unpredictable. Their faith is mutable. The short term memory is good but the remote memory may be poor. They may have fearful dreams, dreams with flying, jumping and running. Their sleep may tend to be scanty and interrupted. Their speech is fast and their pulse may be thready and feeble. They may frequently be poor and may spend money quickly on trifles.

People with the *vata* constitution tend to develop excessive gas, lower back problems, sciatic pains and stabbing pains caused by a variety of disorders affecting the nervous system. They may be more subject to paralysis.

The *pitta* personality may be recognized by sharp, cutting speech. Their pulse tends to be moderate, as is their frame and body weight. Their skin and hair appear soft or oily and the hair may be yellow, early grey or red. The skin may feel warm, and be fair, and red or yellowish. The teeth are moderate in size while the gums are soft and often yellowish. The eyes are penetrating, green, grey or yellow.

The *pitta* personality should display a good to excessive appetite and an excessive thirst. Their elimination will normally be soft, oily and loose. They enjoy moderate physical activity. Their mind is aggressive and intelligent and they are aggressive, perhaps irritable and even jealous in their emotional temperament. They can be fanatical in their faith and their dreams tend toward the fiery, with anger, violence and war, but sleep little and soundly. The subject's memory is sharp. Their financial status usually is moderate and they like to splurge on luxuries.

The constitution of the *pitta* personality is subject to disorders associated with the liver and upper digestive tract. These subjects may suffer from liver disorders, peptic ulcers, highly acid stomachs, gastritis and inflammation of the upper intestinal tract. Their skin may also display rashes and they may be subject to hives.

With the thick frame and often overweight body of the *kapha* personality we may expect to find thick, oily, cool, pale or white skin with thick, oily and wavy hair that may be either light or dark. Their teeth are generally strong and white and their eyes can be big, blue and quite attractive, sporting thick eyelashes.

The *kapha* personality's appetite would be slow but steady, feeding their thick, overweight frame. Their thirst is little and their elimination heavy, slow, thick and oily. They may appear lethargic, have calm, slow minds, and be emotionally attached and greedy. Their memory is slow but prolonged, and they may be slow to forgive. Their faith is steady. Their dreams may tend toward the romantic and have much to do with water, such as rivers, lakes, oceans, swimming and boating (like cruises). Their sleep usually is heavy and prolonged. They are likely to be money savers, spending on food, and may be or become rich. Hoarding could be a common trait.

The *kapha* person is more likely to suffer from problems with bronchitis, tonsillitis, sinusitis and lung congestion. Their weakness appears to be in the respiratory tract.

Ayurvedic medicine gives the fingers significance according both to the five elements, earth, air, fire, water and ether and to several body systems or parts. The thumb is identified with ether and the brain meridian. The index (or as you now know it, the Jupiter) finger is on the lung meridian and represents air. Our Saturn finger is on the intestinal meridian and represents the element of fire. The ring (Apollo) finger is on the kidney meridian and represents the element water. The Mercury finger is on the heart meridian and represents earth.

TRADITIONAL CHINESE PALMISTRY AND THE FINGERS

Traditional Chinese palmistry recognizes the fingers as related to different parts of the family. The thumb relates to the parents. The brother is seen in the Jupiter finger. Self is expressed in the Saturn finger. Relations with the spouse are revealed in the ring finger and children are reflected in the little finger. One looks for any deformity, scar, or other unfavorable signs to show problems in these areas.

The traditional Chinese palmist, while finding the seasons of the year in the palm, will find the months in the hand. Starting with the distal phalange of the little finger, he travels from January down the little finger to March, then moves to the ring finger to travel from April on the nail end to June, then to the middle finger from July at the tip to September on the proximal phalange and finally to the index finger and October represented by the nail phalange to December reflected by the proximal phalange. All twelve months are thus represented for fortune-telling both past and present. The Chinese palmist also looks for deformities, differences, and scars on each phalange to help evaluate their predictive qualities.

From here we will turn our attention to the fingerprints and ridge lines of the hand and the mounts.

CHAPTER SIX

PALM TOPOGRAPHY

The shapes of hands can show the location, capacity, and condition of the reservoirs of energy. These shapes include the mounts and the general areas of formation seen from the layout of the lines. Many characteristics of the subject are found through examination of the shapes of the hands.

THE MOUNTS

There are ten mounts and one plain in modern palmistry (see illustration, p. 15). Five mounts lie directly under the fingers: Mercury under the little finger; Apollo under the ring finger; Saturn under the middle finger; Jupiter under the index finger; and Venus under the thumb. Luna, or the mount of the Moon, is opposite Venus and lies along the percussion, the ulnar (little finger) side of the palm. At the base of the palm is a mount called Neptune between Venus and Luna and below Luna or forming the lower extension of Luna is Pluto. Lying across the palm below Mercury, Apollo, Saturn, and Jupiter are the mounts of upper and lower Mars and the plain of Mars. Upper Mars is under Mercury. Lower Mars is under Jupiter and the plain of Mars is in the middle. Just below lower Mars and above Venus is an area called Vulcan. Some palmists locate the mounts of Neptune and Uranus floating somewhere generally between Venus and Luna. We locate Neptune between Venus and Pluto with Uranus above it. Darlene Hansen[1] substitutes the name Uranus for Apollo. Many palmists, like Roz Levine,[2] substitute the Sun for Apollo, which is reasonable as Apollo was the Sun god. We have also seen palmists set Pluto in Neptune's place, just above the wrist.

Although the books refer to ten mounts, not much is written on Pluto, Neptune, or Vulcan. Generally, Pluto encompasses the deep dream and psychic state of Luna. Vulcan can be confused with the mount of lower Mars or the fiery side of Venus. Neptune lies between the masculine and feminine, yin-yang areas of the hand. When well formed, it shows that the person has a good bridge between these parts of his or her personality. It may also be related to the sixth sense.

Each mount covers certain areas of potential personality, potentials for action and reaction in life. We look at a hand to see which of these areas are well formed and are thus leading areas of potential and support, and which may need support. We see if any areas are inhibiting in appearance or are inhibited and are thus areas of potential strength or weakness. We are looking for the strengths and weaknesses of personality. We look for influence on the directions of instinctive thought and behavior.

There are two somewhat overlapping schools for detecting which are well-formed mounts. The older Western school looks to the size of the mount and its chief proponent is the late nineteenth–early-twentieth-century palmist, Niblo.[3] Others of this school include Leona Lehman,[4] David Brandon-Jones,[5] Jo Sheridan,[6] Yaschpaule,[7] Henri Rem,[8] Lori Reid,[9] Henry Frith,[10] Martini,[11] Joyce Wilson,[12] Judith Hipskind,[13] Elizabeth P. Hoffman,[14] Nancy Frederick Sussan,[15] Litzka Raymond Gibson,[16] Saint-Germain,[17] Julius Spier,[18] Carol Hellings

White,[19] Francis King,[20] Jean-Michel Morgan,[21] Myrah Lawrance,[22] Elizabeth Brenner,[23] Bettina Luxon and Jill Goolden,[24] Walter Sorell,[25] Edo Sprong,[26] Enid Hoffman,[27] Dr. Maria Costavile,[28] and Roz Levine.[29]

Another school of palmists looks for special dermatoglyphic markings and their locations to decide which of the mounts are more favored. One theory for this is that diet plays a strong part in the development of the hand and where the diet is sparse, the mounts will not become prominent. This is one reason we look for other marks on the mounts to find out which are prominent. They will be there whether the mounts are raised or not. When we are concerned with the mounts below the fingers, we are concerned with the location of the triradii. When we find the apices at the center of these triradii we find the apex of each mount.

There are several proponents of this school including the renowned William G. Benham.[30] A leading proponent of the apices marking the mounts school is Beryl Hutchinson.[31] She refers to the 1897 work of Saint-Germain[32] as the first source of this school. But she does not mention that he ignored his work of 1897 on this point in his work published in 1935.[33] Hutchinson is joined by V. A. K. Ayer,[34] K. C. Sen and Noel Jaquin as quoted by Sen,[35] and Rodney Davies[36] and a group mentioned below who hedge their bets.

The apices refer to the apex of each mount, which is its top or summit. This may be in the middle of the mount or it may be located off to one side. In the fleshy interpretation, what one looks for is the fleshiest part of the mount. In the dermatoglyphic approach, on the mounts of Mercury, Apollo, Saturn, and Jupiter, one looks for the location of the triradius on each of those mounts. Usually there is one triradius for each mount. Sometimes one finds a second triradius (see section on dermatoglyphics in chapter 7). While there is generally no triradius on any area of Mars, one may find an axial or border triradius on Luna, Vulcan, Pluto, or Venus. One looks for a triradius near the base of the palm, generally in the area of Neptune. This triradius may be placed from side to side in some hands and be on Venus, Pluto, or Luna. However, that triradius is not generally considered to show the center of these mounts.

There is a third group who hedge their bets. They adopt the triradius for finding the center of the mount, but look for the fleshy part to determine the strength of the mount. They may use either feature to determine where the mount's influence may come from or where it extends. I join this group, which is represented by Elizabeth Daniels Squire,[37] Darlene Hansen,[38] Jo Logan,[39] Esther Newcomer-Bramblett,[40] and Nathaniel Altman.[41]

In addition to these three groups, we have a curious observer, Marcel Broekman, who found "a whorl in the print of the skin" "under each finger."[42] He proposes that the apex of this whorl indicates whether the mount is centered or displaced. Strong qualities are found in mounts where the apex is centrally located. Later we discuss whorls, but they are, as commonly conceived, most likely to be found in fingerprints. Whorls are seldom seen under the fingers. Was Broekman finding whorls indicated by the incomplete patterns of the skin ridges above the triradii? Perhaps he sees triradii as whorls. Because of the rarity of whorls as commonly understood under the fingers, his observation is obscure.

Paul Gabriel Tesla is dissatisfied with using the triradius to locate the center of the mount and joins those who describe the center of the mount as where the flesh area of the mount may be found.[43] Thus Jupiter is commonly found on the palm just below the area between the index and middle finger. Saturn tends to be found over between the bases of the middle and ring finger, Apollo between the ring and little finger bases, and Mercury will commonly be found wrapped around the percussion side of the palm.

Maria Gardini adds a cusp to my observations in locating the high point or summit of a mount, which she finds fairly large in well-developed mounts.[44] The direction of the face of this cusp will determine the direction of the energy of the mount. For example, if the Jupiter cusp is directed downward toward the wrist, the subject expresses his personality in service to others. If it faces Saturn, it expresses a practical personality seeking useful personal goals. If it faces the thenar edge, then the subject's personality faces outward with strong ambition and a spirit of adventure. This subject may lose sight of his or her social duties.

Cheiro adds a bit of astrology to his determination of mount value in his 1916 publication, *Palmistry for All*.[45] He finds the mount of Jupiter positive if the person is born between November 21 and December 20 and it remains so in a minor way for persons born until December 28. Saturn may be considered positive for those born between December 21 and January 20 and it remains so for those born within the following seven days of overlap with the next period in the horoscope. Apollo is considered positive for those born between July 21 and August 20 and it continues to be a generally favorable mount for those born until August 28. Mercury is considered positive for those born between May 21 and June 20 and it continues its positive influence for those born until May 27. Luna is positive for those born between the dates of June 21 and July 20 and it remains a positive influence on births until July 27. Venus is positive for those born between April 20 and May 20 and it remains a positive influence on births until May 27.

Cheiro's 1916 observations might appear curiously at odds with his pronouncements in his 1897 work, *Language of the Hand*, where he defines how he uses the names of these mounts by saying:

As regards the use by cheiromats of the old-time names, such as the Mount of Venus, Mars, etc., I must state that I do not use these names in any sense in relation to what is known as Astrological Palmistry. I do not for one moment deny that there may be a connection—and a very great one—between the two; but I do not think it necessary to consider it in conjunction with this study of the hand, which I hold to be in every way complete in itself.[46]

Perhaps he would just expect that persons with a positive birth for the various planets would show a positive sign of these planets on the mounts of their hands. In the edited edition of Cheiro's works, published in 1968, Robert M. Ockene quotes Cheiro as saying:

Out of astrology was born the study of the hand. It was found that persons who had the planet Jupiter in a powerful position in the horoscope had the same qualities expressed by the first finger of the hand having the base or mount under it large or well developed. If this finger was short or crooked and the mount under it hollow or depressed, the planet Jupiter held an inferior position in the horoscope.[47]

Benham gives us a strong hint of why the triradius was not used until more modern times. He observed that while the apex was easy to see on coarse skin, it can be almost impossible to see on fine skin and by gaslight. Therefore, with nineteenth-century illumination or in the dark, it is almost impossible to locate, even with a magnifying glass.

The apex clearly pictured in his book is what we now call a triradius. Benham seems to confuse the word *capillaries* with the term *ridges*. He refers to photographing the way the capillaries run and accompanies that remark with illustrations of the ridge pattern for the triradius. He then says:

Note that a little triangle is formed by these capillaries. The centre of this triangle is the exact centre of the mount. It does not matter that this apex is not on the most prominent or fleshy part of the Mount. Many students have considered the most fleshy part as the top of the Mount; this is incorrect. It is the centre of the capillary triangle which is its apex. To find and use this apex may appear to be insisting on burdensome and unnecessary detail, but if you expect to get below the surface in hand-reading you must be able to recognize at once the slightest displacement of the tips of the Mounts.[48]

According to Beryl Hutchinson,[49] the apex should be found beneath the midline of the index, the middle, and the ring finger and aligned with the inner side of the little finger. Rodney Davies[50] follows Benham more closely, and reports that, as the apex forms the center of the mount, all apices should ideally lie on the midline of the finger above them.

According to Benham,[51] if the apex is displaced even slightly toward another mount, it signifies that the mount closer to the direction of the displacement is the stronger mount. The mount with the displaced apex gives up some of its "type" (strength?) to the mount it leans toward. I find that the radial or ulnar displacement suggests whether the mount's reflected energy will be inwardly or outwardly directed.

I also look to apex height and can do this by counting ridge lines. When they are within six or seven lines from the first line of attachment with the finger, they are high. If they are fourteen or so lines below that attachment line, they are low. Hutchinson has found that Saturn is habitually higher than either Jupiter or Apollo. I agree. It seems that the higher the mount, the more cerebral, intellectual, or spiritual the influence upon the instinctive thought or behavior. The lower the mount, then the more earthbound or practical are the tendencies.

When the apex of the mount is located toward one side or the other, we can detect which way the influences flow, inward toward the self or outward toward the world. We learn thereby whether the mount reflects introverted or extroverted tendencies or qualities.

Benham describes the padding of the mounts as representing certain qualities of persons. Under his fleshy interpretation, mounts that are prominent are considered strong mounts, flat ones are ordinary, and depressions show weakness and absence of that mount's qualities within a person. Benham and others have modified this. Some also look for strong lines or other features on the mount to modify this interpretation.

Fleshiness and tone are taken into consideration in any hand reading and are the leading indications of strength of the various areas of Mars, Luna, Venus, Neptune, and Pluto. However, any unusual signs or ridge markings on these mounts give them added emphasis. I find that markings on Uranus show more activity of this mount than fleshiness. Fleshiness on Uranus and the plain of Mars can suggest a healthy ability to recover from trauma and disease.

According to Benham and many other Western palmists, if we locate the strongest mounts on the hand, we will locate the leading qualities of the subject. Benham reports that if there is a single vertical line on the most prominent fleshy mount, while the other mounts are normal, this will confirm the opinion that the subject belongs to the character type represented by that mount. This will be further strengthened if the corresponding finger is the most prominent of the fingers by comparative length and size. He says that it is then certain that the subject represents "a practically pure specimen" of the characteristics of that mount. Benham combines the elements of the triradius, along with good and bad signs and with the elements of fleshy appearance, to find the value of the mounts.[52] For example, he finds his Jupiterian: "When the Mount of Jupiter is found full and strong, apex centrally located, finger long and strong, with color of hand pink or red, you have located a Jupiterian."[53]

Benham notes that even in the case of flat mounts, a deep, well-marked vertical line uncut by any cross lines would give that mount an almost equal prominence with any other highly developed mount. While one or more lines add strength to a flat or low mount, they do so in diminishing quantities as their number increases. If they increase, and cross lines are found forming a grille, then the defects of that mount are emphasized.

A mount has good and bad sides. Grilles, crossbars, or crosses increase the prominence of its defects. Color and tone also play parts, with good tone and color strengthening the mount, and anemic or jaundiced colors and weak tone increasing the weaknesses of the mount.

One can find one or more prominent mounts in a hand. Through combining their varied qualities, the reader analyzes the effects they have on the subject's basic characteristics. On many successful businesspersons I have examined, every mount is prominent on both hands.

Parts of the qualities of the mounts seem to extend to the areas and lines below them. For example, I have found stars on the plain of Mars below Apollo. This is a favorable or lucky sign if found on Apollo. Similar favorable indications are associated with a star below Apollo.

Jupiter ♃

Jupiter was the god of gods, the Roman god equivalent to the Greek god Zeus. The Jupiter mount, like the index finger, relates to ego, self-awareness. Jupiter reflects the ego's planning and interest section. It shows the subject's focus on goals and interests in the external world as far as they relate to the subject's present and future position. It indicates how the subject views the greater world for his or her own benefit. Jupiter indicates how the subject presently observes his or her best interaction with the world. It must always be read with the finger and the other mounts and fingers for the subject's best interaction. As such, it is a key to the subject's own perceptive ability: its direction, focus, and clarity. So, as Sprong[54] observes, Jupiter reflects our identification, our personality.

The mount of Jupiter is bordered by that of Saturn, the Jupiter finger, and the heart line or its straight extension. Below it lies the mount of lower Mars.

Jupiter signifies luck, expansion, and achievement. It may also characterize waste, arrogance, excess, and even slovenliness. However, on balance, a well-developed Jupiter will suggest the beneficent qualities of the sign. In astrology Jupiter has been related to energies of expansion and integration in the active world. Jupiter reflects how the subject expands into the outer world and integrates into his or her own character those active experiences. It may also reflect the subject's own parenting process. Does the client encourage, hinder, or ignore this process?

Fenton and Wright[55] describe Jupiter as representing the practical use of the willpower, ambition, and pride. When Jupiter is well developed, one finds executive ability, strong personal beliefs, and direction. If Jupiter is overdeveloped, one finds arrogance, selfishness, unbounded ambition, pomposity, vanity, impertinence, haughtiness, impudence, conceit, presumptuousness, insolence, and snobbery. If underdeveloped, one can find idleness, passiveness, languor, superficiality, laziness, sluggishness, lethargy, shallowness, torpor, and lassitude. These are signs of lack of personal dignity, resentment of authority, and lack of personal discipline.

To Benham, if Jupiter is the dominant mount, then we have the Jupiterian.[56] The Jupiterian is one of the seven types of humanity. This person is an ambitious leader, good, and strong. Benham describes him as neither the tallest of men, that distinction belonging to the Saturnian, nor the shortest, that distinction belonging to the Mercurian. He is large, strongly built, with good muscle tone, and inclined to be fleshy.

Benham wrote at the turn of the nineteenth century when men were more portly and the Pritikin diet and cholesterol were unknown things. Benham believed his Jupiterian's eyes to be large, emotionally expressive, with clear pupils. He would exude honesty and kindly spirit. He is, in short, classified by Benham as one of the good types.

Beryl Hutchinson reports that if the triradius is well aligned in the center of the mount, it is a sign of integrity and high self-respect.[57] She says he may be a gambler or a burglar, yet he will not stoop to meanness nor violate the appropriate code of honor.

She adds that if the apex is toward the Saturn finger, then practical ends control action, those practical ends dealing with the responsibility of family, group, or tribe. This is the nurturing quality we spoke of in relation to the finger shape and inward loop in the fingerprint.

When the apex is placed toward the radial side of the hand, the thumb, there will be a tendency toward adventure, perhaps irresponsibility, and extrovertism. With this feature we are more likely to find the characteristics of arrogance, sloppiness, and waste. Coupled with a strong lunar mount, this expansiveness might be expressed by a desire to own everything and be all things to all people.

Jupiter's close connection to Saturn provides the discipline of that mount. Discipline limits Jupiter and supports its integrative functions. In law, this would be through rule making and drafting formal agreements, actions that tie society together. It may also be expressed in religion. Overattention to these matters reflected in an apex closer to Saturn could also result in a certain arrogance. Arrogance can be found in both the nurturing-mothering qualities and the expansionist proclivities.

Normal development of this mount, as pointed out by Rodney Davies, will emphasize warm, sociable, good-natured, and enthusiastic qualities, affinity for hard work, and honest trading. In the Wu-Hsing system of palmistry, Jupiter and Saturn occupy the major portion of the fire quadrant of the hand with Mars being divided between the fire and air quadrants. Refer back to the discussion in chapter 4 of the four types of hands to understand what additional characteristics the Wu-Hsing quadrants reflect.

Saturn ♄

The mount of Saturn lies below the Saturn finger, bordered by the heart line, and the mounts of Jupiter and Apollo. Below it is the plain of Mars. The corresponding god to Saturn in Greek mythology was Cronos, meaning time. Time is the great discipliner of life.

Saturn used to be considered a bad mount. Stars on it could suggest death by drowning, and strong Saturn fingers and mounts indicate a morose character. However, a strong Saturn is useful to modify overexuberant proclivities of other mounts or fingers. For example, the gambler's finger may be overshadowed as Saturn bends over Apollo. Saturn can return discipline to the excesses found in the other mounts. Strong Saturns return us to reality. That reality is necessary in all life's endeavors. So, in the academic world, a special sign like a star can be a favorable sign on Saturn. It can predict or show the rewards of professional acclaim by one's peers in fields such as science, medicine, law, social studies, and related fields where a certain materialistic grounding is required.

Stars far below Saturn, on Uranus, will disrupt the day-to-day consciousness that typifies Saturn. These bring another energy into play.

Saturn lies at the head of the central axis of the being. It reflects the central role of reason that forms the basis of integration. Do the lines indicate the person's own connection of reason with irrational, emotional states? This thought may be worth further exploration.

Hutchinson believes that the apex of Saturn is always higher than the others, so fewer skin ridges need to be counted to find its relative position.[58]

If the mount of Saturn was dominant, Benham could call the person a Saturnian.[59] Benham describes the Saturnian as a peculiar person. While we may need some of his qualities, it is a blessing that the world is not filled with Saturnians. Saturn is the balance of the character and it exercises caution, prudence, wisdom, and sobriety in keeping the other characteristics in check. Benham sees the Saturnian as the repressor and believes this characteristic is an indispensable part of society. Benham describes this Saturnian as tall, gaunt, and pale; with yellow, dry skin wrinkled in flabby folds or tightly drawn over the bones; a purely bilious type with thick, straight, harsh, dark or black hair. His eyes are deeply set, black, having a sad and subdued expression interspersed with fits of anger and suspicion. He is the epitome of Jacob Marley and the unreformed Scrooge: anemic, jaundiced, decaying, and weak in constitution, repressing all that is vital and enthusiastic. He is a doubter, a cynic, with a tendency to withdraw. The Saturnian may have a love for solitude and the occult and may favor chemistry, mathematics, and medicine. He can be a deep, true scientist.

Fenton and Wright note that Saturn is concerned with practical ambitions, serious thought, earning money, scientific investigation, solitude, and emotional limitations.[60] If it is a predominant mount, watch for a gloomy, pessimistic, and solitary attitude toward life; a person who exercises caution and who becomes easily depressed. In a word, the person will exercise an overabundance of judgment.

In reflecting on an overdeveloped Saturn mount, Rodney Davies brings in the visage of the early Silas Marner before he lost his gold and found the golden-haired Eppie. He was miserly and misanthropic, concerned with his own interest. Low mounts that lack color are little better as they reflect a lack of self-confidence and self-control. Lines on the mount add or detract strength in the same manner as on Jupiter. Davies observes problems for any client with more than three vertical lines on Saturn.[61] Because each line represents an interest, many lines can suggest failure to find success where focus or specialization is required. However, some entrepreneurs, because they must do so many things, may need to be unspecialized to a certain point just to succeed.

Consider an example of multiple Saturn lines. The client had many lines under both Saturn and Apollo. The effect is similar. I chided her for being too scattered. She remonstrated. She said she was the manager of a large convention center and needed to engage in many activities concurrently. She indignantly advised me that she handled all of her activities well. After further discussion, it became obvious that she did not have a problem. Then I learned that the multiple line trait would not be a drawback if the client could control this multidirectional tendency under one or two protocols. This would be exacerbated if the client did not have whorls on the Saturn and Apollo fingerprints. A strong Jupiter mount and finger would help, too. Many working women, for example, have numerous responsibilities while raising children and participating in a family. They appear able to handle them as long as the activities are focused under a couple of umbrellas, such as career and family. When the central focus is lost, the activities are likely to become unmanageable.

If the apex is centrally located, the subject would have a practical attitude toward money and be financially cautious. If toward Jupiter, the subject will be drawn to acquire riches. If the apex leans toward Apollo, the subject may show financial irresponsibility, or at least unconcern, and be a bit of a spendthrift. With the apex set high, the subject will be self-motivated and have ambition and drive. Lower apices may show a more cautious investment proclivity in land and earthy securities.

Julius Spier[62] emphasizes that this mount reveals capacities in philosophic and religious speculation. Too prominent or large a mount not only would emphasize the misanthropic but the self-tormenting and highly sensitive natures of such subjects. If the mount is absent, Spier believes the psyche is overemphasized, preventing harmonious balance. If Apollo leans toward Saturn, and other artistic qualities are strong, we might ask the client if he or she is drawn toward religious or spiritual art.

Edo Sprong observes that the true Saturnian tends to reason matters out through sequential analysis.[63] The thoughts of these subjects appear time-bound and worldly. Saturn is associated with wisdom and the rational sciences. We find this more common if there is a single, strong line centrally drawn through the palm to the mount of Saturn.

Apollo ☉

Apollo, the Sun god, was the god of prophecy, the muses, and the arts. The mount of Apollo is bordered by the Apollo finger, the mounts of Saturn and Mercury, and the heart line. It also lies above the plain of Mars.

I believe that the thumb deserves many Sun qualities. The Sun is the yang or male energy of the universe and the distal two phalanges of the thumb appear as the phallic symbol of the hand. The thumb reflects the will, power, and desire of the person, energies most associated with the Sun. The thumb is opposite the Moon, representing the yin or feminine qualities of the hand. But the thumb is not the traditional finger of the Sun.

The fourth digit is the Sun finger. Here we see the reflection of the Sun god, Apollo. He lends his light to the character of the subject. When the mount is favorable, the energy shines through creativity, charm, outward expressions of love and concern, arts, and hobbies. Scientific talents are enhanced by a well-set mount, particularly with a higher apex. Well-developed mounts suggest sunny people, with good humor and the ability to laugh; they are warm, generous, and optimistic.

Overdevelopment of the mount of Apollo suggests greed, extravagance, and vanity, and a ten-dency to gamble or take unwise chances. David Brandon-Jones warns of an "overwhelming, overbearing egocentricity where good taste is coarsened to the garish, showy style and the person is quite susceptible to flattery."[64]

This is one of the good characters in the Benham seven. Normal Apollonians are healthy and vigorous, and thus happy, genial and attractive. They are not all artists or actors, but they all love beauty, enjoy life, and have a spontaneous nature.

They create through love and share it either with the world or with themselves and those close to them. Apollonians may be highly successful in business and have a natural brilliance and versatility combined with taste. In business, look for strength in the development of the mount and finger of Mercury as well as the strength of Jupiter.

Benham describes the Apollonian as of medium height between Jupiterian and Saturnian.[65] He is neither fleshy like the Jupiterian nor lean like the Saturnian. He is shapely and athletic, with well-defined muscles. His complexion is clear and his eyes have a frank, honest expression that can change to sweetness and sympathy as the emotions play. They sparkle with the brilliance of the brain behind them.

The high apex aids artistic or other creative talent. If it leans toward the second finger, then, according to Hutchinson, one finds psychological complexities.

If the loop is deficient, look for no frills. Look only for survival rations for mind, body, and spirit.

Darlene Hansen calls this mount the mount of Uranus.[66] She notes that persons with flat mounts may feel uncomfortable in social settings, lacking the security and grace to handle the situations. Because Uranus, like Jupiter, forms an antidote to the problems related to Saturn, her renaming this mount is not unreasonable. Uranus reflects the striving to break out of patterns and exudes energy.

Because many attributes of Uranus are malefic and rebellious, we prefer the more traditional name of Apollo for this mount.

Sprong notes that quality of service relates to Apollo.[67] They attract others. They possess such intuitive knowledge that they are conversant over wide subject ranges with no study. These often enthusiastic subjects can inspire others.

Mercury ☿

Mercury was the god of merchants, travelers, and eloquence. The Romans added the purse to the Greek god Hermes, already seen with a caduceus, winged hat, and winged sandals. The mount of Mercury lies on the percussion below the Mercury finger, next to the mount of Apollo and above the heart line. Below it is the mount of upper Mars.

Many subjects come into inquiry on examination of both the finger and mount of Mercury: dependence/independence, sex, intimate relationships, filial relationships, communications, business, science, and math.

Mercury reflects potential separation and the client's ability to overcome separation. Separation can be between the parent and child, the lover and beloved, the male and female, and even the businessperson and client or customer. Even much of the process of math and science reflects the dialectic, the method of question and answer in analysis, exposition, and criticism. Mercury reflects energy the client has to bridge these communication gaps. Like Saturn, Mercury reflects another ability to integrate.

Mercury's power starts with the nervous system and culminates in the mind's power to use successful symbols as means of communication. Here we can see the child's fist banging on the table or the delicate gesticulation of a great performer with the little finger. Those with well-developed Mercury mounts and fingers should show skills with language.

A well-developed mount gives the owner, even when tongue-tied or dumb, the ability to express his or her message, according to Brandon-Jones.[68] He speculates that Helen Keller had good development in this area. Good development also suggests a love for travel, novelty, change, and adventure; an independent spirit and perhaps a flair for science.

Beware the overdeveloped mount of Mercury below the crooked little finger as the combination may reveal, according to Rodney Davies, incipient or actual criminal behavior.[69] It may also signify a weakness for drugs and alcohol (see also the via lascivia, covered under the subject of the minor lines and health lines in chapter 9). It suggests greed, mendacity, and a will to exploit others for personal gain.

Mercury was an interesting god. He was the god of thieves and so there is another, albeit backhanded, reference to business. He was also the messenger of the gods, hence the appropriate relationship to communication, especially verbal or what is popularly considered left-brain, communication. In addition, Mercury was the person who put the gold coins on the eyes of the dead so that they could pay the ferryman to cross the river Styx. Therefore, some look to Mercury for signs of transition.

Benham describes the Mercurian as small, compact, trim, and tidy in appearance.[70] He or she should be strong and have a forceful countenance and expression. The face will be oval and regular, with quick changes of expression mirroring a swift mind. The skin tends toward the olive complexion, and is smooth, fine, and transparent. It may easily flush or drain of color, reflecting mood swings. The forehead is very prominent and the hair chestnut or black with perhaps curly ends.

Males generally grow beards easily and trim them closely.

The Mercurian is the quickest of all the Benham types. He or she is generally successful, being shrewd and an excellent judge of human nature. These persons also seem to possess tireless energy and skillful hands. They can be fine writers, shrewd businessmen, and may be skilled as orators, scientists, doctors or lawyers.

Sprong sees the mount of Mercury as descriptive of how the qualities of the other mounts will be coordinated and expressed in the world. Mercury, like the quicksilver it names, denotes liberty. It also stands for the inquisitive, the collectors of knowledge. Therefore, memory is a faculty of Mercury. Mercury, like Saturn, is associated with wisdom. Mercury can also suggest those who can collect wealth. Mercury and Apollo form most of the air quadrant of the palm in the Wu-Hsing system of palmistry.

Mars ♂

Here is the Roman god of war and agriculture. He was first a farmer, then a soldier. Mars gives us the name of March and his agricultural aspect was honored in May. He is identified with the Greek war god Ares but was more noble, for Ares was a bloodthirsty sort, fond of anger and strife. The mounts and plain follow the more noble god.

Mars is divided into three parts, like a finger laid across the hand. Upper Mars lies between Mercury and Luna on the percussion. It is probably found above a normal extension of the head line if it does no more than gently curve. Lower Mars lies below Jupiter and above the thumb. The plain of Mars lies between.

On the three faces of Mars we experience the interaction of human drives with the areas of higher consciousness. Thus, for example, the drive to survive and procreate, identified through striving for orgasm, may be transformed under Saturn, or Saturn and Apollo, to religious ecstasy. On the mount of lower Mars, above the thumb, the energies of survival and procreation become aggressive with the influence of the expansive Jupiter. The energies of survival and the protection reflected in the womb of Luna transform into the energies of defense and champions of justice as they travel through upper Mars toward Mercury. Saturn and Apollo join all surrounding mounts to modulate the energies reflected on the plain of Mars so that the day-to-day temperament may be displayed.

Upper Mars stands for the characteristics of defense and justice, and lower Mars is a mirror for the aggressive characteristics. The plain of Mars shows temperament. Mars, like Saturn, reflects the embodiment of the ability to distinguish.

Upper Mars reflects the characteristics of courage, tenacity, and the ability to stand in the face of adversity and to defend what is just and right. It is the site of righteousness. When it is overdeveloped, the subject may be argumentative and could be violent, especially if upper Mars is deep red, large and hard.

A thick mount may give resilience and calmness from surprise, while a thin mount may find the subject flabbergasted by the same events. When both the mounts of Mars and Luna curve outward, these are signs of creativity. If straight, the subject, according to Fenton and Wright, is good at interpreting the ideas of others.[71] They say that if the head line penetrates the mount, the person would make an excellent salesperson, even able to sell "refrigerators to Eskimos!"

Lower Mars can be thought of as the seat of aggression. If the mount is fairly large, we have an assertive subject who can be a go-getter and capable. If the mount is small, he could be a whiner.

Lower Mars is identified with action. Over-development suggests contention, hostility, and threat of or actual violence. If lower Mars is under-developed, the person will not stand and fight unless the subject has a well-developed mount of upper Mars.

The plain of Mars is considered by Brandon-Jones as the reservoir for the energies that flow into the crossing rivers and surrounding mounts.[72] When it is deep, flabby, and soft, the subject is lazy and sensual. Brandon-Jones says this person will work for the luxuries but is too ill to work for the necessities.

Thin plains suggest a lack of physical stamina that may be accompanied by a lack of earthy, practical, common sense. This person may be oth-erworldly. The person can be plagued by inse-curity and indecisiveness because, though his intuition for others is generally sound, he fears to use it for his own benefit.

A good mount is characterized by firmness, physical strength, and endurance and feels well padded.

Benham's fifth type is the Martian.[73] He is iden-tified by the two mounts of Mars. Stars, triangles, circles, tridents, squares, and single vertical lines all, alone or in combination, strengthen upper Mars. However, signs found on lower Mars must, according to Benham, be read in conjunction with influence lines on the life line. Grilles, crosses, stars, and all cross lines in the plain of Mars indicate an increase in the temper of the subject. Such marks along with islands show de-fects in upper Mars affecting either health or char-acter. We can concur with this observation as the area of upper Mars relates to the chakras of the head and neck. According to Benham, we look to nails, color, and other markings on the hand to learn whether these marks affect health or character.

Benham emphasizes that the Martian must be estimated by using all three areas of Mars. This allows the combination of both aggression and resistance. While the Martian is a fighter, he is more likely to be found fighting adverse psycho-logical and business elements than being a pugil-ist. Without these qualities, the subject is easily discouraged and defeated in life's struggles. The balance of the two mounts is of great importance. Unbalanced mounts can lead to a lack of push or resolve. Paired large mounts suggest subjects who simply thrust themselves through all obstacles and resist all attempts to be conquered. A whorl on the thumbprint reinforces this observation.

Benham described the Martian as of medium height and strongly built, with erect posture, mus-cular appearance, and one whose posture is ready to immediately react in a carefully measured way to any approach, whether threatening or friendly. He may have a small, bullet-shaped head larger at the base of the skull. The hair may be auburn or red, short, stiff, and sometimes curly. He will have a short, rough beard. The bright eyes are large and bold, dark in color, and surrounded by often bloodshot whites. The thin-lipped mouth is firm and the lower lip may be slightly larger than the upper one, enclosing strong, small, regularly set yellowish teeth. The brows are thick and form a straight line low over the eyes. The nose is long and straight or perhaps of the Roman type with a hump, while the chin is strong, perhaps dimpled or turning up at the end. Connecting the head to the broad muscular shoulders is a thick neck. The shoulder girdle rides on a well-muscled back and expansive chest encasing a strong heart and robust lungs. The torso is supported by short, muscular legs set on broad feet with an instep given to be flat, and supporting a proud, deter-mined gait. This frame is supported by big, strong bones. He is brave, unafraid of conflict, so one would presume he would have whorls on his thumbs.

Sprong notes that upper Mars (he calls it Mars positive) relates to mental resilience whereas lower Mars (Mars negative) describes the body's ability to resist. His key words for positive Mars are perseverance, stability, and self-control. Underdeveloped, these could be changed to fear of disappointment, apathy, and self-destructiveness. When overdeveloped, these characteristics change to an explosive temperament, unreasonableness, and possessiveness. The key words for the well-developed Mars mount are, according to Sprong, enthusiasm, sportsmanship, and physical strength. When overdeveloped, these characteristics become a fiery temperament with strong aggressiveness and a taste for sarcasm. Underdeveloped, these characteristics turn into a lack of determination, low self-esteem, and a feeling of helplessness.

Venus ♀

Venus is the goddess of spring and fruitfulness, protector of gardens, herbs, fruits, and flowers. We find an association of this mount with the earth and vital energies. In traditional Chinese palmistry, the mount is associated with the season of spring and the earth portion of the hand. Venus was later identified with the Greek goddess Aphrodite, the supposed mother of Aeneas, the traditional ancestor of the Romans. In her worship as Venus Genetrix she apparently acquired Aphrodite's power over sexual love for she is also known as the goddess of love. In Hindu mythology, the deity who represents sexual love, Shukra, is a male god. Shukra taught the demons or giants.

This mount lies below the distal two phalanges of the thumb, above the wrist, and is bound by the life line generally. In some, the life line may appear to cut across this mount, reducing the person's vitality, vivacity, and sexuality.

I believe that Venus should be viewed as androgynous. He/she contains both the ovum and the sperm of the person's being. The Moon is the abdominal womb while the upper two phalanges of the thumb form the lingam. On the inward path the thumb figuratively provides the sperm to fertilize the ovum to spark conception. Then the spark of conception attaches to the uterus, the mount of Venus. Here the pregnancy gives birth to desire or the mount may show signs of miscarriage or bareness. The mount of Venus reflects both the uteri of women and the gonads of males. The family line at the base of the thumb above the mount of Venus would reflect the yoni. On the outward path, this ring can be seen as giving birth to the thumb, the subject's child as an expression of the person's will. Indeed, in some respects, the thumb reflects the child in birth.

The mount of Venus may have apices, but this is rare. Hutchinson has found them definitely marked on the hands of Orientals, and strongly marked on Hebrews, but hard to locate on the British.[74]

The ideal mount is rounded, firm but not hard, has good coloration, and extends to about the middle of the hand. It is not cut too sharply or narrowed by the life line.

These mounts are the indicators of physical vitality, good digestive processes, well-working enzymatic and chemical reactions, and good storage and food use. There is a stomach pressure point in the middle of the mount that may be painfully pressed after eating. A well-developed Venus goes along with a well-developed libido, healthy sex drive, and full potency. Deficiencies translate into deficiencies in these areas.

With regard to character, a well-developed mount supports rising spirits, confidence, warmth, and a happy, friendly disposition. It can also indicate a musical affinity and a generous, cooperative, and loving spirit.

Flat mounts may suggest digestive or metabolic problems. Lower levels of energy are expected from narrow, anemic, hard mounts. Such mounts can suggest the hermit or one who is drawn to the monastic life.

Generally, vertical lines on Venus enhance the qualities and horizontal lines increase the worries. Crosses, grilles, islands, and dots would be considered defects in the mount. However, circles, squares, triangles, and single vertical lines strengthen the mount. Stars can show the client is or has been the object of jealousy.

A highly developed Venus, out of proportion to the rest of the hand, with perhaps grilles or strong color, will emphasize the Venusian qualities described by Benham. If it is flat, small, or reduced in size by a narrow curve of the life line, then these qualities may be completely lacking.

The strong Venusian is a highly sexed individual and Benham describes him or her with all the background of his Victorian times. However, he treats this Victorian morality and the Venusian kindly. He finds the well-endowed Venusian to be healthy, happy, even joyous, and pleasant to meet. Benham sees him or her as attractive and furnishing necessary warmth for human companionship. However, he encourages the reader to find other strong qualities in the hand, such as good head lines, before deciding whether these oversexed individuals may keep to the straight and narrow path of morality.

Benham describes the appearance of the Venusian as attractive, even beautiful.[75] He or she is of medium height and shapely, well balanced, and graceful. The skin is soft, pale pink, velvety, and has a transparent, fine texture but of good health. The face is round or oval with no strong prominence, while well-rounded cheeks may show dimples with a smile. Our subject's forehead is lofty. Benham describes a mark of the young Venusian on the forehead as three vertical lines over the bridge of the nose between the eyes. His hair is silky, long, fine, and wavy. The Venusian does not suffer baldness with age. There are prominent, well-defined eyebrows, gracefully curving to sharpened ends and seldom growing over the bridge of the nose. The eyes have a round or almond shape and may be brown or dark blue in color. And when passions are aroused, they cannot be mistaken from his or her voluptuous visage.

A full, soft mount can suggest the subject lacks physical stamina and may be cold and concerned only with the practical areas of life, leaving little or no time to enjoy it.

Sprong has some interesting observations of both Luna and Venus regarding intuition.[76] The mount of the Moon represents the way the subject receives new ideas; Venus shows how the subject figures out their value. Venus represents the power of intuitive discernment. True Venusians prefer to live in harmony, reflecting their receptiveness to intimate relations. If harmonies were their goals, then we should say the true Venusians will have radial loops instead of whorls for thumbprints.

Luna/the Mount of the Moon ☽

Luna, the goddess of the Moon, is identified with the Greek goddess Selene, sister of Helios, the sun, and is also called Mene. Other Moon goddesses of the feminine form from the classical Greek and Roman pantheons were Artemis, Hecate, Bendis, Brizo, Callisto, Prosymna, and Diana. From that pantheon Sprong must have found his goddess of the hunt and unmarried maidens. Artemis was the sister of Apollo and hence this reference by Sprong.[77]

This mount is located on the percussion side of the hand below the mount of Mars and either above the wrist in the case of the seven, or above Pluto, in the case of the ten mounts. It is bounded at the center by the plain of Mars, Venus, the mount of Neptune, and Uranus.

If the percussion appears to bulge, there is a close affinity for water. In Wu-Hsing Chinese palmistry, greater Luna is in the water area of the hand. The person likes to live at or near water. The subject may like to be on the water or in it. In any case, the subject uses water to relax through baths and showers or just by walking beside bodies of water. If the person has any fear of water, a closer examination will often reveal a near drowning experience or other frightening water experience when he or she was very young. This subject's relationship with water is almost as if the person is still reacting to being repudiated by a loved one. The subject still seeks closeness but is afraid to get too close or touch for fear of being hurt.

The mount relates to the unconscious, creative powers, imagination, psyche, intuition, travel, and desire for freedom and change. High mounts may also suggest some linguistic abilities. This is possibly a connection to the Mercury mount qualities. When it is overdeveloped, we tread toward lunacy, unstable psyche, restlessness, very high sensitivity, and possibly depression. It can also be a sign of a very active psyche, clairvoyance, and déjà vu. This person may be too trusting, overgenerous, and always supporting others even against his or her better judgment and instincts.

Flat mounts show lack of these various qualities and may also support a pessimistic personality and a cynicism of all metaphysical subjects. These people are involved in survival with little time for dreaming or creativity. They support conformity and are not easily moved by emotions. With this underdeveloped source they want to forget the past, get away from family, and even deny their present support. We can see this in the cross (horizontal) lines of travel.

Benham calls the person where the mount of the moon is most prominent the Lunarian.[78] When it is thick and forms a conspicuous bulge on the percussion, it is a very strong mount. If unusually large, then we have an excess of Lunarian qualities. In these types, vertical lines add strength while cross ones display defects. The vertical lines, if prominent, may make up for the lack of percussion bulge or thickness of the mount.

Benham divides the mount into three sections: upper, middle, and lower (with no Pluto below it). Each section is useful to locate health difficulties. This is similar to the use of the percussion under my method of locating health problems, except in my method, upper Mars is also used. In my method, the area of the crown chakra (top of the head) would be located just below the start of the heart line, the root chakra (anus and external genitalia area) would be located just above the wrist, and the throat, or throat chakra, would be found by extending a horizontal line across the palm from about the start of the head line. Both methods find that grilles, crossbars, crosses, badly formed stars, wavy lines, or lines with dots or islands will indicate potential health defects in related areas. I have used this approach with considerable success, and I often find corresponding red marks (indicating acute or healing conditions) or darker marks (indicating morbid types of conditions) at corresponding levels of the life line or on the plain of Mars, Uranus, or Neptune areas. Benham believes that the lines at the side of the hand are erroneously named travel lines.[79] However, I do not necessarily concur because it is beginning to be apparent that some lines have more than one function. Unless there is a discoloration of the line or some similar finding, the mere presence of the line or other mark may only signal tendencies or past conditions and not necessarily present afflictions.

Benham describes the Lunarian as tall, well fleshed out, with thick legs and size thirteen triple E type feet. While he may be quite stout, there is a lack of tone to his muscles and his flesh lacks firmness. His decided pallor raises questions of anemia, dropsy, and kidney problems. His head tends to be round, thick at the temples, and bulges over the eyes. He or she may have fine hair that is thick and straggly of a blond or chestnut color. Round, starry eyes, frequently watery, may be bulging and the brows quite scanty and uneven over thick lids, swollen in appearance. The irises may be light blue or gray with a luminescent quality. Finally, the nose is short, nostrils exposed, having that pug nose quality. The lips and mouth are small and puckered. This handsome creature is also seen with large, irregularly placed, yellowing teeth that are both a dentist's and orthodontist's dream provided the pocketbook is well matched. The voice is high and thin with small ears to match, closely held to the head. The entire head is perched on a fleshy neck with folds descending to a flabby chest and a paunch. The large, flat feet seem to shuffle as he walks. His hand is flabby in consistency. The fingers are smooth and short with conic or pointed tips. He has a small thumb with either a pointed tip or shortness.

Benham finds the realm of the Lunarian is imagination and it is the imagination that makes possible communication. He is idealistic, fanciful, and dreamy, but his thoughts may be for naught as they are never put into operation. He is restless and has a hard time settling down in life. He may spend his last dollar on travel. The Lunarian is both physically and mentally lazy and quite an egoist. He tends to become mystical and melancholy, and tends to be superstitious. He displays

slow movements, is extremely sensitive, and of a phlegmatic disposition. Because of his vivid imagination and self-interest, he can become quite introverted as he imagines slights that do not exist. He may love nature and the muses.

Sprong describes Luna as the filter through which all of our senses receive their information of the outside world. It is also a mount through which we reveal ourselves. It shows the manner or attitude by which we relate to the outside world. Strange that this would appear on the passive, introspective side of the hand. Our verbal skills are also observed from this side of the hand in the lines of communication and the mount and finger of Mercury. Well-formed mounts suggest charming, loving people.

Beryl Hutchinson[80] reports that according to some Indian practitioners, an apex found on lower Luna with a line through it or from the center indicates a hard worker whose success will never be recognized. Hutchinson had the mark on both hands, and she felt that the traditional Indian description was all too true.

Neptune Ψ

This Roman named god for the sea has attributes mostly drawn from the Greek god Poseidon. He once held sway over the heavens and earth until supplanted by Zeus. Once he was master of earthquakes, fecundity, and vegetation and was called Genethliosm, the creator. The allusion to fecundity — the ability to bear children — may be one reason Neptune is set just above the wrist. A widow's peak on the upper rascette of the wrist traditionally suggests a problem in carrying or bearing children. Poseidon was possessive but not as strong as Zeus. He was given to fits of rage and was in constant dispute with the gods who owned coastal areas.

This mount lies above the wrist, below the plain

of Mars and between the mounts of Venus and Luna. Hutchinson says that, when present, its effect is strong so that "Life Force seems to flow so freely through the owner that a magnetism is given out."[81] Brandon-Jones's experience with well-formed mounts of Neptune indicates that they bring the owners in tune with the world of the human unconscious.[82] Deficient mounts suggest unhappy, misunderstood subjects who seem to antagonize others without knowing why.

This mount will be the bridge of the gap between the yin and yang portions of the hand, the female and male sections represented by Luna and Venus. Here dreams can be transformed into practical expressions. Many aspects of Neptune are illusory, ill-defined, or unclear. It is the opposite of Saturn's reflection of reality. It defies time and space. Neptune energy forms the heart of the mystic, the Nirvana of the spirit. Here the subject merges to become one with the greater cosmos. Some, like the astrologer Robert Hand,[83] would say that a more appropriate deity for this mount would be Maya. Maya embodies both illusion and the way through illusion to absolute truth. It is the furnace under Saturn, producing the raw energy that Saturn must deal with. The Neptunian is not one of Benham's seven types of persons.

The raw energy and illusory nature of Neptune can be bad for relationships if it is too strong. Under stress, confusion will abound. One can also experience a loss of ego if this is the predominant mount. As a source of psychic energy, it may reflect the connection to identical and fraternal siblings. Shadows and colors may reflect the concerns or conditions of brothers and sisters.

Uranus ♅

Uranus is so old that there is little memory of him. He appears as Heaven and was the child produced by Gaea, earth, unaided. He became the mate of Gaea, and sired the Titans and various monsters. Either through fear or jealousy, he tried to hide these children in the huge body of Gaea. The Titans are considered nature powers of some sort. She found she could no longer endure the strain and begged her children to avenge her. Cronos, the father of Zeus, obliged. He castrated his father, Uranus, as he came to attend his consort. Cronos flung the member into the sea. From its drops that fell on its flight were born the Erinyes, the giants, and the guardian nymphs of manna-ashes. The member floated on the sea and from the foam that gathered around it was born Aphrodite, who some relate to the Roman goddess Venus. The Erinyes were the just but terrible avengers of crime, especially the crimes concerned with kinship. They pursued Orestes after he killed Clytemnestra, a plot that formed the basis of one of Aeschylus's greatest dramas, *Eumenides*. Nymphs generally have prophetic powers and can inspire mortals. Giants of course are capable of great deeds.

Uranus blends the basic drives and energies of the earth with the powers of creation and sires surprises, even titanic surprises, from within us. Even when checked by Cronos, the time god related to Saturn, Uranus still bears fruit. The energies of Uranus are difficult to limit; they break through the illusions of present reality. Stars on Uranus reflect a curious, uncontrollable ability to look through the cracks of time and see glimpses of the future. We have seen clients who have heeded this ability and saved members of their family from dangers. We have often seen clients with Uranian stars who know when they are going to receive a call and who it is from, even before the phone rings. They have this preknowledge even of calls from people they have not heard from in years. Marks on Uranus can indicate psychic experience uncontrolled but manifest.

I recently observed the hands of a newspaper photographer of merit. He had the stars on Uranus as well as whorls on his thumbs, and I readily predicted he would boldly thrust himself in the midst of the excitement and would have the uncanny ability to be ready to shoot the key picture. He would anticipate, through the Uranian break in the cosmic time egg indicated by the stars, the events that would unfold before his camera. The writer with him who knew his skill readily agreed with my assessment.

Uranus may be related to the energy that results in new inventions and scientific theories. It may also feed the energies to challenge old ideas. Uranus is not as totally destructive and transformational as Pluto. Heaven does not bring death to the old. He sires new births of inspiration. These energies are not always pleasant to behold. Uranus reflects energies that appear innovative and even revolutionary, sparking change aimed toward the world of others. It brings the world of intuition into sharp contrast and intimate connection with the world of reason.

I recall reading a woman who had the Hindu sign of the yoni on this area. I found that her great desire was to nurture and give birth to one who would bring revolutionary change to the world. She totally agreed. Children of such a woman should be watched with interest.

We have generally placed Uranus in the center of the palm just below the plain of Mars. Exact borders in this area are hard to define. We can understand why others have seen the relationship to Apollo. Uranian powers are not readily apparent in all palms.

Pluto ♀

Pluto is an alias for the Greek god Hades. This name means *riches* and refers to the wealth in the earth that Hades inhabits and rules. Another alias is Aidoneus and he was a child of Cronos. Pluto was the god of the underworld and wealth, the invisible one. He was both the terrifying and mysterious god of death and generous distributor of wealth. Here is a fit person to be the god of the lower mount of dreams, the psyche.

According to Darlene Hansen, the mount of Pluto is located below Luna in the unconscious, passive zone of the hand. It is in the realm of dreams and may have connection with ancient mysteries.[84] If the mount is flat, while the person may still have creativity, he or she will not use the metaphysical or occult worlds in that creativity. Some others consider Pluto to be located between Venus and Luna at the base of the palm just above the wrist. I would reserve this space for Neptune. However, the borders between Luna, Pluto, and Neptune are not yet well established.

Those who see Pluto at the base of the palm where we describe Neptune may be opposing Pluto to Uranus. That transposition reflects Pluto as completing the radical transformation of the consciousness resulting from breaches of reality structure that may be symbolized by markings on Uranus. Pluto can be seen as the archetype of death and transfiguration or transformation. Whereas Neptune energies can confuse reality, Plutonian energy reflects the breakdown of reality.

In my early practice I met an elder psychiatrist with an unusual head line that traveled straight across the palm, then divided, and both forks went straight down parallel along the percussion into the area of Pluto. He was very distraught when I met him. Unfortunately, at the time, I was too devoted to the Saturnine world to recognize a man on the verge of great transformation. Otherwise, I would have suggested that he use the gates to other consciousness explored by Carl Jung. Now, lines to this area, especially when connected to the head line, immediately alert me to deep transformation the client may experience or the deep depression that will be experienced if this energy is denied. Those in denial of these energies may resort to drugs, alcohol, or hover between madness and sanity. Our realistic, highly urban world, with its Saturnine religions, economics, laws, and morality, provides little alternative to these palliatives. Our denial of this realm denies the potential shamans of our society.

There is no Benham Plutonian, nor for that matter, is there any Vulcanian.

Vulcan — the Second Sun Mount

Vulcan was the god of fire, the Sun, and thunderbolts. Originally, he was associated with volcanoes and had to be placated. Later, he was associated with the misshapen Greek blacksmith of the gods, Hephaestos. However, Vulcan was never an artificer and could not have wrought the chains that bound his wife, Aphrodite, to Ares in their bed of adultery. Perhaps Hephaestos would be the nobler name to honor this area of the hand, for it is in that area where the clever thumb moves in concert with the other fingers to fashion the hand's work. Yet the anger of lower Mars seems to be more the focus of this mount.

The Sun mount lies, according to Hansen, below the second joint of the thumb and in the conscious, passive zone of the palm.[85] This should be distinguished from the Sun mount described by many others, which is also called the mount of

Apollo. Hansen's Sun mount seems to lie in the area of the birth of the major fire line according to the cheirognomy of Wu-Hsing as described by Dukes.[86] This is the area of the inner thenar crease. It seems to be related to lower Mars, for Hansen observes that when it is well developed, "it indicates success through push and will." She believes that if overdeveloped, the "person could be a blowhard" needing constant praise. If flattened, then the person would exhibit insecurity and need encouragement to keep going.

There is another appropriate reason for calling this area Vulcan. Vulcan as Hephaestos is the smith. This is the control area between the hammer of the index finger and the anvil of the thumb. Frequently, one will see many lines that travel from the area like rays of the Sun. Some slice across the life line like swords or spears. Vulcan can be the smith where these new influences are forged. Perhaps as we study tempering and forging, we can better understand the type of influence that approaches and crosses the life line from this area.

Further Mount Information

I refer the reader back to the sections on fingers and the Benham section on forms for further information concerning the energies reflected by mounts under the fingers and the mounts of the Sun, Moon, and Mars. A good palmist, after looking at a thousand or so pairs of hands, will automatically integrate this information.

TRIANGLE AND QUADRANGLE

The areas known as the triangle of Mars, or the great triangle and quadrangle, are areas formed in the palm by being bordered by certain major lines.

The triangle is surrounded by the head, life, and health lines. The Sun line (line of Apollo) can substitute for the health line (also known as the

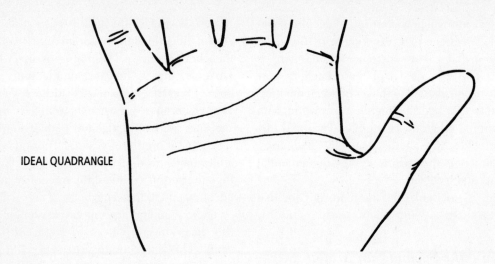

IDEAL QUADRANGLE

line of Mars, hepatic, or liver line). The quadrangle is the area formed between the heart and head lines. Many palmists attach little or no importance to these particular areas.

Francis King[87] attaches great importance to the great triangle when bound by the Sun line, which can happen in the absence of a health line. It can be taken both as a strong indication of achievement and as a sign of intolerance

The Triangle

Francis King believes we should consider the great triangle from three standpoints: (1) as an independent entity, (2) in connection with its upper and lower angles, and (3) the area enclosed by the triangle.[88]

As an independent entity, the area should be as large as possible and clearly marked to show a generous, unselfish nature. If the area is smaller, the person may be subject to intolerance, meanness, and egotism. While the clearly marked sun line cuts down on the area and thus increases egotism and intolerance, it suggests firmness of purpose and chances of success.

The upper angle forms from the junction of the life and head lines. King believes the angle should be easy to see, well pointed, and even, thus aiding clarity and delicacy of mental activity and thoughtfulness toward others. As the obtuse angle increases, that is, the more the head line rises and/or life line falls away, increasing the angle, the more unemotional and common sense thought prevails. Very obtuse angles can suggest impatience, aggressiveness, anger, and a plunge toward self-induced misery.

The middle angle of this triangle is formed by the lines of Mercury (or Apollo) at or near where they join the head line or would join it if extended. Very acute (narrow) angles suggest a neurotic tendency with low physical and emotional vitality. An obtuse angle suggests slow thinking and lack of perception.

The lower angle of the great triangle forms from the junction, real or extended, of the lines of Mercury (or Apollo) and the life line. As the angle

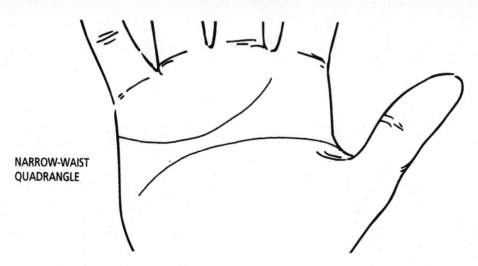

NARROW-WAIST
QUADRANGLE

becomes acute with the Mercury line, it suggests a growing tendency toward lack of physical, emotional, and spiritual energy. Enthusiasm diminishes and what was started may never be finished. As the angle becomes more obtuse, the mental and emotional states grow stronger as does the physical and spiritual energy of the subject. If it is an obtuse angle formed by the Sun line, the open-mindedness and generosity of the subject offsets the acute upper angle of intolerance and narrowness.

The Quadrangle

This is the space between the head and heart lines. Ideally, it should be wide at both ends and even in shape.

Ideal Quadrangle

However, the space may be narrow-waisted in the middle.

Narrow-Waisted Quadrangle

Or it may be wide at the percussion side of the palm.

Quadrangle That Is Wide at Percussion

Or it may be wider at the thenar side of the palm.

Quadrangle That Is Wide at the Thenar Side

The ideal will not be crossed by many lines. According to King, the virtues of the ideal quadrangle are calmness, equable temperament, the ability to make unbiased decisions on any matter, marked intellectual ability, and strong loyalty to friends and others to whom there is a strong sexual or emotional attachment.[89]

Although such a quadrangle should be fairly wide, it should not be too wide or the person will be so broad-minded as to tolerate outrageous be-

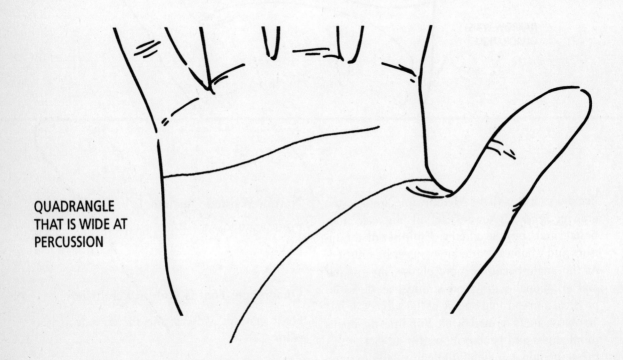

**QUADRANGLE
THAT IS WIDE AT
PERCUSSION**

havior. These people tend to be disorganized and illogical and may well be attracted to unconventional ideas and may be inclined to rash speech, action, and speculation.

When the quadrangle is narrow-waisted in the middle, beware of prejudice (prejudgment) resulting in unfair conclusions. There is also an indication of midlife confusion between the head and the heart.

If it is wider at the Mercury end, the person may

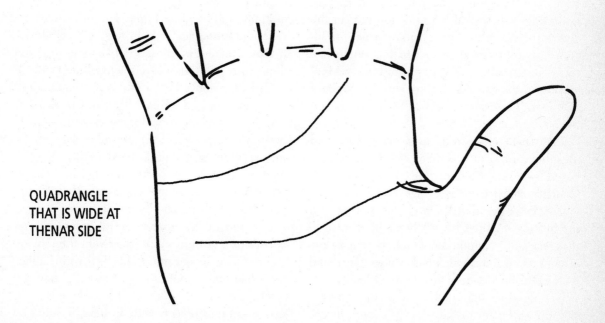

QUADRANGLE
THAT IS WIDE AT
THENAR SIDE

be unconcerned about what others think of him or her. Narrowness at that end can result in the contrary opinion.

If the quadrangle is wider at the Jupiter end, there is an indication of broad-mindedness and tolerance in youth that will diminish with advancing years. Check and see if the flexibility of the dominant hand is less that of the other hand on those over thirty and if the thumb angle is also smaller. Those features support this evaluation.

CHINESE HAND DIVISIONS

In contrast to Western palmistry, traditional Chinese palmistry divides the hand onto eight star mounts and a five-star field according to the five basic elements. It also divides the palm into areas identified with the basic I Ching trigrams: Ch'ien, Chen, K'an, Ken, K'un, Sun, Li, and Tui. A third division of the palm is according to the seasons.

Gettings tells us that Li, while found near the Saturn mount, means flame and indicates brightness.[90] The area is associated with position like career and social standing, those attributes we find playing in the game of "personality" in Western palmistry. These are associated with Saturn and the Saturn line.

Gettings describes K'un as a female principal meaning earth (earth mother?).[91] It is located between Apollo and Mercury. This could explain the sexuality related to the little finger and the outward giving of love found in Apollo. In the west we find the healing striations here. The abilities for intimate, sensitive communications may be found close at hand. The private moments of creativity are found on the little finger side of the mount of Apollo.

Gettings describes Tui, located on upper Luna, as the area linked to the subjects' wives, lovers, friends, and children.[92] He points out that Tui is depicted in Chinese minds as a "joyous lake" relating to the Western water connections for this area. In the west it is an area of daydreams, fantasy, and pleasant thoughts.

Chien is located on lower Luna. Gettings identifies it as the protective palace of the father and associates it with education.[93] Curiously, I also find the matriarch sign in this area, the dominance principal. Could this be the area of the guiding father, the possible mentor, for good or ill? Gettings finds the area strongly related to spirituality and creativity in Chinese application.

K'an fits outside of the lifeline in the area of Neptune. Gettings describes this area as one of great danger, known by the terms *abyss* and *defile*.[94] In Western palmistry it is seen as the bridge between the male and female principals and as the area of raw energy, yet unformed. Gettings sees a connection to the birth of the Saturn line from this area.

Ken occupies the lower area of Venus and in Chinese, according to Gettings, means hard or obstinate and indicates limits. This fits with observations of the subject's ability to give "tough love." It also is related in Chinese to keeping still, and those who give tough love may well be taciturn.

Chen lies above Ken on the Venus mount and occupies some of the area Vulcan and lower Mars. It is the area where the Chinese major fire line is born. Gettings tells us that this palace name means lightning, and indicates an exciting force or quickening force. Western palmists can relate to this interpretation of the elements within the upper Venus, Vulcan, and lower Mars area.

Sun lies in the Jupiter mount area. Gettings advises us that Sun is associated with the moving wind.[95] This Jovian notion fits well with Jupiter, the expansive planet. Gettings observes that the intellect is related to this area, and like the wind, can go around objects without being injured by them. He finds this wind not only related to the expansive nature of Jupiter but also to the intellect that he rules in Western palmistry.

The Chinese Star Division

The student has already learned to look for the quality of areas of the hand and these abilities can be used in identifying the relative strengths and weaknesses of the Chinese hand divisions. We explored the meanings of the elements when we discussed hand shapes. The Chinese geographic areas relate to various characteristics of the sub-

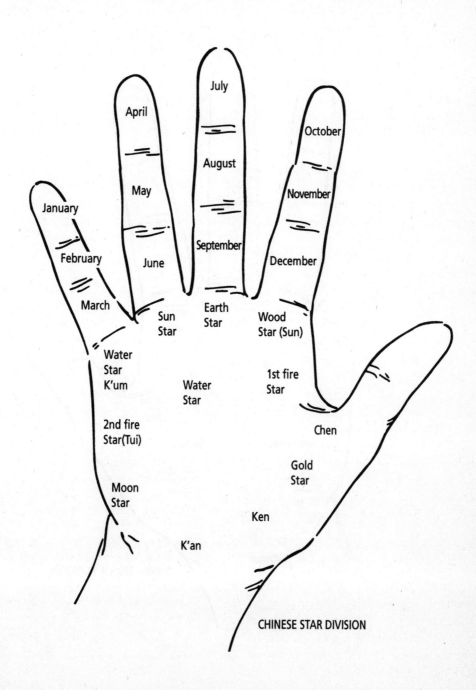

CHINESE STAR DIVISION

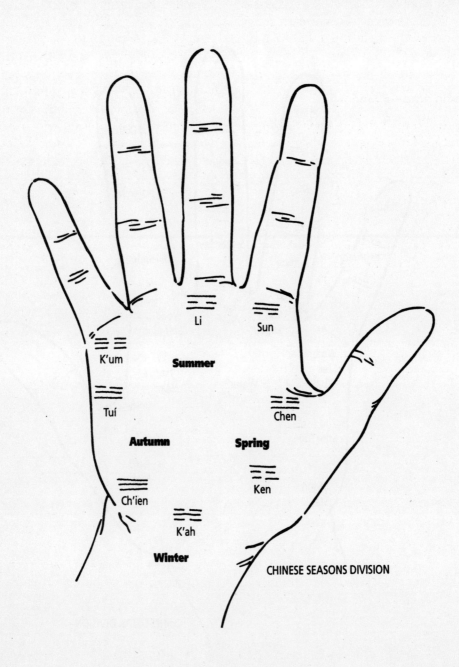

CHINESE SEASONS DIVISION

ject, just as the mounts do. The wood star relates to personality, the earth star relates to determination, the Sun star relates to success, and the water star relates to money.

The Chinese Season Division

The Chinese also use hand geography to reflect the good and bad times of a person's life. This may be useful in the future as I have found the four part divisions of hand shapes useful in the past. Seasons of the year are found starting with the mount of Venus representing spring. The traditional color related to spring is green. Summer is found in the area of the mounts of Saturn and Apollo and is traditionally red. Autumn is found on upper Luna and upper Mars and goes with the traditional color of white. Black is the color of winter and winter is found in the area of Neptune between Luna (Pluto) and Venus, just above the wrist.

CHAPTER SEVEN

PATTERNS

The patterns that appear on the fingers and palms could be viewed as maps guiding the soul to the universe. The whorls trace light paths through galaxies, while loops and arches chart waves among the constellations of life. These patterns indicate the manner and methods best suited for our clients' travel to their anointed goals in life. Some show the dancer, others the digger, while others perhaps the dowser who perceives beyond the visible. We may find in the configurations the drill, the single minded achiever, the press or relentless pursuer, or the bullet of the person who must penetrate to the very core of the challenge. The ridge patterns in the fingerprints and palms lay out the syncope of the client's pace. They advise the best setting of the cadence of life: fast, slow, deliberate; or give us instruction on how to adjust it to waltz time, jazz, or rap, or even if such an adjustment can be made. More practically, the highly specialized surfaces of the palm and sole of the foot serve to enhance friction and touch, a touch more sensitive than any yet accomplished by mechanical means.

Fingerprints have long been a subject of prophecy. Mavalwala[1] describes a two-volume Japanese manuscript by Ashizuka-Sai Shofou dating from 1820 that lists thirty-two different types of whorls and their incidence in various combinations on the five fingers. That manuscript also distinguished between the radial and ulnar fingers (finger patterns?).

Fingerprints attracted the anatomist Malpighius as long ago as 1686 and the first attempt to systematically categorize fingerprint patterns is found in the work of Purkinje in 1823. He used a nine pattern classification. Almost seventy years later, Galton proposed a simpler system that still finds a fairly wide progeny based on whorls, arches, and loops. Such classification systems went on to become the foundations of the classify, file, and identify methods utilized by governments around the world where their reason for existence is to record the print and easily retrieve this information to identify the subject. We typically find this used in the criminal justice systems and armed forces where identification of the subject is the reason for its existence.[2]

I believe that much of the twenty-first-century development of palmistry will be built around a better understanding of the significance of the ridge patterns on the palms and fingers. Therefore, the serious student and practitioner who will contribute to that development must have some grounding in the methods of study of these markings. In other words, the student and practitioner must first know what to look for before making assumptions about any characteristics he or she may believe the subject has when a particular pattern is found. That will also require some knowledge of the frequency of certain pattern types. Then it is suggested that we explore the potential existence of particular characteristics normal to certain patterns.

DERMATOGLYPHICS

The medical study of the ridge patterns of the palm (palmar ridges) and fingers (fingerprints) is called dermatoglyphics. The term is attributed to a Cummings and Midlo publication of 1926 and refers to the arrangements formed by skin ridges on the palms, fingers, soles of the feet, toes, and even the ventral surfaces of the tails of nonhuman primates.[3] The term is used in the zoological study of the hands, feet and tails of nonhuman primates, the anthropological study of human populations, and the general study of genetics. This scientific field also includes the study of skin creases and "white" lines or secondary ridges (those that do not have sweat glands).

PALM PATTERNS

The Fixed Patterns

Patterns tend to fade with age, use of cortisone, and during some illnesses. Restored health usually finds the return of those patterns faded by illness. Pastry bakers are notorious for losing their finger patterns as they burn them off in pulling out hot trays from the ovens. While the size of patterns will vary with the growth of the hand, the configurations and relationships should remain constant.

Even the burned, faded, or defaced patterns can still be found by use of high-tech equipment such as an electron microscope.

The fixed, unchanging nature of the fingerprint and its individuality are cornerstones for law enforcement criminal identification systems throughout the world. This is described in a recent U.S. government publication as "one of the most potent factors in obtaining the apprehension of fugitives."[4] These patterns have also been useful in identification of amnesia victims, missing persons, and unknown deceased persons, such as victims of major disasters, adding a humanitarian aspect to their use. Until the recent advent of DNA identification, fingerprints were considered the most infallible and feasible method of identification.

The static, unalterable nature of the patterns is generally conceded. Hutchinson reports only one tiny change observed by the pioneer in the field, Sir Francis Galton, where a tiny island in a ridge line joined itself into the ridge and thickened it.[5] A friend reports observing a Native American of shamanic powers whom he observed change his prints to "drop out of the system" after being dis-charged from the military. Perhaps some adept could do this, but I have never observed such a change.

Before we consider other various types of maps of the palm, all readers should become familiar with the pattern of the triradius as it forms certain key landmarks for such mapping.

The Triradius

The first pattern we study is called the triradius. It is also mistakenly sometimes referred to as the triadius. It is a demarcation pattern and appears in a number of styles:

Triradii

The triradius is formed where three groups of patterns intersect and generally appears as a Y-shaped hub at the intersection of these patterns. It may be seen on each of the fingers in cases of loop or whorl or even tented arch fingerprints. It is usually seen beneath each finger as well as at the central base of the palm between the mounts of Venus and Luna. It is occasionally seen in other locations on the hand.

The location of the triradius may be used both to describe the types of patterns observed (singular triradii for loops and tented arches, dual triradii for whorls) and the location of the centers of mounts (in the cases of Jupiter, Saturn, Apollo, and Mercury), the starting point for main lines and auxiliary lines, as well as being an otherwise distinguishing characteristic of some hands by its unusual location.

Mount Apices and Other Palm Triradii in Palmistry: While triradii may be seen on fingerprints, and will be discussed there, they also form important landmarks on the palm: the apices of mounts. They are commonly found on the mounts of Apollo, Jupiter, Saturn, Mercury, and Neptune and are sometimes also found on the mounts of Venus and Luna and the plain of Mars.

Recognizing the apex or summit of the mounts

of Jupiter, Apollo, Saturn, and Mercury by the location of the triradii has long been recognized in palmistry, being so described by Saint-Germain in 1897.[6] That, however, was ignored by many over the years, at least until Beryl Hutchinson observed it.[7] We still find a large number of palmists who insist that the center of the mount is found where the hand is most fleshy, including those mounts found under the fingers.

Ideally, the apex of each of the finger mounts will be found in the center of the mount under the middle of that finger, but the apex could be found to either side or high or low on the mount or perhaps not at all. Special adjustments would have to be made to reflect the location of the apex of the mount under our dermatological formula above to pick up any special meanings attributed to its location by palmists. The palmist will consider doing this because tradition has given the location of the apex of each mount special significance.

The significance and location of each of the mounts will be discussed in greater detail in chapter 5.

Palmistry — The Axial Triradius and Health:
The axial triradius has been associated with a number of health problems by palmists. Fenton and Wright assert that the healthy person should have an axial triradius situated "directly above the wrist." Displacement would be symptomatic of heart disease.[8] They could have gotten this from a misreading of Scheimann, who quoted from an article of T. Takashina and S. Yorifuji in the *Journal of the American Medical Association*[9] that the frequency of axial triradii displacement in either hand occurred with significantly greater frequency in patients with congenital heart disease (64 percent) "than in patients with 'acquired' heart disease" (17 percent).[10] According to Nathaniel Altman, referring to some unnamed issue of the *Journal of*

the American Medical Association, a displacement of the axial triradius "to a higher location" indicates "a predisposition to congenital heart disease."[11] Now the student and the reader who has read this chapter will know how much weight to give such statements.

Palmistry Looks at Other Patterns on the Hands

Distinctive patterns in the forms of loops, whorls, and other figures also appear on the palm and have special significance, as do the locations of the triradii. We will deal further with the triradii as we deal with the mounts. Let us look at some of the more common patterns that may be found on the palm.

Loops Between the Fingers and on the Palm:
Between the fingers one may find any one or more of several loops: the loop of humor, the loop of style or vanity, the loop of seriousness, the loop of charisma or the rajah loop, and the loop of courage.

Loop of humor:
This is found between the mounts of Mercury and Apollo. These people can laugh and possess a happy, optimistic approach to life. Enid Hoffman agrees.[12] They can see the ridiculous side of things, feel the humor in things. Hutchinson,[13] who recognizes this sense of the ridiculous, says that when the loop is found in both hands the bearer can be accused of facetiousness.

The loop of humor may be one of those key dermatoglyphic marks that better aids us in appreciating the use of dermatoglyphics as a map of certain brain functions or areas. Dr. Damasio, in his book on emotion, reason, and the human brain, shows the brain areas used in controlling the muscles of the smile so that we can distinguish between a true smile and a put-on smile. This relies on the difference between the voluntary muscle control without the emotional involvement for the put-on smile and the emotional involuntary muscle control for the true smile. Scientific studies have pointed out specific areas of the brain involved in both actions.

In tracing the history of this discovery, Damasio points out that a nineteenth-century researcher, Guillaume-Benjamine Duchenne, discovered the true joyous smile required the combined use of two facial muscles, the orbicularis oculi and the zygomatic major. He further discovered that the orbicularis oculi (controlling certain movements around the eye) could only be moved involuntarily. One could not will it to move (adept yogis possibly excluded). This is probably one reason for the success of actors who actually become the part they play.

In any case, the loop of humor may be representative of some portions — or more precisely — processes of the brain that are involved in the involuntary muscle movement of such things as the smile of joy. It may have to do with increased receptivity and/or production of certain neurotransmitters or neuroinhibitors (chemical agents) in these areas or some other features of the central nervous system we have yet to understand.

Upper Palmar Loops

Bevy Jaegers adds that while one finds a normal sense of humor in those with the humor loop directly between the little and ring fingers, if it lies slightly under the ring finger, the humor is slightly offbeat and advises avoiding making this type of person the butt of practical jokes. She says that if it is placed beneath the ring finger (where others find the loop of vanity) the subject definitely does not enjoy humor at the expense of others but may find "bloopers or misprinted headlines hilarious."[14]

We have found that when paired with a loop of seriousness, the person can have a sharp tongue and be quite sarcastic. Fenton and Wright report that if a whorl is found in the loop, there is a talent for foreign languages.[15] They also report the subject will have a love for animals, but if the loop is crisscrossed with lines, he or she may have little time for them. Look at the size and shape of the loop. After observing a number of them, one can begin to discern the type of humor that might best appeal to the bearer, whether sharp, broad, slapstick, sarcastic, or clever.

Loop of style or vanity: Hutchinson[16] calls it the loop of vanity, as do some others. It is also known as the loop of ego and even relationship. It is a sign of style, some humor, and outward creativity. Others may well heed the warning not to laugh at but rather with people who have this type of loop. Enid Hoffman[17] describes it as a sign of great pride and self-confidence. Style is the kindest observation and quite a large number of those we have observed were noticeable for their striking or very tasteful dress. Jaegers, who calls this loop the ego or relationship loop, finds such people quite introspective, impervious to opinions of others, totally egocentric, and displaying little humor over jokes aimed at themselves or others. She also notes that if found on the left hand with a normal loop of humor on the right, it can indicate extraordinary feeling for the moods and emotions of others.[18] In her newer book she finds the subject extremely self-conscious, one who finds it difficult to be convivial.[19]

Fenton and Wright add that these subjects not only take great pride in their appearance and what they do, but they can be very cutting and sarcastic

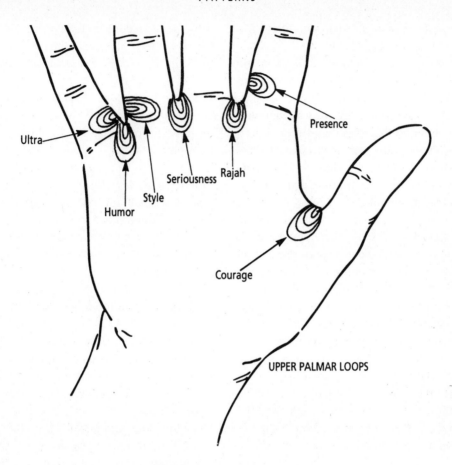

Ultra

Humor

Style

Seriousness

Rajah

Presence

Courage

UPPER PALMAR LOOPS

when crossed.[20] We recall the extraordinary smile that came across one client's face as we told her she had the loop of vanity. "Finally," she exclaimed, "someone has recognized my passion. I have a whole room full of evening dresses that I delight to wear."

Loop of seriousness: Hutchinson calls it the loop of serious intent. These people often readily admit that they are quite serious. They appear to have very serious interests in life. These people do not appreciate wasting their time. It is also known as the loop of common sense. I have found that

many who have it tended to cry as children or even as adults, taking matters so much to heart. Bevy Jaegers calls it the common sense loop and subjects having this mark also have what is known as good horse sense. They have good management abilities in some or all areas of life. She says these people generally know what is best for themselves and give good advice, but may take on burdens beyond their capacity.[21] In her later work she expands her comments concerning these feelings of a sense of responsibility toward others by noting that this is not just directed at family and friends. Doctors, medical researchers, nurses, social workers, and community group leaders may have this mark on their palms.[22]

If the loop is found on one hand only, the seriousness may be expressed in a hobby. If found on both hands, more is implied. Hutchinson finds this loop common in gatherings of councillors and religious groups and theorizes that it represents a blending of the happiness of Apollo with the stability of Saturn to inspire the choice of life activities that are of service to communal living. These subjects do not waste time.

Loop of charisma: This loop was supposed to indicate that one had descended from royalty and is also known as the loop of the rajah.[23] Subjects may display strong hints of personal magnetism that can be useful in seeking to succeed through public recognition. They may find that they are naturally called upon to assume leadership positions. Enid Hoffman describes it as a sign of great dignity often coupled with leadership qualities. On the right hand she noted it lent an executive quality to the subject's action; on the left hand she found it in the hand of a woman accomplished in entertaining her husband's associates with charm and skill.[24]

Bevy Jaegers describes the loop located here as the loop of power and introspection, and describes it (in agreement with Hutchinson) as rare and claims little is known about the significance of the sign. She says the loop is occasionally found on people with a "powerful 'aura' of charismatic attraction." She had, in her earlier work, found only one subject actually descended from royalty, the claim of Indian palmistry tradition.[25] In her later work she finds that those who have it are introspective.[26] She also indicates a loop of charisma in her later work. She adds that those who have it may have a chromosomal disorder, but does not cite her source other than to describe it in her 1974

work as a "recent well-known medical digest" which is not very helpful.[27] I have identified this as the loop of presence. See below for further discussion of this loop.

The subjects we have questioned with this sign commonly respond that they are regularly chosen for positions of leadership without having sought them.

Open field: Hutchinson describes this dermatoglyph that lacks pattern as an indication of a mind uncluttered by introspection. It is found on people who use their rationality and intuition in harmony with nature and who allow their emotions to flow easily without internal discord. Her book illustration refers to what appears to be open fields between all the fingers except the thumb.[28]

Loop of courage: This is located at the point in the hand that the Chinese recognize as the start of the major fire line, and it is associated by location with the mount of lower Mars, the mount for aggressiveness. These subjects admire bravery. If the sign is long and accompanies the family ring around the thumb, then, according to Hutchinson, it could reveal a long and hard fight for the family against numerous difficulties that will succeed through the courage shown.[29] Jaegers calls it the loop of courage and determination.[30] She notes that the courage implied by this loop includes stamina, fortitude, and steady reliability.[31] It could make up for a weak thumb. In her later work, Jaegers adds that in youth we may find tomboys or mischievous boys. These people can make stubborn, loyal friends. She does not find these people argumentative or combative, but defenders of the right to their last breath.[32]

Hoffman describes the subject as having natural strength, great character, courage, endurance, stamina, and fearlessness.[33] Hutchinson seems to confirm such findings attended with a longing to be braver than the appearance of the mount suggests.[34]

Ultra (femininity or masculinity): According to Bevy Jaegers, this loop on the lower (proximal) digit of the little finger, running crosswise, has a special significance in the area of libido/id and the sexual/sensual nature of the bearer. It seems to build up the macho in the men and the femininity in women, indicating strong, uninhibited sexuality. They have no problem in their sex identification.[35]

Loop of presence or charisma: Bevy Jaegers gives this loop the title the loop of charisma. Her loop of charisma is found solely on the proximal phalange of the index finger.[36] It is a sign of leadership. She finds such people capable of selfless service and dedication who leave "an indelible impression" on whoever they meet.[37] They command attention by just walking into the room.[38] One wonders if George Washington had such a loop. These people may have an overpowering presence.[39]

Hoffman anticipated by many years the findings of Jaegers describing the subjects as having magnetic and hypnotic qualities.[40]

Thenar (Venus) Loops: The mound of Venus, the proximal digit of the thumb, can support five possibly musical signs:

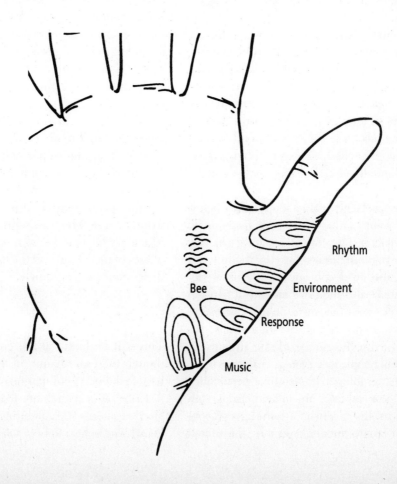

The musical bee loop: The Bee is a cross pattern shaped like an insect body, probably made up of vestiges. It would indicate strong responses to stringed instruments according to Hutchinson.[41] She believes that while there may be a love for music and the subject will be emotionally moved by music, especially stringed music, these feelings will not necessarily be accompanied by the abilities to compose and play. Hoffman finds that ability to compose in some and certainly the musician where she seeks the mark. She does not mention the stringed instruments. Jaegers agrees with either Hutchinson or Hoffman, depending on which of her books one reads, and gives credit to neither of these ladies.[42]

Loop of rhythm — brass loop: This is a loop identified by Enid Hoffman as located at the angle of dexterity, also know as the angle of rhythm or time; the medial radial angle of the thumb. These subjects have a great love of melody and harmony and may possess aptitude in music or dance.[43] Hutchinson finds these subjects respond to brass and martial music with the swing of the rhythm as the paramount element.[44]

Response loop: Jaegers calls a loop slightly below the medial joint of the thumb the response to environment loop. The subject may have a heightened, almost automatic response to rhythm and music and also be deeply moved by his or her environment. It also indicates empathy.[45] In her later work she goes beyond noting the subjects' deep response to music and rhythm and observes that subjects with this rare mark are strongly affected by both people and events. This gives these people a changeable, chameleonlike personality. She finds these subjects are often persons with Mediterranean heritage who are strongly responsive to their environments, especially the moods and emotions of their surroundings. She cautions such people to avoid confining places, such as jails.[46]

Hoffman environment loop: This loop is pictured by Hoffman as formed midway between the medial and proximal joints of the thumb on the first angle above the wrist. Hoffman finds that these subjects have a strong rapport with life, responding quickly to the environment, sounds, music, and nature. This sensitivity can result in wide ranges of moods and wildly fluctuating emotions. These subjects need to find discipline and self-control.[47]

Music loop: The loop entering the mount from the border of the wrist with the thumb would, according to Hutchinson, indicate a strong love for music. However, she cautions, this does not necessarily indicate any talent for artistry or composition.[48]

Hypo-thenar (Lunar) Loops: There are a variety of signs that can appear on the mount of the Moon. The most common are the loops of memory and the loops of nature. Also seen on this mount can be loops of nature and inspiration, and whorls. Those who have signs on the mount of the Moon are likely to be far more susceptible to the phases of the Moon and the tides and should plan their activities accordingly.

Loop of memory:

This will be found at the end of the head line, though the exact nature of this memory may be hard to define by comparing palmists. Hutchinson describes it as a memory that may bloom in relaxed moments and can bring past experience and knowledge to bear to help solve present dilemmas.

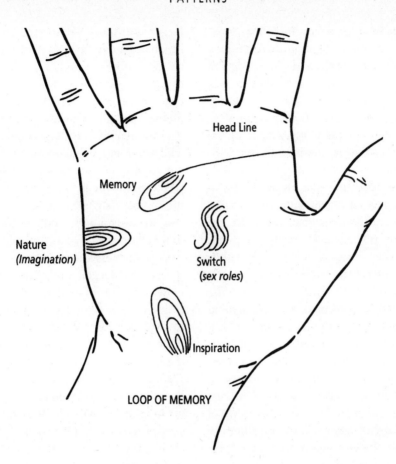

Head Line

Memory

Nature
(Imagination)

Switch
(sex roles)

Inspiration

LOOP OF MEMORY

Sometimes these people just know things and the loop could well be connected to the psychic, at least those who are dowsers seem to believe so.[49]

Andrew Fitzherbert[50] endows the possessor with a little telepathic ability in the nature of empathy for the moods of those who are close. Hoffman takes the psychic abilities much further, finding these subjects not only possess very keen memories but the sign could encourage them to develop their psychic awareness and open their channels to the great universal memory known as the akashic records.[51] We would add that if this is so, the loop is probably accompanied by a head

line that slopes to at least midway on the Lunar mount.

Jaegers believes the memory is excellent, almost photographic. If the head line is straight, the memory is very good for facts and figures as befits a practical person. At the end of a sloping head line, the memory may be better for sounds, images, emotions, and physical feelings. This person may have enhanced awareness of the sounds and tones of music, for example, or excellent recall of physical movement or a beautiful sunset. The lower it is, the more enhanced is the imagination.[52]

Like all lunar loops, there is a practical affinity

for the Moon and a tendency to follow lunar rhythms in life. A whorl in the same area is an even stronger sign of imagination and a sure sign of lunar influences. Fitzherbert believes that the subjects with a whorl on the lunar mount identify themselves with their daydreams because they appear so real.[53] Fenton and Wright speak of the whorl on Luna as a sign of psychic gifts.[54]

Loop of nature: This indicates an awareness of Gaea, mother earth, of her feelings and emanations. Hutchinson indicates that green fingers from gardeners may emanate from this loop and dowsers feel the emanations of the objects they seek.[55] She went on to discuss some findings of a Dr. Debrunner, who found this pattern on the hands of a very high percentage of mongoloid people. The way she uses the term *mongoloid*, it could mean Down's syndrome or any of the trisomy gene problems. She emphatically denied that normal people with the sign show mongoloid tendencies, but she added folklore of the village idiot having the "gift of the bees" or other forms of affinity with nature. Fitzherbert confirms her observation that the loop of nature shows a gift for sensing the vibrations of objects and places.[56]

Fenton and Wright call this the **loop of imagination** and believe that the imagination and intuition will be more purposefully used if the loop is near the mount of upper Mars. They believe it shows a love for the countryside and outdoor sports such as fishing.[57]

Enid Hoffman finds these subjects so keenly aware of nature that this trait adds "an extra dimension" to their psyche. They have an innate understanding of natural phenomena and are most contented in natural surroundings where they can most strongly feel the rhythms of nature and life.[58]

Bevy Jaegers calls it the **ulnar** or **nature loop** and it is also known as the environmental loop.

Jaegers has found some relationship to mongolism, being a significant factor to check in children, although, like the simian line, it is not a sure sign of Down's syndrome. She indicates that it may evidence a latent genetic influence that could include possible Down's syndrome. The natural environment is very important to these subjects who love water, clean air, plants and animals, and the great outdoors. Jaegers finds that when coupled with the medical stigmata (healing striations) the subject may be a natural vegetarian and have a strong love for both medicine and animals (a natural veterinarian?). The subject needs peace, so will avoid closed surroundings with animosities present and Jaegers finds this aspect stronger the closer the loop comes to the mount of upper Mars. It could be a sign of claustrophobia and would undoubtedly be so if there is a ring of Saturn.[59] In her later work, she claims she is right to identify the mark with DNA defects or idiosyncrasies. If it is located about two-thirds of the way from the base of the fingers it indicates something unusual to do with the subconscious mind, perhaps the sign of a poet, metaphysician, fiction writer, or artist. Low in the hand it may indicate health problems.[60]

I have found it, like the bulging percussion, to indicate a subject with a strong affinity to water and the Moon. This seems to be the case with all lunar mount marks. If there is a fear of water, check for a very traumatic experience in early youth, connected to the water. It is found with the loop toward the center of the palm while the lines travel to the percussion on the mount of the Moon.

Double or switch loop: This has been described as a sign of reversal of feelings for sexual roles. Fitzherbert describes it as indicating the feminine subject would display masculine qualities of competitiveness, confidence, and aggressiveness; the male subject would have the feminine qualities of gentleness and appreciation for artistic pleasures.[61] It is not the sign of homosexuality as there is no universal sign of this trait, but it can indicate masculine qualities when found on a woman's hand and vice versa.

Jaegers, who calls it the double loop, has quite a different perspective on the qualities it indicates. She tends to find these subjects living in two different worlds (hardly uncommon in our experience). It may also make the subjects rather childlike in their innocence. She finds it can also indicate either the "chicken little, sky is falling syndrome" or the self-sacrificial martyrdom complex.[62] From her descriptions, one would anticipate more problems with the mark on the water hand than on the earth, fire, or air hands.

Hutchinson discusses finding the composite or intertwined loop. She finds the same duality as noticed below on composite fingerprints, especially thumbs. She sees those marked subjects seem to start off with an idea but raise so many questions about their course that in the end they perform nothing.[63] Some counsel such persons to seize the first idea in their mind and perform it, or else they will always be troubled by indecision.

Proximal Palmar Loops

Inspiration loop: Jaegers, Hutchinson, and Fitzherbert all describe a loop found in the area of Neptune and Pluto to the lunar side of the center of the hand, which they call the inspiration loop. It is nice to have a common name.

Hutchinson tells of subjects who hear music they compose or design from ideas that just "come to them." With her description, this might be called the channeler loop. People with this loop seem to receive inspiration from other universes. She believes that the imaginative powers and intu-

itive gifts are linked by a lively, active pineal gland.[64] Fitzherbert speaks of these very sensitive, creative subjects becoming inspired from their "higher consciousness."[65]

Jaegers believes such people should also be able to inspire, and would have anticipated such a sign on the hands of John F. Kennedy, Martin Luther King, Jr., and Hitler. These people may have to build their own belief systems since organized religions will seem inadequate and perhaps sacrilegious. Here may be a subject who has vision and/or has been granted special revelation and may be able to inspire others through his or her voice and speech.[66] In her later work she adds that these subjects have a great love for color and music.[67]

Parathenar loop: There is a loop referred to by Hutchinson that occurs in the central portion of the lower hand, around the mount of Neptune or between the mounts of Venus and Luna that almost follows the life line, and she calls it the **loop of humanism.** She says it is a rare loop. She was unable to describe its precise qualities, but relates it generally to humanitarianism.[68]

I observe that when it falls into the area of a raised place between Venus and Luna, it falls on the mount of Neptune or Pluto, depending on the name preference, and may be related to the sixth sense, telepathic powers, and clairvoyance.

Palmar Arch or Tented Arch: Hutchinson describes a tented arch (usually found in fingerprints) that she discovered on the lunar mount. She followed her reading of this sign on the fingers as enthusiasm and initiative arising instinctively and felt it fit.[69]

Now we turn to the digits and first we will return to the study of the dermatoglyphic significance of fingerprints.

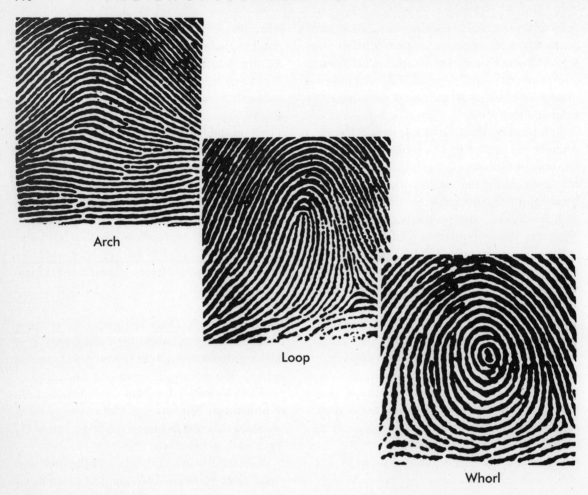

Arch

Loop

Whorl

FINGERPRINTS

Fingerprints in General

Three major patterns of fingerprints are the whorl, the loop, and the arch.

These patterns may also be found on other parts of the hand, and when the loop and the whorl are found elsewhere, they bring to that part of the hand important significance. Fred Gettings mentions one author (Mairs)[70] who distinguishes some thirty-nine different types of fingerprint patterns. We will be satisfied with less. Mavalwala reports that Okros in 1965 had identified as many as ninety-five types of fingerprints, though he is reported to have later indicated that he could eliminate some of the rare types and reduce his working number to sixty.[71] Mavalwala identifies some forty fingerprints for his own uses in dermatoglyphic studies.[72]

The most common fingerprint is a loop, and that is most commonly an ulnar loop (the loop faces the thumb side of the hand and the pattern opens on the ulnar side). The little-finger-facing loop is called a radial loop and we have rarely found it on the thumb and fingers three, four, and five (Saturn, Apollo, and Mercury). We have more often seen it on the second finger (Jupiter). A loop has only one triradius at its confluence and that is its chief distinction from a whorl, which it sometimes resembles very much.

The whorl has been described as any ridge configuration that possesses two or more triradii. One triradius will be found on the ulnar and one on the radial side.[73] They certainly do not have to be an equal distance from the center of the formation.

Fingerprint Patterns Identified by Palmists

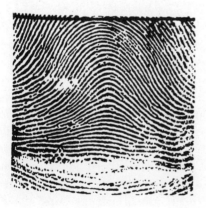

Simple Arch (Earth Element, the Digger): According to many palmists, this refers to a simple type of personality, which follows the fundamental survival motives of security and protection and exhibits shyness, practicality, and perhaps inhibi-tion, though I have seen some very outward and successful persons with this sign predominating. However, many subjects did share the necessity of hard work, for nothing came to them easily. To succeed, those with simple arches had to over-come their basically withdrawn character. The characteristics reflected often include the inar-ticulate, suspicious, and cautious. Terence Dukes relates this, as an earth sign, to group or tribe orientation associated with the fundamental drives of security and feelings of inhibition.[74]

Hutchinson[75] terms these as signs of fixed, reli-able, essentially practical people. She had found those persons with simple arches on their Jupiter fingers to be the salt of the earth, practical, trust-worthy, courageous, and reliable. However, as the number of arches increase, so too does the diffi-culty of oral communication, although writing, sketching, and other artwork can still form outlets for communication, especially when there are four or more arches on the ten fingers. We would observe that any findings of impromptu or sponta-neous speech problems signed by arches could be considered exacerbated by a line showing a blocked throat chakra.[76]

Hutchinson notes that arches on the second finger (Saturn) indicate subjects who demand that religion improve the morality of people and are little attracted by the ceremonial or ornate side unless it is of historical or architectural value. One wonders what the predominant native prints are that are found in Latin countries where religious ceremony is taken so seriously. Perhaps Hutchin-son should be reexamined on this point.

Hutchinson finds few arches on the Apollo fin-ger unless they are part of a complete set. If found, any artistic expression will likely be practical. She gives the example of a world-class knitter who has a whorl on the left-hand Apollo finger and an arch on the same finger on the right hand.

Hutchinson also finds that arches occur on the little finger in relation to complete sets or on a hand predominated by arches. She believes that these people tend to be reserved and that their conversations tend to reflect domesticity, business, or social matters. One wonders how accurate this observation is if one is faced with a person with short proximal and medial phalanges and a long distal phalange on the little finger. In my experience, the proximal phalange represents family conversation, the medial phalange represents social intercourse, and the distal phalange represents the conversations derived from higher consciousness or spirituality. Perhaps business might try to reach this level. I have found those with short medial phalanges are also short on small talk without regard to the type of fingerprint.

Hutchinson finds the arch fairly common on the thumb, frequently accompanying a strong will demonstrated by the distal phalange. These are persons of practicality and efficiency, who are unlikely to bother with theories or abstract ideas.

Jaegers follows Hutchinson's observations and adds that this print is also somewhat sensual, and if several are seen, the owner may be quite sensual.[77] In her later work, she observes that this is a sign of high intelligence and a questioning mind. The subject may also be appreciative or acquisitive of historical objects. The subject is simple, direct, and truthful. Jaegers finds it especially good when found only on the index finger or on the index and Saturn fingers, adding depth of intellect. However, she reserves greater intelligence for the tented arch and apparently measures it by the height of the arch.[78]

Fitzherbert confirms much of Hutchinson and adds that these subjects are slow to believe anything until it is proved. They also prefer to control their own emotions. He sums up the positive qualities as steadiness, realism, and usefulness, while observing negative qualities of reluctance to accept change and a lack of responsiveness. He also notes differences in the higher arches that indicate the subject possesses more skill and is more idealistic.[79]

Fenton and Wright observe that arches do not "bestow an easy life." My own observations generally followed this until I met an elder citizen who took issue with this reading and pointed out that her father had provided very well for her and she had no particular worries. However, another subject with all arches, born in a small village in India and now living on the West Coast of the United States, admitted, figuratively, that he needed a forty-ton crane to lift a strawberry. Still, he showed great inner strength and intelligence, owning his own business after earning two doctorate degrees in subjects as diverse as chemical engineering and educational humanities. Yet Fenton and Wright would describe this man as practical, which is questionable, since he gave up his career with the drug industry to follow a higher goal in the humanities; shy, which he may well be; and quite ordinary, which is very disputable.

Fenton and Wright find such subjects withdrawn, secretive, introspective, and defensive, with possible early unhappiness. The early unhappiness makes such subjects fit in easily with the very large number of subjects common today coming from dysfunctional homes or from backgrounds that provided no grounding in learning about interpersonal relationships other than soap operas on TV, which are not very interrelational.

Fenton and Wright also note that once these people finally become fired by a project, person, or cause, they can become born again enthusiasts and bore everyone in their surroundings with their obsessions.[80]

Tented Arch (Fire Element, the Flame): Dukes describes this as indicating the hyperactive type[81] while Hutchinson uses the word enthusiasm, often for a cause.[82] These people can be of great assistance in getting things started, being both impulsive and full of expression. The location of the triradius distinguishes this pattern from the loop. Here the triradius is located at the base of the arch while in the loop it is located on the side of the loop. When the pattern goes straight toward the tip of the finger, the subjects are dedicated to truth and honesty, not only in themselves but in those around them. Noel Jaquin finds these subjects to be sensitive and emotional, perhaps even high strung.[83] They can be artistic and idealistic.

Given their enthusiasm, Hutchinson finds that if the subject has a tented arch on the index finger allied with a flexible thumb, he or she may be overwhelming to his or her colleagues, as the flexible thumb indicates an ability to return again and again to former work, but with fresh insight, and of course with the enthusiasm reflected in the tented arch.

Fenton and Wright observe that the energy goes straight up the finger, deviating neither to the left nor right, and this signs the subject's character as straightforward. Curiously, they picture a straight loop rather than a tented arch in the print shown. The psychological findings might prove valid for each type if the loop does indeed project directly up the finger. They add that this sign shows a lack of adaptability and difficulty with the unexpected. In confirmation of these authors, I have found that such subjects do not cope well with anyone who approaches life in a devious manner. Fenton and Wright also add that a tented arch on Jupiter attaches tenacity to the subject's character.[84]

Fairchild echoes all of the fixed, conservative, restrictive characteristics noted above for the arch and the tented arch, and adds that those who have an abundance of tented arches tend to entrench themselves in the belief of their own separate existence.[85] They might suffer from what is termed in the drug and alcohol recovery fields as the syndrome of terminal uniqueness.

Jaegers adds that these people are often very good with animals and if there is a kernel enclosed at the base of the tent, they could be very good research workers or in any job requiring creative analysis. They tend toward perfectionism. Perhaps this colors their vision, because she also finds they tend to misjudge others in their desire to see only the best in people.[86]

Loops in Fingerprints

Loop (Water Element, the Dancer): Here we see a smooth flow of energy, either outward or inward or in a few cases (but more likely in the case of the tented arch) straight upward. When straight upward, the subject is dedicated to truth and honesty. Otherwise, the subject can flow with the rhythms of life. These are adaptable, sociable people. They are sensitive, responsive, and may show artistic interests. These people are flexible, but they may lack a certain amount of individuality and drive. They do not like confrontation but would rather dance around life's impediments. Dukes sums the sign up by saying it indicates sensitive and responsive subjects with artistic interests who often lack concentration.[87]

These people live best in the here and now. I like to joke with those clients who have ulnar loops on all of their fingers and say that they are just here for the cruise and should not be concerned with the destination of the boat. These are the people who can make the present bearable for the rest of society. Because of this, it is often difficult to discern their ultimate goals. Their immediate paths are paramount. This conclusion will be modified as we discover other fingerprint patterns intermixed with the loops.

From time to time, I entertain at company parties. I find that patterns quite commonly repeat themselves throughout the employees of a company and reflect the company's prime goals. One summer evening I joined a group of employees on a boat cruise. Loops predominated all fingerprints on the twenty-five to thirty-five employees examined, especially on the Jupiter finger. The business of the company was helping families buy homes through providing home mortgages. Its primary aim was to help the customer achieve his or her immediate goal. It was a service company. The party was on a cruise that started and left from the same dock, going nowhere in particular, but enjoying a pleasant time.

Radial loops are generally found on the Jupiter finger and indicate an inward flow of energy, a nurturing or mothering quality. They can also be found on the thumbs, indicating an inward flow of willpower, but they are seldom seen on other fingers.

Hutchinson indicates that those with the radial loop on the Jupiter finger can be adaptable as long as they are faced with choices within their own interests and as long as they may do the choosing. Ulnar looped persons, however, are more inclined to follow the suggestions of others.[88] A loop on the index finger of the predominant hand signals flexibility, a power to improvise and to vary action. A loop on the subservient side faced with a more fixed sign of a whorl or arch on the dominant index finger gives the person an ability to see clearly to avoid the obstacles in life.

In my experience, the radial loop on the Jupiter finger may be more suggestive of the care and concern of the mother for those within her sphere of interest and protection. When I see the radial loop on the Jupiter finger, I call the person the nurturer. They may tend to be unsure of themselves or self-effacing but live vicariously through those they support. However, they do not lack willpower. I once read at a medical convention where every doctor whose hands I saw had this formation.

Hutchinson and my experience generally find ulnar loops on the Saturn, Sun, and Mercury finger. She wrote that she had never seen a radial loop on the little finger, and I do not believe I have ever seen more than one or possibly two.

To Hutchinson, the ulnar loop on the Saturn finger signals an interest in religion accompanied by an open mind. If it is set high, it is a good sign for the researcher, allowing some flexibility even in a hand otherwise bearing static shapes and marks. If the loop is low, she would counsel entering down-to-earth type of work.[89]

The subject with the ulnar loop on the Sun finger has interests that lie in new fashions and the beauty they represent, according to Hutchinson. Low-set loops indicate interest in worldly endeavors such as decorating, flowers, and clothes. A person with a high-set loop would be interested in art, which might include philosophy, history, and criticism.[90]

Hutchinson believes that an ulnar loop on the little finger is the ideal sign for that finger, and this is good because she further points out that it appears on about 90 percent of those fingers. It helps in all forms of expression, aids in harmonious working conditions, and complements humor.[91]

According to Hutchinson, the ulnar loop on the thumb shows that the will can be easily expressed, provided the thumb shows there is a will to express.[92] I tend to somewhat disagree. I find that so long as communication is friendly and not competitive, a loop may aid the expression of will. Even if there is strong will, I find that those with loops on their thumbs do not enjoy confrontation or argument or head-to-head competition. They are the dancers who would rather go around the obstacles in life and argument can even make many of them sick. So some forms of expression are not eased, no matter how strong the thumb. In a strong thumb I tend to find these people will defend their position but will not push. This differs from the people with a whorled pattern, who will defend and push.

Another interesting finding I have made involves the combination of the loop on the thumb and the whorl on the index finger of the predominant hand. I like to compare these people with sailing ship captains. They can chart a course for a distant port, but they sail using the winds, tides, and currents. They do not approach their goal in a straight line. By contrast, the whorl-whorl pattern is like a super tanker, plowing through all weather. The loop pattern on both of these fingers indicates the person who likes to go out for a day of sailing but doesn't care where the boat goes. However, socially, they are very necessary as they form a pleasant cement for society, smoothing its rough edges and making life bearable.

Bevy Jaegers breaks down the loop into a loop with an arch, a kernel loop radial, a kernel loop ulnar, a loop radial, and a loop ulnar. The loop with an arch is a fairly common print. She believes it indicates open-mindedness, good verbal memory, interest in science or technology, and the capacity for abstract thought. It belongs to readers, thinkers, and even philosophers of sorts.[93]

The kernel loop is described by Jaegers as a loop that encloses a closed formation that rejoins the loop. The radial print indicates self-direction. These subjects are perceptive, often seeing things from a different angle. They may have their own exclusive style and eccentricities. They have good visual memories. On the Jupiter finger it aids the perception of truth; on the Sun finger it indicates the appreciation of color and form. It may also impart a more metaphysical ability to see the patterns behind the forms of reality.[94] The qualities that differentiate the ulnar from the radial kernel loop involve the stimuli that direct the aptitudes. Ulnar loops receive their stimuli more from outside, and the radial indicates a more self-directed subject.

Jaegers views radial looped subjects as a fairly egocentric people who can improvise "for their own choice" at a moment's notice. They are less adaptable and flexible than those with the ulnar loop. Those with more than one radial loop can think fast on their feet and can find the "escape hatches," though their attention span is "often fairly short." Jaegers advises that when considering this sign, think of flexibility of approach and adaptability in working toward a goal. The radial loop is a good sign of a team worker.[95]

Fairchild discusses loops, but I am not sure if he knows what the feature is, as he illustrates the loop with two central pocket whorls, which I sometimes call peacock's eyes.[96] He describes the feature as a lasso that "gracefully swings out to grasp any thought which comes within its range." Fairchild finds the difference in attitude reflected in whether the subject's thoughts and attitude are directed by self-interest (radial loop) or are more generous in acting on the suggestions of others (ulnar loop). He finds that not only is the loop common on the thumb (and I agree) but that it is "usually a radial loop." Our experience is just the opposite. Fairchild describes the subjects with a radial thumb loop as being insecure, effaced, and reserved. With a weak thumb he sees them having conservative attitudes toward life, spreading themselves quite thinly, failing to fight for their rights, and becoming easily victimized.

Fairchild finds easygoing jacks-of-all-trades "who go through life dipping their toes into multiple pools" indicated by the Jupiter looped finger. They have a "driving ambition to take on responsibility" that "stems from a spiritual conviction" energizing "the need to do something constructive for their surroundings." This sounds a little like dilettante water walkers for Greenpeace. He assures us they often make "very loving parents and good friends. Their fluid personalities enable them to adapt to social situations galore." But, we might ask, would such "fluid personalities" be dependable in a pinch, when the chips were down?

I agree with Fairchild that the Saturn loop is usually ulnar in origin. He says such subjects have a wide range of intellectual interests that "they continually tend to lecture . . . others about." While I have not listened to any of their lectures, I have found such people generally to be rather nonjudgmental, seeing issues in various shades of gray rather than in the right-or-wrong mode more associated with the whorl.

Perhaps Fairchild agrees with me, at least in the field of religion and metaphysics, as he finds these subjects with loops on their Saturn finger quite open-minded. Their desire to gain knowledge "causes them to change their beliefs with regular frequency."

Fairchild finds that these Saturn looped subjects seek to find success, regardless of the odds. I have often felt that sort of characteristic depended more on willpower, and aggressive and defensive qualities are more the province of the strengths and weaknesses of the thumb and the mounts of Mars, though of course other mounts and fingers could influence this drive. These people possess a strange personality if they seek success at all odds, because Fairchild describes them as "flighty on first impression." He assures us, however, that they are tenacious and are only hesitant to be assured that when they do act they will win. We must wonder at this hesitancy that he finds, for he says these subjects often lack patience and are always excited about new interests. Furthermore, they "rarely trap themselves in limiting circumstances as their urge to remain open takes precedence." Fortunately for me, many of these subjects have masked this confusing personality.

Fairchild next speaks of the loop on the Venus finger. I presume that he means the Sun-Apollo finger or some sixth finger on the hand. He finds this loop also usually an ulnar loop. The subject appreciates ideas reflecting beauty and harmony and when offended, will walk away seeking other security rather than argue. He apparently has difficulty coping with temper tantrums. He is a lover not a fighter, with a refined nature, sensitive personality, and inspiring to fellow travelers. The subject may have several projects going on simultaneously and has the boundless energy to attend to them and he responds to varied interests. We are happy that at least this time the subject seems a bit more consistent.

Fairchild believes that 90 percent of the Mercury fingers have loops, making these subjects warm and affable, with an optimistic tongue able to persuade the most "inflexible snob" to join in a delightful companionship. We would observe that with such an overpowering number of persons having these traits, we must live in heaven. But it must be so, because Fairchild describes these people as close to angels. These people readily give the benefit of the doubt while relating to their possible opponents. Their helpful human nature makes them always available to act as mediators in discussions, though seldom do they interfere. (Is that why so many discussions seem never to get anywhere?) These subjects have "habitual shoulders to cry on" and their few accusations are always justified. They desire a one-on-one communication and wish to embrace the truth. "This is a warm and comforting finger for the Loop to live on!" Well, fortunately for us all, Fairchild ran out of fingers, for what other qualities should we cover with these lariats of his?

Fenton and Wright sum up most of the qualities that Fairchild tries to enumerate when they describe the subject with the loop as friendly, adaptable, and responsive to people. They are good team workers who need variety in social and work life. Their minds are elastic, quick, and lively, with an appreciation of humor. This type of person tends to be a dilettante. He would fit the astrological sign of Gemini or other mutable signs, and will not be easily cornered as he has likely left himself an escape.[97]

I am not so sure these subjects need variety in social and work life. Rather, I hypothesize that the sign of the loop indicates a certain need to float through certain phases of life or work because of a lack of focus or drive to accomplish any particular goal. To me, the need for these subjects is to fulfill the desire for certain comfortable, stress-free qualities in the area of life represented by the particular finger that the loop appears on. This urge may or may not be compatible with the subject's goals or even his or her desire for variety. Thus, when found on Saturn, we find the nonjudgmental;

when found on Mercury, the easy talker; when found on Jupiter, the person with no great ambition; when found on the thumb, the person who, no matter how strong the underlying will, is not a pusher; and when found on Apollo, this trait might be symbolized by a good but not great cocktail lounge pianist.

Fitzherbert sums these looped people up by attributing to them the good qualities of "flexibility and all-round capability" with negative traits including lack of individuality.[98] I believe this is far too general, as one is likely to find loops on the vast majority of hands read, nearly 90 percent, according to Fairchild and Hutchinson.

Concentric Circles, Targets, or Punch Whorl

Spiral, Shell, or Drill Whorl

Press Whorl

The Whorls: Dukes says this, according to Chinese tradition, is "the tree standing in the desert," which is what Elizabeth Daniels Squire reported earlier.[99] These subjects are individual, perceptive, thoughtful, with opinions clearly formed, independent, freedom seeking, original, self-motivated, often with intensity and frequently talented in some way. This client can be highly secretive and emotionally inhibited.[100] The mark is distinguished by always having two triradii at its base. The whorl can come in three patterns: concentric circles, targets, or punch; the spiral, shell, or drill; and the press. The spiral pattern indicates less intensity than the concentric pattern. I would be curious to note if any palmists find differences between left (counterclockwise) and right (clockwise) spirals.

Being highly perceptive, deeply engrossed, desiring to act only when fully informed, and being very individualistic, the whorled person's reactions will appear slow. They appear to be fast only in the area of immediate interest after these subjects become deeply absorbed and informed. Then, as in the case of trained emergency reactions, they can be extremely fast and self-assured. They can be considered self-centered and orientated toward the inner regions of thought. The pattern has its strongest effect on the index fingers and the thumbs.

My observations indicate different qualities, depending on where the whorl is found. On the thumb, the whorl indicates the person who will not say no, the person who hates to lose, the competitor who will fight to win. On the index finger, it indicates a very focused ego, a long-range planner. Mix a looped thumbprint and a whorled index fingerprint and we find people who should model themselves like the great sailing ship captains and navigators who sailed the world. They can plan their destinations and then use the winds, currents, and tides of life to carry them forward. The whorl on both fingers indicates a person who

is more like the modern motorized ship, sailing almost straight through life to the appointed destination. Add a whorl on the ring finger and give the body a good physique and watch for the tough athletic competitor. Put a whorl on the middle finger and observe one who sees answers to questions in either right or wrong, black or white. Place it on the little finger and behold the person who can act as the sentinel. This person will interrupt conversations to make sure that he gets his point across, even if it has nothing to do with the conversation. These subjects are like the sentinels found in animal groups such as prairie dogs, who can warn the pack of their perceived impending dangers. They are the whistle-blowers.

Jaegers describes the punch like an eye and the drill like a target. When her eye is found on the Jupiter finger, it indicates the gift for perception in one who is good at judging others. On the middle finger it signifies an organizational gift of genius and an ability to see through confusion. On the ring finger it indicates discernment, the ability to spot the flaw or omission. She agrees that all whorl people are individualistic. Their ability to see all sides may cause them to hesitate.[101] I tend to agree with Jaegers on most of these points and would add that when found on the Saturn finger, it seems to accentuate the judgment and the subject does have a very definite opinion of right and wrong. Further, when found on the Mercury finger, the subject will communicate in a very direct manner. Jaegers adds in her later work that the whorl on the little finger signals the gift of communication, and on the thumb it indicates the gift of willpower and forcefulness.[102]

Jaegers finds that the spiral or drill form of whorl indicates the almost complete nonconformist, who will be contrary just to avoid conforming. These people obviously need to be their own bosses. It is an extremely strong print.[103]

Fenton and Wright would agree that the whorl types are self-centered, independent individualists "oriented towards the inner realms of thought." The sign indicates subjects who tend to set their own standards and find their own way. If the sign is on Jupiter, we find the cool, emotionally controlled, calculating, successful antihero for whom doors open. Fenton and Wright notice that while these people are "rarely emotionally vulnerable," they lack understanding of why they receive little from relationships, and they need compliant partners or those who may seek separate careers and interests.

In short, Fenton and Wright find those with whorls on Jupiter to be blinkered, self-centered subjects, focused on career and not distracted by others. On Saturn, the whorl could indicate one who is too serious or even depressive and lonely, though self-disciplined and successful in some highly novel way. Besides ambitions, these subjects may be obstinate, with airs of self-importance. Marriage partners must be suitable. The subject with the Apollonian whorl "sets emotional standards" and believes he or she can mandate the feelings of those emotionally close. Tastes tend to be set early in life. These authors are a little easier on the persons with the Mercurial whorl, finding them to have good teaching ability and a desire to expand their intellectual horizons as they research and reach for answers. They make good broadcasters, journalists, and "seekers after truth." I wonder if this depends on whether or not they have straight little fingers. However, Fenton and Wright add, they could be shy and emotionally insecure.[104]

Enid Hoffman discusses no distinction between clockwise and counterclockwise spiral whorls or concentric (bullet/eye) whorls. She finds they represent an individualized style with strong belief systems and unique qualities that are dependent upon the domain covered by the finger where they are found.

Hoffman observes that a subject with a hand with all whorls is indeed rare and represents one who is truly unusual and exceptional. This subject will have tremendous energy, strong opinions, and will enjoy being around like-minded people. The subject's will is strong, giving him or her the strength to prove his or her credibility.

Little finger whorls indicate to Hoffman a subject who has definite expectations from relationships and who needs to find a spouse with similar values. When the subject has these signs on both ring fingers, he or she has definite tastes in friends, music, and art that are not easily influenced. This person may have a career using creative talents. These signs found on the middle finger bring home, family, and career into the spotlight of importance to the subject. These fields will prove fertile ground for the subject to sow his or her unique talents. When seen on the index finger, the whorl signifies a subject probing the mystery of his or her own identity, and who also has a strong ambition to become quite successful. This person takes charge of his or her personal life and has latent talent to exercise power and authority. The whorl on the thumb is a sign of a powerful will of one who prefers to be the boss. These signs are a good augur of success.[105]

Fitzherbert finds that the spiral and concentric whorls have much the same meaning, but the concentric whorl's qualities are a little stronger. The positive qualities are intensity and general ability, and the negative qualities include isolation and too much self-indulgence.[106]

Fairchild adds that thumb whorls signal a need for recognition that may lead the subject into overdoing anything. He feels this reflects past lives of irresponsibility and self-indulgence and uses this to discuss a moral lesson to be learned in this life.

The Jupiter whorl he finds akin to the loop of charisma, naturally attracting others by the subject's magnetic leadership. These people tend to be strict taskmasters for themselves and willingly accept responsibility. Past lives warn of mating discord because of defensiveness and argumentative natures, and subjects may display fear of rejection. A dutiful homily follows. Saturn's whorl signals past lives built around insatiable acquisitive natures. Venusian (Apollonian) whorled subjects have the knack for locating injustice and teaching morality and truth while demanding freedom for themselves. Their love is unlimited but needs a focus. Their past life was built around discovery and analysis rather than artistic and creative endeavors. The Mercurial whorl indicates a subject capable of using his or her understanding of others to succeed, but he or she may be prone to exaggerate his or her own self-portraiture in hopes of winning over competitors. Past lives seem to have been filled with unrewarded charity and this time the subject is out for the payback. Fairchild advises to watch for the love of money and acquisition of wealth. In each case, Fairchild finds the whorl is a call upon the subject "to break the circle of personal limitations" by widening his or her perceptions.

Some of my friends have little use for past lives. Yet, working as a counseling clinician, these may be a useful tool in opening up insight of the present, even if they are little more than a fairy tale to the rational analyst. They could be thought of in the same fashion as Jung's archetypes. However, one should use them only if one feels comfortable with them, because most subjects can feel any insincerity of the counselor, which will render the work of little value.

Noel Jaquin warns that although the person with the whorl pattern appears to have a healthy regard for law and order and social convention, this is only when it suits his or her needs.[107]

The press is considered a softer form of the whorl pattern. Like other forms of the whorl, it indicates one who becomes deeply immersed in his or her present activities and finds it difficult to make quick changes. All whorl patterned people need time to disengage and to reposition before effectively changing their focus of interest. If you interrupt them with a different subject or new activity when they are busy, don't expect a polite answer or immediate involvement in the new activity. They tend to dislike interruption, as it breaks their concentration. This break triggers an emotional reaction. The press whorl will soften the response. Perhaps the emotional or attachment to the current willful activities of the brain reflected by the press is not as strong as with other whorls, yet it is stronger than that reflected by loops. Rather than drill or penetrate as a bullet to the heart of the subject being explored, this form will slowly but inexorably press toward the accomplishment of his or her well-perceived goal.

Dukes indicates this is a combined water and air sign of subjects who carry emotional overtones to the qualities otherwise signified by the whorl. The person tends to be more considerate, and attitudes will be prompted by emotional experiences.[108]

Composite Whorl (Fire and Air Elements, the Transceiver): This looks like two whorls superimposed side by side, often going in opposite directions. Dukes describes this as an incomplete energy transformation.[109] Most finger pattern observers have said that they see perception with indecision. The ability to see both sides translates into inability to act unless there are other strong features in the hand. If other strong features are present, these subjects may find the ability to be-

to dowse and use the pendulum. Also note that its shape, when extended at a right angle (sideways), looks like the double helix of DNA and the antennae of a transceiver.

There is a current theory in alternative medicine that I will return to in discussing the girdle of Venus. That theory postulates that DNA both sends and receives wave forms from the brain as a means of living communication in addition to the nervous, cardiovascular, and lymphatic systems.[112]

I have found that these people do best by neither trying to dance around impediments or pressing through challenges. They do better by forming clear and precise statements that can be answered with a yes or no, asking the universe these questions in the form of statements, and accepting the answer they get, using their mind and possibly a gadget, like a pendulum, as the magic parts of the transceiver to carry out this communication until they can come to recognize their intuition directly. However, they may be frustrated, as are so many people, responding to our modern world's rational or scientific view with the limitations it places on the modes of successful behavior. Our worldview does not have preconceived slots into which these people fit.

We do not perceive this as a mark of the person's weakness but as a mark of human ability that our society has difficulty accepting within its own paradigms. It reflects greater weakness in society's inability to perceive or accept alternative paradigms.

I often advise these people to study the use of the pendulum and use it for a guide until they feel more comfortable with their psychic connection to the universe. Fortunately, pendulums will give these people yes and no answers that will help them get over indecision.

The use of the pendulum is very simple. One can use a fish weight on a string or pay a fancy price for a very pretty bauble. One holds the string

come good lawyers or administrators or undertake any other profession or occupation requiring the ability to see both sides of a problem.

Composite Whorl

The weakness seen in the composite whorl (also known as the imploding whorl) is indecision and self-mistrust. Where the decision has been made, it may not be laid to rest but must constantly be reexamined, to the subject's continued regret, no matter what course was decided. Fenton and Wright[110] have noted this feature on the thumbs and Jupiter fingers of psychics. This type of thinking has led me to some very interesting speculation and exploration.

I tend to agree with Fenton and Wright that when found on the thumbs or the Jupiter fingers and perhaps other fingers, this may indicate psychic abilities. I call it the dowser[111] because I find that those who have the formation, especially on the thumb and index finger, may have the ability in a completely relaxed hand on a relaxed arm and makes statements that one knows are true or false, such as "My mother is bald." After a while one begins to notice that the pendulum tends to swing one way on true statements and another way on false statements. After calibrating how the pendulum is reacting (and one may need to do this from time to time), one makes statements about matters where one does not have the answer. If there is a present answer, the pendulum is supposed to be the guide. This is the sign from the cosmos to the doubting Thomas.

This is just one form of psychic connection that the hand reveals. The girdle of Venus, discussed later, indicates empathetic connections. The line or crescent of intuition indicates clear hunches. Stars in the area of Uranus can indicate the occasional moment of déjà vu or preknowledge of imminent happenings.

However, people with these abilities are like so many other people who fail to find their calling in the modern world. The limitations placed on the ideas of successful behavior in our modern world generally do not leave room for psychic abilities. That does not mean they do not exist. I remember discussing the problem with the dean of a local nursing school. She advised me that the school trained its nurses to recognize these intuitive moments because that would put them on the ward even before the warning bells went off. We do not perceive these abilities as marks of weakness, but as marks of human ability that our society has difficulty accepting.

One further tale befits the dowser, or as he is sometimes known, the water witch. A man in his middle thirties came to us for vocational advice. He had the broad, strong hand of one who would enjoy the outdoors, and he readily agreed that he would enjoy an occupation in the open air. He had clear, well-formed composite whorls on each

thumb. I suggested he go into water well drilling. He passed it off, and we went on with other reading information, but I came back to the vocational advice several times. Finally, as if exasperated with my advice to go into well drilling, he said, "So you think I ought to go into business with my mother." I had no idea until that moment that his mother was actually a well drilling contractor. The mark does appear to follow a genetic course.

Imploding Whorl

Hutchinson notes that when the mark on the thumb is coupled by a loop on the other thumb, decisions come faster only to be questioned at a later date. However, a whorled companion will indicate increased delays and difficulty getting started. Hutchinson says an arch is a rare partner, and she pictures opposing thumbs becoming quite cross at each other.[113] Fenton and Wright note that a double loop on the Mercury finger *may* indicate bisexuality.[114] Dukes describes this as the imploding whorl and believes it to be related to materialism, inability to adapt easily, and stubbornness. I wonder if this pattern does not better fit into Hutchinson's description of the compound pattern minus the peacock's eye. If that is the case, we should distinguish between the composite whorl, the imploding whorl, and the peacock's eye.

The Gemini: This feature is not truly a whorl, as it may have little or no curvature outside of the first curve. It appears to be a double loop. However, it has the double triradius of the whorl. The energies do not converge; they go off in opposite directions. I am toying with relating this form to the Gemini complex. This may be the sign, on a Jupiter finger, of one who is excitable and easily upset, yet as easily assuaged. He or she may have two or more affairs (business or otherwise) going on at once and is adroit at balancing them. This person can be a good executive by using this flexibility. Being an excellent communicator, he or she may speak from both sides of the mouth. Look for lines of enemies on the percussion. We find they are very good bargain hunters and might do well in the scrap business or as professional buyers. They also give their friends and partners, along with their whorled companions, sore necks as they can totally change directions in a breath. We sometimes call these subjects opportunists, because of their ability to change courses in midstream to seize opportunities that would have passed others by.

Peacock's Eye (Flame, Fire and Water Elements): While on the palm, this may appear as a flame generally pointed toward the fingers. On the fingers, this flame shape points more often toward the palm. Fenton and Wright note that the sign rarely appears on more than one or two fingers and "not necessarily on both hands." In my case, they appear to be on four to five fingers and exhibit what Hutchinson refers to as compound patterns. Mine are like loops within arches. They are central pocket (ulnar) whorls. Where the double triradius exists (the second at the formation of the inner pocket whorl), it is considered a whorl. In Indian palmistry, according to Hutchinson,[115] a peacock's eye on the third finger is a sign of protection from physical danger. Hutchinson confirms this in her experience, and Fenton and Wright[116]

and Brandon-Jones[117] also indicate this. I have it on my right Apollo finger, which is slightly longer than my Jupiter finger, with a well-formed whorl on the same hand. I have walked away from numerous car accidents in younger years, including at least one total loss. Dukes says it shows activity with discrimination when it is a flame or peacock's eye.[118]

I have found that clients with this sign do best when they are performing for others. The whorl intensity is fired by an audience. When left to their own devices with no audience imput, these subjects show more of the loop characteristics.

These signs may also be associated with a high degree of perception, according to David Brandon-Jones.[119] Fenton and Wright believe that the finger where this formation appears will show where the talent lies.[120] The talent will be displayed with the intensity of a whorl and the flexibility of a loop.

Generally, more than one peacock's eye is rare with any subject, although one author indicated seeing three barely distinguishable from arches. I have four or five, depending on whether the one on the left thumb is a peacock's eye or a mere composite. They are located on both little fingers, the right Apollo finger, the right thumb, and perhaps the left thumb. All of the other fingers support whorls and all are concentric except perhaps the Saturn finger on the right hand, which is a very tight spiral. So I have trouble with a lot of whorl analysis.

Bevy Jaegers[121] mentions one other pattern that I have pictured above among the prints on dermatoglyphics: the accidental print. She gives us no explanation of its value, so we are back to research.

One of the reasons this chapter went into so much detail is to open the eyes of both the student and practitioner to the vast world of dermatoglyphics and the fact that palm experts have just barely touched the surface of examination and evaluation of the signs we can see in the palm and fingers of the hand.

Sex and Race Differences for Future Study

I have not really touched here the sexual differences to be found in the hands. Schaumann and Alter point out that the total ridge count is influenced by the number and type of sex chromosomes and tends to be lower in females than in males. Further, females have higher pattern frequencies on average in the hypothenar and fourth interdigital areas, but lower pattern frequencies in the thenar and the first, second, and third interdigital areas. However, this is not a universal trend in all populations.[122]

Different ethnic groups and even groups within ethnic groups exhibit highly significant variations in the frequency of dermatoglyphic configurations. These differences tend to be not only racial but extend to ethnic groups within races and even small population isolates.[123]

Humans are an extremely diverse lot with many talents, and most of them we probably do not even understand. Pity the poor politician, jurist, social scientist, and others who must display some competence to devise political, social, educational, and economic relationships to comprehend, nurture, encourage, and reward such diversity, especially in a nonagricultural or nonhunter-gathering world where we so depend upon our human ingenuity and incomplete paradigms to create our environments, to define, protect, and preserve our rights and powers of life, liberty, and needs for our corporeal reality. Let us not go beyond pity to toleration and acceptance of this poverty that would deny useful talents or fail to understand or provide for them within our societies. Let us continue to push forward our undersanding of humanity by the careful attention to the detail we are trained to see.

CHAPTER EIGHT

THE LINED PALM AND MAJOR LINES

FEATURES AND CHARACTERISTICS

Medically, the skin of the palm displays three linear features: flexure lines, tension lines, and papillary ridges. Flexure lines are those permanent creases or folds at the principal axes of movement in the hands. In some parts of the palm, they are known to the palmist as the mounts. The skin is reactively mobile because the underlying fibrous tissue is heavily loaded with fat. However, the flexure lines are anchored to deep tissue, producing lines of skin stasis, that is, stability. This may have a great influence on the sense of touch, especially in those hands possessing many strongly etched lines that are obviulsy not rooted in very fatty tissue.

Flexion creases and papillary ridges are prone to show genetic abnormalities and/or environmental growth disturbances. Mongolism (Down's syndrome) frequently is accompanied by a simian crease, and the full complement of flexion lines may be absent from the little fingers.

Papillary lines or ridges are covered in chapter 7 under dermatoglyphics. Tension lines occur all over the body as the skin loses its elasticity, often with advancing age. On the hand they may be seen as fine vertical lines on the fingers (phalanges), horizontal lines on the back of the hand (the dorsum), and oblique lines on the thenar eminence (mount of Venus under the thumb).

Dr. Eugene Scheimann,[1] in his *Doctor's Guide to Better Health Through Palmistry*, indicates that he is at least one medically trained person who recognizes a fourth set of lines put upon the palm by nature unaided by the flexion movement of the hand. Most of the subsidiary markings fall into this category, such as mystic crosses and medical stigmata, triangles, and squares.

PALMISTS' POINTS OF INTEREST

One examines the course, depth, width, and color of the major, basic, or main lines. When one looks at subsidiary or minor lines, one relates them not only to these features but also to their starting and ending point and the relationship of these lines to the major lines. In subsidiary lines, the thicker end indicates the starting point of the line. Ascending lines are usually viewed as positive, while descending lines suggest a negative, degenerative, or destructive aspect that can impede character. This is not necessarily so with the life line. Even if these lines do have a negative connotation, be careful to see whether they are necessary to offset over-exuberance and excess energy in some other area. They may bring about more balance.

Many palmists believe that neither physical labor nor movements of the hand cause "the slightest effect upon its shape, expression and lines" as Julius Spier[2] observed. Injuries can and do modify that opinion. Some medical sources will maintain that the hands show evidence of occupation, disease, and to some extent one's temperament and personality, as Dr. John Russell Napier[3] observed.

Dr. Charlotte Wolff[4] statistically surveyed some 1600 handprints of right-handed people and found more accessory crease lines in the left hand than in the right. She points out that no mechanical explanation can account for this. This, she contends, offers irrefutable evidence that crease lines reflect something other than simple movement.

LINE PURPOSE AND REASON FOR EXISTENCE

This section contains some technical data that is of more interest to practicing palmists and advanced students. The beginner is advised to go on to Lines May Change, page 129.

Julius Spier points out that neither manual labor nor hand movements "have the slightest effect upon its shape, expression and lines."[5] We are generally, though not completely, in agreement with this observation. Spier also points out, relying on the right-handed world (as about 90 percent of all persons are right-handed) that while the right hand does more work, the left hand generally has more lines on it. He attributes this to the right hand not being the hand of personality but rather

the ancestral hand that reveals "the unconscious springs of the conscious part of the personality."

The main lines of the palm begin to appear by the seventh week of gestation with the life line (see illustration, p. 47). Then the head line, followed by the heart line, begin to be observed in the ninth week of embryo development. They develop from the thumb side in the direction of the percussion.[6] David Brandon-Jones[7] cites Professor Wood Jones[8] as authority for the proposition that these lines appear on the palm soon after the fingers and before the fingers and palm are the site of any active movement. Schaeuble is reported by Schaumann and Alter to concur.[9] The onset of spontaneous hand movements in embryos of less than 11.5 weeks has not been observed, according to reports by Humphrey.[10] Wurth[11] is also reported to have concluded that these creases develop independently of any palmar or finger movement. But this still does not clearly separate the lines from their future use. Schaumann and Alter caution that these findings do not preclude the possibility that the creases anticipate future hand movements and even abnormal creases in the hand reflect folding movements of the irregular hand. Palmists cannot establish that the lines are totally unrelated to the use of the hand.

Schaumann and Alter present the findings of Popich and Smith[12] of the orthodox scientific conclusions that the life line is the result of the oppositional function of the thumb and thenar muscle pad; the heart line follows an underlying sloping alignment of the third to fifth metacarpal-phalangeal joints (the joints between the middle, ring, and little fingers and the palm); and the head line is influenced on its thumb side by the action of the second metacarpal-phalangeal joint (the joint between the index finger and the palm). Sometimes the proximal and distal transverse creases are replaced by a single transverse flexion line, usually called a simian crease or line. The use of the term *simian* is somewhat of a mystery, as only the pavian monkey shows this line and it is not found on the more closely related gorilla, orangutan, and chimpanzee. These all have several transverse creases. The single transverse crease in its variations can be seen to cross the entire palm.

Another transverse palmar crease that crosses the entire palm is the Sydney line named after the city in Australia where the scientific team Purvis-Smith and Menser first observed it.[13] The Sydney line is the proximal (head) line and the distal crease (heart line) is also present and appears normal. Earlier reports did not consider this crease to be "significantly abnormal," but Schaumann and Alter report later studies showing increased frequencies in those with Down's syndrome, congenital rubella, and leukemia. I have one on my left hand along with a similar extended heart line, but I seem to suffer none of the above problems. However, the principal problem observed with those having Sydney lines have been in children with delayed development, learning difficulties, or minor behavioral problems, which does fit my childhood reading dyslexia. The true Sydney line must reach from the edge of the radial side of the palm to the edge of the ulnar side of the palm.

NECK PAIN, SYDNEY LINES, AND HEALING TECHNIQUES

I have observed that the principal problem with the Sydney line is associated in most people with pains in the upper body, mostly around the neck and shoulder on the side where the Sydney line appears. This is especially so if on the same side there is a break in the fate line about the level of the heart line. I have used and advised the use of a simple mental exercise to relieve this problem and have played with several theories of why it works.

The clients are told to concentrate their attention on the fingertips of the fingers on the hand with the Sydney line. They are asked to advise the reader when they can clearly distinguish these fingertips by their feel and are told the feel may be noticed in a variety of ways such as through warmth, cold, tingling sensations, lightness, or heaviness. Once the subjects have identified the existence of the sensation, they are advised to intensify it. Then they are told to move it to the center of their palm. Then they may be advised that they have just learned the secret art of moving Qui, Chi, Xi, and Kundalini that might have taken them years of study and practice under the watchful eye of a martial arts master or guru. Generally they find this encouraging, and it helps them complete the lesson.

After the subjects have moved the life force energy to the center of the palm, they are instructed to move it by stages across the wrist, along the forearm, around the elbow, up the arm, across the shoulder, across the scapula and back, to the spine in the neck area. They are advised that if there is any blockage, to treat it as a garden gate and open it or as a faucet to be opened. They are advised to leave all gates and faucets open. If they run into pain, they are advised to go around it.

With the energy now concentrated at the neck, the subjects are again advised to intensify it and spread it out to surround any tightness and pain. This they can do by treating it as a balloon that they blow up to fill that side of the chest until it bulges over the shoulder. The subjects are reminded that all gates and pipes down the arm are open. They are then instructed to burst the balloon and reverse the flow, sending all the energy and pain and tightness cascading across over the shoulder, down the arm, around the elbow, out

the forearm, wrist, and finally shoot it out the fingertips into the universe. They are advised to do this every night for several weeks when they are lying in bed waiting to go to sleep. They are told that if they do, and if they keep their shoulders warm, they will probably fall asleep as the energy is leaving the hands for the universe. They will probably awake with relief through the shoulders and neck.

The subjects are advised they have begun to learn to move the Qui, Chi, Xi, or Kundalini energy, known in the West as the life force energy. They are told that this is the secret energy used by the Eastern martial arts experts (to some extent true).

It is a cheap form of therapy and I have used it personally and on a variety of subjects with success. There are several reasons it may work. First, the long head line indicates a thinking process that is hard to turn off. Concentration on the movement of feeling turns off that verbal mind and allows the brain to relax. Second, some people consider the body merely a vast energy source. The Sydney line can be looked upon as a block to the flow of that energy. This is a way of overcoming the block. Third, the concentration on the feeling can trigger the sensory nerves along the path. As they are triggered, they in turn trigger corresponding motor neurons that change the firing instructions to the muscles, allowing the reduction of muscle tone. This reduces tension in the back, shoulders, and neck. Regardless of theories, I have found that if done for several weeks, it has changed some old patterns, giving more permanent pain relief.

LINES MAY CHANGE

Brandon-Jones observes that as the subject leaves his or her inherited molds, these lines change, and if the subject is mentally flexible and adaptable, these changes can occur throughout life. I have not found the Sydney line to change with the relief of the tension in the neck. I have a palmist friend who keeps expecting one of his lines to either get longer or shorter and watches it do the opposite. We are a long way from predicting how the lines will change, but they do change.

All modern palmists generally agree that the lines of the hand can and do change. The change may be rapid or slow. Even Schaumann and Alter, otherwise silent on the subject of line changes, report that the "white lines" that cross fingerprint patterns come and go[14] and that is why they were abandoned as a possible means for personal identification.

Hachiro Asano devotes a section of his work[15] to methods that can be used to alter palm patterns. He asserts that altering personality, environment and lifestyle can change the patterns of the palm and offers suggestions in psychological and physical training to assist the transition. He asserts that Zen-like disciplines used with children will often result in palm pattern changes. He suggests the use of hypnotism and also using palmistry as guidance in autosuggestion. He reports the success of using methods to change prints of the mentally retarded, as well as others. Lest one become too enthusiastic, a good palmist and friend reported to me that when he gave up his former unhealthy lifestyle that included liberal uses of alcohol he expected to see his life line lengthen. However, to his surprise, it shortened.

GENERAL LINE OBSERVATIONS

Charlotte Wolff gives some good advice for looking at lines. She found that the psychological significance of crease lines consists generally on their reiteration of the attributes reflected in the shape of the hand with emphasis on the subject's own personal characteristics. She believed that attaching significance to every line, as suggested in chiromancy, is mistaken because significance cannot be attached to every single line. So if the student forgets from time to time the meaning of every single line, he or she has it on good authority that the reading can proceed with some degree of accuracy.

Although it may be easy to spot the pathological cases and perceive the eccentric patterns, it is difficult to distinguish characteristics of the more normal subjects who are likely to come for read-

ings. This requires long experience and training. An apprenticeship during which at least a thousand pairs of hands are examined and interpreted should be a requisite for any palmist.

Many palmists believe that the shape of lines, their thickness, sharpness, depth, clarity, and even color must be taken into account for interpretation of their meaning. The Chinese Wu-Hsing method divides the lines into four types according to their physical qualities, and these are attributed to the elemental forces air, water, fire, and earth. The characteristics of each of these elements was set forth as I discussed my favorite method of reading hand forms.

The Wu-Hsing[16] method considers the broad, wide, and roughly formed line, often short in length, as an earth line. Earth is a container, self-identified, and preserves experiences. It fears heights, publicity, and lack of distinct definition. Here is the solid, dependable sort.

In Wu-Hsing interpretation, the fine, often pale and wavy lines are described as water lines. Water relates, identifies, or personalizes experience into emotional patterns. Water is nonlinear in approach. It fears fire, insensitivity, and apathy. When we see the hand completely filled by these lines, we observe a subject floating aimlessly through life like a leaf floating on the water.

Should the fine lines be deeper, yet still pale in color, and be either straight or curved, they are, by the Wu-Hsing method, considered air lines. Air communicates, evaluates, or comprehends. Air fears being shut in by people or places, being regimented by emotion or opinion. Air rushes quickly through any opening and fills all vacuums.

If the lines are deep, intense in color, and straight, then in the Wu-Hsing method they are considered fire lines. Fire will challenge the amorphous, mold and cast experiences into recognizable shapes or boundaries of expression. Fire fears water, restriction, or any attempt to envelop its senses. Fire must be fed. It is neither self-contained nor can it have total freedom.

Since the Wu-Hsing method recognizes certain lines as being air, fire, water, or earth, thus, to follow that method, one must understand what the basic characteristic of the line being examined is and also its individual characteristics. For example, the life line, which is a major earth line, may have fire characteristics in places where it crosses some areas of the palm. As each area of the palm also has a characteristic of earth, air, fire, or water, this information would also be blended together in order to interpret the meaning of that particular line at that particular place, which also probably indicates a period in the subject's life.

In the blending, the Chinese may be looking for ch'i (balance) or sha (imbalance). If sha is found, then the Chinese would look to see if it was the result of too much yin power tending to give rise to degenerative diseases, a mixture of change for change's sake, and constant dissolution; or yang excess, indicating rigidity and problems associated with rigidity such as arteriosclerosis and excess body fat.

Traditional Western palmists, starting with Benham,[17] look to the lines as pathways for the flow of energy. They observe the shape and size of the line and picture whether the energy flows smoothly. A deep, fairly straight and unblemished line offers a clear, well-defined channel to carry strong, voluminous currents of energy. Traditional Western palmistry analyzes the lines by looking at their direction or course, shape or form, strength or intensity, and possibly color. Main lines have traditional courses and directions. Subsidiary lines can start anywhere and go anywhere, and one looks to the thicker end of the line to determine the starting point.

Benham hypothesized that the energy enters the lines through the Jupiter finger, passing first into the heart line below the Jupiter finger, then to the head line and the life line along the radial (thumb) side of the hand. He felt that the fate or Saturn line picked its energy up from the end of the life line. Thus, he believed that one should read the heart, head, and life lines from the radial side of the hand and the fate line from the wrist. Most Western palmists would read the heart line from the percussion (ulnar) side of the hand and Spier would read the life or vitality line from the wrist up, rather than down from between the mounts of Jupiter and lower Mars.

The Western palmist would look to see if the lines are proportioned to the palm. A broad earth hand with air lines will immediately alert one to potential conflicts. Benham would point out that if the Jupiter finger were large, then it would attract great amounts of energy and would need lines appropriate to translate this energy throughout the palm. By the same token, those same lines would be inappropriate for a hand with a small Jupiter finger and the energy would tend to be lost in the channels and would meander and flow sluggishly. The channels in effect would not give clear direction. We may consider the energy as analogous to water. It will tend to spread in all directions and lack strength or focus. If the volume is small in a large line, the energy of the current will be used up in trying to fill the width of the line. If the line is small and the volume is large, then the energy may tend to flood the surrounding mount or plain and perhaps sink there, much as a river sinks into the desert sands.

Some Western palmists attempt to simplify the energy hypothesis by merely describing lines. Altman[18] observes that a particularly deep line indicates excessive energy. This singular statement could ignore that part of the Benham hypothesis that the energy must come from outside the lines, in Benham's case, from the universe through the Jupiter finger.

Newcomer-Bramblett[19] believes that the deep lines indicate reincarnation. So when one reads the occasional subject whose hands are full of deeply gravened lines, they may be told they are an old soul.

Are the lines merely reflective of energy at that particular location, or does the hand perhaps reveal a flow of energy? If we use some lines for dating, as all palmists do, then a static energy pattern would seem illogical. However, because subsidiary lines can and do start and stop on all parts of the hand, localized energy sources cannot be ruled out. Like so many things in the art of palmistry, we need to subconsciously balance both hypotheses in developing our own analysis.

Color

Many palmistry books make strong cases for color of the hands and of the lines. However there are many factors that can affect color, including lighting, temperature, and the person's own pigmentation. Fred Gettings[20] observes that the color of the nails is a better reflection of the heart action than hand color. He also advises palmists to draw conclusions based upon more stable parts of the hand. Many palmists maintain that the normal skin color in all races is rosy and pinkish. Some palmists will say that a yellow color in the palms can indicate liver involvement, including the diseases of hepatitis and jaundice, especially on the health line or on the life line. This may be truer of a pale-skinned person than those with olive, brown, or yellow complexions. Bluish hands that are warm may indicate poor circulation or possible heart disease and have been linked to atherosclerosis, certain drug reactions, and Reynaud's syndrome. Others will find that excessive red not only indicates physical heart involvement, but angry temperaments and great energy.

Palmists seeing red or blue dots on the life line will consider serious illnesses or accidents involving a high fever. Such signs on the heart or head line may indicate cardiac or neurological involvement, especially if the dots appear at the same age on both hands. Look to the percussion to see if there is a corresponding line or mark there and this may be of further aid in determining the organs involved.

Length

Length, especially of the life line, is often related to age of death. That is a misconception. We have a friend who is living well beyond the chronological years shown in her life line. Chronological dating will be treated elsewhere. Length of individual lines will be treated under those lines.

Rita Robinson[21] observes that although lines vary in length from hand to hand, it is natural to find long head lines on conic, psychic, and philosophic hands and shorter ones on square and spatulate hands. There longer head lines may have more meaning because they indicate departures from the normal thought patterns associated with these types of hands.

Quality

The ideal line is as deep as it is wide, it is clear, and the depth and width should be even throughout the line. Note any variations of these qualities, for they will have meaning. Particularly deep lines can indicate excessive energy and shallow lines can indicate a lack of focus and strength.

Quantity

An excess of lines indicates hypersensitivity, nervousness, and an inability to focus. This describes a subject needing grounding, discipline, or a feeling of protection and safety. Some palmists believe such persons have the gift of more paths for expressing their talents; others find them so scattered as to lose any effective focus. They become the victims of their own nervousness. However, there may be a need to distinguish between anxiety and nervousness. Andrew Symaniz, while a college student at Abelaid, South Australia, reports that his study indicated fewer lines on the palm showed higher anxiety.[22] This shows the need in many areas of scientific study of palmistry for attempts to duplicate the studies previously reported. In this case, careful attention would need to be paid to exactly what conditions are being studied and compared.

Few lines can indicate a much simpler approach to life. But Symaniz's findings may indicate this is more hope than reality.

Uneven, Broken, and Sprouted Lines

According to the Indians (see V. A. K. Ayer[23]) sprouted lines betoken anxiety or sorrow. Too many lines also can show sorrow. Too few lines can mean poverty. Both suggest shortness of life as can a broken line. Not all writers agree with such assumptions, by any means. Still, broken, pitted, sprouted, splintered, chained, uneven, poorly colored, poorly defined, ill-positioned, and islanded lines all detract from the strengths that can be shown by the lines. It is as if these marks divert the energy being channeled by those lines. Whether absence of lines is a blessing or a curse is a matter open to broader discussion. There may not be any firm answer that covers all lines or the length of all lines.

Forks can reveal either dissipation of energies or a balance of applicable energy. In some cases, a combination of both elements is observed. The writer's fork on the head line indicates the ability to see problems from more than one perspective and also indicates the drawback related to this ability, the added difficulty in coming to a decision.

Comparison of Lines

One should look at both hands and compare each line. Fenton and Wright believe that a mark on the line of the minor hand that does not show up on the dominant one merely shows a past trauma that is still etched on the subconscious, though forgotten in everyday life.[24] One should determine if there are any major differences, and these can indicate potential conflicts within the subject's character.

Fenton and Wright also stress that the minor hand demonstrates what the subject's inner self wants, and the dominant hand shows how the subject is really adapting. This approach may help in understanding conflicts.

Lines at Birth

The life, head, and heart lines are usually in the hand of the newborn. The fate line can appear from birth to age twenty. Spier noted that children born with just the main lines and few or no subsidiary lines seem to be more harmonious and have fewer difficulties in development than those with many lines.[25] One can speculate that the greater number of lines reflects more past-life Karma, or perhaps it mirrors more of the frustrations and difficulties of parents and ancestors.

MAJOR, BASIC, OR MAIN LINES

Depending on which authority one prefers, there are, in Western palmistry, three or four major, basic, or main lines. Some refer to the major lines as the three flexion lines: the life or vitality line, the head or mentality line, and the heart or emotional line. Others add the line of Saturn, also known as the fate or personality line. We will deal with all four lines as basic lines. Sometimes the heart and head lines are totally combined into one line and this is commonly called the simian line, as explained above and in chapter 9.

Life Line

The Indians call the life or vitality line the *pithru* or *gotra rekha*. Wu-Hsing[26] refers to it as the major earth line. Medically, it is known as one of the three flexion creases of the palm, the thenar crease.

Ideal quality dictates a clear, unblemished, well-defined life line. The width and depth should be even. If the line is too deep, there can be excessive energy. If the line is too broad, it indicates a lack of strength and focus. The color should complement the skin. In light-skinned races such as Caucasians, the line should be pink, but as the skin darkens, the line may be pinkish brown to olive to brown. It should be the most deeply colored line of the hand.

According to the Indian ancients (Ayer), and Spier, the life line begins, for reading purposes, at the wrist. Most other palmists seem to follow the beginning of the life line from the space between the thumb and index finger. To the Indian palmists, this line reflects the strength of the family tree.

Long, clear, and well-marked life lines are indicative of strength, vitality, good immune systems, good recovery ability, resilience, and sexual energy, especially if they describe a generous curve around a healthy mount of Venus. This is a person who can meet life's challenges well and, barring some other problems, will probably live a long, healthy life. To the Indians, a long pithru rekha indicates a long line of elders.

Short, clear, and well-marked life lines show more intensity, and indicate good health. Some believe they show a shorter life. Others do not agree. Myrah Lawrance[27] indicates that such a line could, especially after one has lived past the ending of the line, indicate a rather uneventful life. To the Indians, the short line reflects a small family.

Dr. Scheimann noted that in his medical practice he had seen many patients die young with long life lines and many who had reached old age with short life lines. He preferred to call the line the "line of constitution."

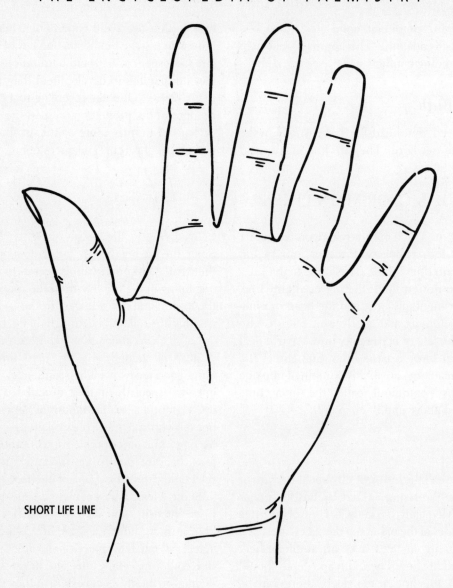

SHORT LIFE LINE

To Dr. Scheimann, a long, deep, and well-marked line was indicative of a strong, vital constitution, and a short, thin, faulty line signified a weak and delicate constitution and immune system.

When the life line is red and deep, it may indicate powerful energy, intensity, and a violent disposition. It could also point to some circulatory complaint.

A wide, undefined line indicates someone easily influenced, not well focused, and possibly lazy. These subjects appear to lack drive or energy. According to V. A. K. Ayer, the Indian palmist, if it

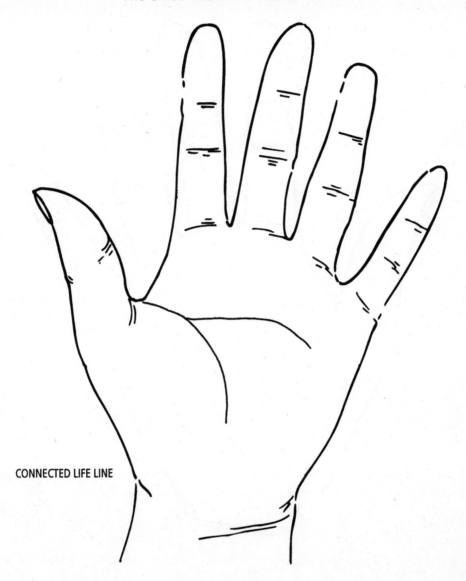

CONNECTED LIFE LINE

is also pale, it indicates poor health, "envy and often bad instincts." If it is thick and red, it indicates brutishness, and if it is uneven in thickness along its course, it shows fickleness.

A long, weak life line is indicative of a weak constitution, and a tendency toward nervousness and indecision. A line that is frayed or chained has this same connotation, showing a tendency toward chronic afflictions and nervousness.

I look to see if the life line is connected to or separated from the head line. This is an indication of early precocity, dependence, or independence.

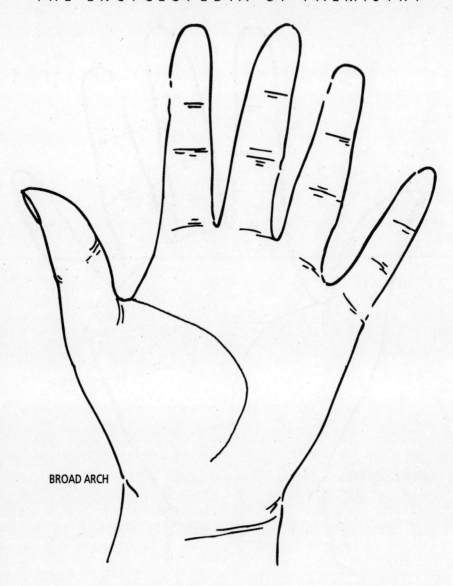

BROAD ARCH

This feature marks the headstrong or cautious and prudent nature of the subject. The longer the lines are together, the longer the subject took to develop independence of mind and the more likely the subject is to be cautious in life. Apparently there has been some statistical study by Dr. Rowan Bayne that confirms that the joinder of the head and life lines indicate restricted, dominated childhoods.[28] The wider the separation of the severed lines, the stronger the indication is of self-confidence, independence, and possibly impulsiveness.

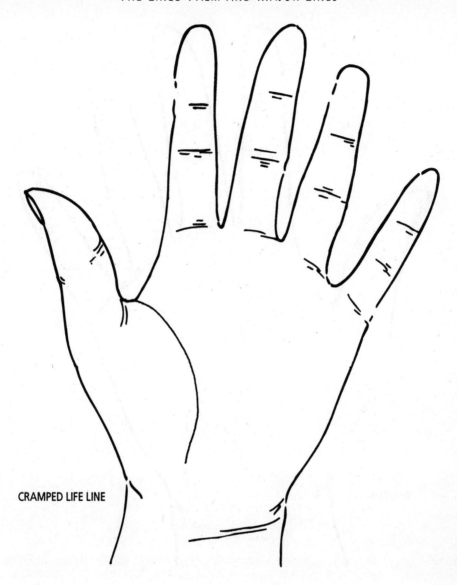

CRAMPED LIFE LINE

We speak of the period when the lines are joined as the period of the group mind. During this period, the subject likes to discuss all major decisions with family or friends before making those decisions. After separation, the subject is free of this need.

Sometimes all three major lines are joined in the beginning. Myrah Lawrance finds that these subjects, though brusque on the surface, are kind, sympathetic, and soft under it all.[29] Yaschpaule[30] finds this a very bad sign. He reports that these subjects are accident prone and unable to learn

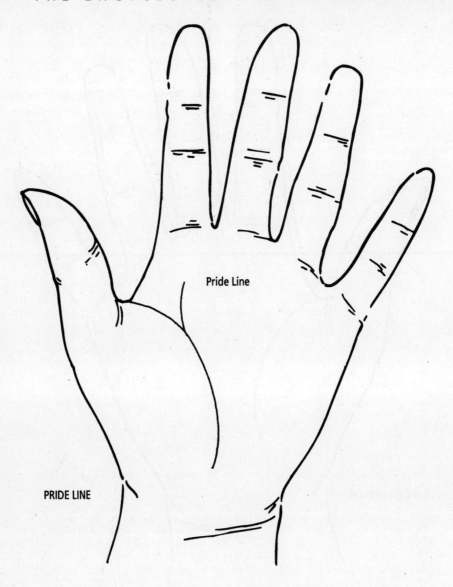

Pride Line

PRIDE LINE

from mistakes. They lack emotional judgment and they have no insight into the causes of their own unhappy emotional states. He says: "Truly, love is blind." Should the sign be found in both hands, he says that sudden death, accident, or illness is likely, though sudden death does not mean dying young, or a premature death.

A broad arch indicates a warm, sensual, and emotionally responsive person.

A line that hugs close to the thumb indicates an

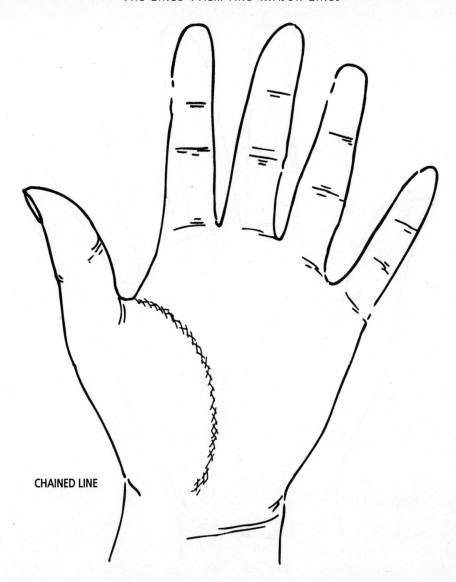

CHAINED LINE

inhibited, cold, unresponsive subject. If the line begins close to the thumb and stays close, it may be a sign of female barrenness or male impotence or sterility. This can be the monastic mark.

When the line moves toward Luna, rather than curving around the thumb, it indicates a restless personality, a person who may well make one or more major geographical moves in his or her lifetime. We have often found this mark on the lower third of the life line on immigrants who came to the country in their younger years. Here is support for those who would read the life line from the

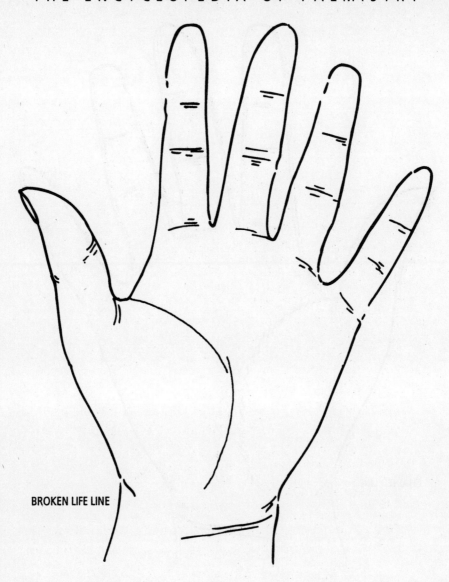

BROKEN LIFE LINE

bottom up. Sometimes it appears that the lines can be read in both directions.

When a branch of the line moves up toward Jupiter, it is commonly called a line of pride or ambition (Jupiter line) and indicates optimism, pride, ambition, and a drive to overcome. To the Indians, when the line reaches the mount of Jupiter, it reflects that the owner has many brothers and sisters and other relatives around him or her. If a branch terminates on the mount of Jupiter, then Ayer indicates it is a sign of holding many titles.[31]

Myrah Lawrance maintains that when the life

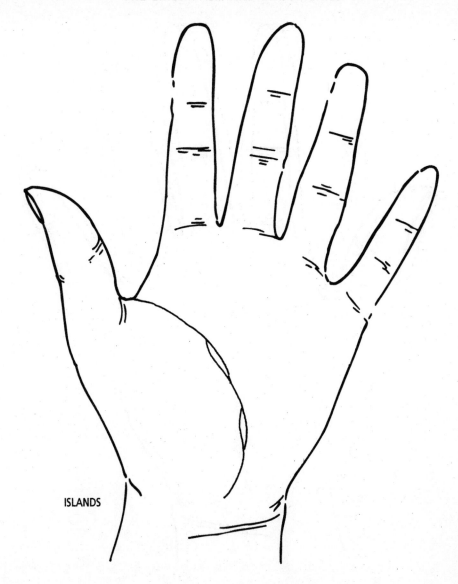

ISLANDS

line begins far over on the thenar side of the hand about midway between the base of the index finger and the top of the thumb, one will discover a subject who always maintains close connections with his or her family, or did so until death destroyed those relationships.[32] By contrast, the line that begins as a pride line would indicate a person who has for most practical purposes severed family contacts fairly early in life.

A chained or poorly marked early life line could mean childhood diseases, trauma, and/or emotional problems. As the head and life lines are

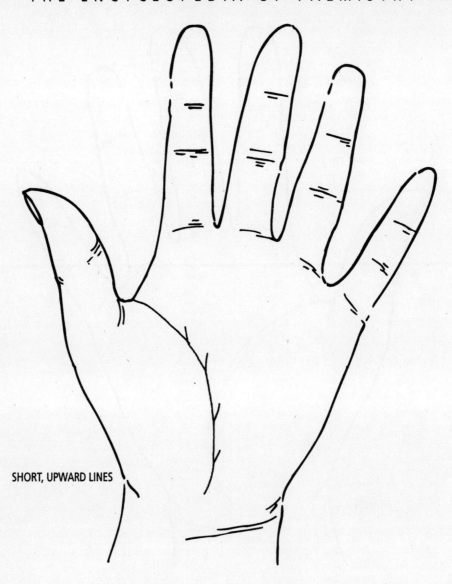

SHORT, UPWARD LINES

often considered to start together, these will indicate that the person was quite mentally upset by the problems and some may even have a poor memory of their childhood. One automatically checks the beginning of the heart line. It will quite often also be chained during the formative years.

One asks if the person had childhood diseases, but these signs could also indicate a dysfunctional early home life.

The broken life line is a warning signal. It is a clear indication to clean up one's health attitudes and actions. Quite often the old life line seems to end, but one can see faint or stronger lines that connect the old life line with the lower part of the Saturn line, the fate, or personality line or even the line of milieu. One may suggest that the person become more active and outgoing, allowing themselves to become warmer, more sensual, open, and emotionally responsive to others if that new line is farther from the thumb. That can become the new life line with a change in attitude and activity. Life lines that are broken in places may indicate abrupt changes in life directions. Wide breaks may indicate a geographic change and will certainly indicate a major life change. If there is no bridge line between the old and the new, the change will be like jumping into the dark.

To the Indians, the breaks in the pithru rekha reflect a splitting of the clan.

Lawrance has noted that a line that connects the life and fate lines is a sign of good protection against accident and bodily harm.[33] Occasionally we have seen the only line available is one closer to the thumb, which has indicated the person is in need of conserving his or her energies and needs to become more reserved and cautious.

According to traditional interpretation, islands are signs of impending disease or dangerous health periods, but perhaps it may only be a time of somewhat reduced or divided energies.

I generally find that the upward lines indicate self-improvement activities. Some that are strongly marked may indicate advanced schooling or major life lessons. Many of these lines indicate the perpetual student.

Lawrance does not seem to agree. She sees lines pointing toward the fingers as restrictions or disappointments, while progress or activity is indicated by lines pointing toward the wrist.[34] I see two possibilities in lines pointing toward the wrist: either an alternative vitality path (living mode and

not necessarily permanent) or a dissipation of energy to some extent.

V. A. K. Ayer maintains that in Indian palmistry the number of upward branches moving toward the fingers indicate the number of claims the subject has on paternal property, and the number of sprouts directed toward the thumbs reflects friends and well-wishers.[35]

Crosses touching the life line may mean family troubles or trouble with a close friend, perhaps death if one of the parallel lines on the inside (Venus side) of the life line comes to an end at that particular point. Lawrance believes that if the cross is between the life line and the thumb, it will indicate a narrow escape, usually from an illness or accident, for the person.

Dots indicate energy suckers. They can indicate uncertain health or danger from some other exposure. Ayer indicates that from the Indian point of view, a black dot at the end of the pithru rekha (which is at the beginning of the Western line for most palmists) indicates a sudden end to life.

Crossing lines to many palmists have bad meanings dating from the time they cross. We have found them to indicate all manner of things from weddings, childbirths, and divorces to illnesses. All seem to reflect some outside influence in the event or cause of the event.

Life lines often have wide branches at the bottom. This indicates a choice of modes of living later in life and can also indicate wider activity and scope of life in later years. The branch toward Luna indicates restlessness and possible moves. Traditionally, the life line that ends on Luna indicates the person will not die where they were born. The branch gives that choice.

When the line is paralleled closely on the mount of Venus so that it appears as a double line, the subject may have a very healthy life and good omens for success. Yvette Grady[36] believes this

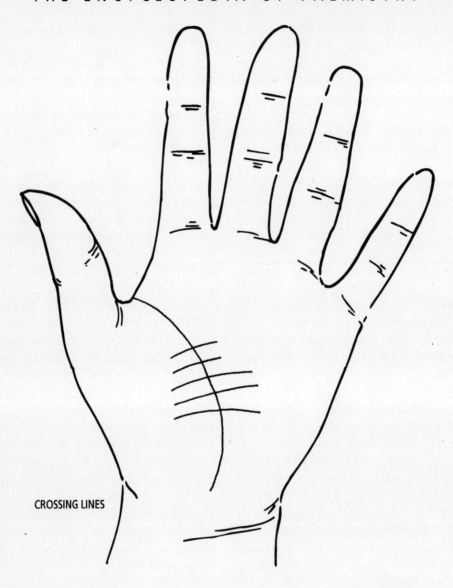

CROSSING LINES

indicates a very passionate person and calls it an inner life line. Brandon-Jones warns us to beware of confusing a far more common Mars line (much shorter and described with minor lines) with a double life line.[37] He has found that those with the double life line lead a dual existence. One should check and see if there are strong lines that divide any of the phalanges. These also can suggest a double life in the area found. The double heart line indicates enough heart for two.

For some time I have been reading early parental influence or lack of it from the lines or lack of

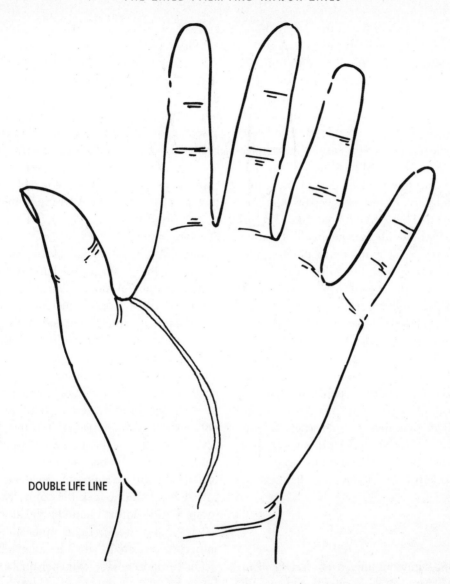

DOUBLE LIFE LINE

them that join the life line in its early phase. I am particularly interested in lines that are deeply red or otherwise discolored. When I see no discolored lines in the area, I can report to the subject that he or she appears to no longer have any childhood-related problems affecting his or her life.

The deep red lines can indicate some force from the parent. It may be love or abuse, but it still exerts a powerful influence on the subject. Lack of parental influence lines can have the same effect if the life line in the area remains red. Sometimes when the line that is red appears to be the early father or mother influence, we question if there were problems either at conception or during gestation.

Using yin and yang theories, I tend to find the right hand as the hand indicating survival qualities and the left hand indicating sensitive qualities. I read the palms of a gentleman in his midfifties who had powerful hands. He had been a chief for one of the world's famous monarchs who had entertained lavishly. When I read his palm, he was a consultant to one of the giant food organizations. He was successful and his hands showed it. There were no red marks on his right hand where the life line begins. But on his left hand there were deep red marks entering the life line from above, from the father area. Upon exploration, it was discovered that his father had been a strict disciplinarian. He had not given his son emotional support. At the age of thirteen, my client had attempted suicide. Tears started to well up as this man remembered the event. He had not yet fully dealt with it. Here was an obvious artist who needed sensitive support from his father and had received strong discipline in its place. I believe that once he integrates that experience into his life, the pain will subside and the redness will go. It took me moments to find this. A psychiatrist might have needed several visits.

Heart Line

The heart line, emotions line, *ayu* or *jeevith rekha* in Indian palmistry, or major water line according to Wu-Hsing teachings, is generally thought to begin from the percussion below the little finger and proceed toward the thumb. It is the upper (more distal) of the two horizontal flexion lines. To the Indians, this line has influence over longevity and is more important on this issue than the life line. It certainly has some significance in lon-

gevity to other palmists, because it is related to the emotions and the cardiovascular system.

There is a disagreement on where this line starts. The Indians and most Western palmists believe this line begins at the percussion under the little finger. However, the Indonesian palmist, Yaschpaule,[38] along with the Western palmist, Benham,[39] believe the line actually starts from the area of the mount of Jupiter and crosses the palm to end on the percussion below the little finger. Schaumann and Alter report that it begins to form from this side of the hand in embryonic development.[40]

Yaschpaule's reasons for starting the heart line toward the thenar side of the hand may appear to be a little easier for some to accept than Benham's reasons. Benham works from a hypothesis that life current flows through the Jupiter finger and is distributed from that side of the hand through the various lines as currents in rivers. Yaschpaule is more pragmatic. He believes that islands on the heart line under the little finger signify high blood pressure and heart weakness. Because these are not generally conditions found in the young, but come with age, he believes we should start the heart line from the other side. Interestingly, there is also some further supporting evidence that indicates that when one feels the palm, if one feels a lump or gristly formation under the little finger on the left hand, it can be an indication that the subject has suffered a silent heart attack.

On the opposite side, from personal experience, I have found a chained or frayed heart line under the little finger often betokening an emotional childhood. Perhaps we need to look at these lines in both directions and perhaps they are really dual gauges of age, depending on what we seek to discover. We have seen the fate line suggested as having this possible quality and it may apply to the other lines.

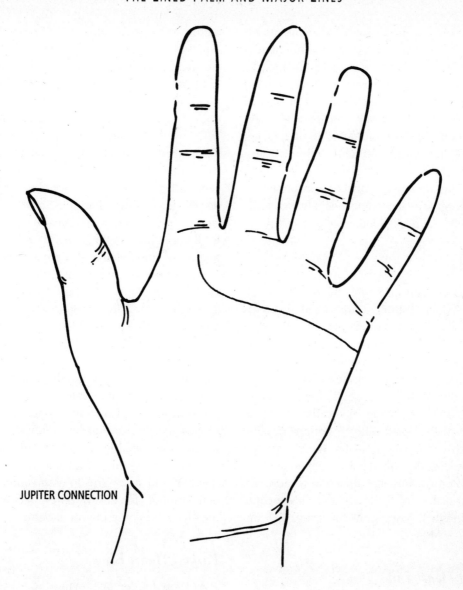

JUPITER CONNECTION

Yaschpaule points out that the heart line must be considered in connection with the mount of Venus. To him, the heart line reflects the higher, more spiritual concepts of love, duty, and moral responsibility, whereas the Venus mount reflects the more basic, supporting instincts of sociability, sex, and lust. The heart line does fall in that portion of the hand related to the aspects of the higher self.

The ideal heart line is deep, well defined, not chained or broken, and either starts or ends from just about the mount of Jupiter. Some believe the best place for it to start is just between the mount of Jupiter and the mount of Saturn. Yaschpaule believes it should start from between the mounts of Jupiter and Saturn because he believes it draws its energy from the mounts where it starts and finishes and thus draws loyalty, idealism, wisdom, and affection from the mount of Jupiter, being qualities of that mount, and sobriety from Saturn. "The subject will feel deeply, but will seldom make an outward show of affection in public."[41] Nevertheless, he or she will feel deeply, be forgiving of faults, and be well balanced and happy.

Jupiter High

If, for Yaschpaule, it starts high, the person will be idealistic. Yet if it is strongly curved and thus starts high, it will reflect a strongly physical attraction and sexual attitude in matters of the heart. Others agree with the sexual and physical attitudes and indicate that if it starts (or finishes) high, either on the mount of Jupiter or between Jupiter and Saturn, then it shows a more physically related response to matters of the heart, complementing warm and sensuous signs in the hand. As I tell female subjects, they like a person who looks good in a set of trunks. Physical attraction is more important in matters of the heart, and these people need a kinesthetic, physically touching, relationship.

Straight Heart Line

Yaschpaule sees the problem with a long line that starts (or ends) on the thenar side of the hand and crosses the hand completely as that it fits the perfectionist. It shows excessive love and devotion to the extent of possessiveness. I would tend to agree. The farther the line progresses over Jupiter, the more one may find the person to be of a jealous

nature. If the line starts high, then it will be a possessiveness of the person, the body of others. If it starts lower, then the possessiveness is of the idea of the person. This latter possessiveness seems to blind the subjects to the real nature of their loved ones. They tend not to see the loved one's faults. They overlook characteristics that do not correspond to their ideal of the loved one. In those cases, the subjects have left themselves open for very rude awakenings. Because they tend to be so possessive, they will hang on to their ideas and visions. This tendency will make it very difficult for them to become forgiving of faults when they finally are compelled to recognize them.

A heart line beginning (or ending) on Saturn is viewed unfavorably. The subject, even Yaschpaule agrees, will tend to be more sensual than truly affectionate. These people seem to know and respond to physical desire, but have real problems relating to concepts of love and affection. Yaschpaule possibly justifies this by relating to Saturn as a malefic planet. It poses more of a study if we were to accept merely his view that the line should receive its strongest influence from the mounts associated with its start and finish and if we view the mount of Saturn as relating to judgment. Yaschpaule warns to observe the character of the mount of Venus with these people as well as the character of the mount of Saturn.

Forked Heart Line

A fork on Jupiter or moving toward the thenar end of the line is favorable. It implies to Yaschpaule[42] that the subject will be both materially prosperous and emotionally well balanced. To others it implies a measure of balance in matters of love between the physical, mental, and emotional qualities of the relationship. Tridents are signs of even better fortune in these areas and

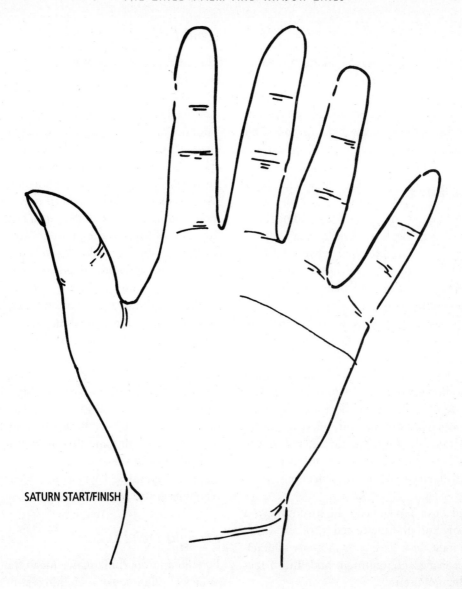

SATURN START/FINISH

the Eastern palmist will see it as another sign of great wealth.

Downward lines are generally considered unfavorable in palmistry. A downward line that touches the head line can be considered a sign of emotional unhappiness. It may be a sign that the emotions are trying to control the practical side of life, the general mental attitudes and processes of life. The emotions cloud the clarity of vision and judgment that one may need to rely upon to make decisions on everyday activities. Spier concludes to the contrary.[43] If a branch of the heart line leads downward to the beginning of the head line, the subject's intellectual processes strongly influence the emotions. The end result may be the same, whichever theory is used, and so perhaps we need better to define our theories. I find that when the heart line crosses the head or life line, by itself or one of its forks, the subjects tend to give their hearts away.

Flirtation Lines

Spier notes that many small, descending lines from or crossing the heart line indicate strong desires for variety in life experiences.[44] Many others, including myself, have found these indicate a flirtatious nature and many small disappointments of the heart.

Although there may be some cause for concern with many interconnected lines between the heart and head line, Spier does not see it that way. For him, such lines indicate that there is a homogenous assimilation of experiences of life by both the intellect and the emotions and when we do not find them, we find a divided personality. Our experience, dating life along the head line, is that the subjects have dificulty with intimate communications until these lines clear.

Chained lines can indicate high sensitivity, a person easily hurt and impressed by others. Such signs can indicate a desire for intimate contact, but with a fear of commitment and thus a tendency to be promiscuous.

Wide or narrow spaces between the heart and head lines are said to indicate not only the influence of these two lines on each other but also whether a person is broad-minded or narrow-minded. The wide space is also said to indicate impulsiveness, impatience, and unconventional behavior.

Head Line

The head line, or line of mentality, the major air line in the Wu-Hsing teachings, or the *mathru* or *dhan rekha*, according to the Indian palmists, is the roughly horizontal line located below the heart line. It seems generally agreed that it begins on the thumb side of the hand and may begin above, below, or in conjunction with or as part of the life line. Each beginning has a different meaning as does each ending, and it may have one or more endings. Typical endings can be found from the plain of Mars to the mount of upper Mars to the depths of the mount of Pluto and anywhere in between. We have examined subjects with more than one head line.

The line is not an IQ line, and length does not indicate genius. It is more indicative of the process and coloration of thinking and how that process effects quality, as well as the quantity of thinking. Generally speaking, the longer the line, the greater time and/or more information the subject will want or need before coming to a decision. However, it may be that those with long head lines that cross the palm and then turn at right angles and go sharply downward, tend to have photographic memories. I would like to have further reactions to this observation.

Straight Head Line

By coloration of thinking we mean the influence or lack of influence of such things as imagination, psychic feelings, intuition, and cold, logical, scientific thought. The straighter the line, the more the thinking is said to be influenced by the practical, logical trains of thought. The more the line curves and the deeper it curves, the more thoughts seem to flow from the imaginative to the intuitive to the purely psychic type of reactions and to what some might have called (and may still call in some areas of the world) madness or spiritual or religious ecstasy. The straighter the line, the more linear the mode of thinking. The more the line curves or is wavy, the more intuitive and nonlinear is the process of thought.

Curved Head Lines

Lines that curve drastically down are often associated in the minds of palmists with depression and suicidal thoughts as well as an imagination that can run wild. We believe that the deeply curved head line offers alternatives to suicidal thoughts or depression if the person will access their own spiritual natures and explore their psychic abilities. We suggest to them that they study trance journies, psychic, and out of body experiences.

The long head line, reflecting the need for more information in making decisions, may also reflect a wider range of interests. Short head lines may indicate thinking that is more limited to mundane affairs.

The formation of the line is important. If the line is long, straight, but too broad, we have the Rio Grande problem. The actual flow of the energy, the flow of the water in the channel, meanders too much and so the thought is scattered and diffused.

Head and Life Lines Joined

When the head line is joined with the life line, it indicates a certain cautious nature of the subject. This comes from being part of a group, family, or clan type mind for that portion of the life indicated by the joinder (with the life line starting above the thumb). Even Yaschpaule, who has the life line start from the wrist, believes that such subjects depend too much on parents, relatives, or friends

for advice when the lines are tied for a long distance.[45] I usually can date a person's mental independence in time from the point where these two lines become separated.

Occasionally, one will find someone whose head line begins on the mount of lower Mars. This is traditionally unfavorable. The thought begins from the feeling of aggression and makes the person argumentative. Yaschpaule[46] sees a like result if the head line ends on upper Mars. However, the lack of self-confidence, oversensitive, aggressive, and highly irritable temperament of the subject with the head line beginning on lower Mars will be replaced by a headstrong person determined to have things his or her own way.

Biccum[47] believes this formation reflects difficulties in the early years of life that result in a disappointing career unless the Apollo and fate lines are good. Even then, there will be struggle. Grady[48] sees these subjects as men with cold ambition who have learned the art of self-control. Perhaps she has observed Biccum's successful ones who have learned their own arts of survival.

Head and Life Lines Separated

A small separation in the beginning of the head line from the life line is a good sign, showing self-confidence, independence of spirit, and probably sound judgment. However, as the space widens, so does the self-confidence, so that the person can become headstrong, impulsive, lack self-control, and take dangerous or unnecessary risks. People with this type of formation will also be sensitive to any criticism that would attack the very high opinion they have of themselves.

A strong head line is indicative of good, clear mental processes while a weak head line indicates lack of concentration or scattered thinking and

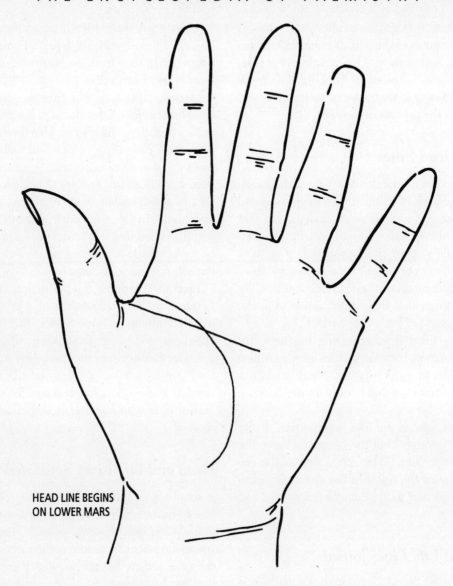

HEAD LINE BEGINS
ON LOWER MARS

lack of focus. Wavy lines can indicate vacillation in purpose.

Islands can indicate difficulty in concentration, head injuries, or psychological disturbances.

A chained head line and a wavy head line are said to be signs of a procrastinator, according to Rita Robinson.[49] She also maintains that breaks in the head line reflect fatalistic views of life, usually brought about by some tragic event that the subject has not recovered from.

The head line will, from time to time, show forks, and these are traditionally known as writer's

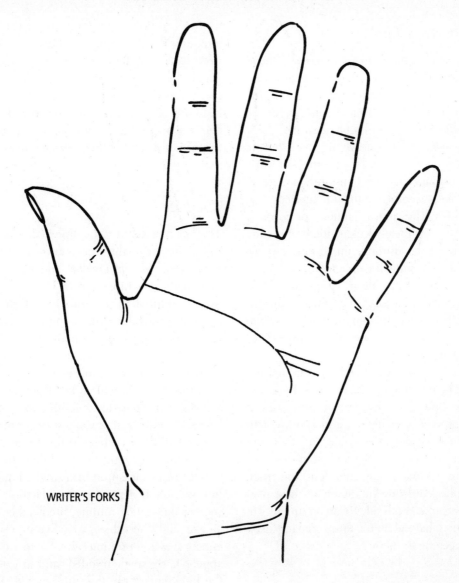

WRITER'S FORKS

forks. Three well-formed forks might indicate a potential fiction writer. What they certainly do indicate is an ability to see from two or more points of view, depending on the number of forks. This has the advantage of giving the subject an ability to have a more thorough understanding of any topic under consideration but the disadvantage of making decisions harder when the views clash. Upturned forks, toward Mercury, like upturned head lines, give the subject an avaricious view, while the downturned lines add fantasy and imagination to the thought process.

Secondary Head Line

From time to time I have run across a second head line. The second head line may not begin until near or after midlife, or it may terminate before the first head line, indicating that at some point the subject will be free of this double identity.

When I suggested to one young man that he had two persona within him, two souls as it were, he agreed and said that they constantly disagreed. One head line was joined to the line up to the age of about thirty, showing a cautious disposition. The other was completely independent of the life line, showing a headstrong, impetuous disposition. I could understand the disagreement. Until a better explanation comes along, I am satisfied that while these two lines overlap, the subject may well have multiple persona. Biccum finds it a good sign of fortune, so I suppose you could say two minds are better than one.

Cheiro[50] confirms the duality of this person, noting that he had that line. He claims these subjects are versatile and have a great command of language, great determination, and can toy with people. Their natures are double and they can combine a perfectly gentle and sensitive personality with one that is cold, confident, and cruel. Brandon-Jones confirms the duality of these people.[51] They can see both sides of an argument. He adds that they have difficult times making decisions and keeping to them.

Secondary Head Line Breaks

As we consider how quickly the person makes a decision, we should carefully examine the head line for breaks. I have frequently found subjects who appear to have a long head line but really make quick decisions. A careful examination of that head line shows a break early in the line with a further line then continuing from very near, or touching the previous line. This person tends to make a decision, then does not announce it immediately, but seeks out supporting rationale or ornamentation depending on the path the continuing head line takes. I have counted two or three breaks and when questioned, the subjects confirm that the anouncement of their decision depends on as many processes.

The Fate Line

The fate line, Saturn line, line of destiny or, as we call it, the personality line, is known to the Indians as one of the *oordhva rekhas*, and is a minor earth line in the teachings of Wu-Hsing. Only a few would count it as a minor line. Others would count it as probably a major-minor line. It appears to record changes in personality, job, and career.

Some would say that a deep, long, clear, and well-cut fate line will indicate favorable effects on the subject. Others will say that this merely reflects a person who sticks to something long after it has become boring, out of some sense of necessity or misguided loyalty. They do this because of their feeling that they must finish all they start.

Success as measured by a single, long, straight line will often depend on two factors: First, the subject may enjoy routine, predictable environs, and second, the subject may live in a world that encourages and promotes those who are steadfast, appear fairly single-minded, and are devoted to the long-range tasks that they started. Such persons may only expect a moderate amount of success in most of the Western world today.

Yaschpaule recognizes the fate line as being able to start from any number of places in the palm. I have counted many fate lines in the same palm, often parallel, some converging, some spreading, and many starting from different

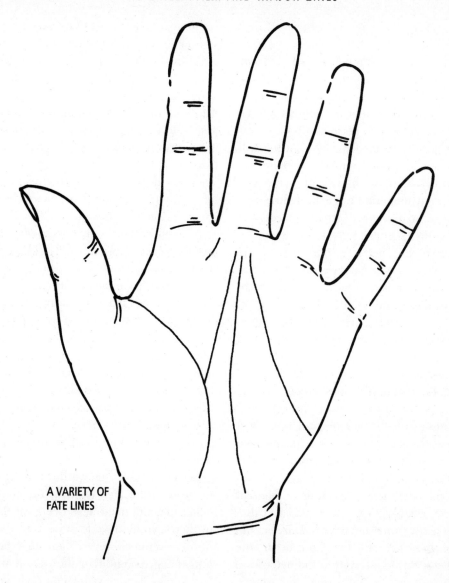

A VARIETY OF
FATE LINES

points. If we look at the position where they start, we can get some idea of the powers that propel them. The plain of Mars can indicate strife, so a line starting there could indicate that the subject will need to struggle hard to accomplish much in life. As Mars and Saturn are hostile, the struggle may indeed be bitter.

Beginnings from Venus can indicate that the subject is strongly influenced by family and friends in choice of career, because that planet symbolizes family and relations. A husband may have a strong influence on the wife's choice of activity (or vice versa). Although the subject may also receive initial support from the family in careers if the fate line begins from the life line, it usually means that thereafter the subject will be self-made and rise through personal merit.

If the line arises from the head line, success will be through mental activity and intense planning. The indication here is that this type of success will only be achieved after middle age. If the line does not begin until the heart line, then the success will come later in life, after age forty or forty-five.

Often we see the fate line starting from the mount of the moon. Luna is related to public appeal, intuition, water, foreign travel, foreign contacts, migration, and female energies. Public-spirited individuals often have such fate lines: doctors, lawyers, politicians, entertainers, hand analysts, and astrologers, to name the ones singled out by Yaschpaule.[52] These subjects will receive help from strangers, outside contacts, the opposite sex, and their own psyche and intuition.

A line starting from the Neptune or Uranus area indicates the self-made person. These people take full responsibility and credit for their personality and fate.

I look at the fate line as indicating, at different points in life, what types of introverted or extroverted personality or personalities the subject has and uses in his or her daily life. Considering the hand divided with the introvert to the percussion side and the extrovert to the thenar side, we can see both tendencies and changes. When we see fate line changes, we look to see if there have been or will be major changes in the subject's activities at the time of the changes as reflected on the other major lines and on the line of Apollo, which is discussed in the next chapter. This may help us decide what will influence the changes we detect.

Some look to the fate line for signs of marriage and new relationships. Katherine St. Hill is credited with finding relationships signaled by small lines rising up from the Saturn line.[53] I have had moderate success using strong lines joining the fate line from below, before the fate line reaches the head line, as indications of marriage in the teens and the twenties. Others have reported that crosses on the fate line are signs of relationships and have dated them in a manner parallel to the life line, from the bottom down. I have not had great success with this method.

Absence of the fate line does not mean absence of fate, success, or wealth. Often I have found such people not only successful, but enjoying life. If anything, it has indicated that these people have lost the care of their own self-importance. They no longer seem to worry about their own personality, but live as if they are the right person in the right place at the right time. This is especially true on otherwise good, healthy hands. They do tend to take charge of their own lives. I read a very successful surgeon who lacked such a line but had a strong Apollo line. He was totally into his work and had no care for himself or his personal reputation.

Some palmists believe the lack of a fate line may mean the lack of luck. But those subjects either may not need luck, being capable of rising by their own hard work, or do not believe in luck in any event. However, there may be a lack of long-range direction in the person who lacks a fate line as they can only comprehend who they are in relation to their present activities and location.

A few palmists have the fate line terminating under mounts other than Saturn. To me, those are not fate lines but other lines and should not be confused with fate lines.

A fate line that terminates high and well on

Saturn traditionally indicates a person who will have a stable financial position, even in old age.

Benham takes the view that the fate line, unlike the other major lines, does not indicate health problems.[54] I disagree and have been successfully following a method suggested to me that I thought had found support in another of Benham's remarks, but I presently cannot locate it. I find the Saturn line to represent the central axis of the body; between the head and heart line represents the spine; the pelvis and hips are represented by the area just below the head line; the legs are represented by the area below that; and the neck and head extend above the heart line. This represents the "backbone" of the subject. From its base, where the feet may be found, to the top of the Saturn mount, where the top of the skull may be found, the lower limbs, spine, and skull may be traced.

By tracing the course of the fate line, I find the head line is usually about the area of the low back, around the fifth lumbar vertebra, and the heart line is usually around the juncture of the cervical and thoracic spine. Just below the head line one gets into the sacrum and hip area, and at about the age of twenty on the fate line, reading from the wrist, one finds the knees.

Breaks, bends, converging lines, and other markings indicate existing or potential problems. I was quite surprised at the accuracy of these observations after one reading in Atlanta. The subject was a slim, tall young man in a white suit who obviously had good posture. But his Saturn line indicated a gross deformity of the spine, which I proceeded to describe to him as a hunchback and a twisted back, a kyphosis and a scoliosis. I apologized for my reading, as I was sure I was in error. He smiled and asked me if I knew what he did. I said no. He then explained that he was a chiropracter and that he had developed a set of daily exercises that allowed him to stand straight. Without them he was a hunchback with a scoliosis.

This analysis has enabled me to spot the low back sufferer, the shoulder and neck problems, the knee problems, weak ankles and feet, and a variety of other problems or potential problems. Because the formations refer also to potential problems, I am not always sure I have identified problems the subject presently suffers from. Sometimes I have discovered past problems that have been corrected by surgery or other therapeutic changes.

Once, when counseling a very well-built, muscular young man, I saw no fate lines where the legs should have been. I advised him not to play American football. He answered that the issue had already been settled for him on his first week out for practice when he and the coach found out that he did not have the legs for the sport. I then explored lifetime occupations. He had the large bulge on the percussion indicating a love of water and the skin of an outdoors type of person. I advised him to go into deep sea diving. This would reduce his lifelong battle with gravity to a minimum. He answered that such was indeed one of the two occupations he was considering. Here is an excellent example of the positive use of palmistry to reduce the potential for long-term pain and serious injury. Attention to these sorts of signals could save the public and industry literally trillions of dollars over the years. My clinical findings should be followed up by serious controlled studies. This type of information should be readily available to every family physician, school, employment counselor, and physical education specialist without the need for expensive scientific apparatus or time-consuming tests.

The right hand appears to reflect the right side and vice versa. Sometimes the client will report trauma or pain to the opposite side of the body. He or she may have suffered an injury or pain to the left knee, although I have detected a weakness in the right knee. Do not be disheartened. The injury may have resulted from a long period of overcompensating for the weaker side. This is a common occurrence.

Endings and Breaks of Fate Line

A trident or forked termination is a most favorable indication if well-formed and clear, traditionally being a sure indication of outstanding success or wealth at the age it appears. Upward branches are also favorable, more so if flawless.

Yaschpaule points out that it is a principle in his hand analysis that two main lines should never clash.[55] So neither the head line nor the heart line should stop the fate line. They do at times.

Should the head line stop the fate line, we have the problem of judgment. Has the subject made a blunder in career or finance? Did he or she get too smart for himself or herself? Look to see if there are recovery fate lines.

Should the emotional line stop the judgment line, have emotional decisions gotten the better of good judgment? Or perhaps the subject has suffered some weakness of the heart. Check for other health signs.

Breaks are serious, as they mean an end to current activities, but they can be aided by overlapping or substitute lines. Often, the fate line may disappear, but one will still find strong Jupiter, Apollo, or Mercury lines or combinations of such lines that can carry on for the fate line.

Wavy and twisted lines are a problem. The subject will lack the consistency and constancy to achieve success and fortune. His material prospects will, like his personality, waver and fluctuate. Yaschpaule even believes such persons will have difficulty in having children, or if they have children, will have difficulties in their parental responsibilities.[56] Good Sun (Apollo) lines can compensate for this and other bad characteristics of the fate line.

CHAPTER NINE

OTHER LINES

SIMIAN LINE (SINGLE TRANSVERSE CREASE)

The simian line is really an alternative major line. It is characterized by one line that completely transects the palm and the absence of any distinctive heart and head line. It may have branches from this one line and it will still be considered a simian line. If there is a girdle of Venus, that may be considered a heart line and the transecting line will then be considered the head line. The differences in appearance probably lead to confusion and may be at least partially responsible for the different percentage of reports of its occurrence observed in healthy populations according to Schaumann and Alter.[1] According to Schaumann and Alter, the reported frequencies this line found in control populations varies from 1 to 15 percent and may be considered higher in those with developmental defects. Thus these have diagnostic medical value.

My favorite story about the simian line was related during a psychic fair from another palmist who had me look at her child's hand. At that time we were insisting on the existence of a single line only as the simian line and thus did not recognize the child's line as a simian line. He could have had a modified simian line. The mother had been told by another palmist when the child was very little that the simian line was a mark of being retarded. This became such an issue for her that she started studying palmistry and became a palmist. The child, as I recall, was quite healthy and intelligent.

But the story illustrates how much nonsense can be conveyed by the ill-informed palmist. While the simian crease does appear in a significant portion of those suffering from Down's syndrome, it also appears in a significant number of those with normal intellectual capacity.

Schaumann and Alter report that a single transverse crease appears in at least one palm in about half of those suffering with Down's syndrome. This is quite contrary to the unsubstantiated reports of Fenton and Wright that subjects with "Down's syndrome are no more likely to have simian lines that anyone else."[2] Differences reported were attributed by Schaumann and Alter to whether variants were counted or not. An increased frequency in this crease has also been found in subjects with other congenital defects.[3]

When the simian line is associated with Down's syndrome, it is often associated with other atavistic characteristics such as a short thumb, curved little finger, and abnormal palmprint patterns such as a wide-angle axial triradius pattern.

Asano[4] finds a simian variation the most common pattern on many Japanese Buddhist statues and says that according to ancient Eastern palmistry doctrines, it is the most noble feature possible for humans and is attributed to kings. It is found on the colossal Vairocana Buddha in the Todai-ji temple in Nada. He reports no more than 7 percent of the Japanese have this feature, and it is often found in families of genius.

The feature is a variant of Asano's F type of hand called in Japan the *masukake type*. Asano indicates in his comparison figures that it is more common with Orientals than Occidentals and tends to run highest in his figures with Gypsies (about 14.3 percent), Chinese (about 13 percent), and Koreans (about 11.2 percent).

Asano reports that subjects with the simian line are strongly individualistic and emotionally irreg-

ular. When they become very angry, they do not display it facially. Although they may care for others, they frequently appear very chilly. Socially, in his culture, they appear among the elite and capture attention as early as in primary school. Asano notes that many leaders in Japan have had this pattern and that it was prevalent among the generals during the Period of Warring States (1467–1568) that just happened to be one of the most bloody eras in Japanese history.

Asano observes that subjects with this feature tend to succeed in occupations that require manual dexterity (surgery, shiatsu, and fine draftsmanship) as well as other fields such at TV entertainment, work demanding original ideas, music, writing, and big business.

Fred Gettings[5] presumed that the simian hand was a sign of criminality as so many criminals were thought to have it. He felt this was a result of the inner conflict between the head and heart line, the restriction of the full line from moving from the conscious to the subconscious spheres of the hand. He relates these people to the cold simian line type and he reports another simian type as the earnest seeker for some inner understanding. They create some form of agony and ecstasy to relieve themselves of the intolerable burdens on their souls. One type appears to be evolving and the other devolving. Gettings reported that he was unable to divine a method of determining which was which. I believe the most modern authors on the subject would not accept the criminal typing of the hand.

Certainly Roz Levine[6] tries to reassure the subject with the simian line not to take older palmists too seriously. She finds these people tend to be laws unto themselves and can face problems exacerbated by their own intensity, especially emotional problems. They should take heart, for it is better to feel deeply than not at all, and the deep,

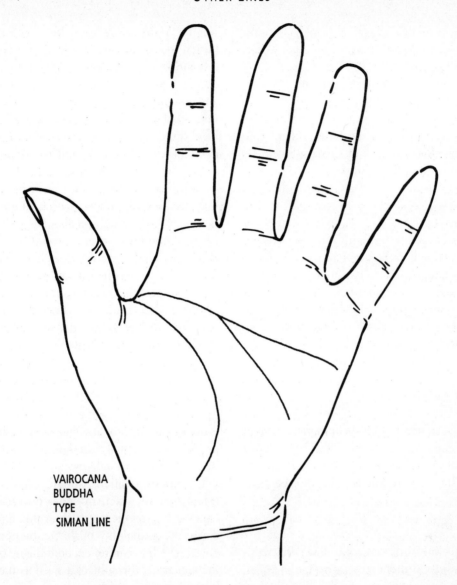

**VAIROCANA
BUDDHA
TYPE
SIMIAN LINE**

often subjective, and passionate feelings can be a source of creativity. The intense powers of concentration will serve well or ill depending on how the subject chooses to use them.

A number of palmists, for example Sorell, Fenton and Wright, Sprong, and Hansen, report that the subject may alternate between emotional extremes where the feelings are in conflict with the intellect.[7] However, the subjects will have a strong tenacity of purpose and a strong capacity for accomplishment. They may well display vigorous energies. If the hand is of an earthy quality, they could be coarse and violent.

Scheimann[8] points to the similarity of many palmists' description of the person with the simian line and the description of the psychopathic personality. The palmists find the simian line refers to the characteristics of single-mindedness and extremism, and the subjects possess "tremendous tenacity or intensity of character" (for good or ill).

The Indian palmist V. A. K. Ayer[9] finds those with the simian line to be highly introspective and egocentric, tending to be problem spouses. K. C. Sen[10] of India reports a similar finding of egocentricity. He does not consider this a happy sign, as people with this sign have difficulty working with others. However, he finds it indicative of an increased determination of character and persistence. Hutchinson notes this increased concentration power.[11] Yaschpaule[12] finds this determination can be dangerous to the subject and others, leading toward extremism in many areas and difficulty in getting along with others. Sen also notes that the position of the line, either in the head or heart line space, will determine whether intellect or sentimentality will rule, a point agreed to by Levine[13] and Yaschpaule.[14]

Some Western palmists, myself included, find that simian line subjects who buy houses, even new ones, immediately set about to remodel them. I have found these subjects also enjoy organizing new offices. This would fit with the subject described by Altman and Fitzherbert[15] who is happiest when creating; and the physically oriented are happiest when building, whether furniture, machines, or houses. It also indicates a need to command and own one's territory.

MINOR LINES

Minor lines generally only bear significance in their appearance, not their absence. They add to a reading, but their absence does not detract from a reading. The Mercury line may be an exception.

Apollo Line

The Apollo line runs vertically down the palm beginning directly under the ring or Apollo finger.

This line is also known as the Sun line, the line of creativity, brilliance, capability or success. M. N. Laffan[16] calls it the personality line. I reserve that designation for the fate line. It can indicate honor, creativity, success, intellectual ability and achievement, artistic ability, and wealth. The Sun is associated with joy. When well-formed, the line can indicate that whatever the subject does, it is done with joy. Creativity is done with love and joy. Indeed, creativity is a description of the activity undertaken through joy and love to effect one's self, environs, relations, and/or neighbors. To the extent that such activity relies on outside influences or the divine spark, then this line may indicate the availability of that influence or influences. The line can reflect both the recognition of the activity of the subject as well as the personal happiness of the subject.

The Sun line does not necessarily indicate artistic talent. It may, when well-formed, indicate a successful businessperson, good teacher, doctor, or, as Yaschpaule[17] notes, even a distinctive thief. "Robin Hood must have had a really good Sun line,"[18] he says.

If the line is deep, prominent, and favorably

formed, it is a sign of good luck or under theories of Karma, a sign of all the past merits earned from previous incarnations. That does not necessarily mean that the subject will be using his past meritorious inclinations in this life. He or she may be the worst crook and still be lucky.

The best marked Sun line is traditionally thought to start at the wrist. It is long, well marked, deep, and extends to the top of the mount of Apollo or even to the Apollo finger itself. That is highly unusual. We believe that this may be best only for some. Visual artistic capacity is more likely reflected by lines starting from the percussion.

Lines that begin from the life line can indicate success through personal effort and ability, though perhaps with initial help from family or friends. If it begins on the mount of Venus, then it increases the influence of the family. The mount of Venus is associated with the family.

A start on Luna indicates more help from outsiders as the Moon brings in foreign influences as well as imagination. If the line is long and favorable, the subject may be charismatic. This can also indicate considerable sex appeal, especially if the mount of Venus is well-formed, elevated, and of good color.

If the line begins from the plane or the mounts of Mars, the indications for success are from struggle and conflict. If it starts on the mounts, this will indicate that the subject's fighting spirit plays a great part in his or her success.

A line starting from the fate line can be a favorable sign. It could indicate, if the line is well-formed, the age when an advantageous opportunity will present itself.

A line beginning from the head line will indicate success from the subject's intellectual abilities and application. If it starts from the heart line, success will be in later life if there are other favorable signs in the hand.

If the line arises from the Mercury or line of hepatica (health), the success could arise from trade, industry, communications, or commerce. It may also show the age that the person starts to display the tendency for sound business judgment and progresses in his or her chosen field.

The line of the Sun complements the fate line, and will make up for a badly formed or missing fate line. But Yaschpaule points out that if both the Apollo and Saturn lines are badly formed at the same level, then the subject is in for some rough times.[19]

When the line ends in several vertical lines, it indicates the use of a diversity of talents. Beware of the tendency of the subject to fragment, to spread his or her talents too thinly and thus find rewards elusive from failure to concentrate. However, if a couple of lines run parallel to the Sun line on each side, this is favorable, indicating both success and a good name.

Some of my observations run counter to these traditional beliefs. I find that strong lines from the percussion indicate that the subject has an eye for beauty that others like to share. While reading in Vancouver, British Columbia, I inspected the hands of two men who both had multiple (two or three) Sun lines coming from the general area of upper Mars. The lines were deep and well formed. I noted that both could be very gifted photographers and that because there was more than one line, they would be gifted in several areas, such as in television or movies. Both turned out to be cinematographers for a very famous Italian film director noted for the visual art in his movies. I have had the camera eye and/or the ability to see what is pleasing to others confirmed many times in relation to this formation.

I warned a lady who had many lines immediately under her Apollo finger to be careful not to try to take on too many activities. Following traditional palmistry, I advised her that she would be spreading herself too thin and could never be a success. She advised me that she was perfectly happy taking on many activities and she did it every day and was quite successful. I asked her occupation. She was the manager of a large, multi-purpose convention center. I learned something. People with many lines, like many Sun lines, can undertake multiple operations or tasks, so long as they are structured under one or perhaps two umbrellas, such as home and an occupation that embraces all of the multiple subjects. The failure seems more related to those who try to perform disconnected multiple tasks.

Line of Fortune

This is a line described by Ayer.[20] He says it usually commences at the wrist and goes right up to the base of the third finger, a description of the Apollo line. He even says that the line is sometimes called the Apollo line. He indicates that it reinforces the fate line. Whereas the fate line indicates the personality of the subject, this line emphasizes divine help. Ayer states that "Education, eloquence and material prosperity or social status depend upon this line. If well-formed, the indicia is overall success and prosperity."[21]

If the line starts from the mount of Venus, then success in the arts or through the influence of one's partner is indicated. A beginning on the mount of the Moon can indicate successful musicians, actors, and painters. If it starts higher on the palm, around the plane of Mars, then the success can be after many difficulties. A beginning from the heart line indicates riches in later life.

If it ends in a bunch of sprouts, it suggests a variety of incomes from several occupations. A branch ending on Jupiter indicates a management post, branches to Saturn indicate great fame, and branches to Mercury indicate success in business, particularly if there is a trident formation.

Beware of any branch that cuts a line of union. It will indicate a miserable marriage. A star is highly desirable anywhere on the line, but a cross is pernicious. Breaks indicate domestic or financial problems, and islands can denote domestic scandals.

Decision Lines

These are fine lines that cut the fate or Apollo lines. If the lower end is on the radial side and they start from that side (are wider on that side at the end) then they indicate the subject will make their own decisions. However, if the starting and lower end is on the ulnar (percussion) side, then someone else will make the decisions. A line that is straight across is a blocking line, which either blocks the subject or forces him or her to act. A line that cuts the fate line and joins the head and heart lines indicates a lack of communication in a relationship.

Lines of Milieu

If there is a line between the fate line and the life line, Julius Spier[22] refers to it as the line of milieu and the area that it springs from (generally the area of the mount of Neptune) as the area of milieu. The milieu line will come to a halt well before the fate line. *Milieu* indicates the social environment of the subject. The line of milieu will indicate for the period it covers that the social environment or cultural setting of the subject projects an impending force in a different direction or even in opposition to the individual tendencies of the subject. The subject may have had to follow educational requirements that did not really suit his or her particular needs or tendencies, or the traditions

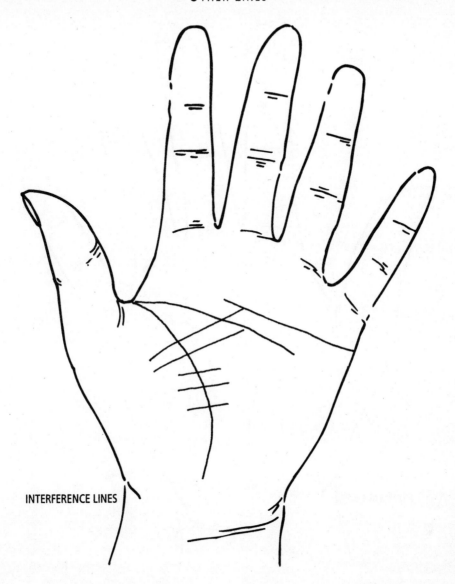

INTERFERENCE LINES

and conventions of his or her family, society, or environs did not complement or were in contrast to his or her own disposition. Certain personality traits thus become entrapped and may fail to develop or become useful. If the line is complete, the subject will be aware of these restrictions, but he or she may not be aware of them if the line is fragmented. The latter case may reflect conflicts between parents or parental repressions or aggressions that the subject may not have consciously experienced but that still had a decisive influence on his or her unconscious emotional life.

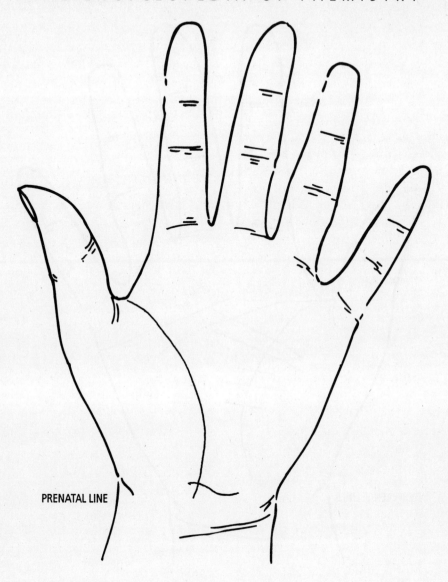

PRENATAL LINE

Spier identifies small marks and groups of lines extending in straight lines between the fate and life lines as marks of milieu.

Spier reflects that if the fate line comes from the life line, then the strength of the milieu is much stronger and more subtle because the person is not conscious of the "very roots of personality" and is "arrested by the milieu."

Interference Lines

These lines originate on the mount of Venus and proceed toward the life line. They are sometimes called worry lines. They have actual impact upon the life of the person if they actually cross the life line. Typically, a hand will show more of these lines in the first thirty-five years of life (provided that the life line is measured from above the thumb). They indicate disturbances or special changes, often external in connection, in the subject's activities or health at the periods indicated. If the line goes beyond the life line and reaches any other major line, then the influence will reach those areas. A line that reaches all the way to the heart line could signify a marriage, divorce, or birth or death of a child or loved one.

Prenatal Line

This is a line identified by Spier as an indication of a psychic link between mother and child. Spier dates the life line from the wrist and says the prenatal line starts earlier than the life line on the lower part of the mount of Venus. It cuts the life line near its beginning (if begun near the wrist) and is "either received by or joins any line, or terminates somewhere in the hand." Something happened during pregnancy that had a decided influence on the psychological development of the child. This could leave the subject with certain unexplained fears or other psychological reactions, the causes of which are consciously unknown to the subject.

Matriarchal Influence Line

Another line, on the opposite (percussion) side of the hand, at about the lower third of the mount of the Moon, may be called the matriarchal influ-

ence line. It should be a fairly strong horizontal line. We find this line on people who have to contend with a matriarch in their lives, a dominating woman, who might be someone such as a mother, a wife, or an aunt. This line is another example of how lines on the percussion can have a variety of meanings.

Sibling Lines

Fenton and Wright tossed these lines into consideration of the practicing palmist.[23] I have had only partial success in confirming any correlation of the lines to the sisters and brothers they are supposed to indicate. The lines are located on the radial side of the mount of Jupiter, are similar to attachment lines, and are supposedly concerned with siblings. My experience is that they sometimes refer to siblings that are strongly regarded by the subject, or close friends who could be considered brothers or sisters. Even so, the frequency of my observation of this phenomena does not give these lines a very high level of predictability. I now look for information on siblings on the mount of Neptune.

Parental Influence Lines

Above the thumb and on either side of the start of the life line, one may find lines or marks that seem to begin from the edge of the hand and connect to the life line and sometimes cross the life line, especially if the head line is separated from the life line. Some lines above the life line have been tentatively identified by Fenton and Wright as sibling lines. These may or may not touch the life line. I do not think I have had as much as 50 percent success in relating these lines to siblings. However, there is another explanation that I have found highly satisfactory. These lines that touch the life line indicate the influence (or lack of

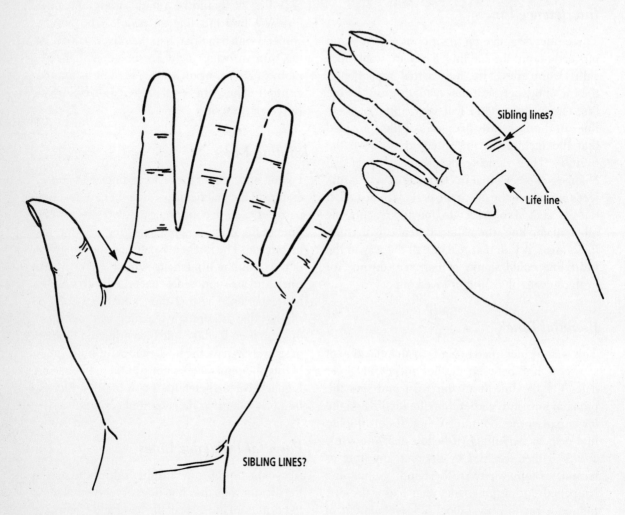

Sibling lines?

Life line

SIBLING LINES?

influence) of the parents of the subject. The father's influence is above the life line, and the mother's influence is below the life line, nearer the thumb. Lack of touching lines can indicate lack of influence.

Sometimes one will see a very strong mark above the life line with no marks going from it to cross the life line. I have found such people had a strong but distant father who was either not home much or had little interaction with the children.

Stronger, deeper lines have indicated abuse, some even physical abuse. I have also found that the lack of the lines can indicate a lack of connection. I have even found connections after death of the parent on clients who describe either coming to terms with or connecting with a departed parent at a point in the life where the influence line crosses the life line.

More recently, I have looked for color variations. If there is a red coloration on this line, I tend

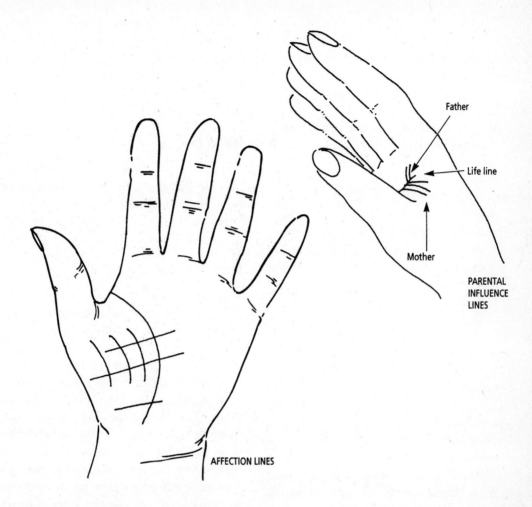

Father

Life line

Mother

PARENTAL
INFLUENCE
LINES

AFFECTION LINES

to find the relationship with the parent indicated by the line is still like an open wound. The subject has not fully dealt with that relationship. It may well be related to present difficulties the subject has with intimacy.

Affection Lines

Both vertical and horizontal lines are frequently found on Venus. Dr. Sen[24] refers to them as affection lines. A heavily lined Venus mount indicates one who is attractive to others as well as attracted by others of the opposite sex. But occasionally those lines are mere figments of an active imagination. Affections present and future will be found on the right hand. If the line does not break the life line, no matter how important the affair may seem, it will not have lasting influence.

When there are a couple of lines side by side, the subject may be running two affairs at once. Again, one of the lines may be a figment of the imagination. When the affair blossoms, Luxon and Goolden see the line moving out to cross the life line.[25]

Luxon and Goolden describe an affection link as a longer line that changes course, usually toward the mount of Mercury, which they coyly remind the reader is the home of marriage lines.

The formation of the line reveals much of the character of the relationship. If it stops at the head line, obstacles are encountered to impair its progress. The obstacle is probably some thought pattern that suggests another course, though Luxon and Goolden mention parental objections, good intentioned interference by others, and decisions to wait.

If the line ends at the heart line, this will mean that the other partner is already married and can not go farther. An affection line crossed by a Jupiter line may indicate that the subject's ambition gets in the way of the affair and terminates it.

If the line ends in an X, the partner is responsible for the termination and it may come as a shock to the subject. If the line hooks down, the subject is happy to be responsible for the split in the relationship.

Breaks in the affection line can indicate a stormy path, but marriage can be the outcome if the line reaches the mount of Mercury. Islands on the line indicate jealousy, and it can be on the part of the subject if his or her heart line indicates that tendency. Otherwise, the partner is jealous.

Those with an avaricious nature will have an affection line that leaves Venus and heads directly toward Jupiter, for that signifies a pair bonding with a rich and successful member of the opposite sex. The line that travels to the mount of the Moon indicates a relationship with a foreigner or one who lives abroad. If there is a strong fork in the lower part of the life line, look to a successful consummation of the relationship and living abroad.

Branches

As a general rule, lines which resemble branches that rise up toward the fingers are good omens, and those that fall indicate loss of energy or other losses.

Family Lines

These lines follow the same curve as the life line and the line of Mars on the mount of Venus within the confines of the life line. Sometimes they represent members of the family. Sometimes they represent other influences on the person, such as friends so close that they could be considered family, guardian angels, or spiritual guides or protectors. The stronger the marking, the more influence the person has over the subject's life. The period of influence is measured by a life line comparison. The lines on the subjective hand will refer more to the biological family, while those of the active hand will refer also to the chosen family (including friends and loved ones).

They may also be called influence lines.

Family Ring

David Brandon-Jones describes this as the line at the joint of the second phalange of the thumb with the mount of Venus.[26] As most people find raising a family or living in a family difficult, these often are chained or have islands. Breaks and incomplete arcs suggest an unsuccessful relationship or unfulfilled desire for children. A strong, emphatic line indicates a deep devotion to family. If the family is of no particular importance, there may be hardly any line at all. If the line starts at the ring and continues through the life line to the fate line, and the fate line is broken up after it is touched by the line, Compton reminds us to look to the family for the fate problems.[27] I have found major tragedy reflected by stars on this line.

If there are two rings, Fenton and Wright[28] suggest the subject may be involved in life with two families and two homes. As one would expect, dots and discolorations indicate troubles. Fenton and Wright propose that lines starting at the rings and crossing the life line are family interference in the person's life. A single, strong line like a light crease, seen radiating from the ring to the life line, can indicate the very strong family loyalty of the subject. If the crease rises toward the fingers, the love goes toward the parents, while if it falls, the love is directed toward the children.

Gibson[29] differentiates lines of family from a formation she calls the thumb chain. The family lines she sees are those curved lines on the mount of Venus that follow the life line path, following courses like the line of Mars. These can indicate friends as well as family members and others who have strong influences on the subject.

The Thumb Chain

Beneath the second phalange of the thumb, Gibson describes a line that separates the thumb from the mount of Venus. A poorly defined, chained line, according to Gibson, indicates an argumentative person who likes to get in the last word. Could this be another of those dual or multiple value lines? Is the family ring wrong, or is Ms. Gibson wrong? Until we can begin to make some

definitive studies of all the palm lines, we may never know.

Girdle of Venus

This was once known as the line of prostitution. It was said to indicate coquetry and sexual license. That is not the accepted view today, especially where the line is well-marked and the other qualities of the hand favor other activities.

Yaschpaule admonishes us all to, "Fit the line to the subject, not the subject to the line."[30] Look at the underlying character of the subject seen from the larger picture — the hand shape and size, the color, the tonus, the dermatoglyphics, etc. — and then see what added strengths and weaknesses or attributes the lines may indicate.

The girdle of Venus forms a semicircle running from the space between the little and ring fingers to the space between the Jupiter and Saturn fingers. It is often incomplete and frequently more than one girdle or partial girdle will be observed. Similar attributes can be found from lines that seem to start on the mount of Mercury and go to the mount of Jupiter that are not true heart lines. Some consider the girdle of Venus a secondary heart line.

I would call it the crescent of empathy or clairsentience. Persons who have it also possess more than normal empathy for the feelings and emotions of those around them. It is an indication of one of the most common of the psychic gifts, clairsentience or empathy, the keen psychic ability to perceive what cannot be observed through the normal senses about the feelings or perceptions of others. Until such persons become aware of what they are doing when they exercise this normal ability, their own emotions and cognitive thinking can be a mystery to themselves. A couple of examples may help to describe this condition.

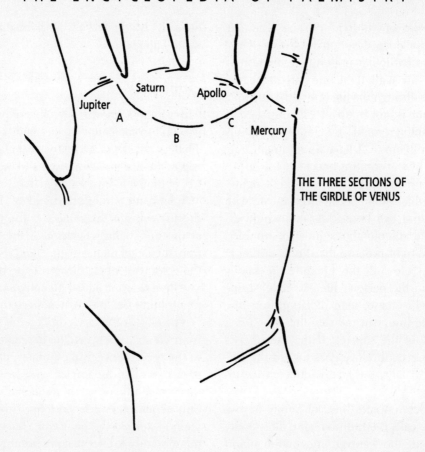

THE THREE SECTIONS OF
THE GIRDLE OF VENUS

Subjects may find that they can watch a comedy at home and never laugh, but if they see the same comedy in a crowded theater or with others who are amused, they laugh heartily. Tears may also flow. They will know when others are happy and sad, but more to the point, they may feel happy or sad without knowing why until they realize that they are mirroring the feelings of others. They may take tests on subjects they know thoroughly in the company of others who do not know the subject and feel the confusion of the other minds when it comes to answering questions. The confusion can be so complete that they can miss answers they know before and after the test when they are no longer in the company of the uninformed persons who were also taking the test. Thus, it is easier for people such as this to become overwhelmed by the excitement and emotions of others. They need to be taught from a very early age to protect themselves so that they can always quickly identify with their true feelings, emotions, and knowledge.

Fenton and Wright divide the girdle of Venus into three sections. If the fate line touches section A while the life line tends toward the fate line, the subject is career minded, and he or she will be married to that career. If the life line curves around the mount of Venus, then he or she will look for emotional fulfillment rather than career.

If A and B are both present, then the person can walk out of the marriage in favor of the career if the marriage interferes with personal ambitions.

Possession of A and C without B indicates a more intellectual empathy, a person drawn by the intellectual aspects of others, the person who can talk well or tends to spiritually communicate.

B is the most sensitive part of the girdle. The subject may tend to be hypersensitive and over-react to any supposed insults or slights. He or she can go through enormous midlife crises.

C is the indicia that these people like to flock together with like-minded souls. They need to communicate, to be understood. As their preoccupations are often rather particular or perhaps intellectual, they will pick and choose friends carefully. Being impressionable, they may seek life teachers. They can find, when older, that they have little left in common with their spouses.

As children, these people, for sheer protection, have become sensitive, shy, and wary of other people. If the head line has curved toward Luna, their intuition and imagination has added to this.

People with this sign often have more difficulty recovering from trauma. They are emotionally as well as physically at risk. Fenton and Wright note that traumas that have happened at the age of about twenty to twenty-one can also be found on the mount of Neptune, in the life line, or the fate line in the form of islands.[31]

The girdle has a history of strong sexual connotation. Vera Compton[32] refers to much of this as she notes that a girdle that travels from the edge of the hands in broken lines that cuts across a line of attachment (relationship line) indicates that the subject will ruin his or her own domestic happiness by sexual unfaithfulness or inconsistency. Even if it only runs from the first finger joint to the edge of the hand, it will indicate a highly sexually imaginative mind. But a line that runs from be-

tween the first two fingers (Jupiter and Saturn) to between the last two fingers (Apollo and Mercury) is a sign of love of harmony and beauty in all forms. A star on the girdle indicates a break in emotional affairs. An island can either mean that the person is clairvoyant or it could indicate the person has an unconventional emotional life.

I have this line on both hands. It is broken. When I was about fifty and was studying irridology, I returned to college to study human anatomy. The course required a lab test of the names of the muscles of a cat we had all dissected. Four of us would take the test together. We would write down the names of the muscles as the assistant lab instructor pointed them out. It was an excellent course, and we even got to observe open heart surgery from the position of the anesthesiologist during the course.

Most of the students in the course were taking it in hopes of entering the medical profession or some related field, so my companions at the test were young premed or prenursing students. They were required to pass the course to go on with their chosen careers. Thus these tests generated considerable emotional energy. However, I was quite composed, relaxed, and confident. The instructor pointed out the first muscle and I drew confusion. I passed that off as the slowness of age. However, when the confusion persisted after he pointed out the second muscle, I decided there was something wrong. Then I recalled my palmistry findings, leaned forward, covered my paper, crossed my legs, and physically shut out the other three students at the table. Immediately I began to recall the names of the muscles. I now understand many of my similar failures in earlier life. I am an empath, highly sensitive to the emotions of others in the immediate vicinity.

This sensitivity, until it is recognized, can play havoc in other areas of life. In conjugal embraces, those who possess it can immediately feel the slightest change of emotion of their partners. This can result in hurt feelings if one does not understand and allow the play of the other's emotions. I can jump to conclusions too quickly and fail to recognize that others still have the right to modulate their emotions by their rational thought processes.

Intuitive Crescent

This is also called the line of the Moon, the intuition line, Diana's bow, or the line of Uranus. It follows an inward curve or crescent beginning in the Luna area, often in the Pluto region, and traveling back toward the percussion in the area of Mercury. Gibson calls it the twin of the cephalic line and those who fancy palmistry as an occult science are convinced that this line is purely a psychic representation. Altman calls it the line of Uranus and notes that it is often found on clairvoyants, mediums, and healers. I found an unbroken one on a professional racetrack tipster. The line should be unbroken if one is to gamble on the hunches that the player subject will form. Branches or frays show a nervous, perhaps irritable disposition while breaks indicate spasmodic, unreliable intuition. Islands may indicate a sleepwalker when found on the subjective palm. If the crescent is found on the active hand, then the gifts are still there, but slower to develop. A reverse crescent indicates the hunches are always wrong. This person has an uncanny ability to miss.

I observed this feature, totally unbroken, on a lady, and jokingly said I would like to go to the horse races with her. She asked, "Do you know what I do for a living?" Having never seen the lady before, I said I did not. As with most of my clients, I had no idea what her occupation was. She said, "I write tip sheets for three racetracks." Curiously

enough, she would lose money at the slot machines in Las Vegas. So I wonder if the intuition must be related to living things. I have heard of others who sense something about slots that tells them which machines are about to pay off, but I have not had the opportunity to see if these people have the line of intuition.

Ring of Solomon

This is a ring or line beneath the index finger and is a traditional sign of wisdom and may be one side of a square that is valued as a teacher's square. It indicates a distinct interest in metaphysical matters. It is like a wedding ring to the occult. It indicates a gift for understanding people and for having psychological insight. It may appear doubled and shows a real talent for psychology and can be useful in business and in practicing law or psychology. David Brandon-Jones[33] distinguishes between the curved ring and the straight line, calling the latter a sympathy line and indicating it reflects sympathy that is wise and universally directed to all fellow creatures.

Some palmists have considered the ring of Solomon rare, but I find it quite often and it is one of the signs I look for when investigating the psychic abilities of the subject. Yaschpaule[34] indicates that when joined by a good head line, strong thumb, and a well-marked fate line, it indicates a mind that probes the depths of human understanding. It shows latent occult studies ability and that the subject may become a good astrologer, palmist, numerologist, or in my own experience, card reader or other psychic reader. Yaschpaule finds the mark on businessmen to be a sign of keen business intuition.

Compton[35] finds this ring associated with a propensity for philosophical studies, and observes that eminent theologians often have this sign.

Fenton and Wright[36] share another palmist's report that the ring belongs to people who help others and that if the heart line reaches into the ring, looking after others may take the place of normal family life.

Sprong describes several types of rings.[37] The one that travels deeply over the full mount of Jupiter suggests that these people retain some lustfulness. They may have higher aims, but they still desire the pleasures of the flesh. They are quite physical when it comes to expressing their love and would make good massage therapists.

Another ring described by Sprong runs just below the upper border of the mount of Jupiter. These people are more cerebral in their love. They would make good psychologists.

The middle position of the ring indicates the capacity for both physical and mental altruistic love. These subjects could be good social workers. Sprong notes that this ring is also called the ring of renunciation, named for the ability of the possessors to renounce attachment to worldly pleasures.

Broken rings indicate the seeker of harmony who has not yet found it, the thin ring indicates the subject has only tentatively found his altruistic self, and islands on the ring indicate that there is disruption in the ability to help others while the desire lingers on. Finally, Sprong notes that a thin ring on a high mount of Jupiter or under an overdeveloped Jupiter finger indicates Jupiter's pride will overcome feelings of altruism and limit action.

Sprong describes the line from his reading of *Hasta Samudrika Shastra*,[38] calls the line *diksha rekha* and describes it as the line of renunciation when it merges into a low-set heart line to form a triangle. Such a feature combines the highest forms of love, duty, conscientiousness, and unselfish devotion to country, to truth, and non-violence with the greatness of the abilities of renunciation.[39] If there is a triangle found in this mark from a fork in the heart line under Saturn to the ring of Solomon, we have the sign of the yogi, that is, a person having union with god.

Ring of Saturn — Balance Line

This is rarely seen. It is a ring beneath the Saturn finger on the mount of Saturn. It is generally considered a destructive mark, perhaps preventing the smooth flow of life forces to and from the fate line. It is a barrier to the fate and personality of the subject. The subject will feel an unsteady fate, may jump from one occupation to another or from job to job. Persistent failure and inability to get along with others may dog the subject. The unfavorable aspects are lessened if the ring is fragmented. Yaschpaule believes that when the ring is found in the hand, not only will the mount of Saturn be badly placed in the hand, but also badly aspected in the chart or conjoined by a malefic planet.[40]

Biccum[41] calls this formation the balance line. It can be present as one line or as two, separated or crossing. He contends that the line shuts out seriousness, wisdom, and balancing qualities. Those who possess such a line can either develop into bad characters or shift from one activity to another with no continuity and end up as failures. The separated line indicates the tendency to jump from occupation to occupation, but it does not necessarily mean failure. Crossed on a bad hand, it could indicate a potential suicide victim.

Asano[42] has a different observation to make of the ring of Saturn. He proposes that it is a sign of interest in homosexuality or such a desire for unusual sexual experiences that ordinary intercourse does not satisfy the subject.

Fenton and Wright[43] concur with most palmists

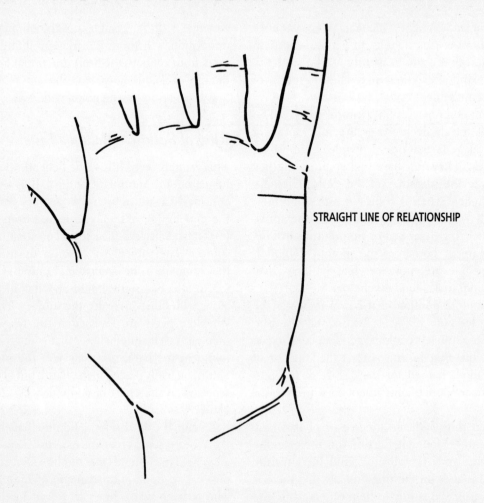

STRAIGHT LINE OF RELATIONSHIP

that the ring cuts off the balancing influence of the Saturn finger from the rest of the person. This they believe forces the subject into the position of a lone wolf who has difficulty relating to others. One wonders what energy exercises using the movement of Chi, Qi, Xi, and Kundalini might do toward healing this break in personality.

There is another much more common feature found under Saturn that is not necessarily always recognized as a ring but has some of the same action. I look to see if the lines (fate, heart, and/or girdle of Venus) form a V or a scattered ring under Saturn. If I find this, I know the person has a natural tendency to feel trapped. They need to live in homes with views and feel that they can escape. They may have a constant need to travel, even if only for short trips. This is not a good omen for the person with a twisted little finger and we could well look for jail in their past and/or future. This could also be true of the person with the pure ring of Saturn.

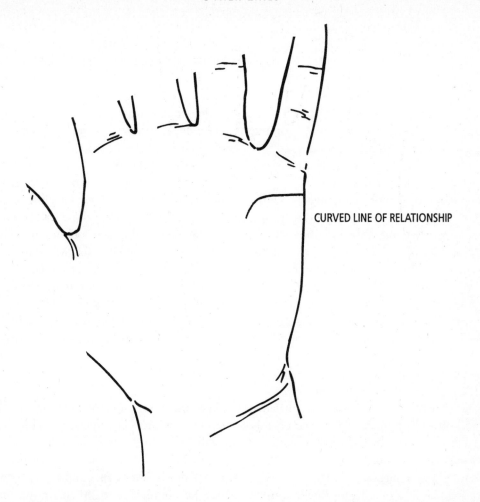

CURVED LINE OF RELATIONSHIP

Ring of Apollo

These are blocking horizontal lines, not to be confused with girdles of Venus, on the mount of Apollo, indicating forces at cross purposes with creative abilities and other influences represented by the line of Apollo. They are horizontal and short. Defects in the Apollo line, such as these, are connected in some traditional palmistry with eye defects.

Ring of Mercury

This is not to be confused with a relationship line. Like rings of Apollo, rings of Mercury are short and horizontal. They are found just below the Mercury finger toward the inside of the mount as opposed to the percussion. Here we have a negative force applied to the good qualities of the Mercury line. It could indicate a break in studies and could be bad news for businessmen or others who depend upon the strength of the matters represented by Mercury.

Relationship Lines (Nesting Lines)

These are also called marriage lines, affection lines, and lines of union. They are found coming from the percussion across the mount of Mercury. They may be seen in a variety of shapes and sizes, some of which are illustrated below.

The configuration pictured on page 177 indicates a good relationship when the lines are deeply etched. If long, extending far across the palm to beneath the Saturn, Apollo, or Jupiter fingers, palmists often say it indicates the relationship is with a soul mate over several lifetimes.

If the line turns down, as it does in the illustration above, it traditionally indicates disappointment in the relationship before it is finished. The disappointment could lead to a divorce, or the partners may tolerate miserable circumstances to preserve the marriage or keep the peace.

When the line turns up, it indicates that the partner will do well in the world. However, this could lead to jealousy or the feeling of being inadequate or left behind. Sprong,[44] by contrast, finds that an upward curve suggests a longing for spiritual freedom, that is, a longing for freedom from attachment. These subjects may not see the necessity of marriage. This may be especially so if the subject tends to hold his or her little finger separate. These subjects understand that partners do not have to be bound physically and traditionally to enjoy a strong spiritual bond.

If the relationship line is cut off by a vertical slash, this indicates a rather abrupt, sudden ending of the relationship or marriage.

If we have a less drastic curve upward than in the third example and there is a branch line, this branch line may indicate a successful hobby or interest of the subject while the partner's success is not so threatening. Roz Levine[45] indicates that if we find a three-pronged fork in the line, we have a problem with a ménage à trois and the middle line represents the interfering lover.

The appearance of a loop on the relationship line indicates illness or some fairly severe problem for the partner. This mark may come and go.

Almost parallel lines show a gradual drifting apart in a relationship. Partners coexist for years, but marriage is not emotionally close or satisfying. They may split up after the children are grown.

If the relationship line touches the heart line it indicates a sad widow or widower who looks back fondly at his or her mate and their relationship. But if the relationship line loops upward toward the Mercury finger, it should not be confused with a ring of Mercury. It denotes the perpetual spinster or widower. It is a bad gamble to marry such a subject if one is looking for a long life. Tradition is that they either never marry or lose their mates through death.

The final variation on relationship lines are companion lines. The relationship line has a fine, parallel line, indicating the subject is not completely fulfilled by a relationship or marriage, no matter how close or successful it is. The subject may be committed to an interesting career or hobby or may need affairs or outside relationships. Look at the heart line. If it curves toward Jupiter but tends to weaken or soften toward the end, the relationship may be sexually unfulfilling. If the heart line curves up, then sharply downward, the subject may need a close relationship with a person of his or her own sex and this could either mean the need of a companion or latent homosexuality. It is difficult to sort these matters out.

Alternative (or confirming) lines of union can be found from lines that start on the mount of the Moon and join the fate line. In strictly monoga-

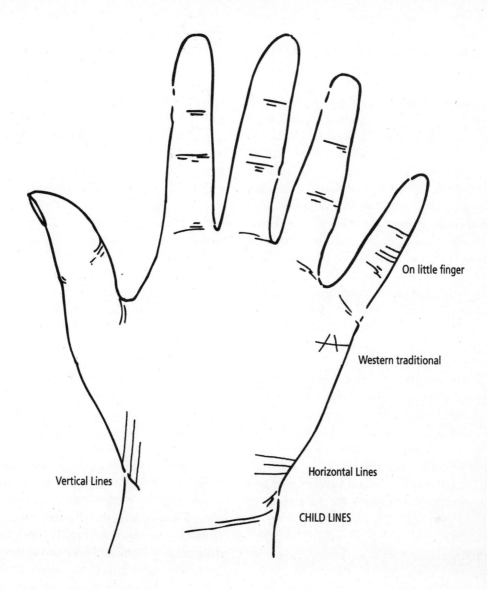

On little finger

Western traditional

Horizontal Lines

CHILD LINES

Vertical Lines

mist societies, the strongest will indicate the line of marriage, and any others will indicate casual affairs. In Western society, they could indicate marriages, affairs, or relationships. I have had some success in dating marriages from strong lines of union in this part of the hand.

Also, in checking for potential times of relationships, I have looked for merely angle lines crossing the line of fate and possible appropriate influence lines that touch both the head and heart and indicate a fate line connection. Hope springs eternal, especially in the mind of the romantic. Or, As Dr.

Sen reminds us, lines grow on hands and we need not be cruel.

We gained great insight into relationship lines at a party for a number of retired, Orthodox Jewish couples. One lady displayed about a dozen relationship lines on the palm of her predominant hand. It was a crowded room and I was a little intimidated by her happy husband of sixty years prancing about under his yarmulke. So we explored, using each relationship line for approximate ages of the lady. Did her marriage become warmer, more cozy, when the line was there? She answered in the affirmative and confirmed that when the line was absent, she and her husband were busy with raising children or other businesses.

Thus we learned that relationship lines do not necessarily reflect different people. They may reflect a period in a person's life when he or she very dearly needs a mate, a companion to build a nest with. When two are very close together and seem to overlap in time, then we find overlapping relationship commitments. These may be represented by work outside of the home or a *ménage à trois*. Usually one line appears to be secondary to the other line. If the secondary line is above, I have usually found that the outside interest has been that of the mate. If it is below, I have found that outside interest to belong to the subject being read.

Child Lines

Since at least the advent of family planning, birth control devices, and the like, these have never been particularly accurate indicators of children. The strong vertical lines are supposed to indicate the sons, while the weaker vertical lines and the diagonal lines are supposed to indicate the daughters. If the lines wander around to the side, they are supposed to indicate wayward children. Broken lines indicate difficult relationships with the child, and islands indicate temporary problems.

I now only look to these lines to see if they confirm strong horizontal lines I find on the lower mount of the Moon, vertical lines on the lower part of Venus, and horizontal lines on the palm side of the middle phalange of the little finger. I average these out, putting particular weight on the lunar lines, and then consider where the subject lives. I have found that those who live in more rural areas seem to have larger families. If not all of the children are born to the subjects, they may marry someone with the added children, or they may treat their pets as children, or perhaps, even figuratively, adopt others as children.

When the number of other vertical lines on Mercury exceed those on the lower mount of the Moon, they may indicate possible grandchildren. I am having a much higher success rate with this approach.

Dr. Sen[46] reports several other places I use to look for children. Child lines can be found at the base of the thumb on the mount of Venus. If the lines are thick and clear-cut, they indicate sons; if they are short, thin lines, they indicate daughters. Another view is to look to the family ring, that ring at the base of the thumb, and count the big islands as sons and the small islands as daughters. I have had no success with this method. Sen reports that children have also been read between the lines of the heart and head, and his drawing shows a number of horizontal lines in this area. I do not use this method. Others have taught that these lines indicate the enemies we draw to ourselves. Dr. Sen further notes that the lines of children in the hands of *yogis* and *sadhus* or monks indicate disciples. Two other places Dr. Sen reports also indicate children. One is any vertical clear-cut lines on the medial phalange of Mercury, with the number of lines indicating the number of children. The second is the medial (middle) phalange of the Saturn (second) finger where similar clear-cut vertical lines indicate children and counting these lines indicates the number of prominent children the subject will have.

Dr. Sen and others warn to be cautious when reading couples and finding a different number of child lines on each subject. This is certainly not unusual in a society like ours, in which broken homes are so prevalent. But in some societies in the world, a careless statement based upon such observations could be quite hurtful.

Inheritance Lines

These are small hash marks between the Apollo and Mercury fingers that are supposed to represent inheritances, though the amounts may not be large. They are some promise of money.

Rascettes of Venus, Bracelets

Rascettes of Venus are also referred to as bracelets. They are lines or chains below the base of the palm on the wrist. There can be one to five. Traditionally, each full bracelet represents twenty-five to thirty years of good health. If the top one tends to be peaked under the mount of Neptune on a lady, then she may have trouble in childbearing. If it is frayed, chained, or, according to Gibson, close or actually on the palm, it will signify that hard work will be necessary to achieve success. If it is well-formed, clear, and well-defined, it adds to the promise of life fairly free of excessive struggle.

Biccum[47] agrees with the pregnancy observations and further indicates that if the rascette tends to rise in the middle in the male, it could indicate a delicacy of the abdominal organs.

Line of Mars

This line runs parallel and very close to the life line on the side of the mount of Venus. It does not touch that line and is regarded as a sister to the life line. As a sister line, it gives strong vitality support to the life line. A well-formed line is a sign of strong physical vitality, courage, and strength. If there is a break in the life line where the Mars line is present, there is protection from illness or accident attributable to the break. Yaschpaule indicates that if the Mars line is very close to the life line, the subject will be quarrelsome by nature and perhaps litigious (look for corresponding lines on upper Mars).[48] Yaschpaule also indicates that should this line cross the life line and go to the mount of the Moon, it will take on the characteristics of the via lascivia. Sprong[49] reports that in women, the support indicated by the line of Mars is generally found in a relationship, whether with a partner, father, or friend, who aids them through life. We have even found a number who have referred to this friend as being a guardian angel or spirit guide. Sprong finds that in macho men this line usually indicates strengthening of the life force, while those who have more of a feminine balance may be found to have a partner, as is the case with women.

Biccum[50] calls this line the warrior line. He agrees that its effect is to strengthen the life line. He explores a number of different endings to the line outside of the mount of Venus. Whether these lines indicate a long and vigorous life, perhaps of great travelers, or whether the person will die suddenly after great excess, exhaustion, suicide, or other self-harm from insanity, or will just become insane, all depend upon accompanying marks, splits, line ending places or, in the case of vigor, lack of marks. In other words, Biccum depends on reading several different characteristics together.

Frustration Lines

These lines appear on the thumb and other fingers. They tend to cross the fingers horizontally. They appear to dam the flow of energy. On the thumb they often represent deeply felt angers. They are frustrations to formulating will when on the second phalange of the thumb, and carrying out will when on the distal, nail phalange of the thumb. Sprong appears to agree with this analysis.[51] We can determine if they have been overcome by looking to see if there are vertical lines that cut through these lines and run along for a distance farther toward the nail ending of the fingers. These cutting lines indicate spiritual or higher conscious growth that has in effect taken the subject beyond that frustration and anger.

Schaumann and Alter[52] describe such lines as white lines. The name is derived from their appearance in fingerprints. They note that these lines can disappear partially or completely. Their incidence appears to increase with age. Their prevalence in normal populations is uncertain. Even the cause is not well understood, with dish washing and water immersion being considered as one of the causes. Even hereditary factors have been considered.

When I see such lines, especially on the distal phalange of the thumb, I suggest to the clients that that they have a coyote or crow as their totem spirit, or that their higher power is a trickster. They will find that directions in life are incomplete or inaccurate. They will take something that must be assembled from the box of life, read the directions to put slot A into slot B, and find their material has two slot A's and no slot B. The frequency of this finding can be determined by the area of the thumb crossed by the white lines. The solution for these people seems to lie in their going within to find directions in life and not relying on the standard advice and directions they receive.

Traditional Travel Lines

These lines that run horizontally on the mount of Mars do not necessarily mean that a trip will be taken, but only that the desire is there. We have seen hands of world travelers with no travel lines. They seem to be at home wherever they are. People with travel lines are restless and imaginative. These clients may not feel comfortable at home and can have a nervous disposition. If one is curious as to where they would like to go, follow the suggestion of Fenton and Wright.[53] Superimpose the globe between the wrist and the mount of upper Mars and look at the lines as representing the longitudes of desired travels. I dumbfounded a client recently by picking out his immediate desire to go to Spain.

Alternate Travel Lines

These lines that branch off from the life line I have found more indicative of actual travel. Altman and Fitzherbert,[54] Reid,[55] Brandon-Jones,[56] Yaschpaule,[57] Brenner,[58] and Grady[59] also find them to be travel lines. Compton[60] refers to one of these lines as the line of restlessness and associates it with traditional travel lines. Only very clear, long branches can be interpreted, according to Hutchinson,[61] as an actual wish to travel. Dating is somewhat easier on these lines, though I can be baffled by the long line indicating a distant move later in life across a sea or continent. Many times I find it reflects an immigration in youth from another continent to North America. Finding travel lines branching downward from the life line is a far cry from the traditional view of Benham that these lines represent a dissipation of energy in the vitality line and at a point where the rising lines stop and the drooping lines begin we find the turning point of life and the fall from the zenith of the subject's abilities.[62]

Lines of Opposition — Litigation Lines

These are referred to by Litzka Gibson[63] as being similar to relationship lines, proceeding from the percussion, but traveling across the mount of upper Mars instead of the mount of Mercury. She says they represent the opposition of others that the subject frequently invites. If short, they signify petty and insignificant matters. As they grow longer, the antagonism grows greater and can indicate lawsuits. A long line that cuts into the lines of Mercury, Apollo, Saturn, the head line, or the life line can threaten fame, fortune, mind, honor, or family, depending on the lines cut. Gibson believes that such a threat is always a litigious one. This could be called the lawsuit line. The line can also curve upward. If there is another fate line and it curves across the heart line, it may mean litigation over affections. Otherwise, it can be a special fate line that indicates drawing personality from one's own strong sense of justice.

Dr. Sen[64] recognizes the two mounts of Mars as seats where palmists may read enemies and reported in his 1960 work that all European palmists agreed that horizontal lines on upper Mars from the percussion reflected enemies. If they are long and strong enough to cross the lines of fate and the Sun, then they indicate persons who will hinder the success of the subject's career and success. He notes that this is also the area where litigation is observed, and if there are small horizontal lines that connect with other lines from the family ring area, they will indicate litigation among members of the family. He further notes that if the lines are seen as coming from lower Mars, the enemies are of the same sex as the subject. The lines they cut can suggest the problems they cause, such as life line and health, fate line and financial losses, head line and mental worries. If the lines come from the mount of Venus, then Dr. Sen holds that they represent enemies of the opposite sex.

I comfort my clients with the advice that the enemies are only there to emphasize a life lesson and once it is learned, they will be free of the problem. Of course, I do not guarantee freedom from the enemies.

Via Lascivia-Poison Bar or Hypothenar Bar

Andrew Fitzherbert[65] calls this a poison bar or hypothenar bar, and Litzka Gibson[66] calls it a cephalic line. Because Gibson's cephalic line is described as a different type of line, we will deal with it separately. Gibson also refers to a line of escape that runs between the mounts of Venus and Luna that indicates the desire to seek some form of escape through wandering, drink, or other indulgences that seems to have a closer connection to our description of the via lascivia. This would be closer to Compton's[67] via lascivia described as an indicator of restlessness, the love of exhilaration, and emotional sensitivity.

Fitzherbert's poison bar or poison line or hypothenar bar and extended poison line describe, in form, location, direction, and reflection, very much what I have learned of the via lascivia. This is also true of Carol Hellings White's[68] line of Neptune and Diana's arrow. The bar extends horizontally across the mount of the Moon and indicates the subject should have strong reactions to drugs, alcohol, and chemicals. He or she is strongly subject to either allergic or addictive reactions or both. The closer it comes to the life line, the stronger is the reaction.

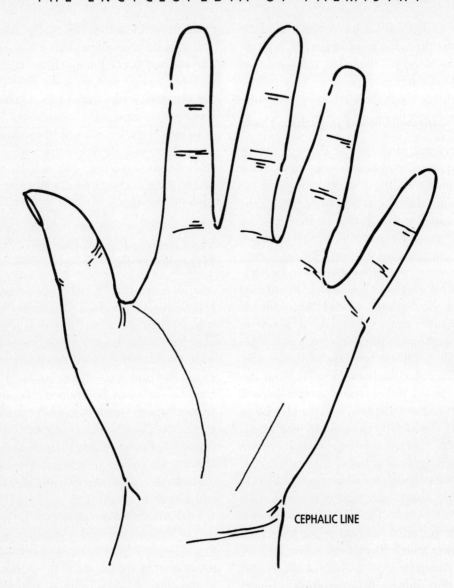

CEPHALIC LINE

Beryl Hutchinson[69] believes these lines show "a strong awareness of affinity with Nature" that drugs unduly affect. She indicates that homeopaths frequently show the transverse mark on their mounts of Luna.

Yaschpaule[70] describes a via lascivia as a cross between a poison line and a cephalic line and as a sister line to the line of Mercury. It should be parallel to the line of Mercury, starting near the base of the mount of Luna and ending near the top of the mount of Luna. Psychos[71] agrees. That is how, Yaschpaule says, it should be formed. However, he says he has seldom found it that way but has found it as a semicircular line from the mount of Luna to the mount of Venus. He finds this formation a menace, indicating the subject will debase himself or herself and yield to temptation, which is very much like falling to allergies or addictions. Should the line be curved and wavy, the subject will have many love affairs and will have a craving for variety and excitement.

Looking at the health lines that intrude from the percussion on the palm, I have found that this line should occupy the area of about the liver-stomach level, about one-third to halfway down toward the wrist from a point on the percussion level with the start of the head line.

Cephalic Line

Gibson[72] calls this line the cephalic line and notes that it is also called the Milky Way and the via lascivia. She runs it parallel to the health line (rather than at right angles to it), more toward the mount of the Moon than the health line, and considers it a sister line sometimes strengthening the health line.

When of good quality, it can add to the energies of the health line and possibly indicate the subject has the ability to conduct two enterprises simultaneously. It also strengthens health line deficiencies unless it crosses the health line. It improves this tendency as it grows longer, but if it crosses the health line, it will indicate a conflict of interest.

If the cephalic line is wavy or curves toward upper Mars, it indicates the subject is given to excesses, dissipation, or extreme sensuality if it is found in combination with weak palms or other similar signs. Stars on these lines indicate riches will be soon squandered, if other indications are bad (such as a weak thumb). So it can indicate a fast-moving wheel of fortune.

From Gibson's description of the cephalic line, we may well wish to consider it a separate line from the via lascivia that runs at right angle to the health and life lines. However, she seems to have agreement from the Indonesian, Yaschpaule.[73]

I also suggest that vertical lines along the edge of the percussion can be associated with liver weaknesses or complaints.

Health Lines or Communication Lines

Health Lines on the Percussion: Traditionally, the Mercury line has been considered the line indicative of health near the percussion. Some of us have had real problems associating the line of Mercury with health. I believe there are far more reliable markings on the percussion. Starting at the wrist and going up the percussion side of the hand, I look to the lines one commonly refers to as travel lines. Upon these I superimpose the major chakras so that the root chakra is near or at the wrist and the crown chakra is at the heart line. I anatomically superimpose the corresponding internal organs for reference.

Roughly where a line running parallel to the heart line from the start of the head line meets the percussion would be the throat chakra area. The external genitalia and anus would be at or just above the wrist and the top of the head at the heart line. I relate corresponding internal organs to any lines seen. A mosaic of potential weaknesses in the body will present itself, on the theoretical order of iris and pupil mosaic foundations of iridology. The spine and central axis of the body is covered under the fate line.

Benham may have been the first to discover the correlation of lines and markings on the percussion to health problems.[74] He clearly challenged calling the lines on the mount of Luna travel lines and reported they were health indicators. However, he did support finding that the Mercury line would indicate the state of the liver and digestive system and related illnesses.[75] I am not so impressed. I have found some tentative correlation between downward sloping lines in the area of Luna, Pluto, and Uranus and some digestive problems such as constipation or diarrhea.

Enid Hoffman[76] pictures a number of lines from the percussion much as I have discussed from Benham's comments on the mount of the Moon and my own experience in studying health and the hand. Hoffman indicates that some of these lines[77] show stress on the spleen (they appear to be at about that level) and conflicts with authority. Another picture is like the ladder of Mercury (see below) and shows multiple horizontal lines along the percussion.[78] Hoffman finds these show inner tension and anxiety that can cause digestive problems. There is a conflict between subjective feelings and objective beliefs and attitudes, she says. I would find such a person to have a fairly delicate constitution and in need of watching his or her health, living in clean air, walking, getting more rest, and watching diet.

Hoffman shows an additional set of lines on the percussion[79] with some of the lines longer than the others, which may indicate stress on the liver and spleen, and she adds that these lines can result from difficulties with relationships with power figures. The lower, longer line looks to me like the matriarchal line and the upper one could be at the level of the spleen, stomach, pancreas, or liver (it is not clear). It might be high enough to encompass the lungs and heart.

To the extent that any of these lines are discolored, reddened (perhaps healing) or darkened (perhaps diseased) we may discern both present and potential future health problems. Lines at the stomach level frequently indicate food allergies and if combined with liver-level lines, alcohol or

other detoxification problems. Lung-level lines can indicate airborne allergies. Many lines can indicate more systemic problems. Frequently, a blocked throat chakra appears, and I know that the subject may benefit from finding alternative modes of expression to speech. The artist or writer may crave expression, so one looks for an Apollo line indicating the auditory artist, or if it curves toward the percussion, perhaps the visual or photographic artist. Widened lines may well indicate prior operations.

Sometimes the color, lack of color, or a black dot will appear on the life line or elsewhere in the hand. I first check to see if there is a corresponding percussion line on the same level and inquire about health in that area, such as pains, nausea, colds, etc.

In all questions of health problems, it is prudent to look for corresponding signs on other parts of the hand. For example, head problems, such as eye problems, may also be reflected through stars on the mount of Jupiter as well as marks on the head line and a mark or line on the corresponding area of the percussion. These may also indicate persons who have a tendency for either getting things in their eyes or bumping their heads.

Often, if health problems have not surfaced, one may find a family history of such problems, with the signs showing in the left hand more likely to be from the mother's family, and right-hand signs more likely those from the father's family.

Several years ago I observed a strong line and especially clouded area at the base of the percussion, the area representative of the anus and external genitalia, on a man in his early twenties. He was feeling a general malaise. I advised him to go to his doctor and have his prostate checked. I did not see him for about a year, when he ran up to me and asked if I could please check the area again to see of he was all right. He had gone to the doctor as

I had suggested, and within two weeks had discovered testicular and related cancer. He wanted to know if it was all cured. Apparently he is doing well, and I saw him in a state of good health a year after our second meeting. It can be wise to have one's palm checked on a regular basis.

TRADITIONAL HEALTH LINES

Mercury Line

Health is covered in a number of areas in this book, from the shape of fingernails, the color of the hand, the form of the major lines, the special significance of the fate line as referring to the condition of the spine, and the special condition of cross lines along the percussion. Despite Benham's[80] caution, the health line is considered one line by many palmists, including Asano,[81] Biccum,[82] Compton,[83] Cheiro,[84] Davies,[85] Reid,[86] Yaschpaule,[87] Grady,[88] Hilarion,[89] Hipskind,[90] Hoffman,[91] Gardini,[92] Newcomer-Bramblett,[93] Saint-Germain,[94] Robinson,[95] Spier,[96] and Altman and Fitzherbert.[97] Others disassociate the line from actually indicating any health problems. Some (see below) even associate the line of intuition with it.

Traditionally, the Mercury line is also known as the health line, the line of hepatica, the liver line, and sometimes the communication line. According to some hand analysts, this line reflects the workings of the liver and digestive system and can reveal physiological malfunctions of these organs. Most traditional analysts believe that if there is no Mercury line, it is a blessing, indicating robust health.

Traditionally, irregular, wavy, and yellow lines indicate a tendency to suffer from nausea, irritability, and liver complaints. A heavily marked line traveling between the head and life lines reveals an overstrained nervous system, so the subject should be careful of his or her health. Rheumatic fever may be shown by red spots or dots on the line. If the line is stopped by the heart line, look for heart problems, perhaps heart-digestive problems (such as suffered from heartburn). Heart problems may also be indicated by a wavy line that has red or bluish spots. It is believed by some that if a branch of the Mercury line touches the life line, it will indicate the age at which severe illness occurs.

Chained lines are traditionally also supposed to be indicative of serious health defects. The subject may have a strong tendency to suffer from gallstones, inflammation of the gall duct or bladder, cirrhosis, or other liver disorders.

Spier,[98] who calls it the gastroenteric line, finds that if the line is darker than all the others and is divided into two parts, liver or gallbladder trouble is indicated, but if it is fragmented into little parts, then the subject is inclined to suffer from kidney or bladder problems. However, if the line starts from the life line and ends on a strong mount of Mercury, then it merely strengthens that mount.

Traditionally, islands, not to be confused with chains, signal a temporary period of health problems and could be associated with such organs as the liver, stomach, intestines, and appendix or other organs such as the heart. A single island can refer to many parts of the body affected by delicate health. If the island is near or above the head line, look to the head, such as the nose and throat, and for tendencies toward increased flows of mucus. According to Yaschpaule, an island stretching over the head line along the health line is a sign of delicacy of the chest and lungs, especially if the nails are long, almond-shaped, narrow, and fluted.[99]

If there are several islands on the line, or one

very long, continuous island, one would traditionally check the nails again and see if they are bulbous and examine the mount of upper Mars for grilles. These signs, according to Yaschpaule, are a very strong sign of extreme delicacy of the throat and lungs.

According to tradition, each of these health conditions and delicacies will affect other areas of life, such as business, marriage, and all areas of happiness. These people must be encouraged to take charge, so far as possible, with the understanding and management of their health as a primary responsibility for their own total well-being.

Stars on the line in women can indicate a variety of female complaints. Stars together with certain signs seen in the rascettes or bracelets may well indicate problems in childbearing.

Yaschpaule has found that a cross high on the line of Mercury accompanied by a circle on the head line is indicative of blindness. We have not observed very many true circles on the head line.

Fenton and Wright[100] disagree with these health pronouncements. They hold that this line does not have much to do with any ailments, but it does indicate someone who is interested in health, eats a good diet, exercises, and lives a good, clean life. Outside of indicating matters concerned with childbirth, such as stars or islands especially near the Luna end, that indicate difficulties but that fade a few years after birth, Fenton and Wright find the line unremarkable as it relates to health. They also indicate that the health lines on those who work with the sick, look after those in poor health, or practice spiritual healing may glow "redly for about an hour after they" complete their work.

Altman[101] and Fitzherbert[102] agree that this line refers to health and more specifically to the intestines and stomach. Weak or fragmented lines indicate possible problems with colitis, ulcers, chronic constipation, parasites, or other forms of intestinal problems.

Litzka Raymond Gibson[103] represents some of those who find psychological problems associated with the health line rather than physical abnormalities. She believes it is a third line of destiny, substituting for the fate and Apollo lines. She finds those with it are keenly discerning. Persons who have this line are directed toward more rapid production and gain and require more than usual energy to keep up in their daily affairs. Because they may lack long-term objectives, purposes, and ambitions, they tend to lose their immediate objectives when their energy falls. Such falls in energy have traditionally been associated with lack of health, hence the name, *health line*. These people will tend to overdo things and exhaust themselves.

She agrees that complete absence of this line is a good sign. Its absence does not restrict the good attributes of discernment from a well-formed mount of Mercury. If well-formed, it may activate the quality of discernment to the expense of all other qualities, but a weak line indicates fits and starts of discernment and business abilities to fill in gaps in other attributes.

Like all lines, the Mercury line should be clear, preferably deep, and it should be fairly thin and colorless. Wide lines lend to the problem of overtaxation. Red lines indicate fever or feverous activity. Those that are yellow indicate the jaundiced disposition. Frayed lines will emphasize the nervous qualities of the subject, and chains indicate sluggishness and depressive moods.

Starting from the life line, the Mercury line can indicate business talents and physical traits derived from the family coupled with a desire for personal accomplishments. Starting from the wrist or rascettes or in the area of Neptune, more originality is indicated in everyday affairs. A lunar starting point could indicate true originality in business and commercial enterprises showing intuition. Forks at the start, while seeming to indicate a combination of these forces, do, according to Gibson, usually show a conflict of these forces.

Traditionally, the line should be straight, for when it is curvy it shows unpredictable and often jealous trends in commercial enterprises. The point of beginning can also be used as an age gauge to the point of influence. If the line carries all the way to the mount of Mercury, then it heralds success in business, but if forked, frayed, or tasseled there, it shows decline in later life.

Breaks indicate business reverses which, according to Gibson, the subject will blame on poor health but that are really due to the subject's incompetence. Overlaps indicate quick recovery. Islands, traditionally, are very serious. They indicate energy failure, so double-check the life line. Triangles at the end of the health line that are part of the line indicate rare genius, and stars indicate extraordinary achievement.

The triangle reflects a sign observed by Saint-Germain. While Saint-Germain reported a number of health-related problems revealed by the condition of the Mercury line, he also mentioned other traits unrelated to health.[104] If the line forms a triangle with the head line and the fate line, it shows an aptitude for occult sciences, and if the lines are very straight and clear, the person is clairvoyant. Niblo,[105] writing about the same time, agrees with Saint-Germain in finding such subjects good at natural magic, electrobiology, and related subjects, having good "intuition, sometimes accompanied by second-sight."

Saint-Germain reports that talent in the occult sciences can also be found if the line forms a clear cross with the head line on both hands, and if it is accompanied by the via lascivia as a sister line (wherever that line may be), it is a sign of great happiness and passion in love. Should it run close to the percussion while crossing a well-developed Luna and should the subject also have a well-developed mount of Mercury, look for capriciousness. Niblo, without reference to the quality of the mount of Mercury, finds a line running across the mount of the Moon is a sure sign of caprice and of change in the course of the subject's life.

Saint-Germain reports that if there is no Mercury line, and the mount of Mercury is well-developed, that is not all that should be well-developed, so look for "vivacity." Niblo again agrees without regard to the quality of the mount of Mercury and finds vivacity in conversation accompanied by an agile and quick manner.

White[106] does not relate the line to health but to behavioral characteristics. She finds that people with the line tend to be direct rather than tactful, may have a sharp, critical tongue, are impulsive or anxious to try anything once, and tend to be overindulgent. She relates the line to communication, finding that these subjects usually have a sharp wit and talent for communications through writing and/or speaking. The law or legal procedures may play an important role in these subjects' lives.

Domin[107] relates the line of Mercury to many nonhealth-related attributes. She relates the unbroken intuitive crescent to a robust constitution and sturdy organs as well as to sensitive temperament and psychic and inspirational abilities. Broken Mercury lines indicate a lack of the power to resist and a failure of self-discipline. If the line is interrupted, the subject is easily distracted and has bad work habits. If the lines are broken, curvy, and wavy, it indicates a degree of empathy feeding an ultrarestless subject. If the line is made up of a series of steps like ladder rungs, the subject is stubborn and hangs on long beyond reason, reversing his or her fortunes. The star on the line shows a scattering of talent that needs to be harnessed into a single career, and if that is done, the professionalism in the subject will allow him or her to succeed more than ever imagined. Islands on the line indicate important dream clairvoyance. Domin goes on to describe another forty characteristics depending on the shape, size, and directions of the Mercury line. It would be nice if she would describe her underlying rationales.

Gibson says the absence of the line is best, because its presence indicates subjects who require more than normal energy to keep up with daily affairs.[108] Many others agree that it is best not to have it, such as Cheiro, Levine,[109] Niblo,[110] Squire,[111] Saint-Germain,[112] and Robinson.[113] Hilarion[114] even contends that the fading of the health line is a good sign because it indicates an improvement to health.

However, Jean-Michel Morgan[115] would disagree with the palmists who say absence is best. According to Morgan, while the missing line of hepatica often indicates great physical agility, it also means "tight, closed skin," and this means the palm does not sweat readily and that, in turn, makes the subject more predisposed "to headaches and migraines."

Niblo reports that a strong health line will counteract the health indications of a poor life line.[116]

Morgan finds that a strongly colored health line demonstrates arrogance and brutality. Niblo agrees, if it is red throughout its length. But if it is merely red on the top, it indicates headache tendencies; in the middle, it is a sign of fever; and at the lower (wrist) end, it is a sign of a weak heart. Saint-Germain agrees and adds that if it is of varying colors but red across the head line, beware of apoplexy. Meanwhile, a yellow color indicates internal complaints.

Morgan finds that if it is tortuous and colored yellow or black, liver disease may be indicated.[117] If a triangle is formed with the head line, Morgan,

like Saint-Germain[118] and Niblo,[119] would find a capacity for the occult sciences.

Rodney Davies[120] agrees that absence is good, but he believes a well-developed line is even better, reflecting both good health and success in business, science, or some other area under Mercury's rulership.

Brandon-Jones[121] warns that much research is needed before any definitive opinion can be expressed on the function of the Mercury line. The only certainties he reports is that the line travels toward Mercury (without regard to where it may come from) and that it is somehow connected to the unconscious mind. He laments that this line presents the reader with an imponderable factor that "upsets and makes nonsense" of those clear and precise reflections ascribed to it.

Where it comes from is important in considering what it reflects. If a branch comes from the fate line, then Brandon-Jones says it indicates prospects in business that depend upon inspiration and insight.[122] Regardless of where the line comes from, Hipskind[123] contends that a good, strong Mercury line is logically associated with business ability. Davies,[124] Reid,[125] and Grady[126] agree, and Grady adds lots of vitality for good measure while Reid goes along with a more prevalent view that a clear, strong, straight, unbroken line starting from Luna indicates good health.

Brandon-Jones contends that the inspiration line (see elsewhere) is a Mercury line.[127] He notes that, common to the intuition line, powers of the "sixth sense" appear heightened when the line comes from deep within Luna. He does find that if the line comes from Venus and leaves a weakened life line behind it, then it has health significance that may be averted if the lines are equal in strength or if the Mercury line is weaker. Robinson[128] contends that the weakened life line indicates cardiovascular disease, often hereditary.

Niblo[129] reports that a health consequence, without reference to the quality of the life line left behind it, is weakness of heart. Reid[130] reports that a line starting from either the life line or the mount of Venus will indicate poor digestion, acidity, and a tendency toward nervous tension.

Brenner[131] reports that one may expect the subject to be concerned with health during the time period indicated by the connection of the health and life lines. If the life line continues with full vigor, the subject recovers fully. But if the life line is weakened, then the subject suffers from some chronic weakness. However, she also says that the subject can take precautions and ease, if not totally erase, the problems.

Brandon-Jones recognizes the line's connection with intuition. Others agree, including Compton, Grady, Gardini, Charlotte Wolff,[132] and Hipskind. Dr. Wolff identifies nine lines as lines of intuition belonging to famous people including Romola Nijinsky, George Bernard Shaw, Maurice Ravel, and Armande de Polignac. Seven of these lines originate from the low middle of the palm and two form the intuitive crescent and all end up on the mount of Mercury.

Gardini finds that when the line begins on the mount of the Moon, it indicates exceptional powers of organization, communication talent, a broad overview of subjects, and extraordinary insight. Compton would tend to agree. Gardini concludes from this that subjects will be not only coherent, but also logical. Having a total respect for the truth, they tend to be direct in their conversation. Does this account for some of White's observations above? If the line is short, ending before the head line, then Gardini finds the talents to be latent. But if the line extends to cross the heart line, Gardini finds exceptional insight. If the subject has square fingers, then his or her advice will be highly prized in business affairs.

Gardini reports other nonhealth-related roles of the line if it originates from the life line or crosses it. If it crosses the life line, there is family pressure to assume roles that are not suited to the subject. The stress can cause health problems. Roz Levine[133] would agree and finds that the illnesses that occur can be a sad and desperate way of avoiding family pressures.

But Dr. Costavile[134] reports that such a line starting on the mount of Venus is a good sign of people who are confident in their personal and professional lives, which they live in a calm and serene manner.

Gardini reports that if the health line originates with the life line, the subject may assume these roles from an internal feeling of moral obligation, not from family pressure. The line indicates that these people tend to be of high moral character and the family roles will be interesting experiences, though probably taken only for a specific time. She contends that the line is common among criminal lawyers, judges, and lecturers. However, if the line begins very high up, it reflects mostly health. Here Dr. Costavile is closer to agreement, as she finds such people have high principles matched with decisiveness, which allow them to achieve fulfillment in life.

Davies[135] holds that the Mercury line is like other ascending lines in that it is more fortunate if it branches, and the most fortunate would be the line with rising branches to all three of the palm's other upper mounts, Jupiter, Saturn, and Apollo. Branches reflect great health and outstanding business, scientific, or academic success. A single branch to the right-hand Jupiter mount indicates acquisition of power or authority, just the thing for the ego. A right-handed branch to Saturn reveals that honesty and hard work sensibly applied will bring business success. The right-handed branch to Apollo signifies shrewdness matched with intellectual brilliance, all with fame and success. Ages of success will be computed from the moment the branch leaves the line (something this author would dispute).

Dr. Costavile finds the location of Mercury important. If found high on the palm, the subject can have problems with communication and accepting events but will have technical and scientific talents. If it is in the lower part of the palm, it indicates an introspective, reflective nature that nevertheless is farsighted, with pronounced imagination and some ambition. The double line and the one flanked by small, vertical lines indicates much nervous energy and need for overload caution.

Dr. Maria Costavile[136] finds other significance in branches. The Apollo branch indicates the life-long student whose intellectual qualities will continue to develop and be enriched by study. A Mars branch indicates not only courage but a strong will to achieve prestige. The branch toward Saturn indicates a serious disposition and an infallible capacity to pick the right career. When numerous branches are found on Mercury, we have a subject who will be loved and possess a wealth of intellectual, emotional, and loving vigor.

Many, like Compton,[137] Asano,[138] Grady,[139] and Hutchinson,[140] consider the psychological link important to physiological or physical disorders.

Related to the psychological observations are the observations of Hutchinson somewhat supported by Hipskind[141] and Squire.[142] Hutchinson finds that wherever in the palm measurement time frame this line appears, the subjects have an awareness of their autonomic nervous system. She observes that the longer the line, the greater the awareness. She finds that such subjects recover when they are pleased and determined and follow their down emotions into illness. She names the line, regardless of its wrist-end origin, the "head line of the subconscious."

A number of writers relate the line to nerves and the digestive tract, including Compton,[143] Davies,[144] Squire,[145] Hipskind,[146] Spier,[147] and Altman[148] and Fitzherbert.[149] Compton observes that unless the digestive tract and the liver are in proper working order, proper function of the mind is out of the question in subjects with this sign. Subjects with poor health lines in both hands, when broken or with islands or other adverse signs, should be concerned with diet throughout life.

I see the Mercury lines as indications of some communicative abilities. I look to other factors in the hand to indicate where these communicative abilities may lie.

Biccum[150] sees a health problem if a line comes from the mount of Venus (regardless of the strength of the life line left behind) and ends up on Mercury, provided the mount has a star, dot, bar, or cross on it and the head line is thin at the start, has chaining during deflection, and a star at the end. This is another of Biccum's warrior lines and this one indicates possible insanity and mental stress due to business concerns that may lead to self-harm.

Biccum disputes that upward branches from the life line can be considered health lines.[151] He contends that the health line starts from the mount of the Moon or Neptune, always outside of the arc of the life line. He, like most palmists, does not regard its absence as a bad sign. Indeed, he finds its absence is a sign of a good constitution that only the subject can abuse.

Biccum describes seventy-seven unisex, one additional male, and seven additional female traits, mostly health, that may be ascribed to the varied appearances of this line. One must admire any researcher who could have recorded and statistically compared the medical histories and hands of literally thousands, perhaps tens of thousands, of subjects and controls that would have had to have been observed to reach the wide variety of distinct conclusions that Gerald Biccum has on this subject. Unfortunately, Mr. Biccum does not discuss his methods in any detail.

When Brandon-Jones published in 1981, he said that the Mercury line was wide open for scientific research and investigation.[152] Biccum,[153] who published in 1989, has claimed that he first organized his information through the use of computers but took ten years to test and verify his conclusions after interviewing thousands of people. The sheer volume of his research is staggering when one observes that during this ten-year period he was able to interview enough people to establish over 1,300 separate palm and line characteristics, distinguish them with particular certainty to various aspects in the lives of the subjects interviewed, and draw from those interviews supportable conclusions.

Domin's book *PalmaScope*, like Biccum's book *Handology*, invites us to review a series of varied pictures to find one that matches one or more features of the subject's hand and then gives an explanation of what that feature means. These books are modern-day competitors with Saint-Germain's book *The Practice of Palmistry for Professional Purposes* of 1897. Saint-Germain also sets forth numerous drawings of the palm for the reader's comparison. Biccum contends his is based upon computer-generated material followed up by ten years of personal verification. Domin says that her material is based upon review of about 3,500 years of written palmistry material from different schools around the globe that has been reassembled into the unified system presented in her book. This book, like *Handology* and Saint-Germain's 1897 work, are all prepared with such extensive pictures as to enable the professional, student, and subject to point and know. Saint-Germain prepared his book from lessons given to students over the years and sought to make it the clearest, most systematic, and most complete book on the subject then available in the English language by reporting two to ten times more reliable observations than any other work then published.

Mercury Ladder

Biccum, Domin, and Saint-Germain all describe a Mercury line in the form of a ladder. Saint-Germain indicates this is a sign of both very severe liver trouble and a succession of business losses. Perhaps Linda Domin partially agrees, because she sees a subject who is too stubborn to let go facing chronic performance problems with business reverses. This person has problems pinpointing the problem and listening to professional advice. Domin does not mention the liver. Biccum says that this indicates the worst form of stomach problems and indigestion and resultant ills, with gastric fever and inflammation of the bowels as possible disorders. This is close to the opinion of Psychos,[154] who adds dyspepsia and catarrh of the stomach or intestines to Biccum's list. These assessments are not exactly alike, with two in the gut and two in business. Perhaps Saint-Germain covered all three best.

Wavy Mercury

Saint-Germain, Biccum, and Domin all describe a wavy line. The wavy line indicates to Domin that the subject is addicted to the wrong food, especially buttery, crisp, and crunchy textures. This potato chip freak just can't stop eating them. Reid[155] would find this an indication of digestive problems. Biccum seems to look at the result. He finds chronic biliousness reflected in such a hand, with attacks of bilious fever and related liver problems. This is frequently complicated by rheumatism. Business is unsteady and subject to many changes or alterations. Psychos[156] and Saint-Germain find biliousness in its worst form. Yaschpaule[157] would agree with the bilious findings. These observations are fairly comparable.

Forked Mercury

Saint-Germain, Domin, and Biccum all discuss the line that appears to end in a fork on the mount of Mercury. Saint-Germain finds languor and weakness, especially in old age. Domin finds the subject's energies split between two goals, and success awaits the choice of goals, with the obvious implication that if no choice is made, there will be no success. She does not mention age, weakness, or languor, but then, weakness and languor might be the result of failing to make a choice. Biccum relates the fork to age and says that the greater success eludes the subject because of division of energies between various talents. So far, the nineteenth-century writers had done well without the use of the computer or the modern reorganization of the various schools' teachings into a unified program.

Branched Mercury

Saint-Germain, Domin, and Biccum do not have drawings to compare with each of their findings on the health line, but they do have at least one further drawing that appears to closely compare. Here the line splits and one (or more in the case of Saint-Germain) fork goes to the mount of Apollo. Domin finds such subjects have agreeable personalities and are shrewd, and with this combination, they will become independent in business. Biccum says that this a good sign on a good health line and a certain indication of success. The subject's life sails over difficulties as he or she floats to success. Saint-Germain says that this foretells changes for the better in business. These are not exactly comparable readings, but they are close enough that if one merely remembers business, differences will never be noticed. One who was seeking some underlying rationale for these findings might ask why the fork on Mercury foretells reduced chances for success while the branch reaching over to Apollo indicates increased chances for success. There would be no answer from Biccum's or Domin's book. Enid Hoffman[158] finds the multiple branching on Mercury suggests an extremely well-balanced and stable person who probably enjoys great health, but then one of her branches falls between the Mercury and Apollo fingers.

Mercury Branched to Apollo

When it comes to health and the line of Mercury, those who find the connection generally agree that it may be involved with the intestines and liver. Yaschpaule[159] may best consider the implications spreading to other health complaints when he observes that the line reflects the condition of the digestive tract and physiological action of the liver and that many of the world's maladies would not exist were these systems in healthy, robust working order.

This is not an exhaustive treatment of the writings or the subjects involved in what has been variously called the health line, the line of Mercury, the hepatica line, and the liver line. That awaits a new book of its own, which may be part of a growing library on health subjects and palmistry; hand, finger, and fingernail analysis; analysis of flexion lines; and dermatoglyphics.

CHAPTER TEN

SPECIAL MARKS: STARS, PROBLEMS, AND CRITIQUES

This chapter is as much a criticism of the present state of palmistry as it is a review of the meaning of stars and my own experiences with these curious formations. It may be of more interest to the professional for future research. The student can read it at leisure and when there is a particular feature that is in need of some explanation. The star can be an enigmatic sign.

Some palmists seldom find stars on the hands they have reviewed. I have encountered them quite often. The discussion of the meaning of stars in the literature on palmistry is quite contradictory, as this chapter will demonstrate. I believe the numerous contradictions point to some funda-

mental weaknesses in the present study and reporting on palmistry, and these weaknesses are reflected in various parts of this book. As one of the aims of this book is to improve the credibility and value of hand analysis studies, I believe that at least one critical chapter of this sort may be helpful for the truly serious student and practitioner.

There are a variety of stars recognized in the literature. Here are the ones I am familiar with: the most common star, Hoffman's star, the pentacle, and the Star of David.

Dr. Costavile[1] describes a star formed by four intersecting lines like this:

195

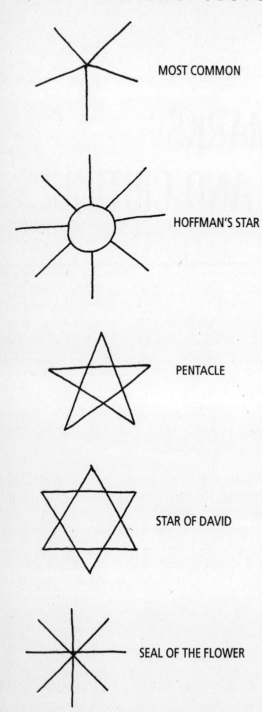

MOST COMMON

HOFFMAN'S STAR

PENTACLE

STAR OF DAVID

SEAL OF THE FLOWER

She brings the seal of the flower from her studies of Chinese palmistry. This sign, she reports, is an indication of social achievement and profit and a good sign for students sitting for examinations. She also describes another star formation from her studies of Chinese palmistry: the star of the south. Her description of its meaning is below and it looks like this:

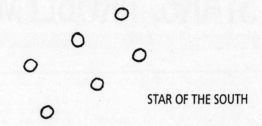

STAR OF THE SOUTH

Star of the South

Of these five types of reported stars, the most common reported in the literature is formed where five or more lines roughly meet at a point, and, as observed by Bettina Luxon and Jill Goolden,[2] this line intersection often appears very much like an asterisk (*). More uncommon is the star reported by Enid Hoffman,[3] which consists of a tiny, round dimple or circle with radiating lines flowing from it.

The third star, the pentacle, or clear portions of it, I have seen only infrequently, and all were on hands of subjects who were available only for quick readings. So I have yet to form a strong opinion on the meaning of the pentacle. I was interested in trying to determine whether it was the top point or the two legs that were up. In some ways one must consider what is the top of the hand; the wrist as one stands anatomically, or the fingers as one holds up the hand. In several of my readings it appeared to be related to protection and the last subject felt as if she could call upon, and at times was surrounded by, an army of angels. The Indians call it the symbol of mercy. The six-pointed Star of David they call the star of Siva.

Dr. Maria Costavile, publishing in 1988,[4] describes the star of the south as being made up of an even number of cavities or small circles on a smooth palm. So long as it is neither pale nor crossed by a line, its meaning is favorable, as it indicates riches. If it is not red but pale, or crossed by a line, or if, perchance, it is seen on two phalanges of the Saturn finger, it is an unfavorable sign.

Enid Hoffman, publishing in 1985, reports that her star is rarely seen and should not be confused with intersecting lines. It is a portent of good fortune or fame. However, if found on the Saturn mount,[5] it bodes no good, suggesting sad or tragic events. She asserts that awareness may make avoidance possible. A star on Mercury is a harbinger of success for those who pursue business, science, or public speaking.[6] A star on Luna could indicate motion sickness or other sicknesses due to water. If it connects to any travel lines, trouble on a journey may be indicated.[7]

Dr. Sen,[8] as published in 1960, would agree that even a star formed by intersecting lines on a travel line has this indication. A star on lower Mars may be a sign of conflict or the loss of a close friend, associate, or family member. On the bright side, it may also indicate a superior military commander.[9] Move the star to upper Mars, and it may be an indication to be health conscious. If it is accompanied by an Apollo line, strong character may enhance notable personal achievement.[10]

Vera Compton reports in 1952 that the most common feature of a star is its indication on lines of a sudden disturbance to the status quo.[11] Henry Frith, publishing in 1952, believes that it indicates situations that the subject cannot control.[12] Jean-

Michael Morgan, publishing in 1975, agrees.[13] Frith also indicates that one should be aware that stars do not suddenly appear but are formed gradually. White also emphasizes the topically unexpected, uncontrollable suddenness of the often unusual events, either good or bad, that a star portends.[14] Niblo, publishing about 1900, emphasizes that stars foretell events over which the subject has no control and that are usually dangerous, but the good or bad aspects of the sign depend upon other palm features, and especially the fate line.[15] He warns never to ignore a star, as it always means something, and in fact, is almost the most important sign found in the hand.

I have seen many hands with stars on them, unlike some of the writers who have reported on them, and I believe the stars, at least the ones with five or six intersecting lines, are not very unusual. I agree that they are probably important marks, and I will illustrate, especially here, the almost total confusion and disagreement among the writers on palmistry over what this sign may mean. This, I hope, will emphasize the need for serious scientific statistical study of these signs and other features of the hands before further broad pronouncements are made concerning their meaning, unless some broad consensus has already been reached. I will now illustrate the lack of consensus on the star.

Lack of Consensus on the Star

There is a difference of opinion on whether stars are good or bad signs. Fenton and Wright,[16] publishing in 1986, say that it is traditionally a bad sign, intensifying the energies of its location and acting like "a stone piercing and cracking a pane of glass." This could refer to a trauma or accident. They do say, however, that traditionally, if found on the mount of Apollo, it is a sign of fame and fortune.

There are many opposed to this view. These include Francis King who, generally speaking, finds the star normally a good sign. King published in 1987. Rita Robinson would agree. Rita Robinson,[17] publishing in 1988, indicates that a star is supposed to be one of the most fortunate of signs, promising success wherever it falls. However, because she prefers to find success in the character and work of her subjects rather than in signs, she does not rely heavily on the star. Spencer Grendahl,[18] publishing in 1990, would agree with the view that stars are signs of success wherever they fall. Rita Van Alen, publishing in 1948, also seems to follow this optimistic view.[19] Even the renowned Cheiro, publishing in the last part of the nineteenth century, would agree, with one or two exceptions, including the star on the mount of Saturn.[20]

Gibson, publishing her revised edition in 1988, while being one of those who generally finds the star favorable, points out that the danger portent of a star is its indication of intensity.[21] It can be the mark of brilliance or an indication of serious repercussions or severe shock if found on the head or life lines. On all other lines and all mounts except the mount of Saturn, and except the plain of Mars, the star is a sign of high achievement, fortune, success, and/or fame. On Saturn it can indicate, through its intensity, an increase in melancholia and on the plain of Mars it can indicate some brief bit of bad fortune.

Yaschpaule, publishing in 1981, finds that an intersecting line star on the mount of Jupiter[22] is a sign of benefit that could indicate a sudden rise in wealth. He believes that as Jupiter is the planet of expansion, such wealth may be the result of the subject's expanding business or activities. If there is a line from Venus that goes straight to Jupiter, it is a good sign of money, and if it ends in a star, it is a sign of extraordinary financial achievement and sudden wealth.[23] A star on the thumb is also a sign of wealth.[24] This follows the Indian palmistry described by Dr. Sen[25] and Mr. Ayer[26] that stars on Jupiter, Apollo, and the second phalange of the thumb denote wealth. But a star on Saturn, like poorly formed rascettes, islands on the fate line, short or low-set little fingers, and fingers that have gaps between them when they are held together outstretched, are, according to Yaschpaule, all signs of poverty.[27] If low-set little fingers are signs of poverty, then 90 to 95 percent of all the Americans I have read in the last seven years are in extreme poverty, which is ridiculous.

Dr. Sen finds a star on the center of the mount of Saturn the mark of a terrible fatality. While it may well be the mark of distinction and fame, it may also be the mark of famous martyrs. If it is off the center of the mark, it may indicate those touched through meeting such martyrs.[28] He finds a star on the fate line blasts the fate of the subject and reading its date determines when the wealthy will be reduced to poverty.[29]

Ayer,[30] publishing in 1962, is another who sees stars as harbingers of good and bad news. Besides the good news if found on Jupiter and Apollo, it can bring fame through communications if found on Mercury. On the plain of Mars it may indicate military honors, but it may also indicate some calamity. Here we might have the Medal of Honor or Victoria Cross awarded posthumously. If found on Saturn, Ayer would follow tradition and find a violent death unless the star is surrounded by a square. It signs danger through water when found on the mount of the Moon and trouble in love if found on the mount of Venus.

Here he may depart somewhat from Dr. Sen, who finds the lunar star is a good mark if accompanied by a good head line and strong thumb. It is the mark of famous poets and novelists. But give it a poor head line or weak thumb, and there is no control over the imagination, so it may run riot and lead to insanity.[31] Dr. Sen acknowledges that other writers on palmistry describe such a star as a portent of suicide or death by drowning.

Dr. Sen does not necessarily see a star on Venus as indicative of trouble in love. He sees it as a sign of animal magnetism.[32] These subjects draw those of the opposite sex, giving them success in affairs of love that will not be denied even by oppositions and jealousies. He goes on to note that if the star is found on the side of the mount, the subject triumphantly carries on grand enterprises and liaisons with people in the field of love.

Following the mount up to the second phalange, Dr. Sen finds a clear star there indicative of wealth. Continuing on to the distal phalange of the thumb, he finds two or three stars on the back the clear indication of famous horsemen and excellent signs of good horsemanship.

Other stars of warning according to Dr. Sen are those found on the life and health lines. If a star is found on the life line, it denotes an accident involving the subject, but he or she may escape it if there is a corresponding Mars line. If a star is formed where the head line and health line cross on the hand of a woman, problems may be expected in the urogenital area with accompanying diseases of the uterus and barrenness.[33]

Francis King relegates those who make dire predictions based upon stars found on the mount of Saturn[34] to history and finds that modern palmists see it as a sign of a dramatic and distinguished career. While not as favorable as the same star on the Jupiter mount, those who have it will still gain some fame and possibly fortune. He agrees with those who predict that intersecting line or ray stars found on Mercury indicate a brilliant career in a field determined by other hand characteristics.[35] A star on the little finger traditionally indicates that anything undertaken, that is, touched, will be successful.[36]

For King, a star on lower (aggressive) Mars (King, like some other palmists, calls it positive Mars) also indicates a brilliant career, but in some military or martial activity.[37] Dr. Sen would agree.[38] However, King observes that if the star is found on upper (defensive) Mars, on what King calls negative Mars, then looks for the success through more passive Martian virtues of courage, patience, and moral dignity.[39] A lunar star indicates success through the use of imagination, or instinctive knowledge springing from the unconscious.[40] The dreaminess of these qualities is enhanced if the head line dips well into the lunar mount. King asserts that the ancient belief that stars found on Luna indicate death by drowning arose from astrological and astronomical relationships in the minds of fatalistic observers and has no substance.

When King finally discusses the star found on the little finger, he gives a caveat about all stars. Success indicated by the stars will only be achieved depending on the other factors found in the hand that supports it. Otherwise, the star is only a mitigating factor.

Mr. King's caveat echoes the warnings of Dr. Sen, who advises us that no single sign on the palm can be read without reference to other signs, lines, and marks on the hand (and, we might add, the absence thereof). He gives the example of a star on Jupiter as being meaningless in the presence of a poor head, fate, and Sun line.[41]

To King, stars found on the mounts of Jupiter or Apollo have more than one meaning, depending on where on the mount they are found. A star low on Jupiter, for example, would indicate a fellow traveler with the famous, but not among the famous. These people would provide the stories for the biographers of the famous. High on the mount, or to the side farther away from the finger (wherever that may be), it indicates strong ambition and likelihood of achieving fame. The Apollonian star[42] connected to the sun line indicates a person widely recognized in the arts. Dr. Sen would find such a star a harbinger of success and wealth, but happiness would elude the subject.[43] King further observes that if the star is centered on the mount, the subject may not achieve great fame, but his or her success will be accompanied by riches.[44] Not so if the star is high or low on the mount. Again, we have the person who merely rubs shoulders with the rich and famous.

Robinson[45] lists her knowledge of the lore of the star to include fame and fortune, possibly as an actor, if found on Apollo; prosperity in business, science, or finance, if found on Mercury; military victory if found on lower Mars; triumph in love on Venus.

Rodney Davies, publishing in 1987, recognizes that the spectacular nature of the star's events are not always positive, even if the placement is fortunate.[46] Davies divides signs from left and right hands, looking generally to left hands for potential or inborn traits and right hands for realization through the efforts of the subject. If the star is found on a mount and not associated with a line, it will herald special success in the area indicated by the mount. While the star on the vertical lines of Apollo, Jupiter, Saturn, or Mercury is fortunate, not so on the horizontal lines if it is seen at the termination of the lines of life, heart, or head. There it signals abrupt upsets to the body part or parts represented by those lines.

One problem with the star appears to relate to its intensity and suddenness. Suppose we find a star on an earth hand. Here we have a person who will feel at home with routine, who will like to plan his or her moves carefully, and who wants to know what is expected. A sudden, intense experience, no matter how fortunate others might view it, may well be an unwelcome experience to the subject, especially if it destroys the careful routine that has been built to support such a person's life. Some have said that the size of the star makes a difference. A small star is like a light being turned on. A large star is like an explosion.

In my clinical experience, I have found that stars toward the middle of the palm in the plain of Mars and on the mounts of the Moon, Neptune, Uranus, or Pluto are very often on the hands of subjects who commonly know what is about to happen in the next forty-eight hours. This they seldom see as a blessing, because they can seldom do anything about the future. However, I recall one woman who said the gift had enabled her to protect her children twice. Typically, subjects will know of impending or immediate death, who is about to call, or who just had a baby or went to the hospital. Some view this as a curse; others as just one of those little annoyances of life they must bear. Few relate that it is of much benefit.

Another recent client indicated some benefit when I described the star as the mark of the shamanic scout in hunter-gatherer societies who could, through his or her psychic gifts, scout out the game. This client was right-handed and had two strong stars on his right hand, one on the mount of Apollo and one in the plain of Mars under Apollo near the lunar mount. He had a corresponding star on the plain of Mars in the left hand, but it was not quite as strong. He had earth hands. He related to being a hunter as his skill was scouting out new locations for the family ethnic food business. However, he mentioned that while he was quite successful, he would expect the success to really be evidenced about two years after he had found the location.

So, if the stars in his hand were related to his gift, are we looking at suddenness? Are we looking at some singular phenomenon or something that may be an ongoing trait? That question could be illustrated by a successful lady lawyer I examined. She had a star under Saturn, which I suggested was the sign of her being very successful in a large case. She said she had been. Then we commiserated together that her problem was readjusting to the mundane level of the practice of law, as that may have been a once-in-a-lifetime phenomenon. But was it?

The following is a partial list further illustrating the wide differences of views of other writers, even when they are reporting stars in similar locations on the hand.

Jupiter Mount: *Bad sign:* Possibly because the Jupiter finger is associated with foresight, some may have concluded that a star there foretells eye problems through illness, accident, or possible head injuries. I have found some subjects with such signs who tended to suffer eye and head accident problems. Squares also may indicate this though more likely they are confined to indicating tunnel vision.

Mixed sign: Newcomer-Bramblett, publishing in 1982, describes this star as indicative of one with the ability to survive in the two worlds of the spirit and flesh (or earth as she calls it). If the characteristic of mediumship is detected, then beware of Dr. Jekyll–Mr. Hyde split personalities. The only problem with this curious reading is the location of the star on the Jupiter mount in her figure on what most other Western palmists call the mount of Venus.[47] Van Alen locates two other stars on Jupiter, one on the thenar edge that she identifies as the guarantee of contact with the rich and famous but no guarantee that it will rub off, and the other, low and toward the middle, allowing personal distinction as well as running with the distinguished folk.[48] Cheiro also found that a star

lying low on the mount, at its base, or cutting the base of the index finger, or resting on the side toward the back of the hand, indicated one who rubbed shoulders with distinguished persons but had no promise of distinction, unless it could be found elsewhere in the hand.[49] Domin, publishing in 1989, describes a star just above lower Mars, which puts it on the lower part of the Jupiter mount. She finds it generally favorable, but then discusses a scenario of it as a sign of unhappiness over a bad out-of-court settlement with an old enemy and suggests that giving a little to patch up an old feud will find ready acceptance on the opponent's part.[50]

Good sign: Always a sign of favorable events; such as unexpected elevation, fortune gained by marriage, and gratified ambition, says Henry Rem,[51] writing in the 1920s. Rita Van Alen, publishing in 1948, agrees, finding no mark the equal to this star.[52] She follows Cheiro on the high mounted star. Cheiro, publishing in 1887, found that the star high on Jupiter promised great honor, gratification of ambition, and final triumphant success, especially when accompanied by strong fate, head, and sun lines.[53] Jean-Michael Morgan, publishing in 1975, follows this hypothesis, finding the subject predestined to be satisfied in love, honors, and ambition, experiencing a sudden rise in the world, and if connected to a cross of union, marriage with one of higher social standing.[54] Newcomer-Bramblett agrees on both counts.[55] Frith agrees with it as a sign of honor and wealth.[56] Niblo agrees with the above, adds luck, and finds the propitious marriage without mention of the cross of union.[57] Kwok Man Ho, Martin Palmer, and Joanne O'Brien, publishing in 1986, find its placement in the traditional Chinese wood star area (shown as placed in the center of Jupiter) as a sign of one who will attain high rank within the army or other disciplined organization.[58] Linda

Domin tells her reader that if he or she has such a star, then that subject may look forward to meeting a distinguished person who will change his or her life and through the subject's inborn ability to speak to all peoples, the subject will rise to the same distinction and be spurred on to further heights.[59]

Saturn Mount: *Bad sign:* Always threatening to Rem, the star announces paralysis, incurable disease, disastrous death or assassination, and is almost always found on the hands of the condemned criminal mounting the gallows.[60] This follows the reasoning of Niblo, who finds it the sign of a great fatality.[61] Newcomer-Bramblett, publishing in 1982, agrees with the paralysis through fear.[62] Leona Lehman, publishing in 1959, finds it indicates death by violence.[63] They follow the opinion of Cheiro, who finds the bearer the pitiful plaything of fate, and whether prince, pauper, hero, villain, or even religious martyr, ending in doom.[64] Cheiro observes that like stars around Jupiter, if the star is off to the side of the mount or protrudes into the fingers, then we have the subject in contact with a doomed one. Frith agrees with violent death unless a square surrounds the star.[65] Domin predicts that a distinguished stranger, promising to make history, will try to lead the subject away from the path of righteousness or the law, and this stranger's path is better avoided because of the notoriety that will be involved.[66]

Apollo Mount: *Good sign:* Van Alen agrees with Cheiro in finding the sign one of fame and fortune.[67] She locates another star, set low between the mounts of Apollo and Mercury, that indicates one who brings the new and original into existence.[68] If she finds the upper star accompanied by a long finger of Apollo and a square-shaped mount of Venus, it is indicative to her of one

blessed with the ability to compose music.[69] Lehman finds predicted fortune may come unexpectedly.[70] Newcomer-Bramblett follows a common belief and finds success in art or in science.[71] Add a good Sun line, and she finds wealth together with the artistic fame. Domin describes a sun ray pattern that is very like the Hoffman star. This sign foretells the rise of one who will gain international repute through strongly motivated extraordinary talent applied through clear thinking.[72]

Mixed sign: Here, beneath the annular finger, is the sign of wealth or fortune that brings happiness to the possessor, declares Rem,[73] but beware, he says, for it portends danger from firearms. He advises the reader to study the life line to determine whether death will result. Cheiro finds that the star on Apollo denotes great expectations of wealth and place, but finds it no guarantee of happiness and muses that the price required for physical or mental health may be too high.[74] Frith agrees without any explanation.[75] Niblo follows this hypothesis if there is no line of Apollo. With a single line of Apollo, Niblo predicts stardom of the talented after struggle, and with several lines, assured wealth.[76] Domin starts with a very good reading, saying the sign was an indication of receipt of quite unexpected wealth and a mark of distinction through following one's natural instincts (mostly in the arts), but it is also a sign of surplus strength that is likely to lead to abuse of the good qualities.[77]

Mercury Mount: *Bad sign:* This signifies the thief, the rascal, the dishonored one, especially on unscrupulous subjects, says Rem[78] (such as those with crooked little fingers?). Frith agrees that it is the sign of a thief or con artist.[79] Morgan also agrees, especially on hands with other adverse indications.[80] All follow Niblo, who makes a similar prediction.[81]

Mixed sign: Newcomer-Bramblett finds this the mark of one successful in using other people's money to make money. This could be a good banker or investor or a thief, depending on what is shown by the rest of the hand.[82]

Good sign: Cheiro found it the sign of one successful in business, science, or eloquent expression according to the hand type. If it is off to the side, it indicates one who associates with such people.[83] Van Alen[84] agrees in finding it is a sign that guarantees success in business or science (so if one is failing with an M.B.A., maybe one should return to school for an M.S. and Ph.D.?). Lehman finds this success comes without much effort.[85] Domin finds it a sign of genius with outstanding reasoning powers, belonging to a truth-seeking visionary whose dreams will someday bear fruit.[86]

Upper Mars: *Bad sign:* Rem finds this foretells serious injury by firearms or death in war.[87] Frith, referring to Mars generically without specifying a location, finds it portends sudden death, perhaps in war.[88] Niblo, without specifying which Mars, said it signifies violence leading to a homicide.[89] We presume he means upper Mars because he writes of it in the same sentence that he describes the star on Mercury.

Mixed sign: Domin finds the silent, unknown fighter who will someday be known for his or her courage in supporting a worthwhile cause, but success depends upon patience, which is often lacking, and this may lead to moods of jealousy and wrath. She advises staying away from sharp objects and firearms.[90]

Good sign: Following Cheiro's[91] footsteps, Van Alen calls it the star of honor through patience and fortitude, so she finds this indicates courage and pays off with the greatest of honors.[92] Newcomer-Bramblett simplifies it to fame from military service or the combative arts but finds

upper Mars where most people locate lower Mars, above the thumb.[93] Domin says that if this star falls between the head and heart lines, it portends ability to achieve inner satisfaction and even rise to great heights in the fields of graphics, science, or banking, utilizing the inborn love for accuracy in detail and reproduction.[94]

Lower Mars: *Good sign:* Cheiro[95] again leads other palmists such as Van Alen in finding this the star of martial glory, predicting honors through military actions.[96] Domin builds a story based somewhat on this rationale.[97] Newcomer-Bramblett calls this mount upper Mars (see above).

Plain of Mars: *Bad sign:* Rem[98] observes that a large star here connected to a line leaving Venus is a time indication of the exact epoch when a catastrophe will befall the subject.

Good sign: Newcomer-Bramblett describes a star within the triangle formed by the fate, life, and head lines, near the life line, as a sign of fortuitous events happening "at that time."[99] (Does she mean the time indicated on the life line or the time of the reading?)

Venus Mount: *Bad sign:* Morgan finds this a sign of death of parents or friends.[100] This is one of several of Rem's conclusions. Newcomer-Bramblett locates a star here in her figure, but her text calls it a star on the mount of Jupiter, so read above about mixed signs on the Jupiter mount. If it is at the base of the mount, Niblo predicts misfortune brought about by female influence.[101] Frith finds it a sign of marital troubles or love relationship problems, and if it is near the life line, it could indicate lawsuits.[102]

Mixed sign according to its location: Rem[103] makes four observations of stars on the mount of Venus: (1) If it is at the beginning of the life line it will be a fortunate sign for the subject according to his or her class and caste. (2) One found at the foot of the mount portends misadventures in love and embarrassments in marriage (though he recognizes a contrary view by Belot as a sign of people happy in love). (3) If it is united with another star on the head line, it indicates lawsuits or divorce. (4) One or more stars on Venus will indicate the death of relatives or those near and dear to the subject. Domin sees it the sign of the successful, passionate lover who nevertheless is followed by trouble associated with the love of his or her life.[104]

Good signs: Cheiro[105] observes that a star in the center or at the highest point on Venus indicates the brilliantly successful lover. We have seen above that he is followed in this opinion by Dr. Sen. A star on the side of Venus, according to Cheiro[106] and Van Alen,[107] suggests that lovers will be distinguished. One at the base of Venus, Van Alen says, guarantees success in love affairs. Lehman tends to agree, finding such a star foretells a luminous marriage, surprising happiness, and wealth.[108]

Lunar Mount: *Bad sign:* Rem, following his saturnine style, agrees with the danger or death by water descriptions.[109] Lehman buys a drowning end.[110] Frith merely says it is a sign of danger by water.[111] Morgan follows this ancient line, but notices it can also indicate bladder problems.[112] Newcomer-Bramblett limits her finding of water and travel mishaps to those stars on travel lines on Luna.[113] Niblo reports that old palmists predicted death by drowning and when on the end of the head line, suicide by drowning, but he predicts that it indicates hypocrisy and deception, with misfortune resulting from an excessive imagination.[114]

Mixed sign: Actually, Cheiro[115] views it as a good sign, indicating great renown arising through the imaginative qualities of the mount. He notes, though, that when the star falls on the end of the head line, it may also be on the lunar mount. In that case, it is to be read as part of the head line, and the lunar part will ruin the balance of the head line and result in insanity and may result in suicide. He observes that water suicide was no longer fashionable in his day, with the subjects more often opting for revolvers or morphine. He does not relate the lunar star to drowning. We might also note that water travel inland had been reduced by his day in favor of better roads, bridges, and railroads, and today, it accounts for a very small percentage of the total miles traveled by the public compared to the total public miles traveled in the eighteenth century and early nineteenth centuries.

Good sign: Van Alen locates two stars on Luna.[116] She follows Cheiro on the one on upper Luna and calls it the star of celebrity, indicating a person who operates through his or her imaginative faculties. The other, low on the Moon mount, she calls the star of supreme adventure, indicating the subject has the psychic ability to participate in supersensory perceptions. Newcomer-Bramblett finds the lower star an indication of multiple births, and if it is accompanied by a good Apollo finger, many new ideas or brain children.[117] Contrary to Cheiro, she finds a star at the end of the head line indicates a brilliantly creative imagination.[118] Domin finds this another sign of the seekers of truth and light whose visions may become the realities of tomorrow.[119]

Neptune Mount: *Good sign:* Newcomer-Bramblett describes a star near the end of the life line as a sign of public recognition in old age.[120]

Quadrangle: *Mixed sign:* A "well colored star," according to Rem,[121] following Niblo's explanation,[122] located here between the heart and head lines, is the sign of a good man who may fall in love with and be easily influenced by a conniving woman and have his natural good instincts perverted. Nevertheless, according to the traditional view, should he lose all his money, his merit will allow him to regain it. If the whole hand is good, it predicts exceptional honors.

Good signs: Domin locates two stars in this area, one under Apollo and one under Saturn. The Apollo-connected star indicates success awaiting in the fields of communication and an ability to be courteously forthright and handle money well.[123] The Saturn star portends an outstanding career in teaching others to help themselves form a personal understanding and ability to make needed changes.[124] Newcomer-Bramblett finds this a sign of fame, fortune, and honor through mediumship.[125]

Life Line: Bad sign: Lehman says such a star predicts threatening illness.[126] Asano, while cautioning that research is still incomplete, finds this formation and similarly situated dots seem to appear in cardiac patients.[127]

Mixed sign depending on location: Rem[128] finds that such a sign at the beginning of the life line signals a misfortune at birth or a "love child." But what of his observations of such a star on the mount of Venus at the same place? A star on the line near the bracelets indicates death in old age, according to Rem.[129]

Good sign: See the comments of Newcomer-Bramblett above, under the Neptune mount. Domin shows the sign and writes about the terrible loss of self suffered by the subject upon losing his or her most beloved and the long time it takes to heal, and predicts that the subject will finally reemerge from withdrawal and go on living life anew.[130]

Head Line: Bad sign: Here again we have bad news as Rem[131] finds this announcing insanity, violent nervous pains, or dangerous head wounds. I have actually had a client experience such a predicted head wound quite unexpectedly after a reading, and almost totally without warning.[132] Clinical experiences such as these are very humbling to my scientific mind. Lehman joins the bad chorus, finding again the sign of the threat of illness.[133] Frith finds such a sign at the end of the head line indicative of "weakness of the brain," whatever that may mean, and a star on the head line near generic Mars is reported to indicate blindness.[134] Morgan is clearer on the star at the end of the head line as he declares it to be a sign of madness or head injury.[135]

Good sign: See Newcomer-Bramblett's findings on this formation under the Moon mount comments above.

Heart Line: Bad sign: Lehman finds a star here also is a sign of threatened illness.[136]

Fate Line: Always a sign of misfortune: Rem confirms this, and if it is at the foot of the line, it indicates loss of fortunes amassed by the parents.[137] Frith warns subjects with it to beware of accidents.[138] If the star joins the line at the base of the Saturn finger, Frith states it indicates violent death. Kwok Man Ho, Martin Palmer, and Joanne O'Brien warn to beware of loss of money if the star is low, but if it is high, guard against suicide.[139]

Not a sign of misfortune: Van Alen sees this star in the middle of the line, as indicating the subject has the necessary aggressiveness to fight any crisis in his or her career.

Apollo or Sun Line: Bad sign: Rem[140] describes a star or a group of small, disorderly lines, located here as indicating a calamity when the Sun line comes to a sudden halt. If the line then continues, the bad luck will be followed by good luck.

Good sign: Lehman finds that such a line crowned by a star indicates dazzling accomplishment, bringing with it renown and wealth.[141]

Girdle of Venus: *Bad sign:* Rem[142] sees this is a sign of a crime of passion and prison if a star ends this line. Such a star cutting the girdle of Venus under Saturn would, according to Rem, indicate a sexually transmitted disease. I might note, in reviewing his observation, the proximity to the ring of Saturn and the emotional charge of the girdle of Venus.

Bracelet, Rascettes: *Good sign:* Rem[143] finds good news, for here is a sign of advantage or inheritance in the future.

Child lines (Percussion at Mercury Mount): *Bad sign:* This is a fatal indication to the child, according to Rem, to result from an accident if there is a dot accompanying the star.[144]

Marriage line (Percussion at Mercury Mount): *Bad sign:* Rem contends that we have a sign of widowhood.[145]

Travel lines (Percussion at Lunar Mount): *Bad sign:* Don't take that voyage, Rem would advise, for such a sign or one described by Enid Hoffman with a hole in it are signs of sinking, journeys plagued with fatality, and just generally bad news.[146] Niblo says it is a certain indication of death by drowning.[147]

End of Thumb: *Curious bad sign:* Here Rem finds the chivalrous profligate.[148]

Thumb, Distal Phalange: *Bad sign:* If found on the back and near the nail, Rem indicates it is a sign of lewdness.[149]

Good sign: Newcomer-Bramblett describes a star located on the side of this part of the thumb as a sign of the self-reliant individualist capable of uncommon feats of willpower.

Thumb, Proximal (Second) Phalange: *Bad sign:* If the star is located just below the flexion line at the base of this part of the thumb, then Rem finds it predicts misfortunes associated with women, often in marriage.[150] Morgan places this star just above the flexion line, but agrees it signifies feminine-caused unhappiness and disastrous marriages, adding that only those with a strong Jupiterian hand can escape or resist.[151] This follows Niblo's rationale, but Niblo places the star on the junction of the proximal phalange (of logic) and the mount of Venus.[152]

Good sign: Newcomer-Bramblett finds such a star a sign of an analytical mind with excellent reasoning ability.[153]

Fingers generally: *Bad sign:* On the ends of any fingers, Rem sees a star as a sign of danger.[154]

Good sign: Cheiro is of the opposite opinion. Stars on the tips of the fingers portend fortunes to be found in anything touched.[155] Niblo agrees as to stars on the distal phalange of any finger, especially Saturn.[156]

Index, Jupiter finger: *Good sign:* Rem finds that a star on the first (distal) phalange of this finger and the auricular (little or Mercury) finger indicates eloquence.[157]

Middle, Saturn finger: *Bad sign:* A star on the first (distal) phalange of this finger, according to Rem, announces a fate beyond the capacity of humanity, thus perhaps madness or "Napoleonic glory."[158] Morgan agrees.[159] Did Hitler have such a sign? Morgan goes on to note this is a sign of paralysis (as with Napoleon in Moscow?), untimely death, incurable disease and, if very pronounced, perhaps even murder. If it is on the proximal phalange, Niblo reports the subject may be assassinated, and if joined by the fate line, an inevitable disgraceful death, the nature of which must be discovered from other parts of the hand.[160]

Good sign: Van Alen is more prosaic, finding such a star is merely indicative of unusual faculties expressed through artistic, poetic, or dramatic modes of living.[161] If it is on the first phalange, then Niblo finds it a sign of good fortune.

Little, Mercury finger: *Good sign:* Rita Van Alen finds a star on a long distal phalange a sign of eloquence.[162] Rem agrees[163] (see Jupiter finger above).

Comment

Obviously, I have not dealt with every palmist who has described the sign of a star and tried to give it one or more meanings, but there are basic points to make about the whole field of palmistry and the star offers an excellent place to continue to make it. Conflicts probably result from several factors. Some of the problems could be related to faults in observation. One might be a lack of careful observation of the star's location. Another source of error may be through relating the star to unrelated psychological characteristics or other unrelated events.

Another problem is characterization of the empirical evidence. Even if characteristics and/or events may bear some relation to the star, the particular characteristic or event may not be described with enough specificity. In other words, the attributes of the quality or event described need to be clarified and perhaps broken down further to determine what part of it might have been signified by the star.

A third problem, I believe, is that palmists tend to report clinical findings as general observations. This may be illustrated especially by the works of Saint-Germain discussed below. Thus there is little or no statistical foundation based upon carefully and scientifically gathered empirical evidence for the conclusions often reached about the significance of various signs or lines.

A fourth problem is the tendency by many palmists, as I think we have now illustrated, to uncritically adopt what they may have read or been taught on the subject without further inquiry. This is a waste of the talents of persons who should be trained observers.

Now we will sample the works of two other authors in the field, Gerald E. Biccum, publishing in 1989, and Comte C. de Saint-Germain, writing in 1897. Both Biccum and Saint-Germain refer to the star as a complement to discussions of other hand formations. Biccum presents approximately 40 situations where the star has some significance.[164] Saint-Germain had already identified about 125 variations of star relationships in hand analysis.[165]

Biccum is quite able to generate most if not all of his forty examples using stars without reference to the large number of star illustrations already displayed by Saint-Germain. Each discusses the star in relationship to some other features of the hand, but without a relationship to the whole hand. The illustrations of each give the impression that no attempt has been made to fully illustrate all aspects of the hand. Furthermore, neither uses these varied observations to support a description of what he thinks is the basic meaning and function of the star without regard to a particular application. Saint-Germain clearly discusses clinical findings in most of his comments on the star. Biccum basically says to trust him on his comments, so there is no clear indication where he got his information.

Biccum shows several stars on the F mount, which is at least lower and perhaps middle Luna. Four he relates to the termination of warrior lines (lines of Mars). All reflect ending years of life. The same reading may be given whether the mark is a star, dot, bar, or cross on the F mount. If this is accompanied by any sign on the head line, then it reflects brain exhaustion through life's rapid pace.[166] If the life line takes off and ends in a star on the mount of Mercury under the little finger, and the head line is thin at the start, goes through a chained deflection, and ends in a star, it indicates "you may become insane at the age indicated."[167] (Which is indicated by what, the thin line, the deflection, the star on Mercury, or the star at the end of the head line?) He also says this indicates mental stress due to business strain that causes self-harm. So, do we have the business found in Mercury and the suicide found by the star at the end of the head line, possibly on the mount of the Moon?

Biccum's next warrior line star is at the end of the line on the F mount and is accompanied by a star in the middle of the head line following a dot on the thenar side. The description below the picture is confusing. Again, Biccum tells us that we will find insanity "at the age indicated" followed by self-inflicted death.[168]

The last of Biccum's warrior line stars also appears at the end of the warrior line on the F mount, clearly Luna, and is accompanied by a star at the end of the head line that is preceded by an island and a dot. Here we have possible insanity "at the age indicated" (by what: where the warrior line crosses the life line, where it ends, where the dot, or the island, or the star on the head line appears?). Anyway, this also indicates that insanity is followed by possible death due to mental strain causing self-harm.[169]

Biccum finds a couple of other stars on the Moon mount (or the F mount). One is an imperfect star on the F mount with a corresponding star at the junction of the health and head lines. This indicates very serious "female weakness" causing great difficulties in childbearing.[170] The other star is on the F mount and is accompanied by a dot on the life line with a line to the Saturn finger and a line to the F mount with an imperfect star apparently on the mount. Here he says there is a chance of disease of the joints that is increased "by a chance line and a mark on the 'B' mount."[171] The B mount is the Saturn mount. Taken together, such observations are of little help in discerning the significance of the star found on the hand. We doubt they show serious study of the predictions made (that is, if Biccum did do follow-up studies to indicate causes of death). At best, one or more might be a clinical observation.

Saint-Germain often, but not always, writes as if his observations were clinical observations. He likes to embellish his observations. He says a star on the lunar mount indicates the danger of drowning, while if on a travel line, the danger of shipwreck. Curiously, if the star is on the lower part of the mount, he finds the danger of dropsy and relates one of his clinical stories of a woman operated on three times for dropsy.[172] So, even there, water is prevalent.

Saint-Germain reports on three stars at the end of the head line. On the one sloping to the mount of the Moon, he follows tradition and finds it an indication of death by drowning, often by suicide in a fit of insanity (one wonders how many corpses Saint-Germain, Biccum, and others examined to make such predictions). The second star he discusses as a clinical type finding where the sloping head line ending in a Moon mount star is accompanied by a big cross under the star, and another star lower on the same mount is connected by a forked line to the life line. The subject's fate line is straight, clear from Neptune, and unbroken, ending on the Saturn finger. The liver line (a strong communication line from Neptune to Mercury) is also deep and straight and the subject had a double girdle of Venus. This case was reported according to Desbarrolles. The lady was considered wise in money matters but deteriorated into some form of insanity with a persecution complex.[173] The third star is found at the end of the head line that reaches or almost reaches the rascette in its slope. Here he describes it as the sign of brilliant fortune, following Desbarrolles.[174]

When the star is found on the lunar mount on a branch of the heart line reaching that mount, Saint-Germain finds it is an indication of hereditary madness of an erotic form.[175]

A star on the Saturn mount, according to Saint-Germain, may indicate death on the scaffold, paralysis, or an incurable disease. On a clinical subject who died at thirty-six from sexual excesses, it was coupled with a star on the mount of the Moon and a much rayed and crossed Moon mount as well as a heart line that also started from the life and head lines.[176] No mention is made whether the subject was male or female or how he or she died.

Finally, he states that finding a star at the end of the fate line on Saturn together with another star on the mount of the Moon on the same hand indicates a tendency toward suicide.[177]

Here is the same problem that we have commented on with regard to the work of Asano and we could mention Domin, whose work is another obvious candidate. If any given shape, line, or sign has a particular identifiable meaning, the sheer number of examples of its use coupled with meanings that conflict or vary from use to use does not give us any core description of the meaning or value of that sign, shape, or form. Given that nature has at her disposal an almost unlimited ability to combine various shapes, signs, and lines, we are not given any basic meanings to correlate or values to assign to the signs, shapes, or forms and thus we cannot even begin to form any rules to discern their correlations and possible meanings.

Palmistry is plagued with nonsequiturs and baseless assumptions and this, more than anything else, hinders it from being taken as a serious study. It is fine to report clinical findings, so long as they are clearly described as such, but until we can start to gather a mass of such clinical findings, and/or support them with statistical studies, we might refrain from building broad conclusions concerning the meanings.

Unless we palmists can agree to ground our theoretical work in some basic known assumptions drawn from the smallest common denominators supported by replicable empirical observation, our activities defy serious scientific consideration. Until then, we remain fortune-tellers and clinical psychologists mostly without portfolio and of unknown value.

The Chinese may have avoided this difficulty by grounding their palmistries onto basic philosophical assumptions of the universe generally accepted in their culture. Western palmists who do not have the cultural luxury of such philosophic grounding, despite the supposed prevalence of the Western scientific method. They generally either avoid any grounding of their work or combine it with pop science and psychology and with magic, myth, and nonsense to obfuscate their lack of foundation and basic knowledge of what they are observing. Add to this the latest trend to even avoid common language uses, such as Biccum's F and B mounts and handology, and our common work is disintegrating.

This does not mean that palmists are bad. Some of us are damn good observers and may have insights at times that are far beyond those who claim the support of more traditional scientific methods. But we need to learn more about the process of analysis, the process of description, and the need for replication of the simplest observations. We need to be able to critically appraise our own work. To do this, we need to appreciate our own shortcomings and our own lack of fundamental understanding of what we are observing, and we need to cultivate a humble appreciation of the great mysteries in every hand we are tendered.

Just as this book is readied for showing to publishers, my friend and fellow palmist, Jean Christensen, advises me of another star she found on the lunar mount on both hands of the wife of a high official from one of the Islamic Middle Eastern countries. This lady had perfectly formed Stars of David. I would like to know more of this lady. Perhaps others will share with me before this book goes into a second edition.

CHAPTER ELEVEN

A LIST OF SPECIAL MARKS

I have always felt palmists could use a ready source for unusual signs. I do not claim, however, that this represents all of the signs one may find in the hand. Abayakoon, an Indian astropalmist, claims there are at least 90 basic signs. When these are related to the planets, signs, the twenty-seven asterisms (mansions of the Moon), and fixed stars, Abayakoon claims there are 10,000 signs and signatures.[1] I will not begin to approach that number, but will give the top seventy as I have found them.

Many of the signs in the hand are revealed in sanskrit verses or slokas, according to Dr. Sen, and thus the study of them is very old indeed.[2] Sen has found marks of special help in the absence of lines of fame and fortune. He could not understand why some persons who were rich and respected did not display clearly defined fate and Sun lines. He was dissatisfied with explanations reputedly given by Cheiro and Saint-Germain that he must bear in mind the shape and type of hand and that dim lines on wealthy persons might have little significance as they "set no store by their fortune." So he returned to the Hindu schools of palmistry to restudy the special marks and signs. Those bearing his comments below he claims to have seen. This is not the case with all writers, myself included.

There are a wide variety of special signs or markings that may be found in the hand. Usually, their significance relates to the location in the hand where they are found, such as on a mount, under a finger, or on a line. Some may be significant merely because they are found in the hand or on the wrist. For example, Dr. Sen finds on close examination of a print of William Jennings Bryan, perennial democratic presidential candidate at the turn of the twentieth century and later notorious opponent to Clarence Darrow in the Scopes (Monkey) trial, the mark of the temple on his wrist. That would have indicated his extraordinary success in an otherwise unremarkable hand.[3]

Andrew Fitzherbert cautions us in looking for these signs that finding them is generally up to the imagination of the reader.[4] You are invited to draw your own conclusions.

HOW TO LEARN SIGNS

The student shoud approach this chapter on signs in three parts.

1. The student should master the following signs: bars, breaks, chains, crosses, dots, grilles, healer's marks, islands, spots, squares, triangles, tridents, and tassels.
2. The student should become familiar with the circle, crescent moon, fish, flags, stray lines, stripes, sun, and tree.
3. The student should be aware that other signs are here for future reference.

We will now consider the following marks on the hand: bars, circles, conches, crosses, dots, fish, flags, flowers, grilles, healer's striations, islands, rays, scars, spots, squares, stray lines, temples, triangles, trees, tridents, warts, X's, and some other exotic lines. Just a little over half of the books in my own library devote some space to marks, and most of those only to stars, crosses, bars, grilles, triangles, and healer's striations.

Some signs have a fortunate meaning, some have unfortunate connotations, and some have a variety of meanings depending on size, shape, and location. Many palms have no special marks at all and the absence of these marks may not be significant. For example, the failure of the hand to show special signs of fame, fortune, or high recognition does not mean that the subject will fail to achieve any of these attainments. If the hand is otherwise strong and the subject is willing, success, fame, fortune, and high recognition may be all achievable.

Signs of fortune on otherwise weak or bad hands may neutralize the deficient tendencies but then may not really indicate the same success that they would if found on a good hand.

Fenton and Wright[5] advise us that we should seek confirmation of the mark's significance in other parts of the hand and that marks may well indicate more immediate (temporary) expectations, since they tend to come and go.

Some palmists believe there is a difference in whether the sign appears on the right or left hand. Students may wish to translate the right hand into the active or conscious hand and the left hand into the passive, hereditary, or unconscious hand in order to understand these palmists, or they may find my own yin-yang hand explanation useful.

Because there is not as much difference of opinion about the significance of these signs as there was on stars, I will not attempt to fully annotate all the observations on the value of these signs. When I refer to Vedic astrology, I am referring to the works of Bepin Behari.[6]

Arrow

An arrow marking can appear as having one or two prongs pointing in any direction. Ayer reports that a person with such a sign will have large, landed estates.[7]

In Vedic astrology it is one of the symbols of Saturn. It is also the symbol of Pushya, the eighth nakshatra ruled by Brihashpati, the Vedic Jupiter. Here we may have a subject showing great spiritual magnetism who can vacillate between emotional instability and the tranquil mind. Corresponding symbols are the circle and the flower.

Ashton or Eight-Sided Figure

This eight-sided octagonal marking has been identified by Dr. Sen, but it is not further explained.[8] Abayakoon identifies an eight-cornered star that may also be related to this sign.

Balance

Two triangles hanging from the ends of an inverted "V" indicate balance. Dr. Sen reports that this sign is sometimes found in the hands of shopkeepers.[9] Does it indicate one who takes the weight and measure of the produce and commodities of the material world offered in exchange in order to find a way to make a profit?

Bangles

Small, concentric circles are often called bangles. While Ayer reports the existence of the bangle,[10] his books in my possession do not describe it. Dr. Costavile describes the one shown above from Chinese palmistry. She says they are always positive, and if red in color, they announce material and emotional riches.[11]

Bars

Bars are hindrances to the flow of force through the line. They appear as hatch mark crossings on major lines and represent hindrances to the activities represented by the line. When they appear on fingers, these horizontal lines indicate frustrations to the activities represented by that finger and that portion of the finger. The frustration is relieved or the hindrance is overcome if that line or new energy lines on fingers or mounts flow through the bar.

Bed

Abayakoon pictures beds without any explanation. In Vedic astrology, the small bed symbolized Uttara Phalguni, the twelfth nakshatra, while the small cot symbolized Uttarashada, the twenty-first nakshatra. Uttara Phalguni is ruled over by Aryaman, the wooer, who entices the bearer with ambition aided by black magic to raise the latent powers in man. Uttarashada, on the other hand, is ruled by Viswa Deva, the universe as god, overseeing the drive toward cosmic unity through the contrapositioning of humility with self-centeredness. Ambition, self-centeredness, and the desire to use black magic, which can mean tainted means, to succeed, may well bring material riches but at the cost of evolving in this lifetime.

The Bow

This marking of a bow with drawn arrow can also appear to be a loop and bar on a major line.

This is a rare sign reported by Dr. Sen to be found on princes and kings. He says that on the hand of a millionaire the mark is made by two head lines denoting a rich man, even though the lines are shadowed by Apollo and Saturn lines.[12] Ayer reports that it, along with the sign of the sword, signifies great warriors' fighting qualities.[13] It is one of the symbols of Saturn in Vedic astrology.

The bow is also the symbol of the seventh nak-shatra, Punarvasu, ruled over by the visible infin-ity, Aditi. Another symbol is the house. Here we find the drive to unite sound and the divine con-sciousness. Have we possibly the musician or com-poser? Passion and discipline play roles in the nature of the bearer of this mark.

Braid

A concentric circle with a half-moon outlined along one side is referred to as a braid. This sign in Chinese palmistry presages high positions and honors, according to Dr. Costavile.[14] It seems to hold particular significance for those in the mili-tary.

Breaks

Palmists would agree with Yaschpaule[15] that here we have the force of the line interrupted and that the wider the break, the greater the danger. Look for repair signs, sister lines, triangles, squares, or overlaps.

Canopy or Umbrella

A half circle with a line running down the center and continuing out the bottom appears to be an open umbrella. Ayer reports that this sign will be found on a future emperor or empress who will bear royal children.[16] Dr. Sen believes this sign is found on the best of men and was supposed to have been on the soles of the feet of Shri Krishna. Dr. Sen claims that he saw the sign on the British nineteenth-century prime minister Gladstone, as well as on C. P. Ramaswami Iyer and Ra-bindranath Tagore, Bengali poet and Nobel prize winner.[17]

The umbrella along with the earring are sym-bols of Jyestha, the eighteenth nakshatra, who is ruled by Indra, the lord of the Vedic gods. Here the bearer experiences the drive of the Kundalini, that life force energy nesting at the root of the spine. In the drive for perfect Nirvana, the bearer must travel a true path because he or she is balanced between arrogance and divine benediction. This is a transformation sign and the soul may experience the end of the materialistic desires and be driven to new goals. Others, observing the subject, may believe he or she is a hypocrite as the subject ascends, balanced between two planes, the mate-rial and spiritual. The bearer of the mark is little concerned with the feelings of others so long as they do not obstruct his greater designs.

Chains

When these appear on a line, they can indicate a lack of stamina, confidence, assertiveness, weak health, or a difficult and confusing life. The for-mation of a line of chain links is like a continuous series of obstructions, observes Yaschpaule.[18] This seems to be generally agreed to by palmists. Sasha Fenton and Malcolm Wright indicate chains un-der Saturn are a sign of headaches or migraines.[19] Dr. Sen notes that if all three rascettes are chained, life will be hard, and money will be earned by hard labor.[20]

Checkerboard

Dr. Costavile writes that if a checkerboard pattern of lines is found on the mount of Venus, it reflects depression and reduction of ability to cope with difficulties. If this sign (which also looks very much like a grille) is found elsewhere on the hand, it promises changes for the better with the possibility of resolution of even the most difficult problems.[21]

Circles — the Large Wheel

A large circle is a rare sign. Esther Newcomer-Bramblett finds it a favorable sign if on a mount but not so auspicious if on a line.[22] Jo Logan finds it a favorable sign except when found on Luna.[23] Cheiro, on the other hand, finds it an unfortunate sign except when found on the Apollo mount,[24] and Yaschpaule agrees with Cheiro.[25]

Ayer reports favorably on the sign if on the mounts of Jupiter, Saturn, or Apollo, but, according to Indian lore, a circle on Luna suggests drowning (as it did to Cheiro). Under the head line on the Apollo line it may indicate a vehicular caused accident. On the heart line it denotes heart trouble, and if found on the life line, beware of eye trouble. Under such systems, if the circular mark is found on the female thumb it will indicate a boisterous, overbearing, quarrelsome, scolding woman of easy morals. A similar mark on the Jupiter finger indicates inheritance, but beware of other lines thereon as these will indicate expenses beyond income. A circular mark on the thumb or the figure of a lotus flower will indicate inheritance from the father's side. An inheritance can also be expected if the circle is on the Saturn finger, but the source will be unexpected. Income can be expected from many sources if the circle is found on the Apollo finger and will come from business or industry if found on the little finger. Other lines will indicate losses through the same channels.[26]

Dr. Sen agrees that the only favorable location of the circle is on the Apollo mount. On all other mounts it indicates the subject's success will be interfered with: if on the mount of the Moon, drowning; if on the heart line, loss of sight; and anywhere else it may indicate the subject will be entangled in misfortunes, freedom from which will be difficult to achieve.[27]

Dr. Costavile describes a similar sign that she names the *large wheel*. This is an ambivalent sign that is favorable on the mounts but unfavorable on the lines. If found on the thumb, it indicates a lively intelligence, and when found elsewhere it may be one of those signs indicating mysticism.[28]

Dr. Sen speaks of another circle on the tips of the fingers. He also discusses a shell at the same location. I wonder if he means the two types of whorl fingerprints, the drill and the bullet. In any case, he reports as follows: one circle is a clever person; two, good looking; three, luxurious; four, poverty; five, learned; six, clever among scholars; seven, a hermit and recluse; eight, a poor man; nine, a king; and ten, a government servant. If it is a shell then: one, a raja; two, a wealthy man; three, a yogi with great spiritual powers; four, a poor man; five, wealth; six, a yogi; seven, poverty; eight, riches; nine, a yogi; ten, definitely a poor man. Another reason why I think he may have referred to fingerprints is he says to read these on both hands.[29] In Vedic astrology the circle is another symbol of the eighth nakshatra. See the arrow sign above. It symbolizes that the individual's path to completion is now laid out and the means are at hand to enable the subject to take the path.

Conch

Conches or shells appear to be elongated circles with rounded or pointed protuberances at the top or side. Often there are parenthetical lines inside the conch. To Yaschpaule, the conch is another of the signs indicating great wealth if the subject is a materialist.[30] Dr. Sen agrees, if the sign is found on the wrist or on Jupiter.[31] However, Yaschpaule also finds it one of the signs of a possible scholar. This he determined from three readings and, I presume, his own studies.

According to Indian palmistry (Ayer) the sign of

the conch on the hand of men will make them great intellectuals, commanding universal respect.[32] Dr. Sen notes that the conch was another of the signs reputed to have been on the palm of Lord Krishna, thus denoting the scholar living a pure life and renouncing the world.[33]

Crosses

A cross, as Yaschpaule[34] points out, must be made up of independently formed lines, not by the mere crossing of the major or minor lines identified already in palmistry. In Indian palmistry, according to Ayer,[35] a cross on the mount of Jupiter indicates a happy marriage and on Saturn bad luck. Ayer goes on to note the Indians find that a cross on Apollo will indicate the mind of a pervert or one who is dogmatic, and on Mercury, one who is given to petty larceny. On Venus, he says, beware the unhappy love affair. If it is on the heart line or any marriage line, beware of shock in love life. Ayer indicates that such a sign on the mount of the Moon indicates a great imagination.

Although in Western palmistry it has a generally negative meaning, in the Chinese practice of palmistry (Dr. Maria Costavile) it represents the word *ten* and can have a variety of meanings, not all inauspicious. It could be a sign of good fortune, unexpected assistance, or even a serene life.

Gibson[36] sees the cross as a representative of hindrances whenever it touches a line. On mounts, it can represent the following: Saturn, a fatalistic attitude; Apollo, thwarted fame; Mercury, evasion or bad bargains; the mount of the Moon, self-deception; Venus, family problems; and on Mars, quarrels, violence, or danger from enemies. If found on Jupiter, she follows Saint-Germain,[37] Ayer above, Yaschpaule,[38] and others in saying that it foretells great affection or a happy marriage (a cross of union), though she contends it

can be a token of infidelity. Saint-Germain warns not to confuse this cross with a bar on an upward branch of the life line, which means social ambition thwarted. My friend Robin Gile no longer supports the idea that it indicates matrimony or riches, but feels that it indicates that the possessor will meet his or her match, his or her foil.

Of course, a cross in the quadrangle is the famous mystic cross, which may mean nothing or you may delight your subject by noting that he or she may have psychic or other metaphysical gifts.

A cross made up like an X is a better sign. See X below.

The Devil

A squared-top letter "A" has been called an unfavorable sign in Chinese palmistry, according to Dr. Costavile.[39] Cowardice, indecision, and deceit are foretold. It is a temporary sign, not easily seen, and the hand must be examined carefully to identify it.

Dots

These are like little holes or whirlpools in the channels of the lines, which suck the energy from them. Ayer finds that dots on the life line indicate sickness or sorrow; on the head line, mental strain; on the heart line, emotional loss or heart trouble; and on the fate line, bad luck or other misadventure. If found on the mount of Jupiter, loss of stature; on Mars, loss of possessions; and on Luna, debt.[40] Yaschpaule points out the temporary nature of the illness and that it is often nervous in origin.[41] I recall one reading of five dots on the heart line when I advised the client he would have five heart problems, only to later learn that he had five areas of blockage in his arteries that could lead to these problems. Yaschpaule advises to observe the color of dots and that yellow ones on the life line could indicate bilious problems.

Dr. Sen combines dots with spots. A red one on the head line is indicative of head trauma, while blue or black dots are indicative of nervousness. Red dots on the liver line are indicative of fever, and if on the life line the disease will resemble a fever. Yellow spots on life, head, and heart lines indicate liver problems (biliousness) and foretell irritability.[42]

Dr. Sen separates the black dot from the other dots and reports that if it is found in the center of the palm, if foretells constant acquisition of wealth. If it is on the sole of the foot, it is a sign of government position and the love of having authority.[43] For further information, see the sign *spots.*

The Double Boat

This is another of the Chinese signs reported by Dr. Costavile.[44] It looks like the infinity sign or a tilted figure 8. It is unfavorable, foretelling problems or disagreeable surprises. The figure must be clearly defined without breaks in the lines.

THE DOUBLE WELL

The Double Well

Dr. Costavile warns that this Chinese sign is easy to confuse. If it can be clearly distinguished, then Chinese palmistry finds it a favorable mark foretelling material and moral satisfaction.[45]

Earth (the Chinese Word for Earth)

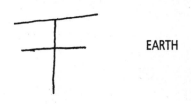

EARTH

Do not confuse this with the sign for *hand.* Dr. Costavile indicates this Chinese sign evidences a cold-hearted, disloyal behavior in the pursuit of personal gain.[46]

Extension

A square box dissected by a cross is referred to as an extension. This Chinese ephemeral sign is described by Dr. Costavile as always favorable, indicating extinction of unfulfilled desires and achievement of success.[47] The extension should not be confused with the field sign, which is described later.

Eye of the Elephant

EYE OF THE ELEPHANT

Dr. Costavile describes this favorable "Z" shaped sign as appearing seldom and indicating the qualities of honesty, fairness, and loyalty when seen.[48]

Fire *(the Chinese Word for* Fire*)*

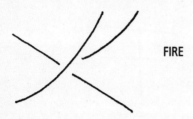

FIRE

Dr. Costavile warns that this is an ambivalent Chinese mark that can be read in different ways.[49] She says the reader should be on guard for any other indications in the hand that symbolize fire, such as anger and hasty decisions.

Fish

An oblong circle with a pointed rear, a squashed triangle with overlapping end lines, even a whorl or dot forming an "eye" are all fish-like markings. According to Rodney Davies,[50] apparently drawing on Indian palmistry lore, the fish on the mount of Jupiter symbolizes power, eminence, honor, religious principles, and respect. If found at the end of the right-hand life line, it promises good fortune throughout life.

Dr. Sen notes that in India the clear sign of a fish on the hand of a woman is a good sign, meaning she will have great wealth, children, and a husband who will outlive her, for it has been considered a great misfortune in India to be a widow, especially a young one.[51]

Dr. Sen regards this as one of the four signs and lines indicative of wealth the subject may be expected to enjoy. It invariably accompanies a strong Jupiter mount in the same hand. It is a sign of leadership of good-natured, charitable, and religious persons.[52]

According to Ayer,[53] under the Indian system,

the fish is a very favorable sign, indicating a man who will achieve enormous success. Yaschpaule agrees.[54]

Yaschpaule also asserts that a clearly formed fish will be found on a subject with Jupiter well aspected in his or her horoscope.[55] Besides a good heart, strong finances, learning, and enjoyment of a post of authority, the subject will have a philosophical bent. For the housewife, it is an indication that her husband will be financially successful, especially if found in her right hand, which according to Indian palmistry, reveals the material prospects of the husband.

The fish can be found anywhere on the hand and may or may not have an eye. If the face is toward the wrist, prosperity is expected in middle age; if the face points toward the fingers, it foretells an earlier prosperity. Once it occurs, wealth follows throughout the life.[56] Dr. Sen agrees generally on wealth being found and states that if the fish is pointed toward the fingers or side of the hand, the subject will enjoy happiness and prosperity throughout his life, while if it points downward, the benefits come late in life.[57]

A fish symbolizes Revati, the twenty-seventh and final nakshatra. Do we find some connection with Pluto? Revati is ruled by Pushan, the nourisher. This nakshatra stands for the womb, resting place for the Sun before it begins the new cycle. In completion, it signifies dissolution and may find its impulse in nihilism. The bearer is suspended between equanimity and complete destruction. The fish is the great fertilizer for the new creative force through its own decay. The old cycle ends and pregnantly awaits the new birth of creation.

I love what Yaschpaule and Dr. Sen say, but must report that at the age of fifty-seven, my two right-handed fish have failed to be signs of early prosperity.* That is very frustrating as one is on the mount of Apollo. Maybe I am looking at confusion, as one fish may be pointing toward the fingers from just above the wrist and the other may be pointing toward the wrist from the Apollo mount. Could that narrow the focus?

Chinese Fish: Chinese fish appear as open-ended triangles or check-marks. Dr. Costavile treats this Chinese mark as an auspicious sign of the serene life. If it crosses a finger like the tail of a fish, it indicates money (so check the month of the digit crossed). If it appears on two fingers, there will be both money and honors.[58]

Field

The field is a square box with a cross firmly planted in the center. The lines forming the cross do not overlap the edges of the square, unlike the extension mark as described earlier. The field is a happy sign, according to Dr. Costavile's reports on Chinese signs, which foretells success in business and good fortune.[59] The clearer, cleaner, and deeper the marks, the stronger is the interpretation.

Flags

Flags are triangular protuberances shooting out from vertical lines. According to Davies,[60] this sign, which is attached to one or more of the main palm lines, can represent wealth and success. More frequently it signifies faith, perseverance, virtue of heart, purity of mind, and a desire for spiritual enlightenment. Davies looks for it in the hands of the spiritually advanced.

Dr. Sen finds this a mark on men with the virtues of renunciation, purity, and strength of character, and it is also the sign that the person will be rich, enjoy material prosperity, and own many interests. He has found the mark in imprints of hands of persons like the British prime minister of the nineteenth century, Gladstone, and the American author, Mark Twain.

Flight of the Geese

Dr. Costavile describes this as a favorable sign composed of five wavy lines that do not touch, and it indicates success and prestige.[61] These should not be confused with flying needles which follows.

Flying Needles

Described by Dr. Costavile[62] as short, parallel lines that are usually not perpendicular and are identified by their intense red color. These lines announce success unless crossed by another line. If they are crossed, this presages a serious difficulty.

Flower, Lotus, and Octagon

Eight-sided flower-like markings have several interpretations. A lotus or an octagon, according to the Indian system (Ayer), indicates a man who will be fabulously rich and live a long life. Ayer couples the lotus with the circle in discussing inheritance (see above).[63] Dr. Sen reports that this sign or the fish or the swastika is generally found on women who will be outlived by their husbands.[64] The sign is called Padma in sanskrit and Yaschpaule believes the subject bearing this

---

* This is so, even though Jupiter is 17°39′ Capricorn retrograde in the third house, trine with the Sun at 19°28′ Virgo retrograde in the eleventh house, trine with Mercury at 23°00′ Virgo in the eleventh house, trine with Neptune at 18°44′ Virgo in the eleventh house, and trine with Uranus at 13°27′ Taurus retrograde in the seventh house, and has semisextile involvements with the Moon and Mars, quinxunxes with Venus and Mercury and a semisextile with the ascendant. That sounds like pretty heavy Jupiter.

sign will not be much interested in the cares of this world but rather follow divine pursuits.[65]

Dr. Sen points out that this is another sign to be found on the hands or feet of avatars such as Lord Krishna and Shri Rama and claims he saw the sign on the British nineteenth-century prime minister Gladstone, as well as on C. P. Ramaswami Iyer and Rabindranath Tagore.[66]

A flower is a third sign of Pushya, along with the arrow and circle described above. This flower symbolizes all flowers in the blooming of latent abilities. The lotus, by contrast, indicates spiritual perfection. I suspect that a really fine Indian palmist would distinguish the marks of the flower and the lotus.

The lotus flower symbolizes Anuradha, the seventeenth nakshatra, which falls under the sign of Mars. It is ruled by Mitra, a sun. Spirit and matter mix in the primary impulses and we may see the use of occult powers for quite selfish ends as part of the evolution of the bearers of this mark. They may be caught in a whirlpool of materialism, yet the lotus flower contains all the creative energies or entire creative process. Our subject could rise unknown from poverty and achieve greatness and high spirituality as he or she puts aside ignorance and is purged of his or her clinging materiality. The sign does not promise an easy life.

Lotus (Chinese Style): Dr. Costavile describes another Lotus found in Chinese palmistry[67] made up of two converging lines that do not actually meet. If clearly defined, it is another mark of mysticism and withdrawal from reality. Overall, she says, it is considered a favorable sign.

Grilles

A series of crossed lines which form a mark resembling graph paper have been named grilles. Under theories that reflect the lines as passageways for the energies of the hand, a grille would indicate an abundance, indeed an overabundance, of energy in that particular area of the palm. Because the grille is made up of many crosses, it would indicate that such energy is working at cross purposes. The sign is almost uniformly considered bad.

Ayer considers the sign on Jupiter to indicate superstition and selfishness; on Saturn, restraint; on Apollo, narcissism; on Mercury, a thief; on Venus, lust; and on the mount of the Moon, a brooding and moody nature preoccupied with death.[68] In these findings he follows Cheiro, who finds the grille on Jupiter indicates egotism, pride, and dominating spirit; on Saturn, it indicates a melancholy nature and morbid tendencies leading to misfortune; on Apollo, folly through vanity and the desire to be a celebrity; on Mercury, unstable and unprincipled subjects; on Luna, it indicates restlessness and discontent; and on Venus, caprice in passion.[69]

Gibson, following similar reasoning, finds a grille on Jupiter indicative of a person who shifts personal blame for lack of success onto bad luck.[70] On Saturn, she sees it as a sign of resignation that may well produce the disappointments feared by the subject.[71] On Apollo, she sees it as a sign of those with inflated self-worth who may believe their own publicity.[72] On Mercury it indicates failure in ventures.[73] She finds a grille on Luna indicative of a confused imagination often disturbed by thoughts of ailments.[74] A grille on Venus shows increased ardent desires. Such a feature on upper Mars indicates a violent temper.[75]

Fenton and Wright point out, following the line-energy channel hypothesis, that the vertical lines represent excessive wants, and the horizontal lines represent cross purposes or confusion. This could lead to obsessive-compulsive behavior in the areas represented by that particular mount.[76]

Rita Robinson finds a grille on the Jupiter mount is possibly a good sign, especially if the mount is well developed and the finger long. In this case, it can be the sign of a good leader if that person can hold his or her excessive demands in check. However, on Apollo, it indicates a scattering of energies; on Mercury, bad business decisions (hasty decisions born of two much energy?); and on Saturn, a detraction from the person's charm. On the mount of the Moon it can detract from the imagination.[77]

Hand (*the Chinese Word for* Hand)

HAND

This is another auspicious Chinese ephemeral mark reported by Dr. Costavile[78] that is not always easy to identify and needs to be distinguished from the Chinese word for *earth* as described previously. It indicates pure feelings and loyalty.

Healer's Marks, Striations, Medical Stigmata, and Samaritan Lines

To find these marks, look between the Apollo and Mercury fingers. You will find either a series of perpendicular lines unattached at the base, or attached, creating a broom effect. I like to call the perpendicular marks the sign of the old-style doctor with the good bedside manner. These indicate people who are just nice to have around. They are nice to hug. They tend to be demonstrative, act as good listeners, and leave one feeling better. They may be quite unaware of their talents. They tend to draw to themselves dependent types of people. Rita Robinson, among many others, would agree.[79]

Dr. Sen has found such lines are signs of "psychological gifts and talents for scientific studies."[80] Vera Compton records that three or more of these lines are an indication of the person's aptitude for some phase of the medical profession and they are also known as Samaritan lines.[81] I have been told by at least one other palmist that the physician would more likely be marked with five parallel lines, and those working in other health professions would tend to have fewer lines.

The broom was shown to me by another palmist on my own left hand. Here the perpendicular marks are drawn together by another angular mark so that we see the rough outline of a broom. I recall asking the particular significance of this mark and was told it was a sign of someone who works with herbs. That fit, as I have a rather extensive closet filled with herbs, including some of the more powerful, less common ones such as tansy and wormwood.

On a later occasion, reading for a meeting of hospital administrators, I encountered one obviously skeptical subject who was all business. When I looked at her hand and told her she had an affinity for herbs, she looked dumbfounded. She had two loves in her life: her work and her herb garden. In my experience, these people react more favorably to herbal medicine than alopathic or homeopathic remedies, at least for minor ailments.

Hooked Fish

This mark, which resembles parentheses, is reported by Dr. Costavile to be a favorable Chinese sign of power and personal satisfaction.[82]

Islands

Random loops or pools attached to lines are called islands. Islands indicate a temporary division of the energies and could indicate a period of limitation, misfortune, depression, or ill health. Most palmists whose work I have read agree that the island diminishes the qualities of the line or mount. Dr. Sen notes that any line running into an island on any portion of the palm is a bad sign.[83]

For example, Ayer gives these meanings to islands on various lines: on the life line, it indicates a period of delicate health with a possible cure; on the health line, it depicts periods of worry, headache, and mental strain; on the heart line, it is the mark of misplaced affection and misfortune in love; and when found on the fate line, it foretells an adverse time in one's career, perhaps undeserved.[84]

Fenton and Wright warn to always take islands seriously, for they indicate difficult times because of the sudden splits of energies of the line affected. They advise to check to see if there are other disturbances in the hand corresponding in time, in which case the island may indicate a sudden, life-changing event. If it is alone, it may indicate a health problem.[85]

Fenton and Wright describe several islands not connected to health problems: a large one at the beginning of the life line indicates childhood unhappiness; a thin one early in the life line can indicate the shock of a marriage before the person has really faced adult reality; a long one on the Venus side of the life line indicates a period of restriction, such as raising children; and one on a line leading to the fate line could indicate relationship difficulties.[86]

Carol Hellings White describes this oval formation as "a symbol of isolation or separation." Reflecting that it is a common marking found on most major lines, she observes that it may indicate illness, mental stress, emotional upheavals, difficulty in love, loneliness, or just isolation and that big islands are worse than a chain of small islands.[87]

Rodney Davies reports islands as harbingers of children. He advises examination of the lowest crease in the thumb for islands. Those on the right thumb indicate natural children; those on the left indicate the ones that may come into one's life through adoption or marriage. The little ones are girls, the big ones boys, and their order can be determined from placement in the right thumb with the lower island being first.[88] This observation has not worked out well on the author's hand.

Davies also reports one island to be a most fortunate sign if clearly formed, large, and centrally placed on the knuckle line between the distal and medial phalanges of the thumb.[89] It indicates a happy life with all things being beneficial to the possessor in the end. So this author only hopes he lives so long.

Jupiter

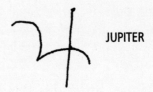

JUPITER

The sign of Jupiter is reported by Saint-Germain, despite his admission that he has never seen the sign.[90] Nevertheless, he reports that when it is found on the mount of Jupiter, it intensifies the good qualities of the mount.[91] When the sign is found on Saturn, it indicates a desire to gain fame through some philosophical discovery.[92] Obviously, it could mean eloquence in statesmanlike discourses when found on the Sun mount.[93] On the Mercury mount, Saint-Germain would expect power reached either through verbal communication or science.[94]

Enter the "insatiable conqueror," whether on the field or in the bedroom, when this sign is seen on upper Mars, says Saint-Germain.[95] Lower the sign to the mount of the Moon, and conquest drops into extravagant dreams of power and position.[96] Move the sign of Jupiter to the mount of Venus, and Saint-Germain predicts that the bearer will love those who flatter his or her vanity.[97]

Another sign of Jupiter, according to Abayakoon, is the Christ thorn leaf.

Lascivious Desires

These thin, crooked and closely parallel lines are commonly found on the mount of Venus and Dr. Costavile tells us that these marks indicate sexual love in Chinese palmistry.[98] If found in those of advanced age, they are good indications of continuing sexual abilities.

Mars

Similar to the symbol for "male," the Mars mark is a concentric circle with an arrow pointing upward toward the right.

This is another of those elusive astral signs reported by Saint-Germain that he has never seen,[99] yet so great is his confidence in the archetype meaning of this sign that he is able to predict a military genius if it is seen on the mount of Jupiter.[100] When found on Saturn, it is indicative of a combative spirit in disputes over religion or politics and could be found in the hands of fanatics and inquisitors.[101] Though he has never seen it, Saint-Germain can still report that it is "frequently

in the hand of a painter or writer of military subjects."[102] The sign of Mars on Mercury indicates the highwayman type (modern-day mugger) who combines violence and theft.[103]

Mars on upper Mars merely intensifies the mount, according to Saint-Germain.[104] The Moon graced with the Mars sign would be a strong indication of brain fever or of raving mania.[105]

Another sign for Mars, according to Abayakoon, is the lentil.

Mercury

The sign of Mercury is a well-rounded circle with a cross hanging from the bottom.

Another sign for the powers of Mercury is the scorpion senna, according to Abayakoon.

Saint-Germain continues to follow the archetype analysis of this astral sign when he reports that, although he has never seen the sign, if it is found on Jupiter, it will indicate administrative ability and statesmanship.[106] He reports that it is a sign of aptitudes for high mathematics and astronomy when found on the mount of Saturn.[107] Watch for the person with this sign on the Apollo mount as it is a sign of "remarkable money making talent."[108] Mercurial signed Mercury would intensify the features otherwise shown in the mount.[109]

The gambler may well be found with a sign of Mercury on upper Mars, according to Saint-Germain, for here we have the person with the ambition for conquest, wherever the competition.[110] Put the sign of Mercury on Luna, and the subject's taste for speculation will be pushed to extremes, including financial ruin.[111] Mercurial Venus would be a sign of the prostitute who is mercenary over love (or for that matter the spouse who marries for gold or the employee who sleeps with the boss to get a raise).[112]

Moon (Crescent Moon)

Crescent-shaped ovals or half-circles symbolize the Moon powers, according to Abayakoon.

Ayer believes that those graced by the Moon sign on their hands will lead happy lives.[113]

Saint-Germain does claim to have observed this astral sign on several occasions.[114] He reports that found on Jupiter, it indicates ambition led astray by imagination.[115] When found on the Saturn mount, it signifies a morbid imagination and often insanity.[116] Combined with the mount of Apollo, we may expect to find an increase, possibly an excess, of imagination in artistic and literary work, "sometimes to the point of incoherence."[117] The wild con artist or schemer, one who deceives both himself and his friends and associates, is predicted if this sign is found on Mercury.[118]

When the Moon sign shines over its neighbor, upper Mars, Saint-Germain predicts violent insanity.[119] Lunacy would be the most obvious expectation of Saint-Germain in finding the sign of the Moon on the mount of Luna. He calls it "diseased imagination, nightmares, insanity."[120] The lunar signed Venusian mount, while a bad sign, might appeal to those who would like to get together with a subject who has an erotic imagination.[121]

Dr. Costavile finds the crescent moon in Chinese palmistry to be a favorable sign, foretelling good fortune in business and love, so long as it is not crossed by a line. When crossed by a line, the sign turns unfavorable, particularly with regard to work.[122]

Nail (the Chinese Word for Nail)

The nail marking is a distinct capital letter "T."

This unfavorable Chinese sign is described by Dr. Costavile as representing some difficulty in overcoming obstacles. She indicates it might be considered a key sign, directing the subject to go around the obstacle rather than meeting it head on.[123]

Pitcher

A vase-like shape, identified by both Yaschpaule and Ayer, who calls it the water pot, report this as a sign of high office for the subject.[124]

Precious Spiral

Dr. Costavile describes this uncommon Chinese sign as the harbinger of achievement through work and in social life. If it remains on the hand for "some time," then honors and personal satisfaction accompanied by financial gain may be expected.[125]

Rays

These shooting vertical lines, wherever they fall, are believed by Esther Newcomer-Bramblett to enhance any trait.[126]

Roof

Two lines forming an angle is another simple sign from Dr. Costavile's report on Chinese ephemeral marks and is also known as the sign of two branches.[127] It is not a good sign if the angle is acute. The more obtuse the angle (greater than ninety degrees), the less unfavorable the sign. It is another indicator of temporary problems.

Samaritan Lines

See healer's marks, above.

Saturn

Picture a lower case letter "h" with a long tail on the right to identify this sign. Saint-Germain reports seeing it once.[128] He further reports that if it is found on Jupiter, it indicates caution, because here is a lover of occult sciences.[129] When found on Saturn, it indicates a student of the mysterious, religion, philosophy, occult sciences, and the like.[130] Saturn adds a weird quality to the mount of Apollo, perhaps macabre artistic genius, and on a bad hand, it is an indication of the misuse of occult sciences.[131] When the sign is found on Mercury, we should find the doleful talent.[132]

On upper Mars, Saint-Germain would expect the subject with the Saturn sign to display a morbid, even murderous disposition incited by such motives as revenge rather than by love of money.[133] Religious insanity would be expected from the subject with the sign of Saturn on his or her Moon mount.[134] When found on Venus, he would expect an unnatural kind of love full of melancholy and morbid connotations.[135]

We have mentioned that the arrow, bow, and javelin are alternative signs for this mark. Abayakoon adds the thorn apple.

Serpents

Dr. Sen finds this an unfavorable sign, indicating opposition from enemies.[136]

Vedic astrology gives more possible depth to the sign. The serpent symbolizes the ninth nakshatra, Ashlesha, ruled over by Naga, the serpent king. The serpent symbolizes the rising of the Kundalini, opening the wisdom and spiritual enlightenment of the subject. But if mishandled, the subject must understand it is a deadly, poisonous energy. These subjects must cleanse their lives in order to manifest their goals and achieve that Nirvana promised by the rising of the Kundalini. The serpent is bipolar and is capable of good and evil. The subject will probably be continually regenerating just as the serpent renews its skin. So the subject does not fit well into society's slots. They tend to outgrow whatever they enter.

Six Flowers

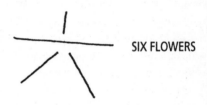

SIX FLOWERS

This is very uncommon, but one of the most favorable ephemeral Chinese marks described by Dr. Costavile, signifying success in everything: love, business, and social life, and it includes well-being and prestige with advancing age.[137]

Spots

These can indicate temporary problems or where one stabbed oneself with a pin or pencil when a child. When they indicate a problem, they usually refer to health. I like to differentiate between spots and dots. The dots may be recognized as depressions, and the spots may merely be discolorations. The palm books do not necessarily make this distinction, so compare my remarks on both subjects.

Rita Robinson says that dark spots, especially on the head line, refer to emotional illnesses, and red spots indicate fever.[138] My observations are that dark spots indicate more serious conditions, with possible transformation even in the form of death, while the red ones indicate either an acute period, such as an acute infection, or a healing period.

Cheiro believes that the spot indicates a temporary illness, with a bright red spot on the head line representing shock or injury from some trauma, and on the health line or life line it usually denotes an illness with a fever. A black or blue spot indicates a nervous illness.[139]

There is a rumor that certain adept palmists can press the hand and a spot of color appears at the appropriate place in the life line to indicate where the person is in his or her life. I have not been able to accomplish that, but I have seen such mysterious colors appear when a hand is being examined by my friend, Robin Gile. Robin may not agree that the spot will always indicate the age, for he has maintained that after the subjects have sufficiently matured, they have some freedom to travel back and forth on the life line in choosing experiences.

Spear and Spearhead

Think of the head of a spear or rounded arrow when looking for these marks. Dr. Sen identifies both of them and advises that the spearhead is an excellent sign on any mount where it is found.[140] He shows the spear on the right foot of Lord Krishna and the left foot of Shri Radhika.[141]

The javelin is one of the signs of Saturn, along with the bow and the arrow.

Squares

Generally, these are considered as protective signs. Benham developed the theory of energy channels. When the line was broken, the energy of that line would flow over the entire palm, seeping aimlessly into the sands of the palm. But a square around such a break would keep the energy within the normal channel area and act as a protection from the loss of that energy.[142] Most palmists agree with the protective nature of squares. They can offset unfavorable signs on any mount where they are located.

On the mount of Jupiter, the square is seen as a sign of a teacher or a manager. However, it may indicate some tunnel vision. Even rectangles that do not have all four sides fully closed are potent signs in this area. Gibson points out that no side of a square can be formed by a general line.[143]

Rita Robinson finds that the square offers protection from heartbreak on the heart line, financial loss if on either the lines of fate or Mercury, excesses of passion if on the mount of Venus, emotional problems if on the head line, death if on the life line, notoriety if on the mount of Jupiter, and morbidity if on the mount of Saturn.[144]

Cheiro devotes a whole chapter to squares, finding them the most interesting of the lesser signs and noting that they are usually called the marks of "preservation," because of their indication of protection from any danger menacing at that point. While Cheiro generally finds squares a good sign, there is a caveat. When one is found touching the life line but lying outside of it on the plain of Mars, it means "imprisonment or seclusion from the world."[145]

While Dr. Sen agrees generally that the square is a sign of protection, he also agrees with Cheiro that if found adjacent to the life line on the plain of Mars, it is indicative of imprisonment or retirement from the world. He also adds that if it encloses the heart line, it indicates heavy problems with a loved one but heartbreak will be averted, though if the sign is under Saturn, the loved one will be the target for misfortune.[146]

Staircase of Jade

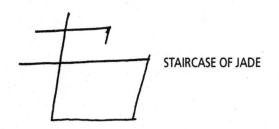

STAIRCASE OF JADE

Dr. Costavile describes this unusual Chinese sign as a bearer of glad tidings. It foretells prospects of high social standing and academic success in examinations.[147]

Stray Lines

Lots of tiny lines which "stray" across the palm indicate many distractions. These subjects show a lack of direction and are nervous. However, tiny lines tend to come and go, so one looks to the formation of basic lines to understand the true potential of the person and to counsel them on this potential. These subjects can often benefit from taking up a directed course of meditation, martial arts, or exercise. Activities that aid their self-discipline will really assist them.

Cheiro speaks of palms covered with fine lines spreading like a net over the palm that tell of an intensely nervous and sensitive person, worried over what others might consider inconsequential matters. This he finds is particularly so with soft-handed people, but not so if found on the hard, firm hand. In the latter hand, these lines indicate a rather selfless type who is energetic and excitable over the cares of others and more successful for them than for himself.[148]

Stripes

Morgan describes stripes as more or less parallel lines. Medical stigmata could be stripes. A series of bars on the fingers could be stripes. The most common stripes, that come with age, are the lines that ascend the fingers. Morgan contends that when there are a large number of stripes located on a single mount or finger, they indicate some sort of "electrical energy" of a quality associated with the mount.[149] Perhaps the term "cosmic" energy might be more appropriate.

Favorable stripes, according to Morgan, should always be ascending. Unfavorable stripes are like bars, horizontally crossing the hand. For Morgan, the more heavily striped the finger, the greater the aptitude represented by the stripes. Thus, a heavily striped Mercury finger represents a person especially active in the pursuits indicated by Mercury, gifted in all of them and particularly in medicine. Such stripes on Saturn will indicate aptitudes in mining or prospecting (look for the corresponding dowser's fingerprint on the thumb), botany, chemistry, or agriculture. On Jupiter, he believes it shows diplomatic or administrative abilities.

Morgan finds ascending stripes from the life line are always favorable, often indicating strokes of good fortune coming from the subject's own personal merit. When we look at the mounts below the heart line, such stripes indicate a high degree of irritability that he finds most true with the unspecified mount of Mars, where they represent violence of action and bronchitis or disorders of the larynx. We suspect by his reference to health matters that he is really referring to upper Mars. In support of this assumption, he goes on to note when the stripes are found on the mount of the Moon, diarrhea is indicated. As a further observation, he notes that the smooth mount of Mars, especially if the lunar mount is also smooth, indicates a "spirit of resignation" that would indicate a few lines might be helpful to a fighting spirit.

Vertical stripes independent of and above the head line that do not intersect that line and are present in small numbers indicate, according to Morgan, the triumph of the subject's intellectual ideas. But similarly situated above the heart line, they serve no useful purpose and can be "positively harmful." He says they rarely occur. But I see them as possible additional parts of girdles of Venus.

Deeply etched, closely packed, or numerous stripes on the mount of Mercury are signs of an aptitude for science. This finding confirms that of Dr. Sen on medical stigmata, mentioned above.

Morgan reports that it is unusual for all fingers to be striped. This is contrary to my own finding. I observe that striping seems to follow the course of life. As people satisfy the initial needs of hearth and home reflected by each of the fingers, the proximal phalanges of the fingers become striped. As they adjust to the social needs of their own lives as reflected by each of the fingers, the middle phalanges of the fingers seem to acquire stripes. Finally, as they tackle and accomplish the higher spiritual and intellectual goals of their lives as reflected in each of the fingers, the distal phalanges seem to become striped. As all of this happens, the stripes seem to extend through the bars and the former barriers to accomplishment, and it appears as if the stripes seem to bleed the bars of their potency as each stripe reflects the internal understanding, personal power, and spiritual growth of the subjects.

String of Coins

Dr. Costavile reports that this ephemeral Chinese mark predicts financial gains and high social status.[150]

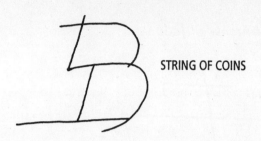

STRING OF COINS

Sun

A round circle with a dot in the center or rays protruding from the sides is known as a sun mark.

Ayer reports that the sun sign on the hand foretells a happy life.[151]

Saint-Germain reports that if this sign is found on the mount of Jupiter, it heralds eloquence and a love of the fine arts.[152] A Sun on Saturn brings brightness to that mount as a sign of the lover of beauty in nature and eloquence in expression of thoughts.[153] The Sun on the Sun mount is sunny indeed, indicating artistic genius.[154] A sunny Mercury identifies one with talent for natural philosophy or astronomy, an ardent ecologist, one with an "intense admiration of God's creation."[155]

Traveling to upper Mars, Saint-Germain finds the Sun sign a sign of vanity displayed in love of show, vivid colors, bright uniforms, or conspicuous gems.[156] Saint-Germain has little good to say for the astral signs found on the mount of the Moon, as he finds even the Sun sign an indication of folly of wealth and extravagance in poetical and artistic expressions.[157] The Sun found on Venus would indicate an idealistic, platonic lover.[158]

Swastika

Dr. Sen merely reports that this is a favorable sign to have.[159] He shows it as one of the signs reported to have been on Lord Krishna's right heel.[160]

Sword

A bladelike edge has been called the sword mark. The Indian name of this sign is the *kuthar rekha*, and Dr. Sen reports that if it is found on the mount of Apollo, it is a sign of trouble in life.[161]

In Vedic astrology, the sword symbolizes Purva Bhadra, the twenty-fifth nakshatra ruled by the one-footed goat, Ajaikapada. The impetus of the sign is cosmic stability, which the bearer approaches fearlessly, but he or she may face sorrow and anguish on the road. The sword has two edges and is an enigmatic weapon used for both good and evil. It can lead to the murderer or martyrdom. The bearer is likely to be caught up in some zealous pursuit motivated by inner urges. The rest of the hand must be read to determine what paths may be taken.

Tassels

Most palmists would agree with Peter West that these, along with breaks and chains, all indicate dissipation of the natural energies of lines and with tassels they are commonly thought of as signs of age.[162] Fenton and Wright observe that when found on the head line, it may be a sign of lack of calcium fluoride or potassium or just much worry that could signal depression of senile dementia (senile psychosis).

Temple

Yaschpaule reports this is a sign of great wealth if it is found on a materialistic hand.[163] It is a rare sign also found on great reformers and famous social workers. It indicates high social position. Davies sums it up by saying it indicates "eminence through wealth, holiness, or by virtue of good works." Dr. Sen states it may be found on royalty, prophets, and saints, and was on the sole of the foot of Shri Krishna and on the imprints of hands of Tagore and William Jennings Bryan. If one line forms a branch from the life line to the Apollo mount, the subject will attain top honors of his or her profession.[164] It is referred to as the mark of shivalaya.

Ten (the Chinese Word for Ten)

See Dr. Costavile on crosses above.

Then (the Chinese Word for Then)

THEN

Dr. Costavile reports this as a negative Chinese mark that foretells problems, even inabilities, in achieving long-term aims.[165]

Three Cats

Three marks appearing like the letter "T" in a configuration is always favorable. This Chinese sign described by Dr. Costavile foretells long life and fortunate love.[166]

Tortoise

While announcing attainment of fame and honors, this complex sign described by Dr. Costavile is hard to identify, but should not be confused with other signs of similar appearance.[167]

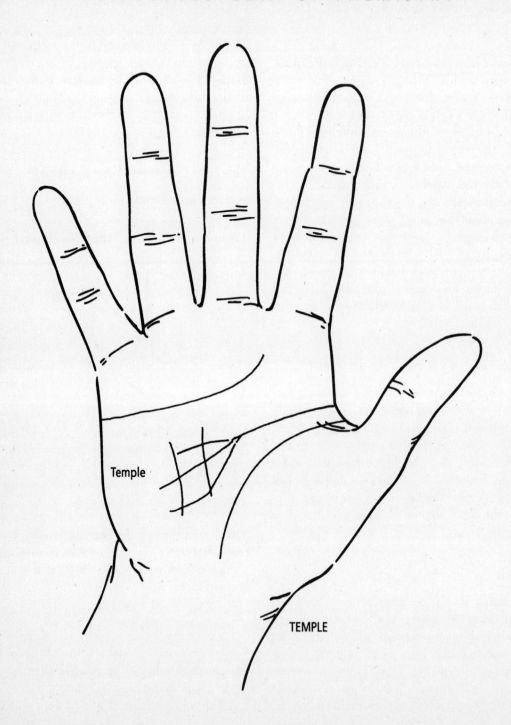

Temple

TEMPLE

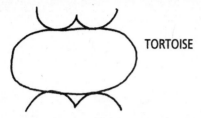

TORTOISE

Triangles

Davies notes that while this sign can be formed by the junction of three lines crossing, it has an even more fortunate meaning when it appears independently. It is, for him, always a good sign.[168]

Yashpaule, like most palmists, agrees that it is always a favorable sign. He notes that it can indicate either intellectual success or material gain. He combines astrology with triangles found at the present age on the fate line to forecast good results from investments.[169]

Dr. Sen discusses triangles in several locations. Small ones on the life or perhaps heart line indicate men who will acquire agricultural land and a home through their own efforts. If a big triangle is formed on the health or head line, look for a famous subject, one who is influential and has a keen intellect. One formed by the head, health, and fate lines (very common) is supposedly indicative of divining the future by one who masters the sciences and deeds of otherworldliness. A triangle found on the head line is indicative of inheritance of property and money from the mother's side, and one on the life line indicates the inheritance will come from the father's side. One on the fate line indicates money from unforeseen sources, and one on the rascette denotes taking over of wealth belonging to others as well as honors.[170]

Davies discusses triangles found on the mounts.[171] If found on either Jupiter mount, the subject will have a stable and mature mind, the power of leadership, and honest, upright ambitions. If it is on the right hand it will indicate these qualities are applied and result in personal gain of honor. On Saturn, the indication is an inborn interest in metaphysics and mystical matters on a subject with a balanced, gentle temperament and love of the outdoors. The right-handed sign further betokens development of a concerned person who achieves spiritual success.

Davies goes on to describe triangles located on the left-handed mounts of Mercury or Apollo as symbols of mental astuteness, which may be turned to artistic success if found on the right-handed Apollo mount or could be turned into success in business, science, or politics if found on the right-handed Mercury mount. Happiness should follow. On either of the mounts of lower Mars it indicates enthusiasm, which is steadily applied with great presence of mind and good fortune. If triangles are found on both mounts of upper Mars, they indicate focused resolve leading to success.

The creative imagination is evidenced, according to Davies, by triangles on Luna, which will be put to successful and good use if found on the right-handed mount. On Venus, it is a sign of sexual drives being held under control and directed toward establishment of strong, loving pair bonds. He finds such are marks of mature and responsible subjects.

Fenton and Wright report that a line that splits into an island shaped like a triangle or diamond is not good. On the head line it will indicate intense frustration and feelings of restraint (possibly prison or sickbed type of confinement). Independent triangles come in for good marks with Fenton and Wright, being signs of talent, even brilliance. But they admit finding no support for the psychic powers reported evidenced by triangles formed like the mystic cross, between the heart and head lines.[172]

Luxon and Goolden find psychic powers indicated by a triangle on Saturn but advise not to exploit the gift because the mount is slightly unfavorable and the results might follow the indications of the mount. These writers note that when found on the Sun mount, it indicates perhaps unexpected radical changes in lifestyle, environment, or career that bring about unexpected rewards, which could come as quite a surprise if found on the right hand only. A Mercurial triangle indicates promotion and acquisition of new skills.[173]

Dr. Costavile treats the triangle in Chinese palmistry as an ambivalent sign that can signify success but also difficulty and bad behavior.[174]

Tree

This refers to two or more rising branches from a vertical palm line. These are said to represent successes in the areas covered by that particular palm line. A fate line with a tree would be a harbinger of a successful career if on the active hand. It is another one of those marks of fame, fortune, and wealth and high position. See Davies.[175]

Dr. Sen considers it a very important mark that might be seen on the hands of all successful people. This is because it is a principle of hand reading that all branches that tend to shoot up are lines of promise tending to bear good fruit. He pointed out that the hands of Annie Besant (of Theosophy fame), the famous nineteenth-century English prime minister Gladstone, and the Indian, Vivekananda, had such signs and it was also one of the signs on the feet of Lord Krishna, so Dr. Sen presumes it was on his hand.[176]

Tridents

Tridents resemble a three-pronged pitch fork with a curved base. This is another favorable mark. Unlike the star, the trident is favorable at the ends of the head, heart, and life lines. It is a mark of outstanding good fortune. Yaschpaule finds it a sign of wealth or fame on the mount of Jupiter[177] and Dr. Sen believes that when it is so located, it foretells success in ambitious pursuits. He goes on to say that on the Sun mount it foretells power through wealth and celebrity status in public life or literature.[178] On the life line it signifies dignity and happiness in later life and a peaceful death.

Tripods

Tripods are also three-pronged but the connecting point at the base is pointed, not round.

Dr. Sen gives these excellent marks on any mount where they may be found.[179] Ayer reports such a sign "will make a man a king" who will be generous and pious.[180]

Valley (the Chinese Word for Valley)

Two parallel lines preceded by a curved, arch line indicates a very favorable sign according to Dr. Costavile's report of Chinese ephemeral signs.[181] Everything from good relations with others, good fortune, and long life to success at work are foretold by this sign.

Venus

This mark is the symbol for "woman" as we know it today—a circle with a cross hanging off the bottom. Saint-Germain claims no personal sight of this sign, yet he reports that if found on the mount of Jupiter, it indicates deep, dignified, and constant love.[182] When found on the mount of Saturn, it signals the combination of passion and despondency in love of the opposite sex.[183] On Apollo we should expect it to indicate a connection with "idealization in the love of poetry and art."[184] When Venus lies on the mount of Mercury, we look for the loving partner who sensibly thinks of the mutual benefits for both mates.[185]

Moving to the sign of Venus on upper Mars, Saint-Germain would expect violence in amorous affairs.[186] If found on the lunar mount, he would predict the subject will constantly seek strange, new sensations.[187] Venus on Venus increases the qualities of the mount.[188]

Wells of Gold

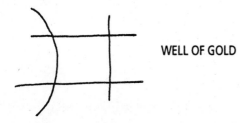

WELL OF GOLD

Dr. Costavile observes that because this sign resembles others, it is difficult to find. When found, it heralds success in business, especially in the purchase and sale of real estate or other property.[189]

Woman

Dr. Costavile reports that this Chinese sign of sensuality will have various meanings depending on where it is found.[190] It can mean support from others or a happy family because of the woman's position, prosperity, or a good social position. If the sign is crossed by a line, the meanings are de-

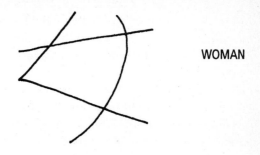

WOMAN

creased and become negative if the line is deeply cut.

"X"

Esther Newcomer-Bramblett indicates this is a favorable sign as there is no horizontal line to impede its forces.[191]

Yav, Yava

A yav is a small oval marking. Dr. Sen reports that this is another rare, unusual sign mentioned in the books on Indian palmistry.[192] Unfortunately, it is not clear from his book just what this sign might look like if it is a separate sign and not a generic term. V. A. K. Ayer, in his *Sariraka Shastra*, describes the sign *yava* as a sign like the canopy, wheel, or spear, and says that one who has it will enjoy luxurious foods and other edibles.[193] Yava in sanskrit can mean barley or grain. Dr. Sen says that when the sign is found on the thumb, it indicates the distinguished scholar who will become rich and a credit to his family and race.[194] "It is a sign of happy existence." Attention all astrologers plagued with subjects who do not know the time of day they were born. Dr. Sen advises that when this mark is found on the right hand, it indicates the subject was born in the dark of the moon, during the daytime; if on the left hand, the birth must have occurred during the bright of the night. Only if the sign is on both hands and is crossed by a line can the time of birth not be told.

Dr. Sen further advises that if found on the base of the thumb, the subject will have a boy child, but only by adoption if found only on the left hand. When found at the base of all fingers, it indicates a licentious subject who may end up drowning (or perhaps in modern parlance, dying in an auto crash on wet pavement).

If the yav is found at the beginning of the Saturn (fate) line, Dr. Sen predicts that it indicates loss of parents at an early age. If in the center of the fate line, the subject will be tempted by the opposite sex (so it must be a common sign). When found on the head line, it foretells promiscuous intermingling of sexes between castes. Yet if the heart line ends on Jupiter in the sign of the yav, death in a holy place shall be the ultimate fate of the subject.

Yoni, Vagina

YONI

This represents the female creative energies. This is another sign of the mother, the carrier of the creative energies. The bearer wants to provide the womb wherein the creative forces can receive nourishment for future expression. With bad signs, it may indicate an overindulgence in sex. It symbolizes Bharani, the second nakshatra, ruled by Yama, the god of death. The subject will be evolving through investigation of metaphysical laws and must avoid excessive indulgence in sex. He or she will probably be drawn to tantric practices.

OTHER SIGNS AND THOUGHTS ON SIGNS

Yaschpaule names a variety of signs. He says the signs of the hill, bangle, yoni, human face, or pitcher will all bestow a high political office on the subject. He warns beginners not to despair if they have trouble locating many of the Indian signs, as it takes much practice and the diagrams of them do not always accurately reflect what may be found in the hand.[195] He names the crocodile as another sign along with the conch, temple, and fish that foretells great wealth.[196] He also mentions the elephant, horse, and club.

Abayakoon finds that the fish, square, umbrella, elephant, rectangle, plough, violin, door, mountain, sword, garland, cart wheel, flower, circle, palanquin, seat, horse, tree, double fish tail, and a formation that looks like a W or M are all very benefic signs if found on the hand or the foot.

Ayer reports several signs not seen here: the elephant, the horse, the bangle, the head of a man, and the "parts of a woman." The first two indicate the subject will lead a happy life. The latter, along with the water pot (pitcher) and bangle, will indicate a subject who can become a minister of state.[197]

Dr. Sen looks for combinations of favorable marks, though he says that even if only one is found, it is enough to indicate greatness. He agrees with Yaschpaule that it takes practice to locate and recognize the fortuitous signs. If one looks for princes, kings, and those of great wealth, the favorable signs are conch, fish, bow, lotus, tree, circle, canopy, and temple. If one examines the hands of saints and great men, then one looks for the temple, flag, square, conch, circle, lotus, swastika, and the *diksha rekha* (line of renunciation, see previous chapter on lines).[198]

Saint-Germain notes that if his archetypical astral signs (Jupiter, Saturn, Sun, Moon, Mars, Mercury, and Venus) are found on exaggerated mounts, then these signs should be interpreted as indicating the defects of their signs, rather than the qualities reported above.[199]

Dr. Costavile emphasizes that the ephemeral marks in Chinese palmistry may appear and disappear in a relatively short period of time, so they are quite the prize to catch. I have not seen most of them. Their meanings can vary according to when they appear, how long they are present, and how clearly and deeply they are etched into the hand.[200]

EPILOGUE

IS THERE A FUTURE FOR PALMISTRY?

I believe there is a future for palmistry, provided that palmists are willing to act like professionals and add discipline to the profession.

I hope this rather critical analysis of the current state of palmistry will herald a new beginning rather than a conclusion. I have been encouraged by other recent works, such as Andrew Fitzherbert's *Palmist's Companion*. We are at a point where much needs to be done to build a common language. If we can build respect as professionals, then we are also at a point where we could share our work with other trained researchers and gather credible evidence to support our conclusions. Such evidence would include gathering population samples with proper controls. It would be scrutinized, where possible, by standardized tests and by applying accepted statistical methods.

We now have the tools from other fields to assist us in this task. But we have some basic tasks that need to be accomplished to gain credibility.

Standardize Terminology

It is obvious that at the end of the twentieth century, palmistry is a very confusing subject. There is disagreement on basic terminology and interpretation. That is a problem palmistry shares with almost every field of human interest. We can either do nothing or look to other fields where the problem has been faced and learn that we do not have to grow into confusion.

We could spend some profitable time reexamining our terminology and perhaps even consider convening an international symposium to formulate a basic convention on terminology. This would greatly aid communication.

We could determine whether we would recommend the continuation of multiple names for the same areas of the hand. We could ask ourselves seriously how necessary it is to have multiple names for the same topographic places and

237

features on the palms. We should face our growing tower of Babel.

Should we encourage the mount of Apollo to also go by the name of the Sun and even be called the mount of Uranus? Should the Apollo finger be both finger number four in science yet remain as Ms. Hutchinson named it, number three, and should it even be known as Venus? What of other palmists who recognize a separate mount of Uranus in the lower middle of the palm? What of Altman, who recognizes the line of Uranus where others call it the line or crescent of intuition, and Gibson calls it the cephalic line? The health, mercury, liver, communication, and hepatica lines all may refer to the same formation. The Apollo line can also be found under the names of creativity, brilliance, capability, personality, fortune, career, or success. The Saturn line is known as the Fate line, the personality line, and the career line. The Mars line has been renamed by Biccum as the warrior line. The cephalic line might also be mistaken for the via lascivia, which may also be called the poison bar, hypothenar bar, the line of Neptune, or Diana's arrow. The Venus we thought was a mount under the thumb, we now find is a name Fairchild gives to the Apollo finger. Several palmists have a hard time distinguishing, at least in writing, between lower and upper Mars. New mounts are named, such as Vulcan, with no explanation of their meaning.

Indeed, the whole subject of palmistry has been renamed handology, and we now have a palmascope. The academic and scientific communities, probably in order not to be tainted with any reputation of charlatanism from palmistry, label their studies under the term dermatoglyphics. Hand analysis is also a popular name. We have such an abundance of modern names for our craft that we hardly ever use the traditional ones of chirognomy, chiromancy, chirology, and chirosophy.

Given all of this confusion, an international convocation on terminology would be useful.

Standardize Reporting Methodology

It is far less likely that we would reduce the diversity of interpretation by a conference. However, we might at least discuss acceptable methods of reporting our findings. We could agree that if we truly have tests, population samples and statistical data should support our interpretations, and the collections of these materials should be standardized and presented in as intelligible and detailed a manner as necessary to enable others to understand what was done and attempt reliable replication. Otherwise, we could treat our findings as clinical findings and report them merely as our clinical findings subject to further research.

Peer Review

By standardizing our terminology and methodology, we could also make it possible to begin to bring peer review to our work. Peer review could train us to be knowledgeable about our own shortcomings and enable us to be less gullible and more critical of our work. This would give the whole field much needed credibility. We might make a book such as this into a real textbook with editors, contributors, and periodic updates.

Encourage Multidiscipline Collaboration

By standardizing our language and methodology and incorporating peer review, we could raise the credibility of the whole field in a manner to encourage outside scientific disciplines to collaborate in our work. This would do much to demystify it and make it more acceptable in the Western world, as it becomes understood within modern academic and scientific disciplines. This would lay the foundation for valuable connections for future collaboration.

WHAT DOES PALMISTRY HAVE TO OFFER?

Palmists offer trained eyes and folklore traditions that will be useful today in giving the whole scientific field a leg up. Scientists who doubt this should take a page from the history of pharmacology. Pharmacology now recognizes the usefulness of folklore herbalism and has long and profitably studied this ancient art. Witness the discovery of salicin from white willow bark. Herbal medicine used it to reduce pains. It was conclusively shown to reduce aches and pains in 1874. In 1853 and 1893, researchers produced acetylsalicylic acid from salicylic acid, and this new product became known as aspirin. White willow bark produces the salicylic acid within the body through oxidation.[1]

Give Up Parochial Ideas

Palmistry offers a tremendous growth field in the twenty-first century in science, education, and industry, but we may have to give up some parochial ideas.

It may be true today, as Bevy Jaegers said in 1974, that one does not need any medical or psychological background, at least to read in fairs or for friends. Yet we must be far more careful in statements that can be read by the general public. It is not good for us to open our mouths only to prove our own uselessness or ignorance.

To be credible, one cannot make such statements as Jaegers made in her 1992 book concerning the double loop fingerprint that "if this appears on your hand in childhood, you may have lived in a 'fantasy' world, had an invisible friend or companion." In the first place, most people turn away and say that fantasy play is typical of most children, at least in this culture. Far more critical is the fact that Jaegers, who holds herself out as an expert on the hand, displays an ignorance of the fact that fingerprints are formed in the third through sixth month of gestation. That sort of statement immediately turns off serious inquiry.

I believe a good grounding in anatomy, physiology, and some human psychology, even if it is merely practical psychology from experience, is very useful in the future of palmistry.

It is time to establish an interdisciplinary chair in palmistry at some of our leading universities.

THE FUTURE OF PALMISTRY

We are on the verge of using our talents to make major contributions to the twenty-first century's growth in the fields of health and human resources. When I speak of health, I speak of the total area of health care. Human resources could cover the entire fields of interaction of humans in education, work, and the marketplace. We are on the leading edge of human growth potential, which includes education and total self-awareness.

The Fields of Medicine, Including Pharmacology

The field of orthodox medicine has already accepted the study of dermatoglyphics as legitimate. We need to expand that entire study to include personality inventories and other signs of behavior and health conditions related to specific types of patterns on the hands, even if we can only do it on a significant statistical basis.

Our work may form a basis of prediagnostic planning for total health care, including preventive medicine, in the twenty-first century. It may be naturally complemented by iridology and other diagnostic aids such as Oriental pulse and aruvedic tongue reading. A combination of these practices could form the basis of a noninvasive prediagnostic profession that can aid in low-tech, low-cost, total health care. Such cost savings in health care and preventive medicine would be welcome to the economies throughout the world. Such information should be readily available to the family physician and local health care specialists long before any expensive lab tests are considered.

As we come to understand the relationship of the patterns on the hands to the human production and uses of various enzymes, neuropeptides, and other chemical substances, our studies may provide vital information on the types and dosages of various drugs and other medical therapies that could be recommended or contraindicated. The entire pharmaceutical industry should be vitally interested in conducting parallel dermatoglyphic tests with all new drugs. Each drug may have pattern-specific applications or contraindications. According to Michael Talbot, some Germans had, in 1989, already developed a piece of test equipment that can compare up to 10,000 prints scanning each tested hand for some fifty distinctive patterns.[2] The means are at hand.

As our cultures go forth boldly into genetic engineering, they will face the same question we must face. What is a normal pattern, and when is there danger? Those who study dermatoglyphics have really not laid out the basic framework to build on. Will the geneticists find the same problem? In genetics it might be stated as: When is a particular gene a "defective gene" that will always result in a genetic defect?

Palmists constantly are faced with new combinations, and new combinations provoke speculation. Judging the combination based upon a single factor is very dangerous unless we feel relatively certain how the interrelationship of all the factors work together. The wide disagreements on value of the star supports this point.

Value judgments may give palmists their largest problem. So many clients want to know what is "good" or "bad" in their future. I have come to tell most of them in my practice that such judgments cannot be finally made until the meal, that is life, is practically complete, and even then the judgments may only be tentative. Take the frustration lines one sees upon the distal phalange of the thumb. These signify blocks to carrying out the will of the subject. Often they indicate that the subject has misinformation even when the subject is following standard approved practices. I like to tell the subject that they have a Native American spirit guide like a fox, or coyote, or crow, who is a trickster. The trickster's game is to encourage some subjects to go within and seek new paths to success and not to rely upon the standard accepted guidelines of conduct. This provides humanity with a constant stream of people who cannot blindly follow given paths leading to an evolutionary dead end.

We have a lot to learn in playing god and hand-ing out value judgments. Science can teach us something of this. One can think of sickle cell anemia. The red blood cell carries the oxygen necessary for life. The sickle cell is an abnormal red blood cell. Its abnormality is due to an abnormal amino acid in the globin chain resulting in a distortion and fragility of these erythrocytes (red blood cells). Simply put, it is a hereditary disease that is passed along by abnormal genes. However, this genetic factor has been very beneficial to natives from equatorial Africa by increasing their resistance to the malaria parasite so common in that area of the world.[3] But it is debilitating to blacks in America who do not have to face that African disease, and it results in joint pain, thrombosis, fever, and chronic anemia with abnormal enlargement of the spleen, lethargy, and weakness, and it can be fatal.

Psychology and Human Resources

In the fields of psychology and human resources, significant research and perhaps even mass testing could be anticipated in the next several decades using the Minnesota Mutiphasic Personality Inventory (MMPI) and related tests. Given the initial success in statistical sampling in certain fields, we might expect that the results could have many benefits. Correlative results would be especially beneficial in areas where the subjects may not have developed the knowledge or articulation to assist in the evaluations. This can include early education assistance, emergency care, and entry employment placement and counseling.

If statistically reliable guidelines can be developed, hand examination can be less expensive, nonintrusive, and far less time consuming than conducting an MMPI or other written or verbal screening tests. It might be superior to DNA sampling by being nonintrusive as well as possibly less expensive.

To the extent that long-range health could be indicated, such as possible structural defects to the body that would be aggravated by particular work, great savings financially and in human suffering could be anticipated through preemployment hand analysis in connection with hazardous or heavy work assignments.

WHAT WILL HAPPEN TO THE ROMANCE OF IT ALL?

Science and romance are not two opposite ends of a pole. Science seems to have a little bit of romance in it these days. The magic has not disappeared. What if we could provide reliable, credible statistical support for some of our stranger findings, such as those that deal with psychic powers and future events?

Science is beginning to recognize certain psychic skills, such as psychokinesis. Talbot reports a number of studies such as the work of Robert G. Jahn, professor of aerospace sciences and dean emeritus of the School of Engineering and Applied Science at Princeton University. Jahn's studies seem to confirm that many people can affect both the unpredictable nature of random movement of radioactive decay particles and the fall of 9,000 three-quarter-inch marbles (microscopic and macroscopic universes) through a test apparatus by their thought processes.[4] The test results differed depending on subjects, and apparently those whose signatures (measurable thought effects on the process) were stronger on the microscopic level were also stronger on the macroscopic level. How would we be able to recognize such individuals? Again, palmistry may divulge the clue.

We believe that palmistry might help us to not only statistically confirm psychic abilities but to identify those who have special talents, talents our children may be able to develop.

PALMISTRY FROM ANCIENT TIMES TO TODAY

Bishop John Shelby Spong points out that the roots of the book of Job are ancient.[5] It, with the books of Ruth and Jonah, form the counterpoints to the structured work of the Old Testament. In Job we find that the life we are marked for may not be fair. Some might say that God plays with loaded dice. Modern humans challenge the roll of those dice. To do so, we must still seek to find how the dice may be loaded. Therefore, it is advisable to look to the underlying mark, the DNA in modern science, or the hand in the Bible. Job 37:7 in the King James Version of the bible says: "He sealeth up the hand of all men; that all men may know his work."

This seventeenth-century translation of the Bible used a word then common to all the English because the seal had been used through the complete social scale from the princes of the realm and the barons through the gentry to the small landholders and even to the commoners. All men (and even some women) seemed to have the right to have seals. It enabled every man to be his own notary. He could authenticate his own documents with his own individual signum and name, even if he was unable to manipulate his pen. Indeed, as Clanchy points out, the seal was more convincing than a notary's *signum* because the seal came from the maker of the document and was kept on him and was among his treasures.[6] The seal combined a device, the *signum*, such as a picture of a horse or a seated king or knight on horseback, with a name and thus was more than a mere signature. It was a representation of the person both by name and to some extent by status. In medieval times Clanchy tells us seals were the tangible, visible objects that symbolized the "wishes of the donor."[7] They did, in fact, individually and personally identify him both by name and sign.

The divine not only placed a person's name in his or her hand, the divine went further and designated the subject's calling according to divine wishes. Perhaps modern science is ready again to delve into the mysteries of Job and the plans for each person's existence. If so, then we palmists are ready to join hands in this great investigation.

APPENDIX: INSTRUCTIONS FOR PRINTMAKING

Ink prints are usually preferable to copy machine prints because of clarity. When the hand rests on the glass in a copier, the ridges and lines get blurred or may not be copied. I teach my students to use the ink roller method. Some prefer the ink pad method, but many times the ink with the ink pad method is not washable. I encourage the use of washable ink. Clients do prefer it and it should be available in tubes from any good art store.

INK PAD METHOD

You will need:

1. small, soft sponge
2. White unruled letter-size paper
3. Sharp pencil
4. Inked ink pad

Place paper on hard, smooth surface or on computer mouse pad. Some successfully use a slightly spongy surface. If middle of palm has a deep hollow (so it will not copy) place spongy material such as powder sponge or some cotton or tissue paper under paper where middle of palm will rest.

Rub sponge, inked from pad, gently over hand until palm side is fully covered. Be careful not to get ink too thick or blotchy as it will interfere with showing the lines clearly.

Spread fingers and thumb apart and place hand firmly on paper.

While hand is held motionless on paper, make an outline of the hand and fingers on the paper with the pencil so that the outline shows around the print.

When the outline is completed, lift the hand straight from the paper so as not to smear or otherwise mar the print.

Then print each fingerprint, marking the thumb with a T, the index finger (first finger next to the thumb) with a J, the next (middle) finger with an S, the next (ring) finger with an A, and the little finger with an M.

Then print the little finger (ulnar, i.e. percussion) side of the palm so as to show the lines that curve around that side of the palm. This you do as if you were resting the side of your hand on the table.

Finally, fold the paper over the side of the table and print the inside of the thumb and palm area with the palm resting against the top of the table and the thumb pressed against the side of the table.

INK ROLLER METHOD

Washable printer's ink, a roller, and glass, tile, or other surface to roll out the ink and spread the ink smoothly over roller surface, can be used in place of the pad and sponge. I bought some cheap tiles at a hardware store that do very well. The rollers can be obtained at an art supply store.

Squeze some ink on the tile. Spread some of it with the roller so that the roller is coated evenly. The roller is then used like the sponge to coat the hand. When doing the fingerprints, ink the fingers directly from the tile.

COPY MACHINE METHOD

Do not press hard on the glass as that will distort and flatten the lines so that no clear print can be made.

Drape a white towel or handkerchief over the surface of the hand not being copied so that the background is white rather than dark shadows. This clarifies the palm print.

INKLESS COPY

This method was described by Jon M. Aase and Richard B. Lyons.[1] Prints of children, babies, and even adults can be obtained by use of entirely transparent, wide, vinyl-based, self-adhesive tape in 8-inch (20-cm) widths (3M type 2VEF tape), carbon paper or graphite applied with a powder puff, and siliconized backing paper. The elasticity of the vinyl tape permits the coverage of curved surfaces.

Prior to applying the blackening agent, the tape should be prepared. Cut strips long enough to cover the surfaces to be printed and affix to siliconized paper so that it will peel off easily.

Hands should be dry. On adults and children, the blackening agent can be ordinary cheap black carbon paper. On infants, powdered graphite is suggested. Rub the carbon paper lightly and evenly over all palmar surfaces of the hand and fingers. Apply the graphite in the same way with a powder puff. Pay attention to the hollow areas between the mounts and in the middle of the palm and the sides of the palm and finger.

Remove backing from the tape and affix one end of tape to the proximal part of the palm and over the wrist crease and smooth the tape upward, toward the fingers, over the palm and the fingers, taking care that the hollows and sides are covered.

Peel tape off the hand and smoothly affix the tape to the siliconized backing sheet. The prints should be ready for examination.

OTHER METHODS

Lynn Robertson-Neufeld and Jeffrey Murray report another inkless method in Jamshed Mavalwala's *Dermatoglyphics: An International Perspective*.[2] Blanka Schaumann and Milton Alter[3] report a number of different methods including both ink and inkless methods, a transparent adhesive tape method, a photographic method, and special methods including hygrophotography, radiodermatography, use of plastic molds, and automatic pattern recognition.

METHOD OF THE FUTURE

We would like to see developed a full natural color with an infrared alternative display, three-dimensional, holographed, full-hand picture that can be flexed, turned, and parts can be greatly magnified. This would require constant lighting and color for holograph prints made at different times, a problem that plagued iridology for many years, leading to all sorts of inaccuracies. The print should be on a computer disk for use in a computer software program.

NOTES

INTRODUCTION

1. Murray H. Seltzer, Chris C. Plato, and Kathleen M. Fox, "Dermatoglyphics in the Identification of Women Either With or at Risk of Breast Cancer," *American Journal of Medical Genetics*, 37 (1990), 482–488.

2. Julius Spier, *The Hands of Children* (London: Routledge & Kegan Paul, 1955; New Delhi, India: Sagar Publications).

1. WHERE WE ARE AND HOW WE GOT THERE

1. V. A. K. Ayer, 2nd ed. trans., *Sariraka Sastra* (D. B. Taraporevala, 1960, 1965). The work translated is described as nearly 400 years old.
2. Terence Dukes, *Chinese Hand Analysis* (York Beach, Maine: Samuel Weiser, 1987).
3. Hachiro Asano, *Hands: The Complete Book of Palmistry* (Tokyo: Japan Publications, 1985).
4. *Eros in Antiquity*, photographs by Antonia Mulas (New York: Erotic Art Book Society, 1978). Satyr and Maenad, pictured on page 23.
5. William Harlan Hale, *The Horizon Book of Ancient Greece* (American Heritage Publishing Company, 1965).
6. Fred Gettings, *The Book of the Hand: An Illustrated*

History of Palmistry (Feltham, Middlesex: Paul Hamlin, 1965).
7. Andrew Fitzherbert, *The Palmist's Companion: A History and Bibliography of Palmistry* (Metuchen, N.J.: The Scarecrow Press, 1992).
8. Fred Gettings, *The Book of the Hand*, 159.
9. An Act Concerning Outlandish People, Calling Themselves Egyptians. 22 Hen. VIII (1530), ch. X. Pickering's Statutes at Large.
10. The Vagrancy Act of 1824 (5 Geo IV c. 83) described "any persons pretending or professing to tell fortunes, or using any subtle craft, means, or device, by palmistry or otherwise, to deceive and impose ..." as rogues and vagabonds subject to

criminal penalties. 3 Halsbury's Laws of England, Vol 10, §18, ¶1337.

11. Fred Gettings, supra, 195.

12. William G. Benham, *Laws of Scientific Hand Reading* (Putnam & Co., 1900). Reprinted as *The Benham Book of Palmistry*, with foreword by Rita Robinson (A Newcastle Metaphysical Classic, 1988).

13. Andrew Fitzherbert, *The Palmist's Companion*, 54.

14. Ibid., 13–14.

15. Ms. Yael Haft-Pomrock also appears published as Yeal Haft and is described as a member of the Israel Association of Psychotherapy and National Expressive Therapy Association and as the founder and head of the Center for the Study and Research of Modes of Consciousness. She is also described as the Chief Director of the Government Mental Hospital, Talbieh, Jerusalem. See her work *Hands* cited in the bibliography.

16. The reference to Ben-Gurion University and the study are found in Fitzherbert's *Palmist Companion*, 16.

17. See Fitzherbert, *The Palmist's Companion*, 25 (references to J. Rothmann, *Keiromantia*, trans. George Wharton, and included in *The Works of George Wharton* [London, 1683]; J. Indagine, *The Book of Palmistry and Physiognomy* [London, 1676]; Richard Saunders, *Physiognome and Chiromancie, Metoposcope* [London, 1653]).

18. Ibid. (Philip May, *La Chiromancie Medicinale* [The Hague, 1665] and *Chiromantia Medica* [Dresden, 1667]).

19. Ibid. (Katherine St. Hill, *Medical Palmistry* [London: Rider, 1929]).

20. Ibid. (Noel Jaquin in *Hand and Disease* [1926], Ina Oxenford in *Modern Palmistry* [1900], and John Spark in *Scientific and Institutional Palmistry* [circa 1894]).

21. Ibid. (Henri Mangin, *Introduction a l'Etude de la Chiroscopie Medical* [Editions Oliven, 1932] and *Precis de Chiroscopie Medicale* [Paris: Chacornac Freres, 1939]. Ernest Issberner-Haldane, *Die Medizinische Hand-Undnagel-Diagnostik* [Berlin: Falken Verlag, 1925]).

22. Ibid., 27. (Noel Jaquin's other books favorably mentioned by Fitzherbert were *The Hand of Man* [London: Faber, 1933] and *The Human Hand — the Living Symbol* aka *Practical Palmistry* [Bombay: Taraporevala, 1958]).

23. Ibid. (Beryl Hutchinson, *Your Life In Your Hands* [London: Sphere, 1967]).

24. Ibid. (Walter Sorell, *The Story of the Human Hand* [London: Weidenfeld & Nicholson, 1967]).

25. Ibid. (Dennis B. Jackson, *The Modern Palmist* [London: World's Work, 1953]).

26. Theodore J. Berry, M.D. F.A.C.P., *The Hand As a Mirror of Systemic Disease* (Philadelphia: Davis, 1963). See also Fitzherbert, ibid.

27. Eugene Scheimann, M.D., *A Doctor's Guide to Better Health Through Palmistry* (West Nyack, N.Y.: Parker Publishing Co., 1969); Eugene Scheimann, M.D., and Nathaniel Altman, *Medical Palmistry: A Doctor's Guide to Better Health Through Hand Analysis* (Wellingborough, Northamptonshire: Aquarian Press, 1989).

28. H. Cummings, "Dermatoglyphic Stigmata in Mongolian Idiocy," *Anat. Rec.* 64:11, 1936. Cummings had reported earlier studies of the hand in "The Configuration of Epidermal Ridges in a Human Acephalic Monster," *Anat. Rec.*, 26:1, 1923.

29. Amrita Bagga, *Dermatoglyphics of Schizophrenics* (New Delhi: Mittal Publications, 1989), 20.

30. Ibid., 20.

31. See note 3 above.

32. A. C. Bogle, T. Reed, and R. J. Rose, "Replication of Asymmetry of a-b Ridge Count and Behavioral Discordance in Monozygotic Twins," *Behavior Genetics*, 24:1, Jan. 1994, 65–72.

33. Blanka Schaumann and Milton Alter, *Dermatoglyphics in Medical Disorders* (New York: Springer-Verlag, 1976).

34. Jamshed Mavalwala, ed., *Dermatoglyphics: An International Perspective* (The Hague: Mouton Publishers, 1978).

3. WHICH HAND TO STUDY?

1. Charlotte Wolff, *The Human Hand* (New York: Alfred A. Knopf, 1943), 144–154.
2. Antonio R. Damasio, M.D., *Descartes' Error, Emotion, Reason, and the Human Brain*, 1994, 133.
3. Ibid., 134.
4. Ibid., 140.
5. Ibid., 144.
6. Ira B. Perelle, Mercy College, Dobbs Ferry, New York, and Lee Ehrman, SUNY, Purchase, New York, "An International Study of Human Handedness: The Data," *Behavior Genetics*, 24:3, 217, 1994.
7. One recent study found some genetic markers through fingerprints (Stanley Coren, Department of Psychology, University of British Columbia, "Are Fingerprints a Genetic Marker for Handedness?," *Behavior Genetics*, 24:2, 141, 1994). Others have studied sex, generational and family handedness for clues; see Marian Annett, Department of Psychology, University of Leicester, in "Handedness as a Continuous Variable with Dextral Shift: Sex, Generation, and Family Handedness in Subgroups of Left- and Right-Handers," *Behavior Genetics*, 24:1, 51, 1994. Perelle and Ehrman, ibid., found eating with a fork not very helpful but found more use in behavior such as stroking a pet (p. 218). They point out that the investigators' approach to the behavior that answers the question of what is a left-hander will determine the proportion of the left-handers found by that investigator (p. 219). Questionnaire analysis relying on reported behaviors of subjects seems to have resulted in some unreliable assumptions when the behavior was one of the following: throwing, bowling, sewing, writing, the use of marbles, a knife, a spoon, a hammer, a saw or scissors. Of course, since most scissors are right-handed, this could be a very unreliable tool. Others have measured dexterity through handwriting tests, other hand uses as well as hand grip endurance and strength. The mirror-image effect of monozygotic twins have been a consideration. However there are studies of singletons (single births), dizygotic and monozygotic twins that have noted no significant variation in left-handedness (p. 222). Education, birth order, and mating have also been considered.
8. Terence Dukes, *Chinese Hand Analysis* (York Beach, Maine: Samuel Weiser, 1987).
9. Julius Spier, *The Hands of Children* (New Delhi: Sagar Publications, 1955).
10. Charlotte Wolff, *The Human Hand*, 149.
11. Hachiro Asano, *Hands: The Complete Book of Palmistry* (Tokyo: Japan Publications, 1985).

4. FROM FORM TO CHARACTER ANALYSIS

1. D'Arpentigny, *La Chirognomie ou l'Art de Reconnaitre les Tendencesde l'Intelligence d'Apres les Formes de la Main* (Paris, 1853).
2. Carl Gustav Carus, *Uber Grund und Bedeutung der Verschiedenen Formen der Hand* (1848).
3. Kwok Man Ho, Martin Palmer, and Joanne O'Brien, *Lines of Destiny: How to Read Faces and Hands the Chinese Way* (London: Rider & Co, 1986).
4. Terence Dukes, *Chinese Hand Analysis* (York Beach, Maine: Samuel Weiser, 1987).
5. Nathaniel Altman, *The Palmistry Workbook* (Wellingborough, Northamptonshire: Aquarian Press, 1984), and *Sexual Palmistry* (Wellingborough, Northamptonshire: Aquarian Press, 1986).
6. Nathaniel Altman and Andrew Fitzherbert, *Career, Success and Self Fulfillment: How Scientific Handreading Can Change Your Life* (Wellingborough, Northamptonshire: Aquarian Press, 1988).
7. Rodney Davies, *Fortune-Telling by Palmistry: A Practical Guide to the Art of Hand Analysis* (Well-

ingborough, Northamptonshire: Aquarian Press, 1987).

8. Fred Gettings, *The Book of the Hand: An Illustrated History of Palmistry* (Hamlyn Publishing Group, 1965), *Palmistry Made Easy* (North Hollywood, Ca.: Wilshire Book Co., 1973); *The Hand and The Horoscope* (London: Triune Books, 1973); and *The Book of Palmistry* (London: Triune Books, 1974).

9. Jemma Powell, *The Stars in Your Hand* (New York: Macfadden-Bartell, 1971).

10. Lori Reid, *Family Matters, Palmistry* (London: Artillery House, 1990) (but see her earlier work, *The Female Hand: Palmistry for Today's Woman* [Wellingborough, Northamptonshire: Aquarian Press, 1986], where she used five categories: square, conic, two spatulate, and psychic, which trace back more to the d'Arpentigny approach).

11. Richard Webster, *Revealing Hands: How to Read Palms*, chapter one, (St. Paul: Llewellyn, 1994).

12. Dennis Fairchild, *The Handbook of Humanistic Palmistry* (Ferndale, Mich.: Thumbs Up Productions, 1980).

13. Dylan Warren-Davis, *The Hand Reveals* (Rockport, Mass.: Element Books, 1993), 51–57.

14. Andrew Fitzherbert, *The Palmist's Companion: A History and Bibliography of Palmistry* (Metuchen, N.J.: Scarecrow Press, 1992), 68.

15. Cyrus D. F. Abayakoon, *Astro-Palmistry: Signs and Seals of the Hand* (New York: ASI Publishers, 1975).

16. Elizabeth Brenner, *Hand in Hand* (Millbrae, Ca.: Celestial Arts, 1981); *The Hand Book* (Berkeley, Ca.: Celestial Arts, 1980).

17. Cheiro (Count Louis Hamon), *Book of the Hand* (London, 1891), *Cheiro's Complete Palmistry, from the works of Count Louis Hamon*, Robert M. Ockene, ed. (New Hyde Park, University Books, N.Y.: 1968), *The Language of the Hand* (London Pub. Co., 1897, 1949), reprinted (New York: Prentice-Hall, 1987); *Palmistry for All* (New York: G. P. Putnam's Sons, 1916); *You and Your Hand* (Originally published by Jarrolds Publishers London) (New York: Doubleday Doran & Co., 1931),

revised by Louise Owen (1969), reissued (New York: Berkley, 1971).

18. Henry Frith, *Palmistry Secrets Revealed.* Edited by John Malcolm (North Hollywood, Ca.: Wilshire Book Co., 1952).

19. Maria Gardini, *The Secrets of the Hand.* Translated by Judith Spencer (New York: Macmillan, 1985).

20. M. N. Laffan, *Handreading* (New York: Kegan Paul, Trench Trubner, 1931), (Philadelphia: J. B. Lippincott, 1933).

21. Martini, *Palmistry at a Glance* (Baltimore: I & M Ottenheimer, 1953).

22. Jean-Michel Morgan, *Palmistry: The Art of Reading Hands.* Translated by David Macrae (Barcelona: Ariane Books, 1975).

23. Niblo, *The Complete Palmist* (North Hollywood, Ca.: Newcastle Publishing, 1982).

24. Elizabeth Daniels Squire, *The New Fortune in Your Hand* (New York: Fleet Press, 1960); *Palmistry Made Practical: Your Fortune in Your Hands* (North Hollywood, Ca.: Wilshire Book Co.).

25. Linnea Eckhardt, *Hands of Time* (Denver: Mission Press Research & Development, 1990).

26. Joseph Renald, *Hands of Destiny: Your Life's Fate in the Lines of Your Palm* (New York: Greenberg, 1931).

27. Peter West, *Life Lines: The Secrets of Your Character Revealed in Your Hands* (Pentagon, 1987).

28. Yaschpaule, *Your Destiny and Scientific Hand Analysis* (Petaling Jaya, Selangor, Malaysia: Heinemann Educational Books, 1982).

29. Richard Webster, *Revealing Hands: How To Read Palms*.

30. Maria Costavile, *How to Read Palms* (New York: Crescent Books, 1988).

31. Litzka Raymond Gibson, *How to Read Palms*, rev. ed. (Hollywood, Fla.: Fell Publishers, 1989).

32. Bettina Luxon and Jill Goolden, *Your Hand: Simple Palmistry for Everyone* (New York: Crown, 1983).

33. Enid Hoffman, *Hands: A Complete Guide to Palmistry* (Gloucester, Mass.: Para Research, 1985).

34. Myrah Lawrance, *Hand Analysis* (West Nyack, N.Y.: Parker, 1967).

35. Leona Lehman, *The Key to Palmistry* (New York: Bell Publishing, 1959).

36. Roz Levine, *Palmistry: How to Chart the Lines of Your Destiny* (Simon & Schuster, 1992).

37. Holmes W. Merton, *Descriptive Mentality from the Head, Face and Hand* (Philadelphia: David McKay, 1899).

38. Pearl L. Raymond, *Palmistry Explained* (New York: Vista House, 1958).

39. Henri Rem, *What Your Hand Reveals* (New York: E. P. Dutton, 1922).

40. Rita Robinson, *The Palm: A Guide to Your Hidden Potential* (Van Nuys, Ca.: Newcastle Original, 1988).

41. Julius Spier, *The Hands of Children* (New Delhi: Routledge & Kegan Paul, 1955).

42. Joyce Wilson, *The Complete Book of Palmistry* (New York: Bantam Books, 1985).

43. Yale Haft-Pomrock, *Hands, Aspects of Opposition and Complementarity in Archetypal Chirology* (Einsiedeln, Switzerland: Diamon Verlag, 1992). Haft-Pomrock describes four hands: the oval, the conic, the spatulate, and the square. The conic and spatulate seem to integrate some of my ideas on the shape of the A and V types in that order. The oval could include the bulgy percussion. The square could be either the earth or the air hand. I also believe that fire and water hands could be observed that do not fit neatly in her patterns.

44. M. M. Gaafar, *Ilm-Ul-Kaff* (Egyptian palmistry), 2.

45. Cyrus D. F. Abayakoon, *Astro-Palmistry: Signs and Seals of the Hand*, 28. Abayakoon presents the Hindu method of hand analysis based upon ancient texts coupled with a thorough knowledge of Vedic astrology.

46. Peter West, *Life Lines: The Secrets of Your Character Revealed in Your Hands*, 23–24.

47. Walter Sorell, *The Story of the Human Hand* (Bobbs-Merrill, 1967).

48. Charlotte Wolff, *The Human Hand* (Alfred A. Knopf, 1943), and *The Hand in Psychological Diagnosis* (Methuen & Co., 1951).

49. Francis King, *Palmistry: Your Fate and Fortune in Your Hand*, 1976 (New York: Crown Publishers, 1987).

50. Hachiro Asano, *Hands: The Complete Book of Palmistry* (Tokyo: Japan Publications, 1985).

51. Ernest Kretschmer, *Korperbau und Charakter* (Berlin, 1931).

52. Fred Gettings, *The Book of Palmistry* (London: Triune Books, 1974).

53. William G. Benham, *The Benham Book of Palmistry*. Preface by Rita Robinson (North Hollywood, Ca.: Newcastle Metaphysical Classic, 1988). Mostly a reprint of Benham, *The Laws of Scientific Hand Reading*, (New York: Putnam 1958) (original 1900). I have a Health Research, Mokelumne Hill, Ca., reprint of the January 1912 printing. See also Benham, *How to Choose Vocations from the Hand* (New York: Knickerbocker Press, 1900), (G. P. Putnam's Sons, 1935), (New Delhi: Sagar Publications, 1967).

5. THE FINGERS

1. Elizabeth Brenner, *Hand in Hand* (Millbrae, Ca.: Celestial Arts, 1981).

2. Sasha Fenton and Malcolm Wright, *The Living Hand: A Unique Guide to Modern Hand Analysis* (Wellingborough, Northamptonshire: Aquarian Press, 1986).

3. David Brandon-Jones, *Practical Palmistry* (Reno: CRCS Publications, 1986).

4. William G. Benham, *The Laws of Scientific Hand Reading*. Preface by Rita Robinson (New York: Putnam, 1958) (original 1900), and *The Benham Book of Palmistry* (North Holly-

wood, Ca.: Newcastle Metaphysical Classic, 1988).

5. Darlene Hansen, *Secrets of the Palm* (San Diego: ACS Publications, 1984).

6. Cheiro (Count Leigh de Hamong), *The Language of the Hand* (Rand, McNally & Co., 1900), 59.

7. Eugene Scheimann, M.D., *The Doctor's Guide to Better Health Through Palmistry* (West Nyack, N.Y.: Parker Publishing, 1969).

8. See note 2 above.

9. Beryl B. Hutchinson, *Your Life in Your Hands* (London: Neville Spearman, 1967).

10. Judith Hipskind, *Palmistry: The Whole View*, 2nd enlarged edition (St. Paul: Llewellyn Publications, 1983).

11. Julius Spier, *The Hands of Children* (New Delhi: Sangar Publications, 1981).

12. Judith Hipskind, *The New Palmistry: How to Read the Whole Hand and Knuckles* (St. Paul: Llewellyn, 1994).

6. PALM TOPOGRAPHY

1. Darlene Hansen, *Secrets of the Palm* (San Diego: ACS Publications, Inc., 1985).

2. Roz Levine, *Palmistry, How to Chart the Lines of Your Destiny* (Simon & Schuster, 1992).

3. Niblo, *The Complete Palmist* (North Hollywood, Ca.: Newcastle Publishing, 1982), 79–81.

4. Leona Lehman, *The Key to Palmistry* (New York: Bell Publishing, 1959), 68.

5. David Brandon-Jones, *Practical Palmistry* (Reno: CRCS Publications, 1986), 91.

6. Jo Sheridan, *What Your Hands Reveal* (New York: Crown, 1963), 44.

7. Yaschpaule, *Your Destiny and Scientific Hand Analysis* (Petaling Jaya, Selangor, Malaysia: Heinemann Educational Books, 1982), 44–49.

8. Henri Rem, *What Your Hand Reveals* (New York: E. P. Dutton, 1922), 114–116.

9. Lori Reid, *The Female Hand: Palmistry for Today's Woman* (Wellingborough, Northamptonshire: Aquarian Press, 1986), 36–39.

10. Henry Frith, *Palmistry Secrets Revealed*. Edited by John Malcolm (North Hollywood Ca.: Ward Lock, Melvin Powers Wilshire Book Company), 38–48.

11. Martini, *Palmistry at a Glance* (Baltimore: I & M Ottenheimer, 1953), 47–52.

12. Joyce Wilson, *Complete Book of Palmistry* (New York: Bantam Books, 1985), 74.

13. Judith Hipskind, *Palmistry: The Whole View*, 2nd enlarged ed. (St. Paul: Llewellyn, 1983), 116–118.

14. Elizabeth P. Hoffman, *Palm Reading Made Easy* (New York: Simon & Schuster, 1971), 58–61.

15. Nancy Frederick Sussan, *Palmistry: All Lines Lead to Love* (New York: Lynx Books, 1988), 71–72.

16. Litzka Raymond Gibson, *How to Read Palms* (rev. ed.) (Hollywood, Fla.: Fell Publishers, 1989), 14, 18, 50–53.

17. Comte C. de Saint-Germain (Edgar de Valcourt-Vermont), *Practical Palmistry: Hand Reading Simplified* (Chicago: Albert Whitman, 1935), (Mokelumne Hill, Ca.: Health Research, 1970), 79–91.

18. Julius Spier, *The Hands of Children* (New Delhi: Sagar Publications, 1955), 58–62.

19. Carol Hellings White, *Holding Hands: The Complete Guide to Palmistry* (G. P. Putnam's Sons, 1980), 24, 27–28, 31, 35–36.

20. Francis King, *Palmistry: Your Fate and Fortune in Your Hand* (New York: Crown, 1987), 15–16.

21. Jean-Michel Morgan, *Palmistry: The Art of Reading Hands*. Translated by David Macrae (Barcelona: Ariane Books, 1975), 33.

22. Myrah Lawrance, *Hand Analysis* (West Nyack, N.Y.: Parker, 1967), 117–122.

23. Elizabeth Brenner, *The Hand Book* (Berkeley, Ca.:

Celestial Arts, 1980) 36–38, and *Hand in Hand* (Millbrae, Ca.: Celestial Arts, 1981), 77–80.

24. Bettina Luxon and Jill Goolden, *Your Hand: Simple Palmistry for Everyone* (New York: Crown, 1983), 26–27.

25. Walter Sorell, *The Story of the Human Hand* (Bobbs-Merrill, 1967), 62–67.

26. Edo Sprong, *Hand Analysis: The Diagnostic Method* (New York: Sterling Publishing, 1991), 72.

27. Enid Hoffman, *Hands: A Complete Guide to Palmistry* (Gloucester, Mass.: Para Research, 1985), 193–194.

28. Maria Costavile, *How to Read Palms* (New York: Crescent Books, 1988), 46.

29. Roz Levine, *Palmistry: How to Chart the Lines of Your Destiny.* See particular mounts for descriptions.

30. William G. Benham, *The Laws of Scientific Hand Reading,* (originally published in 1900) (New York: Putnam, 1958).

31. Beryl Hutchinson, *Your Life in Your Hands* (London: Sphere Books, 1969), 108–115.

32. Comte C. de Saint-Germain (Edgar de Valcourt-Vermont), *The Practice of Palmistry for Professional Purposes* (Chicago, 1897), (London: Newcastle Publishing, 1973), 87.

33. Comte C. de Saint-Germain, *Practical Palmistry: Hand Reading Simplified,* 79–91.

34. V. A. K. Ayer, *Sariraka Shastra: Indian Science of Palmistry (the Kartikeyan System)* (Bombay: D. B. Taraporevala Sons, Treasure House Books, 1960), (2nd ed., 1965), 54.

35. K. C. Sen, *Hast Samudrika Shastra: The Science of Hand-Reading Simplified* (Bombay: D. B. Taraporevala Sons, 1960), 24.

36. Rodney Davies, *Fortune-Telling by Palmistry: A Practical Guide to the Art of Hand Analysis* (Wellingborough, Northamptonshire: Aquarian Press, 1987), 80.

37. Elizabeth Daniels Squire, *The New Fortune in Your Hand* (New York: Fleet Press, 1960), 76–77, 79.

38. Darlene Hansen, *Secrets of the Palm,* 54–55.

39. Jo Logan, *The Prediction Book of Palmistry* (Poole, Dorset, England: Javelin Books, 1985), 23–24.

40. Esther Newcomer-Bramblett, *Reading Hands for Pleasure or Profit* (Austin, Texas: Woods Publications, 1982), 111–113.

41. Nathaniel Altman, *The Palmistry Workbook* (Wellingborough, Northamptonshire: Aquarian Press, 1984), 26–28.

42. Marcel Broekman, *Complete Encyclopedia of Practical Palmistry* (Englewood Cliffs, N.J.: Prentice-Hall, 1972), 128, no. 110.

43. Paul Gabriel Tesla, *The Complete Science of Hand Reading* (Osiris, 1991), 161.

44. Maria Gardini, *The Secrets of the Hand.* Translated by Judith Spencer (New York: Macmillan Publishing, 1985), 66.

45. Cheiro (Count Louis Hamon), *Palmistry for All* (New York: G. P. Putnam's Sons, 1916), 150, 154, 158, 162, 168, 174.

46. Cheiro (Count Louis Hamon), *The Language of the Hand* (New York: Prentice-Hall, 1987), 63.

47. Robert M. Ockene, *Cheiro's Complete Palmistry, from the Works of Count Louis Hamon* (New Hyde Park, N.Y.: University Books, 1968), 106.

48. William G. Benham, *The Laws of Scientific Hand Reading* (New York: G. P. Putnam's Sons, 1900), 194.

49. Beryl B. Hutchinson, *Your Life in Your Hands* (London: Sphere Books, 1969).

50. Rodney Davies, *Fortune-Telling by Palmistry: A Practical Guide to the Art of Hand Analysis.*

51. William G. Benham, *The Laws of Scientific Hand Reading,* 194–195.

52. Ibid., 184–344.

53. Ibid., 200.

54. Edo Sprong, *Hand Analysis, The Diagnostic Method.*

55. Sasha Fenton and Malcolm Wright, *The Living Hand* (Wellingborough, Northamptonshire: Aquarian Press, 1986).

56. William G. Benham, *The Laws of Scientific Hand Reading,* 199–218.

57. Beryl Hutchinson, *Your Life in Your Hands,* 111.

58. Ibid.
59. William G. Benham, *The Laws of Scientific Hand Reading*, 219–237.
60. Sasha Fenton and Malcolm Wright, *The Living Hand*, 35–36, 99.
61. Rodney Davies, *Fortune-Telling by Palmistry*, 85.
62. Julius Spier, *The Hands of Children*.
63. Edo Sprong, *Hand Analysis*, 89.
64. David Brandon-Jones, *Practical Palmistry*.
65. William G. Benham, *The Laws of Scientific Hand Reading*, 238–255.
66. Darlene Hansen, *Secrets of the Palm*, 62–63.
67. Edo Sprong, *Hand Analysis*, 71, 94.
68. David Brandon Jones, *Practical Palmistry*, 103–104.
69. Rodney Davies, *Fortune-Telling by Palmistry*, 88.
70. William G. Benham, *The Laws of Scientific Hand Reading*, 256–275.
71. Sasha Fenton and Malcolm Wright, *The Living Hand*, 32.
72. David Brandon-Jones, *Practical Palmistry*, 105.
73. William G. Benham, *The Laws of Scientific Hand Reading*, 276–296.
74. Beryl Hutchinson, *Your Life in Your Hands*, 114.
75. William G. Benham, *The Laws of Scientific Hand Reading*, 322–344.
76. Edo Sprong, *Hand Analysis*, 75–80.
77. Ibid., 75.
78. William G. Benham, *The Laws of Scientific Hand Reading*, 297–321.
79. Ibid., 300–301. This point will be covered later when we discuss health lines. Benham pointed the way for possible fruitful study that was largely ignored by the twentieth-century palmists who I have read.
80. Beryl Hutchinson, *Your Life in Your Hands*, 115 and fig. 59, p. 133.
81. Ibid., 27.
82. David Brandon-Jones, *Practical Palmistry*, 107.
83. Robert Hand, *Horoscope Symbols* (West Chester, Pa.: Schiffer Publishing, 1981).
84. Darleen Hansen, *Secrets of the Palm*, 68.
85. Ibid., 73.
86. Terence Dukes, *Chinese Hand Analysis* (York Beach, Maine: Samuel Weiser, 1987).
87. Francis King, *Palmistry, Your Fate and Fortune in Your Hand*.
88. Ibid., 48–51.
89. Ibid.
90. Fred Gettings, *The Book of Palmistry*, 76–85.
91. Ibid., 78.
92. Ibid., 81.
93. Ibid.
94. Ibid.
95. Ibid.

7. PATTERNS

1. Jamshed Mavalwala, ed., *Dermatoglyphics: An International Perspective* (The Hague: Moulton Publishers, 1978), 19.
2. Ibid., 22–24.
3. Ibid.
4. United States Department of Justice, Federal Bureau of Investigation, *The Science of Fingerprints: Classification and Uses* (Rev. 12-84), iii–iv.
5. Beryl Hutchinson, *Your Life in Your Hands*, 91.
6. Comte C. de Saint-Germain (Edgar de Valcourt-Vermont), *The Practice of Palmistry for Professional Purposes* (Chicago: 1897), (London: Newcastle Publishing, 1973), 87.
7. Beryl Hutchinson, *Your Life in Your Hands*, 92.
8. Sasha Fenton and Malcolm Wright, *The Living Hand* (Wellingborough, Northamptonshire: Aquarian Press, 1986), 140.
9. T. Takashina and S. Yorifuji, "Palmar Dermatoglyphics in Heart Disease," *JAMA*, Aug. 29, 1966.
10. Eugene Scheimann, *The Doctor's Guide to Better Health Through Palmistry*, 70–71.

11. Nathaniel Altman, *The Palmistry Workbook*, 105.
12. Enid Hoffman, *Hands: A Complete Guide to Palmistry*, 230.
13. Beryl Hutchinson, *Your Life in Your Hands*, 118.
14. Beverly Jaegers, *Beyond Palmistry: The Art and Science of Modern Hand Analysis*, 55.
15. Sasha Fenton and Malcolm Wright, *The Living Hand*, 135.
16. Beryl Hutchinson, *Your Life in Your Hands*, 116, 118.
17. Enid Hoffman, *Hands: A Complete Guide to Palmistry*, 229, 230.
18. Bevy C. Jaegers, *Hand Analysis Fingerprints and Skin Patterns—Dermatoglyphics*, 43, 46–47.
19. Beverly Jaegers, *Beyond Palmistry*, 56.
20. Sasha Fenton and Malcolm Wright, *The Living Hand*, 135.
21. Jaegers, *Hand Analysis Fingerprints and Skin Patterns—Dermatoglyphics*, 47.
22. Beverly Jaegers, *Beyond Palmistry*, 56.
23. Sasha Fenton and Malcolm Wright, *The Living Hands*, 134; Beryl Hutchinson, *Your Life in Your Hands*, 116–117.
24. Beryl Hutchinson, *Your Life in Your Hands*.
25. Beverly Jaegers, *Dermatoglyphics*, 43, 47–48.
26. Beverly Jaegers, *Hand Analysis Fingerprints and Skin Patterns—Dermatoglyphics*.
27. Ibid., 48.
28. Beryl Hutchinson, *Your Life in Your Hands*, 125, 90.
29. Ibid., 119.
30. Beverly Jaegers, *Dermatoglyphics*, 48.
31. Ibid., 48–49.
32. Beverly Jaegers, *Beyond Palmistry*, 63.
33. Enid Hoffman, *Hands: A Complete Guide to Palmistry*, 231.
34. Beryl Hutchinson, *Your Life in Your Hands*, 119.
35. Beverly Jaegers, *Dermatoglyphics*, 58–61, and *Beyond Palmistry*, 73.
36. Beverly Jaegers, *Beyond Palmistry*, 52, 56, and *Dermatoglyphics*, 43, 62.
37. Beverly Jaegers, *Hand Analysis Fingerprints and Skin Patterns—Dermatoglyphics*, and *Beyond Palmistry*, 53.
38. Beverly Jaegers, *Dermatoglyphics*, 62–64.
39. Beverly Jaegers, *Beyond Palmistry*, 65.
40. Enid Hoffman, *Hands: A Complete Guide to Palmistry*, 231.
41. Beryl Hutchinson, *Your Life in Your Hands*, 120.
42. Hutchinson published in 1967. Compare Enid Hoffman (*Hands*, published in 1983), who finds the mark one of musical genius, perhaps a composer but certainly a musician. Then compare both with the more cautious approach of Jaegers in her earlier work, *Hand Analysis*, published in 1974, which restates the Hutchinson hypothesis, and then her later work, *Beyond Palmistry*, published in 1992, which leans toward Hoffman.
43. Enid Hoffman, *Hands: A Complete Guide to Palmistry*, 231.
44. Beryl Hutchinson, *Your Life in Your Hands*, 120.
45. Jaegers, *Dermatoglyphics*, 50–51.
46. Beverly Jaegers, *Beyond Palmistry*, 61–63.
47. Enid Hoffman, *Hands: A Complete Guide to Palmistry*, 230.
48. Beryl Hutchinson, *Your Life in Your Hands*, 120.
49. Ibid., 121.
50. Andrew Fitzherbert, *Hand Psychology*, 251, 253.
51. Enid Hoffman, *Hands: A Complete Guide to Palmistry*, 229, 230.
52. Jaegers, *Dermatoglyphics*, 43, 52–56.
53. Andrew Fitzherbert, *Hand Psychology*, 249, 251.
54. Sasha Fenton and Malcolm Wright, *The Living Hand*, 135.
55. Beryl Hutchinson, *Your Life in Your Hands*, 122.
56. Andrew Fitzherbert, *Hand Psychology*, 249, 250.
57. Sasha Fenton and Malcolm Wright, *The Living Hand*, 135.
58. Enid Hoffman, *Hands: A Complete Guide to Palmistry*, 229, 230.
59. Jaegers, *Dermatoglyphics*, 43, 53–55.
60. Beverly Jaegers, *Beyond Palmistry*, 56–58.
61. Andrew Fitzherbert, *Hand Psychology*, 249, 251.
62. Beverly Jaegers, *Beyond Palmistry*, 71–73.
63. Beryl Hutchinson, *Your Life in Your Hands*, 124.
64. Ibid., 116, 122.
65. Andrew Fitzherbert, *Hand Psychology*, 249, 250.

66. Jaegers, *Dermatoglyphics*, 43, 55–57.
67. Beverly Jaegers, *Beyond Palmistry*, 58–60.
68. Beryl Hutchinson, *Your Life in Your Hands*, 116, 123.
69. Ibid., 124–125.
70. Fred Gettings, *The Book of the Hand: An Illustrated History of Palmistry* (Hamlyn Publishing Group, 1961, 1968).
71. Jamshed Mavalwala, ed., *Dermatoglyphics: An International Perspective*, 23.
72. Ibid., 28–35.
73. Blanka Schaumann and Milton Alter, *Dermatoglyphics in Medical Disorders*, 33.
74. Terence Dukes, *Chinese Hand Analysis* (York Beach, Maine: Samuel Weiser, 1987), 108.
75. Beryl Hutchinson, *Your Life in Your Hands*, 94.
76. Ibid., 100–101.
77. Jaegers, *Dermatoglyphics*, 69.
78. Ibid., 41–42.
79. Andrew Fitzherbert, *Hand Psychology*, 173.
80. Sasha Fenton and Malcolm Wright, *The Living Hand*, 42.
81. Terence Dukes, *Chinese Hand Analysis*, 108.
82. Beryl Hutchinson, *Your Life in Your Hands*, 105–106.
83. Noel Jaquin, *The Signature of Time* (London: Farber & Farber, 1940), 95.
84. Sasha Fenton and Malcolm Wright, *The Living Hand*, 44.
85. Dennis Fairchild, *The Handbook of Humanistic Palmistry*, 59–61.
86. Jaegers, *Dermatoglyphics*, 70–71.
87. Terence Dukes, *Chinese Hand Analysis*, 108.
88. Beryl Hutchinson, *Your Life in Your Hands*, 95.
89. Ibid., 96.
90. Ibid.
91. Ibid.
92. Ibid.
93. Jaegers, *Dermatoglyphics*, 72.
94. Ibid., 73.
95. Ibid., 75–76.
96. Dennis Fairchild, *The Handbook of Humanistic Palmistry*, 61–63.
97. Sasha Fenton and Malcolm Wright, *The Living Hand*, 43–44.
98. Andrew Fitzherbert, *Hand Psychology*, 173.
99. Elizabeth Daniels Squire, *The New Fortune in Your Hand* (New York: Fleet Press Corporation, 1960), 184.
100. Terence Dukes, *Chinese Hand Analysis*, 109.
101. Jaegers, *Dermatoglyphics*, 77.
102. Beverly Jaegers, *Beyond Palmistry*, 46–48.
103. Ibid., 78.
104. Sasha Fenton and Malcolm Wright, *The Living Hand*, 43.
105. Enid Hoffman, *Hands: A Complete Guide to Palmistry*, 233–234.
106. Andrew Fitzherbert, *Hand Psychology*, 172–173.
107. Noel Jaquin, *The Signature of Time*, 92.
108. Terence Dukes, *Chinese Hand Analysis*, 109.
109. Ibid.
110. Sasha Fenton and Malcolm Wright, *The Living Hand*, 42–43.
111. I thought I got the term *dowser* for this formation from Beryl B. Hutchinson, but I have been unable to locate the source. I have found it appropriate on the index finger and the thumb.
112. Harry Oldfield and Roger Coghill, *The Dark Side of the Brain: Major Discoveries in the Use of Kirlian Photography and Electrocrystal Therapy* (Longmead, Shaftesbury, Dorset: Element Books, 1988), 92–127. The authors theorize that the cells transmit via the resonance of their DNA paired bases' hydrogen bonds. A "correct frequency" must be broadcast by a large number of cells binding the organism together. The palm and fingerprints may also be the key or part of the key, along with the iris of the eye, to the "correct frequencies" that need to be broadcast and received between the brain and the cells at the DNA level to achieve the harmonies of health.
113. Beryl Hutchinson, *Your Life in Your Hands*, 104–105.
114. Sasha Fenton and Malcolm Wright, *The Living Hand*, 42–43.
115. Beryl Hutchinson, *Your Life in Your Hands*, 106.

116. Sasha Fenton and Malcolm Wright, *The Living Hand*, 44.

117. David Brandon-Jones, *Practical Palmistry*, 135–136.

118. Terence Dukes, *Chinese Hand Analysis*, 111.

119. David Brandon-Jones, *Practical Palmistry*, 136.

120. Sasha Fenton and Malcolm Wright, *The Living Hand*, 44.

121. Jaegers, *Dermatoglyphics*, 80.

122. Blanka Schaumann and Milton Alter, *Dermatoglyphics in Medical Disorders*, 85.

123. Ibid.

8. THE LINED PALM AND MAJOR LINES

1. Eugene Scheimann, M.D., *The Doctor's Guide to Better Health Through Palmistry* (New York: Parker Publishing, 1969).

2. Julius Spier, *The Hands of Children* (New Delhi: Sagar Publications, 1955).

3. John Russell Napier, *Hands* (New York: Pantheon Books, 1980). Not a palmistry book but a scientific book on hands.

4. Charlotte Wolff, *The Human Hands* (Alfred A. Knopf, 1943).

5. Julius Spier, *The Hands of Children*, 67.

6. Blanka Schaumann and Milton Alter, *Dermatoglyphics in Medical Disorders* (New York: Springer-Verlag, 1976), 103.

7. David Brandon-Jones, *Practical Palmistry* (Reno: CRCS Publications, 1986).

8. Wood Jones, *Principles of Anatomy as Seen in the Hand.*

9. See note 5 above and J. Schaeuble, "Die Entstehung der Palmaren Digitalen Triadien," *Z. Morphol. Anthropol.*, 31:403, 1933.

10. T. Humphrey, "Some Correlations Between Appearance of Human Fetal Reflexes and the Development of the Nervous System," *Prog. Brain Res.*, 4:93, 1964. Reported in Blanka Schaumann and Milton Alter, *Dermatoglyphics in Medical Disorders*, 104.

11. A. Wurth, "Die Enstehung der Beugefurchen der Menschlichen Hohland," *Z. Morphol. Anthropol.*, 36:187, 1937. Reported in Schaumann and Alter, *Dermatoglyphics in Medical Disorders*, 104.

12. G. A. Popich and D. W. Smith, "The Genesis and Significance of Digital and Palmar Hand Creases: Preliminary Report," *J. Pediatr.*, 77:1017, 1970. Reported in Blanka Schaumann and Milton Alter, *Dematoglyphics in Medical Disorders*, 105.

13. S. G. Purvis-Smith and M. A. Menser, "Dermatoglyphics in Adults with Congenital Rubella," *Lancet*, 2:141, 1968. Reported in Blanka Schaumann and Milton Alter, *Dermatoglyphics in Medical Disorders*, 109.

14. Blanka Schaumann and Milton Alter, *Dermatoglyphics in Medical Disorders*, 124.

15. Hachiro Asano, "Hands," *The Complete Book of Palmistry*, 172–178.

16. Terence Dukes, *Chinese Hand Analysis* (York Beach, Maine: Samuel Weiser, 1987).

17. William G. Benham, *The Laws of Scientific Hand Reading*, originally published in 1900 (New York: Putnam, 1958). A recent reprint has been done with preface by Rita Robinson (North Hollywood, Ca.: Newcastle Metaphysical Classic, 1988) under the title *The Benham Book of Palmistry.*

18. Nathaniel Altman, *The Palmistry Workbook* (Wellingborough, Northamptonshire: Aquarian Press, 1984).

19. Esther Newcomer-Bramblett, *Reading Hands for Pleasure or Profit* (Austin, Texas: Woods Publications, 1982).

20. Fred Gettings, *The Book of the Hand: An Illustrated History of Palmistry* (Hamlyn Publishing Group, 1968).

21. Rita Robinson, *The Palm: A Guide to Your Hidden Potential* (Van Nuys, Ca.: Newcastle Original, 1988).

22. Andrew Fitzherbert, *The Palmist's Companion: A*

History and Bibliography of Palmistry (Metuchen, N.J.: The Scarecrow Press, 1992), 16.

23. V. A. K. Ayer, *Palmistry for Pleasure and Profit* (Bombay: Taraporevala Sons).

24. Sasha Fenton and Malcolm Wright, *The Living Hand* (Wellingborough, Northamptonshire: Aquarian Press, 1986).

25. Julius Spier, *Hands of Children*, 68.

26. Terence Dukes, *Chinese Hand Analysis.*

27. Myrah Lawrance, *Hand Analysis* (West Nyack, N.Y.: Parker Pub., 1967).

28. Andrew Fitzherbert, *The Palmist's Companion: A History and Bibliography of Palmistry.*

29. Myrah Lawrance, *Hand Analysis*, 72–73.

30. Yaschpaule, *Your Destiny and Scientific Hand Analysis* (Petaling Jaya, Selangor, Malaysia: Heinemann Educational Books, 1981, 1982).

31. V. A. K. Ayer, *Palmistry for Pleasure and Profit*, 67.

32. Myrah Lawrance, *Hand Analysis*, 72.

33. Ibid., 73.

34. Ibid.

35. V. A. K. Ayer, *Palmistry for Pleasure and Profit*, 65–66.

36. Yvette Grady, *Hand-Picked Men* (New York: Hippocrene Books, 1989).

37. David Brandon-Jones, *Practical Palmistry*, 190.

38. Yaschpaule, *Your Destiny and Scientific Hand Analysis*, 190.

39. William G. Benham, *The Laws of Scientific Hand Reading*, 386.

40. Blanka Schaumann and Milton Alter, *Dermatoglyphics in Mental Disorders*, 103.

41. Yaschpaule, *Your Destiny and Scientific Hand Analysis*, 189.

42. Ibid., 191.

43. Julius Spier, *The Hands of Children*, 84.

44. Ibid., 83.

45. Yaschpaule, *Your Destiny and Scientific Hand Analysis*, 150.

46. Ibid., 158.

47. Gerald E. Biccum, *Handology: How to Unlock the Hidden Secrets of Your Life* (Hillsborough, Ore.: Beyond Words Publishing, 1989).

48. Yvette Grady, *Hand-Picked Men*, illustration 3.2 H, 49, and 109–121.

49. Rita Robinson, *The Palm: A Guide to Your Hidden Potential*, 82.

50. Cheiro (Count Louis Hamon), *The Language of the Hand* (New York: Prentice-Hall, 1987).

51. David Brandon-Jones, *Practical Palmistry*, 212.

52. Yaschpaule, *Your Destiny and Scientific Hand Analysis*, 220.

53. Andrew Fitzherbert, *The Palmist's Companion: A History and Bibliography of Palmistry*, 51.

54. William F. Benham, *The Laws of Scientific Hand Reading*, 531.

55. Yaschpaule, *Your Destiny and Scientific Hand Analysis*, 240.

56. Ibid.

9. OTHER LINES

1. Blanka Schaumann and Milton Alter, *Dermatoglyphics in Mental Disorders* (New York: Springer-Verlag, 1976), 107.

2. Sasha Fenton and Malcolm Wright, *The Living Hand* (Wellingborough, Northamptonshire: Aquarian Press, 1986), 82–83.

3. Blanka Schaumann and Milton Alter, *Dermatoglyphics in Mental Disorders*, 169, 210. Other congenital disorders include trisomy 8 mosaicism and rubella embryopathy.

4. Hachiro Asano, *Hands: The Complete Book of Palmistry* (Tokyo: Japan Publications, 1985), 17, 71.

5. Fred Gettings, *The Book of the Hand: An Illustrated History of Palmistry* (Hamlyn Publishing Group, 1968), 144–145.

6. Roz Levine, *Palmistry: How to Chart the Lines of Your Destiny* (Simon & Schuster, 1992), 90–91.

7. Walter Sorell, *The Story of the Human Hand* (Bobbs-Merrill, 1967), 76–83; Sasha Fenton and

Malcolm Wright, *The Living Hand;* Edo Sprong, *Hand Analysis: The Diagnostic Method* (New York: Sterling Publishing, 1991); Darlene Hansen, *Secrets of the Palm* (San Diego: ACS Publications, 1985), 95.

8. Eugene Scheimann, M.D., *The Doctor's Guide to Better Health Through Palmistry* (New York: Parker Publishing, 1969), 117.

9. V. A. K. Ayer, *Palmistry for Pleasure and Profit* (Bombay: Taraporevala Sons), 70.

10. K. C. Sen, *Hast Samudrika Shastra, the Science of Hand-Reading Simplified,* 7th ed. (Bombay: Taraporevala Sons, 1960), 102.

11. Beryl Hutchinson, *Your Life in Your Hands* (London: Sphere Books, 1969), 149.

12. Yaschpaule, *Your Destiny and Scientific Hand Analysis* (Petaling Jaya, Selangor, Malaysia: Heinemann Educational Books, 1982), 167.

13. Roz Levine, *Palmistry: How to Chart the Lines of Your Destiny,* 91.

14. Yaschpaule, *Your Destiny and Scientific Hand Analysis,* 167.

15. Nathaniel Altman and Andrew Fitzherbert, *Career, Success and Self Fulfillment: How Scientific Handreading Can Change Your Life* (Wellingborough, Northamptonshire: Aquarian Press, 1988), 99.

16. M. N. Laffan, *Handreading* (New York: Kegan Paul, Trench Trubner, 1931).

17. Yaschpaule, *Your Destiny and Scientific Hand Analysis.*

18. Ibid., 257.

19. Ibid., 256.

20. V. A. K. Ayer, *Sariraka Sastra, Indian Science of Palmistry (the Kartikeyan System),* 2nd ed. (Bombay: D. B. Taraporevala Sons, 1965).

21. Ibid., 82.

22. Julius Spier, *The Hands of Children* (New Delhi: Sagar Publications).

23. Sasha Fenton and Malcolm Wright, *The Living Hand,* 117.

24. K. C. Sen, *Hast Samudrika Shastra, the Science of Hand-Reading Simplified,* 143.

25. Bettina Luxon and Jill Goolden, *Your Hand: Simple Palmistry for Everyone* (New York: Crown, 1983), 58–62.

26. David Brandon-Jones, *Practical Palmistry,* 241(e), 247.

27. Vera Compton, *Palmistry for Everyone* (Westport, Conn.: Associated Booksellers, 1956), 86.

28. Sasha Fenton and Malcolm Wright, *The Living Hand,* 122–123.

29. Litzka Raymond Gibson, *How to Read Palms,* rev. ed. (Hollywood, Fla.: Fell Publishers, 1989), 160, 161.

30. Yaschpaule, *Your Destiny and Scientific Hand Analysis,* 317.

31. Sasha Fenton and Malcolm Wright, *The Living Hand,* 114.

32. Vera Compton, *Palmistry for Everyman,* 87.

33. David Brandon-Jones, *Practical Palmistry* (Reno: CRCS Publications, 1986).

34. Yaschpaule, *Your Destiny and Scientific Hand Analysis,* 338–339.

35. Vera Compton, *Palmistry for Everyman,* 88. The Index Ring.

36. Sasha Fenton and Malcolm Wright, *The Living Hand,* 123. Reporting on the conclusions of Sheila McGuirk.

37. Edo Sprong, *Hand Analysis: The Diagnostic Method,* 151.

38. Ibid., 150. My editor asked if this was spelled wrong or if Dr. Sen's book was misspelled. I cannot say that Mr. Sprong refers to Dr. Sen's book so I do not know if there is any misspelling.

39. K. C. Sen, *Hast Samudrika Shastra, the Science of Hand-Reading Simplified,* 169–171.

40. Yaschpaule, *Your Destiny and Scientific Hand Analysis,* 327–333.

41. Gerald E. Biccum, *Handology: How to Unlock the Hidden Secrets of Your Life* (Hillsborough, Ore.: Beyond Words Publishing, 1989), 166, 302.

42. Hachiro Asano, *Hands: The Complete Book of Palmistry,* 168.

43. Sasha Fenton and Malcolm Wright, *The Living Hand,* 123.

44. Edo Sprong, *Hand Analysis: The Diagnostic Method*, 143.

45. Roz Levine, *Palmistry: How to Chart the Lines of Your Destiny*, 88.

46. K. C. Sen, *Hast Samudrika Shastra, the Science of Hand-Reading Simplified*, 140–142.

47. Gerald E. Biccum, *Handology: How to Unlock the Hidden Secrets of Your Life*, 167, 303.

48. Yaschpaule, *Your Destiny and Scientific Hand Analysis*, 333.

49. Edo Sprong, *Hand Analysis: The Diagnostic Method*, 146–147.

50. Gerald E. Biccum, *Handology: How to Unlock the Hidden Secrets of Your Life*, 163, 300–302.

51. Edo Sprong, *Hand Analysis: The Diagnostic Method*, 28.

52. Blanka Schaumann and Milton Alter, *Dermatoglyphics in Medical Disorders*, 122–126.

53. Sasha Fenton and Malcolm Wright, *The Living Hand*, 125.

54. Nathaniel Altman and Andrew Fitzherbert, *Career, Success and Self Fulfillment: How Scientific Handreading Can Change Your Life*, 182.

55. Lori Reid, *Family Matters, Palmistry* (London: Artillery House, 1990), 79.

56. David Brandon-Jones, *Practical Palmistry*, 194.

57. Yaschpaule, *Your Destiny and Scientific Hand Analysis*, 143–145.

58. Elizabeth Brenner, *The Hand Book* (Berkeley, Ca.: Celestial Arts, 1980), 56.

59. Yvette Grady, *Hand-Picked Men* (New York: Hippocrene Books, 1989), 43–44.

60. Vera Compton, *Palmistry for Everyman*, 61.

61. Beryl Hutchinson, *Your Life in Your Hands*, 161.

62. William G. Benham, *The Laws of Scientific Hand Reading*. Originally published in 1900 (New York: Putnam, 1958).

63. Litzka Raymond Gibson, *How to Read Palms*, 157.

64. K. C. Sen, *Hast Samudrika Shastra, the Science of Hand-Reading Simplified*, 147.

65. Andrew Fitzherbert, *Hand Psychology* (London: Angus & Robertson, 1986), 115–119, 242.

66. Litzka Raymond Gibson, *How to Read Palms*, 149–150.

67. Vera Compton, *Palmistry for Everyman*, 88.

68. Carol Hellings White, *Holding Hands: The Complete Guide to Palmistry* (G. P. Putnam's Sons, 1980).

69. Beryl Hutchinson, *Your Life in Your Hands*.

70. Yaschpaule, *Your Destiny and Scientific Hand Analysis*, 343–347.

71. Psychos, *The Mystery of Your Palm* (Philadelphia: David McKay), 133.

72. Litzka Raymond Gibson, *How to Read Palms*, 149–150.

73. Yaschpaule, *Your Destiny and Scientific Hand Analysis*, 343.

74. William G. Benham, *The Laws of Scientific Hand Reading*, 300–302.

75. Ibid., 584.

76. Enid Hoffman, *Hands: A Complete Guide to Palmistry* (Gloucester, Mass., 1985), 173, 174.

77. Ibid.

78. Ibid.

79. Ibid.

80. William G. Benham, *Laws of Scientific Hand Reading*, 298–299.

81. Hachiro Asano, *Hands: The Complete Book of Palmistry*, 169.

82. Gerald E. Biccum, *Handology: How to Unlock the Hidden Secrets of Your Life*, 150–160, 292–298.

83. Vera Compton, *Palmistry for Everyman*, 85.

84. Cheiro (Count Louis Hamon), *The Language of the Hand* (New York: Prentice-Hall, 1987), 109–110.

85. Rodney Davies, *Fortune-Telling by Palmistry: A Practical Guide to the Art of Hand Analysis* (Wellingborough, Northamptonshire: Aquarian Press, 1987), 121–124.

86. Lori Reid, *Family Matters, Palmistry*, 109–111.

87. Yaschpaule, *Your Destiny and Scientific Hand Analysis*, 298–314.

88. Yvette Grady, *Hand-Picked Men*, 68–69.

89. Hilarion, *Body Signs* (Ontario: Marcus Books, 1982), 125–128.

90. Judith Hipskind, *Palmistry: The Whole View*, 2nd enlarged ed. (St. Paul: Llewellyn, 1983), 215.

91. Enid Hoffman, *Hands: A Complete Guide to Palmistry*, 171–176.

92. Maria Gardini, *The Secrets of the Hand*. Trans. by Judith Spencer (New York: Macmillan, 1985), 109–110.

93. Esther Newcomer-Bramblett, *Reading Hands for Pleasure or Profit* (Austin, Tex.: Woods Publications, 1982), 206.

94. Comte C. de Saint-Germain (Edgar de Valcourt-Vermont), *Practical Palmistry: Hand Reading Simplified* (Mokelumne Hill, Ca.: Health Research, 1970), 182–188.

95. Rita Robinson, *The Palm: A Guide to Your Hidden Potential* (Van Nuys, Ca.: Newcastle Original, 1988), 106–110.

96. Julius Spier, *The Hands of Children*, 93.

97. Nathaniel Altman and Andrew Fitzherbert, *Career, Success and Self Fulfillment: How Scientific Handreading Can Change Your Life* (Wellingborough, Northamptonshire: Aquarian Press, 1988), 72.

98. Julius Spier, *The Hands of Children*, 93.

99. Yaschpaule, *Your Destiny and Scientific Hand Analysis*, 305–311.

100. Sasha Fenton and Malcolm Wright, *The Living Hand*.

101. Nathaniel Altman, *The Palmistry Workbook* (Wellingborough, Northamptonshire: Aquarian Press, 1984).

102. Andrew Fitzherbert, *Hand Psychology*; and Nathaniel Altman and Andrew Fitzherbert, *Career, Success and Self Fulfillment: How Scientific Handreading Can Change Your Life.*

103. Litzka Raymond Gibson, *How To Read Palms.*

104. Comte C. de Saint-Germain, *Practical Palmistry: Hand Reading Simplified*, 200–208.

105. Enid Hoffman, *Hands: A Complete Guide to Palmistry*, 139.

106. Carol Hellings White, *Holding Hands: The Complete Guide to Palmistry*, 92.

107. Linda Domin, *PalmaScope: The Instant Palm Reader* (St. Paul, Minn.: Llewellyn, 1989), 131–147.

108. Litzka Raymond Gibson, *How to Read Palms*, 145.

109. Roz Levine, *Palmistry: How to Chart the Lines of Your Destiny*, 107.

110. Niblo, *The Complete Palmist* (North Hollywood, Ca.: Newcastle Publishing, 1982), 138–139.

111. Elizabeth Daniels Squire, *Palmistry Made Practical: Your Fortune in Your Hands* (North Hollywood, Ca.: Wilshire Book Co., 1979), 179.

112. Comte C. de Saint-German (Edgar de Valcourt-Vermont), *Practical Palmistry: Hand Reading Simplified*, 186.

113. Rita Robinson, *The Palm: A Guide to Your Hidden Potential*, 106.

114. Hilarion, *Body Signs*, 127.

115. Jean-Michel Morgan, *Palmistry: The Art of Reading Hands*. Trans. by David Macrae (Barcelona: Ariane Books, 1975), 78–79.

116. Niblo, *The Complete Palmist*, 138–139.

117. Jean-Michel Morgan, *Palmistry: The Art of Reading Hands*, 79.

118. Comte C. de Saint-Germain, *Practical Palmistry: Hand Reading Simplified*, 201.

119. Niblo, *The Complete Palmist*, 139.

120. Rodney Davies, *Fortune-Telling by Palmistry: A Practical Guide to the Art of Hand Analysis*, 121.

121. Ibid., 232–235.

122. Ibid., 223.

123. Judith Hipskind, *Palmistry: The Whole View*, 215.

124. Rodney Davies, *Fortune-Telling by Palmistry*, 121.

125. Lori Reid, *Family Matters, Palmistry*, 110.

126. Yvette Grady, *Hand-Picked Men*, 68.

127. David Brandon-Jones, *Practical Palmistry*, 232.

128. Rita Robinson, *The Palm: A Guide to Your Hidden Potential*, 108.

129. Niblo, *The Complete Palmist*, 138.

130. Lori Reid, *Family Matters, Palmistry*, 111.

131. Elizabeth Brenner, *Hand in Hand* (Millbrae, Ca.: Celestial Arts, 1981), 68.

132. Charlotte Wolff, *Studies in Handreading*. Preface by Aldous Huxley (New York: Alfred A. Knopf,

1937), 21, 35, 55, 69, 87, 103, 105, 107, 110. On page 109 she calls the same line the line of health.

133. Roz Levine, *Palmistry: How to Chart the Lines of Your Destiny*, 106–107.

134. Maria Costavile, *How to Read Palms* (New York: Crescent Books, 1988), 28.

135. Rodney Davies, *Fortune-Telling by Palmistry: A Practical Guide to the Art of Hand Analysis*, 122.

136. See note 81 above.

137. Vera Compton, *Palmistry for Everyone*, 85.

138. Hachiro Asano, *Hands: The Complete Book of Palmistry*, 169.

139. Yvette Grady, *Hand-Picked Men*, 68–69.

140. Beryl Hutchinson, *Your Life in Your Hands*, 174–177.

141. See note 123 above.

142. Elizabeth Daniels Squire, *The New Fortune in Your Hands*, 164; *Palmistry Made Practical*, 179.

143. See note 137 above.

144. See note 124 above.

145. See note 142 above.

146. Judith Hipskind, *Palmistry: The Whole View*, 214–215.

147. Julius Spier, *The Hands of Children*, 164.

148. Nathaniel Altman, *The Palmistry Workbook*, 103.

149. Andrew Fitzherbert, *Hand Psychology*, 240.

150. Gerald E. Biccum, *Handology: How to Unlock the Hidden Secrets of Your Life*, 163, 300.

151. Ibid., 150.

152. See note 127 above.

153. Gerald E. Biccum, *Handology: How to Unlock the Hidden Secrets of Your Life*, 1.

154. Psychos, *The Mystery of Your Palm*, 131.

155. Lori Reid, *Family Matters*, *Palmistry*, 111.

156. Psychos, *The Mystery of Your Palm*, 130–131.

157. Yaschpaule, *Your Destiny and Scientific Hand Analysis*, 301.

158. Enid Hoffman, *Hands: A Complete Guide to Palmistry* (Gloucester, Mass.: Para Research, 1985), 176.

159. Yaschpaule, *Your Destiny and Scientific Hand Analysis*, 298.

10. SPECIAL MARKS

1. Maria Costavile, *How to Read Palms* (New York: Crescent Books, 1988), 75.

2. Bettina Luxon and Jill Goolden, *Your Hand: Simple Palmistry for Everyone* (New York: Crown, 1983), 70.

3. Enid Hoffman, *Hands: A Complete Guide to Palmistry* (Gloucester, Mass.: Para Research, 1985), 203.

4. Maria Costavile, *How to Read Palms*, 72.

5. Ibid., 207.

6. Ibid., 212.

7. Ibid., 214.

8. K. C. Sen, *Hast Samudrika Shastra, the Science of Hand-Reading Simplified* (Bombay: Taraporevala Sons, 1960), 152. Dr. Sen would also classify breaks, islands, and crosses with stars as bad signs on travel lines, showing extreme danger.

9. Enid Hoffman, *Hands: A Complete Guide to Palmistry*, 215.

10. Ibid., 217.

11. Vera Compton, *Palmistry for Everyman* (Westport, Conn.: Associated Booksellers, 1956), 93.

12. Henry Frith, *Palmistry Secrets Revealed*. Ed. by John Malcolm (North Hollywood, Ca.: Melvin Powers Wilshire Book Company, 1952), 121.

13. Jean-Michael Morgan, *Palmistry: The Art of Reading Hands*. Trans. by David Macrae (Barcelona: Ariane Books, 1975), 81.

14. Carol Hellings White, *Holding Hands: The Complete Guide to Palmistry* (G. P. Putnam's Sons, 1980), 102.

15. Niblo, *The Complete Palmist* (North Hollywood, Ca.: Newcastle Publishing, 1982), 144.

16. Sasha Fenton and Malcolm Wright, *The Living Hand* (Wellingborough, Northamptonshire: Aquarian Press, 1986), 131.

17. Rita Robinson, *The Palm: A Guide to Your Hidden*

Potential (Van Nuys, Ca.: Newcastle Original, 1988), 117.

18. Spencer Grendahl, *Romance on Your Hands: Palmistry for Lovers* (Simon & Schuster, 1990), 219.

19. Rita Van Alen, *You and Your Hand* (New York: Greystone Press, 1948), 177–182.

20. Cheiro (Count Louis Hamon), *The Language of the Hand* (New York: Prentice-Hall, 1987), 121–124; *Palmistry for All* (New York: G. P. Putnam's Sons, 1916), 104–106; and *Cheiro's Complete Palmistry, from the Works of Count Louis Hamon.* Ed. by Robert M. Ockene (New Hyde Park, N.Y.: University Books, 1968), 191–194. He says there are one or two exceptions.

21. Litzka Raymond Gibson, *How to Read Palms,* rev. ed. (Hollywood, Fla.: Fell Publishers, 1989), 167–168.

22. Yaschpaule, *Your Destiny and Scientific Hand Analysis* (Petaling Jaya, Selangor, Malaysia: Heinemann Educational Books, 1982), 406–407.

23. Ibid., 212–214.

24. Ibid., 410.

25. K. C. Sen, *Hast Samudrika Shastra, the Science of Hand-Reading Simplified,* 165.

26. V. A. K. Ayer, *Palmistry for Pleasure and Profit* (Bombay: Taraporevala Sons, 1962), 110–111. Mr. Ayer does not mention the thumb.

27. Yaschpaule, *Your Destiny and Scientific Hand Analysis,* 414–415.

28. K. C. Sen, *Hast Samudrika Shastra, the Science of Hand-Reading Simplified,* 52.

29. Ibid., 53.

30. V. A. K. Ayer, *Palmistry for Pleasure and Profit,* 110–111.

31. K. C. Sen, *Hast Samudrika Shastra, the Science of Hand-Reading Simplified,* 52–53.

32. Ibid., 53.

33. Ibid.

34. Francis King, *Palmistry: Your Fate and Fortune in Your Hand* (New York: Crown, 1987), 54.

35. Ibid., 55.

36. Ibid., 57.

37. Ibid., 55.

38. K. C. Sen, *Hast Samudrika Shastra, the Science of Hand-Reading Simplified,* 52.

39. Francis King, *Palmistry: Your Fate and Fortune in Your Hand,* 52, 56. Dr. Sen would agree with this conclusion and add the qualities of fortitude and exceptional willpower.

40. Ibid., 56.

41. K. C. Sen, *Hast Samudrika Shastra, the Science of Hand-Reading Simplified,* 53.

42. Ibid., 54.

43. Ibid., 122.

44. Francis King, *Palmistry: Your Fate and Fortune in Your Hand,* 54.

45. Rita Robinson, *The Palm: A Guide to Your Hidden Potential,* 117.

46. Rodney Davies, *Fortune-Telling by Palmistry: A Practical Guide to the Art of Hand Analysis* (Wellingborough, Northamptonshire: Aquarian Press, 1987), 132–133.

47. Esther Newcomer-Bramblett, *Reading Hands for Pleasure or Profit* (Austin, Tex.: Woods Publications, 1982), 223.

48. Rita Van Alen, *You and Your Hand,* 179, 180.

49. Cheiro (Count Louis Hamon), *The Language of the Hands,* 121.

50. Linda Domin, *PalmaScope: The Instant Palm Reader* (St. Paul, Minn.: Llewellyn, 1989), 187.

51. Henri Rem, *What Your Hand Reveals* (New York: E. P. Dutton, 1922), 277–281.

52. See note 48 above.

53. Cheiro (Count Louis Hamon), *The Language of the Hand,* 121.

54. Jean-Michel Morgan, *Palmistry: The Art of Reading Hands,* 81.

55. Esther Newcomer-Bramblett, *Reading Hands for Pleasure or Profit,* 121.

56. Henry Frith, *Palmistry Secrets Revealed,* 121.

57. Niblo, *The Complete Palmist,* 144.

58. Kwok Man Ho, Martin Palmer, and Joanne O'Brien, *Lines of Destiny: How to Read Faces and Hands the Chinese Way* (London: Rider, 1986), 168–169.

59. Linda Domin, *PalmaScope: The Instant Palm Reader*, 166.
60. Henri Rem, *What Your Hand Reveals*, 277.
61. Niblo, *The Complete Palmist*, 144.
62. Esther Newcomer-Bramblett, *Reading Hands for Pleasure or Profit*, 221.
63. Leona Lehman, *Key to Palmistry* (New York: Bell Publishing, 1959), 88.
64. Cheiro, *The Language of the Hands*, 121–122.
65. See note 56 above.
66. Linda Domin, *PalmaScope: The Instant Palm Reader*, 168.
67. Rita Van Alen, *You and Your Hand*, 179, 181.
68. Ibid.
69. Ibid., 179, 182.
70. See note 63 above.
71. Esther Newcomer-Bramblett, *Reading Hands for Pleasure or Profit*, 222.
72. Linda Domin, *PalmaScope: The Instant Palm Reader*, 174.
73. See note 60 above.
74. Cheiro, *The Language of the Hand*, 122.
75. See note 56 above.
76. See note 61 above.
77. Linda Domin, *PalmaScope: The Instant Palm Reader*, 173.
78. See note 60 above.
79. See note 56 above.
80. See note 54 above.
81. See note 61 above.
82. See note 71 above.
83. See note 74 above.
84. See note 67 above.
85. See note 63 above.
86. Linda Domin, *PalmaScope: The Instant Palm Reader*, 177.
87. Henri Rem, *What Your Hand Reveals*, 278.
88. See note 56 above.
89. See note 61 above.
90. Linda Domin, *PalmaScope: The Instant Palm Reader*, 189.
91. Cheiro, *The Language of the Hands*, 123.
92. See note 67 above.
93. Esther Newcomer-Bramblett, *Reading Hands for Pleasure or Profit*, 223.
94. See note 90 above.
95. See note 91 above.
96. See note 67 above.
97. Linda Domin, *PalmaScope: The Instant Palm Reader*, 187.
98. Henri Rem, *What Your Hand Reveals*, 279.
99. See note 93 above.
100. See note 54 above.
101. Niblo, *The Complete Palmist*, 145.
102. See note 56 above.
103. See note 98 above.
104. Linda Domin, *PalmaScope: The Instant Palm Reader*, 183.
105. See note 91 above.
106. See note 91 above.
107. See note 67 above.
108. Leona Lehman, *The Key to Palmistry*, 89.
109. Henri Rem, *What Your Hand Reveals*, 278.
110. See note 108 above.
111. See note 56 above.
112. Jean-Michel Morgan, *Palmistry: The Art of Reading Hands*, 82.
113. Esther Newcomer-Bramblett, *Reading Hands for Pleasure or Profit*, 222.
114. Niblo, *The Complete Palmist*, 144.
115. See note 91 above.
116. Rita Van Alen, *You and Your Hand*, 179, 181–182.
117. See note 113 above.
118. See note 113 above.
119. Linda Domin, *PalmaScope: The Instant Palm Reader*, 182.
120. Esther Newcomer-Bramblett, *Reading Hands for Pleasure or Profit*, 223.
121. Henri Rem, *What Your Hand Reveals*, 279.
122. Niblo, *The Complete Palmist*, 145.
123. Linda Domin, *PalmaScope: The Instant Palm Reader*, 191.
124. Ibid., 192.
125. See note 120 above.
126. See note 108 above.

127. Hachiro Asano, *Hands: The Complete Book of Palmistry* (Tokyo: Japan Publications, 1985), 124.

128. See note 121 above.

129. Henri Rem, *What Your Hand Reveals*, 281.

130. Linda Domin, *PalmaScope: The Instant Palm Reader*, 183.

131. See note 121 above.

132. I told a lady that, according to the books, the sign of a star on the head line that she had could be indicative of a head wound. I saw the same subject about a year later, and she related to me that about six months after I had advised her of the possible head wound, she was working in a nursing home. Two patients got into a fight, and she stepped in to break it up. One patient was swinging a board, it broke, part of it hit her on the head, and she suffered severe brain damage and was still in recovery when she saw me six months after the accident.

133. See note 108 above.

134. See note 56 above.

135. Jean-Michael Morgan, *Palmistry: The Art of Reading Hands*, 81.

136. See note 108 above.

137. Henri Rem, *What Your Hand Reveals*, 280.

138. See note 56 above.

139. Kwok Man Ho et al., *Lines of Destiny: How to Read Faces and Hands the Chinese Way*, 162–163.

140. See note 137 above.

141. See note 108 above.

142. See note 137 above.

143. Henri Rem, *What Your Hand Reveals*, 281.

144. Ibid.

145. Ibid.

146. Ibid.

147. See note 122 above.

148. See note 143 above.

149. Ibid.

150. Ibid.

151. See note 135 above.

152. See note 122 above.

153. See note 120 above.

154. See note 143 above.

155. Cheiro, *The Language of the Hand*, 124.

156. See note 122 above.

157. See note 143 above.

158. See note 143 above.

159. See note 135 above.

160. See note 122 above.

161. Rita Van Alen, *You and Your Hand*, 180.

162. Ibid.

163. See note 143 above.

164. Gerald E. Biccum, *Handology: How to Unlock the Hidden Secrets of Your Life* (Hillsborough, Ore.: Beyond Words Publishing, 1989), 73, 74, 88–93, 95, 99–101, 103, 105, 110, 113, 114, 118, 137, 143, 145, 159, 160, 162, 163.

165. Comte C. de Saint-Germain (Edgar de Valcourt-Vermont), *Practical Palmistry: Hand Reading Simplified* (Mokelumne Hill, Ca.: Health Research, 1970), 94, 98, 100, 102, 110, 114, 115, 118, 119, 121, 153, 169, 171, 183–193, 195, 207, 208, 210, 215, 234–238, 257, 261, 263, 269, 275, 281, 283, 287–290, 306, 320, 322, 323, 326, 327, 331, 334, 337–340, 344.

166. Gerald E. Biccum, *Practical Palmistry: Hand Reading Simplified*, 163, 300.

167. Ibid.

168. Ibid.

169. Ibid., 163, 301.

170. Ibid., 160, 298.

171. Ibid., 106, 263.

172. Comte C. de Saint-Germain, *Practical Palmistry: Hand Reading Simplified*, 114–115. Dropsy is now know as hydrops, indicating an abnormal accumulation of clear, watery fluid in a body tissue or cavity such as a joint or the abdomen, middle ear, gallbladder, or fallopian tube.

173. Ibid., 261–262.

174. Ibid., 236–237.

175. Ibid., 257.

176. Ibid., 99.

177. Ibid., 288.

11. A LIST OF SPECIAL MARKS

1. Cyrus D. F. Abayakoon, *Astro-Palmistry: Signs and Seals of the Hand* (New York: ASI Publishers, 1975), 9. See chapter 1 generally.

2. K. C. Sen, M.A., Ph.D., *Hast Samudrika Shastra, the Science of Hand-Reading Simplified* (Bombay: Taraporevala Sons, 1960), xiii.

3. Ibid., xiv.

4. Andrew Fitzherbert, *The Palmist's Companion* (Metuchen, N.J.: The Scarecrow Press, 1990), 79.

5. Sasha Fenton and Malcolm Wright, *The Living Hand* (Wellingborough, Northamptonshire: Aquarian Press, 1986), 129.

6. Bepin Behari, *Myths and Symbols of Vedic Astrology.* David Frawley, ed. (Salt Lake City: Passage Press, 1990).

7. V. A. K. Ayer, *Palmistry for Pleasure and Profit* (Bombay: Taraporevala Sons, 1962), 114.

8. K. C. Sen, *Hast Samudrika Shastra, the Science of Hand-Reading Simplified*, 40.

9. Ibid., 60.

10. See note 7 above.

11. Maria Costavile, *How to Read Palms* (New York: Crescent Books, 1988), 71.

12. K. C. Sen, *Hast Samudrika Shastra, the Science of Hand-Reading Simplified*, 60.

13. V. A. K. Ayer, *Palmistry for Pleasure and Profit*, 113.

14. Maria Costavile, *How to Read Palms*, 71–75.

15. Yaschpaule, *Your Destiny and Scientific Hand Analysis* (Petaling Jaya, Selangor, Malaysia: Heinemann Educational Books, 1982), 59–60.

16. See note 7 above.

17. K. C. Sen, *Hast Samudrika Shastra, the Science of Hand-Reading Simplified*, 58.

18. Yaschpaule, *Your Destiny and Scientific Hand Analysis*, 60.

19. Sasha Fenton and Malcolm Wright, *The Living Hand*, 142.

20. See note 12 above.

21. See note 14 above.

22. Esther Newcomer-Bramblett, *Reading Hands for Pleasure or Profit* (Austin, Tex.: Woods Publications, 1982), 216.

23. Jo Logan, *The Prediction Book of Palmistry* (Poole, Dorset, England: Javelin Books, 1985), 93.

24. Cheiro (Count Louis Hamon), *The Language of the Hand* (New York: Prentice-Hall, 1987), 130.

25. Yaschpaule, *Your Destiny and Scientific Hand Analysis*, 62.

26. V. A. K. Ayer, *Palmistry for Pleasure and Profit*, 110–115, especially 113.

27. K. C. Sen, *Hast Samudrika Shastra, the Science of Hand-Reading Simplified*, 54.

28. See note 14 above.

29. K. C. Sen, *Hast Samudrika Shastra, the Science of Hand-Reading Simplified*, 59.

30. Yaschpaule, *Your Destiny and Scientific Hand Analysis*, 63, 407.

31. K. C. Sen, *Hast Samudrika Shastra, the Science of Hand-Reading Simplified*, 165.

32. V. A. K. Ayer, *Palmistry for Pleasure and Profit*, 113–114.

33. K. C. Sen, *Hast Samudrika Shastra, the Science of Hand-Reading Simplified*, 58.

34. Yaschpaule, *Your Destiny and Scientific Hand Analysis*, 58.

35. V. A. K. Ayer, *Palmistry for Pleasure and Profit*.

36. Litzka Raymond Gibson, *How to Read Palms*, rev. ed. (Hollywood, Fla.: Fell Publishers, 1989), 166–167.

37. Comte C. de Saint-Germain (Edgar de Valcourt-Vermont), *Practical Palmistry: Hand Reading Simplified* (Mokelumne Hill, Ca.: Health Research, 1970), 94.

38. See note 34 above.

39. See note 14 above.

40. See note 13 above.

41. Yaschpaule, *Your Destiny and Scientific Hand Analysis*, 59.

42. K. C. Sen, *Hast Samudrika Shastra, the Science of Hand-Reading Simplified*, 50.

43. Ibid., 61.
44. See note 14 above.
45. Ibid.
46. Ibid.
47. Ibid.
48. Ibid.
49. Ibid.
50. Rodney Davies, *Fortune-Telling by Palmistry: A Practical Guide to the Art of Hand Analysis* (Wellingborough, Northamptonshire: Aquarian Press, 1987), 136.
51. K. C. Sen, *Hast Samudrika Shastra, the Science of Hand-Reading Simplified*, 166.
52. Ibid., 57.
53. See note 13 above.
54. Yaschpaule, *Your Destiny and Scientific Hand Analysis*, 407.
55. Ibid., 62–63.
56. Ibid.
57. See note 33 above.
58. See note 14 above.
59. Ibid.
60. Rodney Davies, *Fortune-Telling by Palmistry: A Practical Guide to the Art of Hand Analysis*, 136–138.
61. See note 14 above.
62. Ibid.
63. V. A. K. Ayer, *Palmistry for Pleasure and Profit*, 113–115.
64. K. C. Sen, *Hast Samudrika Shastra, the Science of Hand-Reading Simplified*, 133.
65. Yaschpaule, *Your Destiny and Scientific Hand Analysis*, 63.
66. See note 33 above.
67. See note 14 above.
68. V. A. K. Ayer, *Palmistry for Pleasure and Profit*, 112.
69. Cheiro, *The Language of the Hand*, 131.
70. Litzka Raymond Gibson, *How to Read Palms*, 75.
71. Ibid., 77.
72. Ibid., 78.
73. Ibid., 80.
74. Ibid., 81.
75. Ibid.
76. Sasha Fenton and Malcolm Wright, *The Living Hand*, 131.
77. Rita Robinson, *The Palm: A Guide to Your Hidden Potential* (Van Nuys, Ca.: Newcastle Original, 1988), 115.
78. See note 14 above.
79. Rita Robinson, *The Palm: A Guide to Your Hidden Potential*, 119.
80. K. C. Sen, *Hast Samudrika Shastra, the Science of Hand-Reading Simplified*, 199–200.
81. Vera Compton, *Palmistry for Everyman* (Westport, Conn.: Associated Booksellers, 1956), 61, 88.
82. See note 14 above.
83. K. C. Sen, *Hast Samudrika Shastra, the Science of Hand-Reading Simplified*, 51.
84. V. A. K. Ayer, *Palmistry for Pleasure and Profit*, 112–113.
85. Sasha Fenton and Malcolm Wright, *The Living Hand*, 132.
86. Ibid., 133.
87. Carol Hellings White, *Holding Hands: The Complete Guide to Palmistry* (G. P. Putnam's Sons, 1980), 102.
88. Rodney Davies, *Fortune-Telling by Palmistry: A Practical Guide to the Art of Hand Analysis*, 70–71.
89. Ibid., 71.
90. Comte C. de Saint-Germain, *Practical Palmistry: Hand Reading Simplified*, 92.
91. Ibid., 96.
92. Ibid., 100.
93. Ibid., 103.
94. Ibid., 107.
95. Ibid., 111.
96. Ibid., 116.
97. Ibid., 120.
98. See note 14 above.
99. See note 90 above.
100. See note 91 above.
101. Comte C. de Saint-Germain, *Practical Palmistry: Hand Reading Simplified*, 101.
102. Ibid., 104.
103. Ibid., 108.

104. Ibid., 111.

105. Ibid., 117.

106. Ibid., 92, 96.

107. Ibid., 100.

108. Ibid., 104.

109. Ibid., 108.

110. Ibid., 111.

111. Ibid., 117.

112. Ibid., 121.

113. See note 7 above.

114. See note 90 above.

115. Comte C. de Saint-Germain, *Practical Palmistry: Hand Reading Simplified*, 97.

116. Ibid., 101.

117. Ibid., 104.

118. Ibid., 108.

119. Ibid., 111.

120. Ibid., 117.

121. Ibid., 121.

122. See note 14 above.

123. Ibid.

124. Yaschpaule, *Your Destiny and Scientific Hand Analysis*, 65; V. A. K. Ayer, *Palmistry for Pleasure and Profit*, 114.

125. See note 14 above.

126. See note 22 above.

127. See note 14 above.

128. See note 90 above.

129. See note 91 above.

130. Comte C. de Saint-Germain, *Practical Palmistry: Hand Reading Simplified*, 100.

131. Ibid., 103.

132. Ibid., 107.

133. Ibid., 111.

134. Ibid., 117.

135. Ibid., 120.

136. See note 12 above.

137. See note 14 above.

138. Rita Robinson, *The Palm: A Guide to Your Hidden Potential*, 118.

139. See note 24 above.

140. K. C. Sen, *Hast Samudrika Shastra, the Science of Hand-Reading Simplified*, 55.

141. Ibid., 40.

142. William G. Benham, *The Benham Book of Palmistry*. Preface by Rita Robinson (North Hollywood, Ca.: Newcastle Metaphysical Classic, 1988) (Reprint of *The Laws of Scientific Hand Reading*), 369.

143. Litzka Raymond Gibson, *How to Read Palms*, 168.

144. Rita Robinson, *The Palm: A Guide to Your Hidden Potential*, 117.

145. Cheiro, *The Language of the Hand*, 127–128.

146. See note 42 above.

147. See note 14 above.

148. Cheiro, *The Language of the Hand*, 134.

149. Jean-Michel Morgan, *Palmistry: The Art of Reading Hands*. Trans. by David Macrae (Barcelona: Ariane Books, 1975), 94–96.

150. See note 14 above.

151. See note 7 above.

152. See note 91 above.

153. See note 130 above.

154. Comte C. de Saint-Germain, *Practical Palmistry: Hand Reading Simplified*, 103.

155. Ibid., 107.

156. Ibid., 111.

157. Ibid., 117.

158. Ibid., 120.

159. K. C. Sen, *Hast Samudrika Shastra, the Science of Hand-Reading Simplified*, 61.

160. Ibid., 40.

161. Ibid., 60.

162. Peter West, *Life Lines: The Secrets of Your Character Revealed in Your Hands* (Wellingborough, Northamptonshire: Aquarian Press, 1987), 97.

163. See note 65 above.

164. See note 12 above.

165. See note 14 above.

166. Ibid.

167. Ibid.

168. Rodney Davies, *Fortune-Telling by Palmistry: A Practical Guide to the Art of Hand Analysis*, 124.

169. Yaschpaule, *Your Destiny and Scientific Hand Analysis*, 61.
170. See note 29 above.
171. Rodney Davies, *Fortune-Telling by Palmistry: A Practical Guide to the Art of Hand Analysis*, 134.
172. See note 76 above.
173. Bettina Luxon and Jill Goolden, *Your Hand: Simple Palmistry for Everyone* (New York: Crown, 1983), 72–73.
174. See note 14 above.
175. Rodney Davies, *Fortune-Telling by Palmistry: A Practical Guide to the Art of Hand Analysis*, 135–136.
176. See note 12 above.
177. See note 54 above.
178. K. C. Sen, *Hast Samudrika Shastra, the Science of Hand-Reading Simplified*, 55.
179. Ibid.
180. See note 7 above.
181. See note 14 above.
182. Comte C. de Saint-Germain, *Practical Palmistry: Hand Reading Simplified*, 92, 96.
183. Ibid., 101.
184. Ibid., 104.
185. Ibid., 108.
186. Ibid., 111.
187. Ibid., 117.
188. Ibid., 121.
189. See note 14 above.
190. Ibid.
191. See note 22 above.
192. Comte C. de Saint-Germain, *Practical Palmistry: Hand Reading Simplified*, 57.
193. V. A. K. Ayer, *Sariraka Sastra, Indian Science of Palmistry (the Kartikeyan System)*, 2nd ed. (Bombay: Taraporevala Sons, 1965), 22.
194. See note 192 above.
195. Yaschpaule, *Your Destiny and Scientific Hand Analysis*, 65.
196. Ibid., 407.
197. See note 7 above.
198. K. C. Sen, *Hast Samudrika Shastra, the Science of Hand-Reading Simplified*, 62.
199. See note 115 above.
200. Maria Costavile, *How to Read Palms*, 69.

EPILOGUE

1. Daniel B. Mowrey, Ph.D., *The Scientific Validation of Herbal Medicine* (Cormorant Books, 1986), 224.
2. Michael Talbot, *The Holographic Universe* (New York: HarperCollins, 1991), 117.
3. Horace Freeland Judson, *The Eighth Day of Creation: The Makers of the Revolution in Biology* (New York: Simon & Schuster, 1980), 301–303.
4. Michael Talbot, *The Holographic Universe*, 122–124.
5. John Shelby Spong, *Rescuing the Bible from Fundamentalism* (San Francisco: HarperCollins, 1991), 64–69.
6. M. T. Clanchy, *From Memory to Written Record: England, 1066–1307* (Harvard University Press, 1979), 245–247.
7. Ibid., 207.

APPENDIX: INSTRUCTIONS FOR PRINTMAKING

1. Jon M. Aase and Richard B. Lyons, "Techniques for Recording Dermatoglyphics," *Lancet*, Feb. 1972, 432.
2. Jamshed Mavalwala, ed., *Dermatoglyphics: An International Perspective* (The Hague: Moulton Publishers, 1978), 3–6.
3. Blanka Schaumann and Milton Alter, *Dermatoglyphics in Medical Disorders* (New York: Springer-Verlag, 1976), 13–26.

GLOSSARY

BASIC TERMS

Chirognomy or **cheirognomy**: The study of seeing the basic character, disposition, and potential of people from the size, shape, and outward appearance of the hand. Derived from the Greek words *kheir* or *cheir* meaning hand, and *gnomou* meaning one who knows.

Chirology or **cheirology**: The language of the hand.

Chiromancy or **cheiromancy**: The art of divining the past, present, and future from the signs and lines of the hand.

Chirosophy or **cheirosophy**: Knowledge of the hand. Derived from the Greek words *kheir* or *cheir* meaning hand, and *sophia* meaning wisdom.

Dermatoglyphics: The empirical study and classification of the skin ridges (dermatoglyphics) of the fingers (fingerprints), palms, and feet primarily used in America, Germany, and India for prediagnosis in the treatment of latent physical and mental illness. Also used in anthropological studies.

Herewith follows a general quick reference glossary to various terms used in this book. Some signs may not be included here but are listed alphabetically in chapter 12.

GENERAL TERMS

Active Mars: See *lower Mars, mount of.*

Allergies: See *via lascivia.*

Angle of dexterity: Also called the angle of rhythm. If well developed, the person can be a good craftsman and prefers tasks that have good physical rhythm. Angle formed by the medial joint of the thumb when fully extended along side of the palm.

Angle of generosity: The angle formed between the thumb and the index finger when the fingers are gently spread until resistance is felt. Angles of ninety degrees or more indicate a disposition to control loved ones through giving in and an inability to establish boundaries between self and loved lones typical of codependency. Also, when differences are detected

271

between the hands, it can be a sign of which side of the brain may be predominant in controlling day-to-day activities. In general, this angle indicates the generous spirit of the subject, or, if small, the lack of that generosity.

Angle of harmony: Formed by the proximal joint of the thumb (next to the wrist) when the thumb is fully extended along the side of the palm. The angle can indicate the subject's natural sense of harmony and balance. The greater the length between the angles of dexterity and harmony, the warmer the personality.

Apex: The highest point of the mount, particularly the mounts under the fingers (for those who follow Benham's approach to reading strengths of mounts). Location may be identified either by height of flesh or by the location of the triradius.

Apex of the mount: The triangle area on the mount formed by the skin ridges (derma patterns) on the mounts of Mercury, Apollo, Saturn, and Jupiter. It is considered the true center of the mount. If nearer the top, it elevates the qualities of that mount. If nearer another mount, it is influenced by that other mount and gives of its attributes to the stronger mount. If in the center, the mount is well placed and strengthened.

Apollo: Refers to both the ring finger and the mount below. Associated with creativity, brilliance, artistry, material success, prosperity, optimism, and luck. Also known as the finger or mount of the Sun.

Arc: This is an imaginary line joining the four points where the fingers intersect.

Art, finger of: The ring finger or Apollo finger.

Asterisms: In Vedic astrology, the Moon resides in each constellation for a day and the term refers to the mansions of the Moon. There are twenty-seven of them. See *Nakashatras*.

Astro-palmistry: The name given to a branch of palmistry that tries to combine astrology and palmistry. The masters of this art are supposed to be able to lay out the birth chart from the hand. I have not yet found any reliable source of teaching material on that skill.

Attachment lines: See *marriage line*.

Autumn: In traditional Chinese palmistry, this season is found in the area of Upper Mars and Luna, and the traditional color associated with it is white. As one's eye becomes trained, one will detect slight variations of color tones on the palm. These shadings will run from light colors, that indicate a white covering, to reds and darker colors such as greens and blacks. When observing the hand for favorable upcoming seasons, one looks for these hints of color variation.

Bars: These are found on lines and formed by influence or cross-purpose lines indicating hindrances to the flow of energy in the dominant line crossed.

Beau's lines: Transverse ridges or dents found on the nails. These may be associated with acute infection, traumas, nutritional deficiencies, or nervous shock. Can date the onset by considering the nail grows out in about five to six months.

Branches: Lines that have their origins in other important lines. If they rise, they are good omens. If they fall, they may be bad omens. However, some believe angled falling lines from the life line may indicate alternate paths or travel potentials. Numerous falling lines from the heart line may indicate a flirtatious nature. See also *influence lines*.

Capillary lines: Fine lines that appear and disappear on the palm. These may give advance warning of the approach of an event.

Chains: Indicate lack of stamina, lack of assertiveness, and lack of confidence, and could indicate weak health, lifelessness, and ineffective character. Often seen at the beginning of both the life and heart line, indicating a traumatic, emotional childhood or other childhood illness or disability.

Chance lines: Vertical lines found on the percussion side of the mount of Mercury.

Children lines: Vertical lines found on the percussion side of the mount of Mercury. There are similar lines on the percussion side of lower Luna that may also serve as both health and travel lines and vertical lines at the base of Venus as well as horizontal lines on the middle phalange of the little finger. Check all sources for more accurate reading.

Circles: These are fairly rare when formed by lines. Can be favorable or unfavorable depending on where found.

Color: Should be judged of a calm person in a seventy-degree room. These may vary according to race and complexion tone. Colors range from white to pink, red, ash, yellow, brown, blue, and purple.

Companion lines: These fine lines will parallel a relationship line, indicating that the subject is not completely fulfilled by the relationship and needs a career, outside interest, or lover.

Conch: The name refers to a sign in the hand shaped something like a conch shell and is one of the Eastern signs of success and/or great wealth.

Conic: Refers to cone shape of hand or fingers indicating artistic appreciation or qualities. See *rounded, elegant hand.*

Consistency: Refers to the hardness or softness of the hand under pressure, the resistance, elasticity, and resiliency of the hand.

Core: The center of the ridge pattern area is termed the core. In loops, it is the point at the terminus of the most central ridge. In whorls and composites, the core can be the termination of the spiral ridge line or the center of the innermost concentric circle.

Cross: Here a line crosses another line or two lines cross on a mount and the meaning can vary according to where the cross is.

Curve of Creativity: See *percussion.*

Curve of strength: See *percussion,* especially around upper Mars.

Cyanosis: Bluish discoloration found on hands or nails indicative of local circulatory disturbances or more serious congenital heart diseases or congestive heart failure.

Decision line: Fine lines cutting the fate or Apollo lines including a line that cuts the fate line while connecting the heart and head line.

Deletion line: A line that will appear at the end of a relationship line when it is breaking up or indicating it will break up rather suddenly. It may vanish after a divorce.

Diamonds: Besides being a girl's best friend, they exist when lines split into diamond shapes, and can indicate nasty problems or show intense frustration and feelings of confinement.

Distal: Refers to the more distant part of the body, for example, the finger side of the palm and the nail end of the finger.

Dorsal: A directional term that refers to the back. On the hand, it refers to the back of the hand as opposed to the palm.

Dots: These show illness or stress. They are like craters or vortices that suck the energy out of the mount or line where they appear.

Doubled lines: Such lines can show split energies. They can also show a doubling of energy. Could also indicate a double type of response, such as hot and cold emotions in a doubled heart line.

Effort lines: Upward (distal) moving lines, frequently from the life line.

Elementary hands: These have few lines, are squarish, supposedly reflect dullness, perhaps even regressive tendencies.

Father influence area: The area above the life line on the radial side of the hand.

Family aggravation lines: Lines that radiate out from the mount of Venus, especially the Vulcan area, indicative of family type of worries or concerns, or new thought forms.

Fish: Special signs on the hand in the shape of fish, generally considered favorable.

Flags: Triangles formed by two angled influence lines on a main line that may be considered favorable to success, wealth, or in spiritual matters.

Flexibility: Flexible hands mean flexible minds and flexible attentions. There are drawbacks from either too stiff or too flexible hands. Notice whether the person is more apt to break under pressure (too stiff), or blow with the wind (right-angle flexibility of the fingers). Can indicate how adaptable the subject is to external pressure.

Flexion crease lines: Medical terminology for the life (longitudinal flexion crease), head (proximal transverse crease), heart (distal transverse crease), and fate lines.

Flowers: These are lotus or octagon-shaped marks on the hand indicating certain favorable potentials for the subject.

Girdle of Venus: Semicircular pattern of a line or lines that runs from between Jupiter and Saturn to between Apollo and Mercury above the heart line. Signifies empathetic personality with open heart and needs for emotional, financial, and career security and respect. When unbroken, may be a sign of selfishness. Under older palmistry, was often called the line of prostitution, signifying connubial love with many people. That significance may still exist if line is multi-plied, and there is a large mount of Venus and/or other signs from the heart line indicating strong physical desires. If present under Saturn finger with a space on the line between Saturn and Apollo mounts, and if line is crossed with fate line, person could walk out on relationship in favor of career. Opposite may be true if present under Apollo and crossed by Sun line. The presence here also indicates a need to be around like-minded people. Presence in area between Apollo and Saturn can indicate overreactions or oversensitiveness and hence, when line is fully formed, a tendency toward selfishness.

Grilles: These point toward obsessive behavior associated with the mount on which they appear. The vertical lines are excessive wants; the horizontal lines indicate cross purposes and confusion.

Hair: When present, especially on fingers, can indicate strength.

Hargate line: Named after American novelist J. B. Hargate. This line is also known as an obstruction line. This is a long, clear line from the base of the thumb to the fate line. Indicates changes in private life at corresponding age.

Head line: Usually begins either with the life line or between the life line beginning and the base of the mount of Jupiter on the radial side of the palm above the thumb. Sometimes may be crossed by the life line. Does not indicate IQ but rather thought and decision making processes. It can show strength of mental powers, concentration, rational or intuitive logic, depression, decisiveness or indecision, rashness or long deliberation, and potential shoulder, upper thoracic, and cervical spine pains and tightness.

Healing lines: Also called medical striata. There can be two or more lines located above or in place of help lines. Important for professional qualities that they be parallel. Five are indicative of the doctor personality, lesser numbers may be indicative of other health professional tendencies.

Health line: Also called a line of Mercury, the line of hepatica, the communication line, or the liver line. Described as a line that may begin from the wrist area around the mount of Neptune (space between Luna and Venus) and runs upward toward the little finger. No bad health significance found in its absence.

Health lines: Distinguished from the health line. These are lines that appear on the percussion, horizontal to the wrist, and may be found between the wrist and the mount of Mercury, where the heart line is normally found. The top of this space represents the crown chakra (at the top of the head) and the base the root chakra (anus, external genitalia, hip area). The space in between represents the body in between. These lines can duplicate as travel lines, the lower ones as children lines, and the upper ones as enmity lines.

Heart line: Usually appears to run from the ulna side of the palm near or on the percussion between the mounts of Mercury and upper Mars and extends toward the radial side, with the radial extension starting from one or more of a variety of beginnings from below the life line on lower Mars, to various positions on the mount of Jupiter, to between Jupiter and Saturn or even under Saturn. Some are even shorter. Some believe it begins from the percussion and others believe it begins on the other side of the hand. It will be found above the head line.

Helping lines: Feathery or flowery lines just above the heart line and below the space between Mercury and Apollo.

Hippocratic nails: Sometimes called watch glass nails. They are frequently found in connection with such ailments as tuberculosis, lung tumors, chronic heart disease, and cirrhosis of the liver. The nails are lustrous and convex, curved in the shape of a watch crystal.

Inclining fingers: Indicates that the leaning finger energy has become associated with the finger toward which it leans. It may dominate (as in the case of Saturn) or be inhibited by the finger toward which it leans.

Influence lines: Can refer to any minor unnamed line that reaches toward another line or mount. Often used to refer in this book to rays from father or mother areas of influence and in other writings to those rays from the thumb across the mount of venus toward the life line.

Interdigital areas: These are the areas of the palm between the fingers. In medicine they are numbered from I to IV, starting with the space between the thumb and index finger.

Intuition line: A line that appears to form a semicircle between lower Luna (Pluto) and the mount of Mercury or upper Mars on the ulna side of the hand. It can be intermixed with the health line. If it curves toward the center of the palm in the middle and if it is unbroken, it is considered a very good sign of accurate intuition. Curvature in the opposite direction indicates the opposite effect.

Island: An encased area on one of the main lines. Not to be confused with a split.

Jupiter: Refers both to the index finger and the mount below it. Associated with ego, ambition, pride, leadership, honor, love of nature, the head, and the eyes.

Knot: An enlarged knuckle. Indicates a type of blockage or constriction in the flow of energy indicating the subject has a tendency to hold on either to ideas (the distal knuckles) or things (the medial knuckles). The distal knuckle enlarged indicates the philosopher or the one who will dispute for the sake of disputing to show his or her grasp of any subject. The medial enlargement is more the collector or pack rat.

Lateral: Refers to that portion of the body that is farther from the middle. Anatomically, the hand is held with the palm facing the front for directional purposes. Thus the little finger is always on the medial side of the hand, while the thumb is on the lateral side of the hand.

Life line: Also known as the vitality line. Usually encircles the third phalange of the thumb and marks the outer boundary of the mount of Venus. Is indicative of the strength of constitution and can indicate areas of major change.

Line of Mars: A parallel line to the life line located inside of the life line on the mount of Venus. There can be more than one and they can signify close, protective friendship or health protection of something in the nature of a guardian angel.

Lines: The major lines are the life (vitality), head (mental), heart (emotional), and fate (Saturn or personality) lines. Sometimes the heart and head lines are totally combined and that is called a simian line. Sometimes the fate line is totally absent. An Apollo, Mercury, or even Jupiter line can substitute for the absent fate line, generally in that order. The minor lines include Apollo, celibacy, children, companion, enmity, girdle of Venus, health lines, hepatica, influence, intuition, Jupiter, liver, Mars, Mercury, obstruction, sibling, Sun, travel, worry, and various rings including Mercury (celibacy), Apollo, Saturn, Solomon (Jupiter), and family.

Liver line: See *health line*.

Longitudinal nail ridges: Can indicate chronic health problems that could be hereditary.

Loop: Loops are patterns formed by dermatoglyphics. The ridge lines form a loop that is rounded on one end and generally open at the other end, at least on the fingers. They are commonly seen on the fingers and will also be seen on various places in the palm. Commonly found loops are of humor, imagination, memory, seriousness or serious intent, style or vanity, rajah, royalty, power or charisma, courage, musical genius, nature, rhythm responsiveness, and environmentalism.

Loop of charisma: This is located between the Jupiter and Saturn mounts. It is also known as the loop of rajah, power, royalty, or introspection. Traditionally, it is a sign of royal descent. Often related to a subject of dynamic personal attraction, hence the charisma. Could be, especially with other favorable signs, a dynamic leader. Bevy Jaegers finds it rather rare, but I have seen it on occasion although it is more rare than humor, Saturn, or vanity loops. I have seen it more often than courage loops or musical loops. Jaegers contends that medical digests report the loop signifies a hereditary factor that may have to do with hormonal balances relating to chromosomal abnormalities and has been found in a great number of patients with mental and emotional problems. She also finds it to be on persons who are extremely introspective. See also *loop of presence*.

Loop of common sense: This is located between the Saturn and Apollo mounts. I have related this to a loop of seriousness and have found that many who have it have tended to cry as children or even as adults, taking matters seriously. Jaegers finds the loop related to good common sense and that the person who has it may have good management in all areas of life. She says these people generally know what is best for themselves and give good advice but may take on burdens beyond their capacity.

Loop of courage: This is located on the lower

mount of Mars. This loop indicates a strong aggressive ability, emphasizing the powers displayed by lower Mars. Jaegers calls it the loop of courage and determination. It could make up for a week thumb. She notes that the courage implied by this loop includes stamina, fortitude, and steady reliability.

Loop of ego: This originates between the bases of the Apollo and Mercury fingers and lies on the Apollo mount. It is also known as the loop of vanity or style. Style is the kindest observation and quite a large number of those I have observed were noticeable for their striking or very tasteful dress. Jaegers finds such people quite introspective, impervious to opinions of others, totally egocentric, and displaying little humor over jokes aimed at self or others. She also notes that if found on the left hand with a normal loop of humor on the right, it can indicate extraordinary feeling for the moods and emotions of others.

Loop of humanism: There is a loop referred to by Hutchinson that occurs in the central portion of the lower hand, around the mount of Neptune or between the mounts of Venus and Luna that she calls the loop of humanism. She says it is a rare loop. She was unable to describe its qualities but relates it to some humanitarian qualities. When it falls into the area of a raised place between Venus and Luna, it falls on the mount of Neptune and may be related to the sixth sense, telepathic powers, and clairvoyance. It may also be called the parathenar loop and closely resembles Jaegers's loop of inspiration.

Loop of humor: This is located directly below the space between the Mercury and Apollo fingers and between those mounts. It indicates a good sense of humor and one who enjoys laughter. When coupled with a loop of seriousness (common sense), the person may have a sharp

tongue and be given to biting sarcasm. Fenton and Wright report that if a whorl is found in the loop, there is a talent for foreign languages. They also report the subject will have a love for animals, but if the loop is crisscrossed with lines, he or she may have little time for them.

Loop of imagination: See *loop of nature* and *loop of memory*. A whorl in the same area is an even stronger sign of imagination and a sure sign of lunar influences.

Loop of inspiration: This loop begins from about the beginning of the dermatoglyphic patterns at the wrist on the medial surface of Luna or Pluto or even Neptune as described by some authors. It tends to be looped toward the center of the palm. Here may be a subject who has vision, and/or has been granted special revelation and may be able to inspire others through his or her voice and speech.

Loop of introspection: See *loop of charisma*.

Loop of memory: This may be at the end or slightly below the end of the head line. If the head line is straight, the memory is very good for facts and figures as befits a practical person. At the end of a sloping head line, the memory may be better for sounds and images, emotions, and physical feelings. This person may be able to better feel the sounds and tones of music, for example, or recall physical movement or a beautiful sunset. The lower it is, the more enhanced is the imagination. Like all lunar loops, there is a practical affinity for the Moon and a tendency to follow lunar rhythms in life.

Loop of music: See *loop of rhythm*.

Loop of musical genius: This curious sign is also know as the bee. As such, it may not even be a loop but almost an independent set of dermatoglyphics found on the upper part of the heavy pad of Venus sometimes also called

Vulcan or the mount of the Sun. Here we find the potential performer or composer.

Loop of nature: This can also be known as the ulnar loop or the environmental loop and may be associated with a green thumb and is certainly associated with a strong affinity to water and the Moon, as are all lunar mount loops. It is found with the loop toward the center of the palm, while the lines travel to the percussion on the mount of the Moon. Jaegers has found some relationship to mongolism, being a significant factor to check for in children, but like the simian line, it is not a sure sign of Down's syndrome. She indicates that it may evidence a latent genetic influence that could include possible Down's syndrome. The natural environment is very important to these subjects who love water, clean air, plants and animals, and the great outdoors. Jaegers finds that when coupled with the medical stigmata (healing striations) the subject may be a natural vegetarian and have a strong love for both medicine and animals (a natural veterinarian?). The subject needs peace, so will avoid closed surroundings with animosities present and Jaegers finds this aspect stronger, the closer the loop comes to the mount of upper Mars. It could be a sign of claustrophobia and would undoubtedly be so if there is a ring of Saturn.

Loop of power: See *loop of charisma*.

Loop of presence: See also *loop of charisma*. This transverses the proximal (lower) phalange of the index (Jupiter) finger. Bevy Jaegers gives this loop the title the loop of charisma. It is a sign of leadership. She finds such people capable of selfless service and dedication who leave "an indelible impression" on whoever they meet.

Loop of rajah: See *loop of charisma*.

Loop of response: This is located on the lower lateral edge of the thenar (Venus) mount, just below the medial joint of the thumb. The subject may have a heightened, almost automatic response to rhythm and music and also be deeply moved by his or her environment. It is also an empathetic indicator. Jaegers calls it also the loop of response to environment.

Loop of rhythm: This is found originating at or near the wrist edge of the dermatoglyphic patterns opposite the area where the loop of inspiration would be located and on the proximal (lower) part of the mount of Venus. Jaegers finds it a rare formation found on people who automatically respond to rhythm of any kind. One of several good signs for competitive sports as well as for dancers and other musical performers.

Loop of royalty: See *loop of charisma*.

Loop of seriousness: See *loop of common sense*.

Loop of style: See *loop of ego*.

Loop of ultrafemininity or masculinity: This loop transverses the lower (proximal) phalange of the little finger with the loop end generally pointed medially (toward the outer edge of the hand). Seems to enhance the sexuality of the subject, i.e., macho man and ultrafeminine woman.

Loop of vanity: See *loop of ego*.

Love line: See *heart line*.

Lower Mars, mount of: Part of the three mounts of Mars that transverse the central area of the palm from the medial to lateral side. This part is on the lateral (radial) side of the palm above the thumb and below the mount of Jupiter. It is indicative of courage, aggressiveness, action, and fight or flight tendencies, dependent upon development.

Luna: It is found below upper Mars on the lower ulna, unconscious, medial side of the palm. The mount is also known as the mount of the Moon and the lower portion, next to the wrist, is sometimes called Pluto. It is associated with the unconscious mind, the psyche, with mysticism, intuition, imagination, fancy, and the love of the sea, rivers, water, and travel.

Managing marks: Squares found on the mount of Jupiter are often referred to as marks of a good teacher or manager. See also *teaching marks*.

Marriage line: Also known as the line of union or line of relationship. Horizontal lines found at the percussion in the mount of Mercury.

Medial: That portion of the body that is closer to the middle. Anatomically, the hand is held with the palm facing the front for directional purposes. Thus the little finger is always on the medial side of the hand, while the thumb is on the lateral side of the hand.

Medical striata: See *healing lines*.

Mee's lines: These are formed on the nails and are similar to Beau's lines. They are longitudinal (transverse) white lines not causing ridges or dents. They may indicate high fevers, arsenic poisoning, and coronary heart disease.

Meissner corpuscle: A rapidly adapting tactile organ nerve ending but not quite as rapidly adapting as the Pacinian corpuscle. Also has a higher threshold for activation than the Pacinian corpuscle. One of four neurosensory tactile skin endings that also include slowly adapting response Merkel's cells and Ruffini endings. Meissner corpuscles have very small receptive fields, in contrast to Pacinian corpuscles, which have fields that can cover an entire finger or a large part of the palm.

Mercury: Refers to the little finger and the mount below it. It is associated with business acumen, quickness, communication, sexuality, filial love, independence or dependency, nervous energy, shrewdness, industry, scientific interests and mathematics, and quickness. The shape of the little finger is also related to honesty (or lack thereof) and sometimes self-sacrifice.

Mercury ring: This is a curved line originating on the palm at the intersection of the Apollo finger and the Mercury finger that crosses the mount of Mercury, but rarely reaches the percussion. Indicates a need for personal freedom and sexual change.

Mesoderm: The middle of the three cell layers of the developing embryo that lies between the ectoderm and the endoderm. Bone, connective tissue, muscle, blood, vascular and lymphatic tissue, and the pleura of the pericardium and peritoneum all develop from this tissue.

Metacarpal: A bone in the finger. There is the distal, proximal, and middle metacarpal bone in each finger.

Military stigmata: Certain lines at the base of the thumb on lower Mars.

Mixed hand: Shows qualities of a variety of types of hands and is considered by some to be an indicator of versatility.

MMPI: Minnesota Multiphasic Personality Inventory, probably the best-known and most widely used personality inventory test in the field of psychology, at least in North America.

Monkeylike hands: Fenton and Wright describe this hand as having slim, grasping fingers. It is pictured as a small air hand with thin fingers and a prominent thumb. The subjects are quick, clever, and talented but slippery and untrustworthy.

Moons: The whitish half circles that form at the base of the fingernails. There is no significance if missing on small nails, but there may be an indication of a lack of energy, perhaps from deficiencies in the endocrine system, if absent in larger nails. Misshapen or ragged moons also could indicate health problems.

Mother influence area: This is the area below the upper start of the life line on the radial side of the palm above the thumb.

Mounts: These are areas of the palm. Nine are traditionally referred to. Starting under the index finger and reading clockwise on one's own right hand they are: (1) Jupiter under the index finger; (2) Saturn under the middle finger; (3) Apollo (sometimes called the Sun or Uranus) under the ring finger; (4) Mercury under the little finger; (5) upper Mars under Mercury; (6) Luna or the mount of the Moon under upper Mars; (7) Pluto under Luna; (8) Venus under the thumb; and (9) The plain of Mars in the middle. Pluto is a newer mount. Even newer than Pluto is Neptune, a floating mount that can be found along the inside edge of Luna above Pluto when Pluto is found more at the base of the palm between Luna and Venus. Uranus is also identified as above a floating Neptune and these two mounts may not always exist. Vulcan has also been identified as that portion of Venus at the base of the thumb just below lower Mars and it has also been called the mount of the Sun.

Mouse: When the hand is partially closed and the thumb lies along its side, this protuberance forms between the thumb and the back of the hand. When well formed and prominent, it indicates a naturally good current state of health, good resistance, and powers of recovery.

Mystic cross: A well-formed cross usually in the quadrangle below the mount of Saturn, supposedly signifying occult powers, though many palmists may be skeptical.

Nakashatras: Used interchangeably with the term *asterisms*, a division of the astrological chart into twenty-seven mansions of the Moon. Moon mansions are used in Vedic, Chinese, and Arabic astrology. It is believed that the signs are composites of the influences of the nakshatras that fall within the sign. Each sign has two and a quarter asterisms or nakshatras. I believe that many of the signs related to Vedic astrology are used in Indian palmistry and I have turned to Vedic astrology for more detailed explanations of the meaning of some of the signs discussed.

Neptune: This mount is described as being above the wrist and between the mounts of Luna or Pluto and Venus by most literature that describes it. It is also described as a floating mount that can be found along the inside edge of Luna above Pluto when Pluto is found more at the base of the palm between Luna and Venus. It is associated with harmony and communication, including communication between the conscious and unconscious mind, and is also associated with bridging the yin and yang energies with personal magnetism and healing abilities.

Obstruction line: See *Hargate line*.

Pacinian corpuscles: Sensory receptors associated with end organs, such as hands, situated deep in the skin (dermis) as well as in connective tissue, muscles, the periosteum of bones, and the mesentery of the abdomen. It is constructed to signal rapid changes in touch-pressure and that construction may account for why our sense of steady pressure on the skin fades away. Appears to be important to our tactile perception of objects and textures.

Pallor: This refers to an unnatural paleness or absence of color in the hand. Can be an important sign of anxiety or anemia or even internal bleeding. Check to see if major lines are also pale and if so, a medical checkup could be in order. It might also indicate an unrealistic person or one who is selfish or unemotional.

Palmar: The palm side of the hand, as opposed to the dorsal side; the back of the hand.

Papillary ridges: These are the skin ridges that form the dermatoglyphic maps of the palms and fingers.

Passive Mars: See *upper Mars*.

Percussion: The ulna or medial edge of the palm.

Phalange: Refers to one section of the finger from joint to joint. The distal phalange is the most distant from the hand, i.e., the nail or tip section. The proximal phalange is the nearest, while the medial phalange is in the middle. The distal phalange is associated with the spirit, with emotional and spiritual matters, and matters of higher consciousness. The medial phalange is associated with mundane yet often essential mental matters, business, and social relations. The proximal phalange is associated with the physical appetites. On the thumb, the distal phalange is associated with the carrying out of will. The medial phalange of the thumb is concerned with the ability and constrictions on the planning to carry out will, sometimes referred to as the logic or reasoning of will. The proximal phalange of the thumb, the mount of Venus, is concerned with desire, the primal energy and urges that initiate the exercise of will. Phalanges are counted downward, from distal to proximal, with distal being number 1.

Phalanx: See *phalange.*

Philosophic hand: Shows traits of analysis and tendencies for disputation and debate. Noted for knots around the joints in the fingers, especially the distal joints.

Plain of Mars: This is the area in the center of the palm between upper and lower Mars. It is associated with immediately available energy and reserves of energy, physical stamina, endurance, enthusiasm, and ability to relax. Gives much information through palpation (touch) by the reader.

Pluto: See also *Luna.* This is located generally on the lower, ulna, medial, unconscious side of the palm between the mount of Luna and the wrist. Gile seems to locate it more between Luna and Venus, just above the wrist. Associated with rest-lessness, the need to travel, the ability to translate theoretical ideas into practice, and perhaps siblings.

Proximal: Refers to that portion of the body closer to the center. Thus the wrist is more proximal than the fingernail.

Psychic hand: Shows qualities and traits of clairvoyance, etc.

Quadrangle: The area between the heart and head lines roughly bounded on the ulna side by the health or intuition line and the areas where these would be found. Characteristics of intellect, intimate communication abilities, and disposition may be found here, according to some palmists.

Radial: This is the name of a nerve that reaches the thumb and first three fingers. Directionally, it refers to the thumb side, the lateral side of the hand. The radius is the name of the bone in the forearm on that same side.

Radial loop: In medicine, this is a loop that starts from the radial (thumb) side of the hand with the rounded portion facing in a general distal and/or medial direction (toward the nails or more toward the little finger).

Rajah loop: See *loop of charisma.*

Rascette: One of one or more creases at and below the wrist that traditionally indicates health of the subject.

Rays: These are vertical lines that are believed to enhance traits.

Relationships, line of: See *marriage line.*

Ridge counts. This is a count of the number of ridges that cross a straight line drawn between the triradius and the core of the pattern. When done on lateral pocket loops, it is done using the cores closer to the triradius, whereas on double loops the upper core is consistently counted toward the left triradius and the lower core is associated with the right triradius.

Ridge lines (or ridges): These refer to the dermatoglyphic raised portions of the patterns found on the palmar surfaces of the hands and fingers and the soles of the feet.

Ring of Saturn: Faint, often poorly marked V or semicircle of lines on Saturn mount at base of middle finger. May indicate a feeling of being trapped, and the semicircular formation may also, according to some, emphasize occult powers. Robin Gile notes that if the little finger is also twisted, beware of real jail time.

Roman arc: A rounded arch or arc. Indicates harmonious psychophysical balance and tendency to bring harmony to those about the subject. May accept innovation but rarely initiates it.

Rounded, elegant hand: See also *conic*. Indicative of creative, sensible people who are warmhearted and enjoy good humor, family, and peaceful surroundings.

Rubor: Indicates extreme redness, usually associated with increase in temperature of the hand resulting from blood vessel dilation. May have emotional or medical significance or draw attention to heightened activity in a region of the subject's life indicated by the area where the rubor is observed.

Saturn: This is the name of the middle finger between the index (Jupiter) and ring (Apollo) fingers and the mount below it between the mounts of Apollo and Jupiter. It forms the dividing line between the introspective and extroverted and the conscious and unconscious mind where the balance between the two may be established. Saturn is associated with wisdom, accumulated knowledge, sobriety, balance, stability, love of tradition, melancholia, gloom, introversion, materialism, and caution. It may also be related by some to spiritual leanings and the ability to finish things started.

Shadow lines: These are thin lines that may come in pairs or threes and follow the life line. They may indicate friendships, spirit guides, or guardian angels.

Shadows: From time to time these appear, especially in the Pluto area, and may indicate a draining of energy or problems of siblings (or both). Only a practiced eye will even begin to pick these up.

Short, plump, energetic hands: A small, plump hand that is not soft. These people are described by Fenton and Wright as proud, energetic, and somewhat impatient subjects, but otherwise kindly. The lines tend to curve, the nails appear spatulate shaped, and the mounts rather full. The nails may be bluish mauve in color.

Short, wide hands: The fingers of these hands are described by Fenton and Wright as being distally tapered and the thumb will hyperextend and appear to curve outwards. I like this type, finding in them good friends who are realistic, practical, and possessing a terrific sense of humor. They are dexterous, generous, and supportive.

Sibling lines: According to suggestions of Fenton and Wright, these may be found around the outer edge of the mount of Jupiter. Robin Gile looks for sibling markings in the area commonly called the mount of Neptune, just above the wrists and between lower Luna (Pluto) and lower Venus, the same area considered as representing winter in traditional Chinese palmistry.

Signs or marks: Secondary and miscellaneous lines on the mounts or major lines. They often come and go.

Simian line: Where the heart and head line seem to be formed into one solid line. Some palmists, including the author, would argue that the true simian line should be without branches. Others would agree with medicine and say the simian line may have branches.

Soft hands: If the reader leaves an imprint that is slow to rebound on the palmar side of the hand while gently palpating the mounts, then the hand feels soft and a soft hand can be indicative or age, illness, or in young women, pregnancy.

Soft, squashy hand: Fenton and Wright observe that such people obviously do no manual work but try to lead the easy life, free of much physical effort. They seem to be clever in business, may be quite innocent in facial appearance, masking a very active and manipulative mind.

Solomon's rings: Semicircular line formation (or sometimes straight lines in similar formation) found on the mount of Jupiter. It is sometimes called a *caring line*. Can indicate healer tendencies and if connected to the heart line, a need for a caring career. Also an indication of interest in the metaphysical, and referred to as a marriage ring to the metaphysical.

Spatulated hand: Shows qualities or traits of activity and originality. A type where the fingers come to a point is reminiscent of constipation of energy, while the V-shaped hand that spreads at the fingers and is narrow at the wrist is reminiscent of diarrhea of energy.

Spinster line: It is also known as the *widowhood line*. This runs from the percussion to the open space between the fingers of Mercury and Apollo.

Spoon nails: These nails are concave on the outer surface and may be found in nutritional deficiencies, skin disorders, hypothyroidism, and some other physical and mental health problems.

Spots: Can have health or emotional indications if found on nails or on lines.

Spring: In traditional Chinese palmistry, this is located on the mount of Venus. Its preferred color is green. As one's eye becomes trained, one will detect slight variations of color tones on the palm. These shadings will run from light colors, that indicate a white covering, to reds and darker colors such as greens and blacks. When observing the hand for favorable upcoming seasons, one looks for these hints of color variation.

Square: This formation is considered a protection around breaks on major lines. While it may protect, it may also restrict or constrict free passage. See also *teaching marks*.

Square hand: Shows qualities and traits of dependability, regularity, love of tradition, and need for a regular routine in daily life.

Square, slim hands: Fenton and Wright create another variation on either the earth or air hand (without a picture it is not possible to decide which). The only description of this practical, decisive, honest, good-natured, and energetic person who is straightforward in approach is that he or she has slightly tapering fingers.

Star: Traditionally, it is a bad sign. It acts like a rock breaking a glass pane, or an explosion. If small, it may be like a light going on. The larger it is, the more devastating is its potential. It intensifies the area where it appears and could indicate a shock or an accident. For example, on the Jupiter mount, it may indicate loss of sight or head or eye problems. But on Apollo it could indicate sudden success, as it might also on the other three mounts under the fingers. But this can be a mixed success, like fleeting fame, only to leave a bitter taste in the mouth.

Straight line arc: Uncommon in advanced societies. Very self-confident and unlikely to admit mistakes or tolerate opposition.

Stray lines: Tiny lines indicating frayed energies and distractions.

String of pearls: A condition where the skin ridges become broken up and appear to be badly formed. Fenton and Wright indicate this is due to emotionally based disturbances, but Beryl B. Hutchinson might look to other potential causes. Altman notes they may indicate some form of neurosis.

Summer: In traditional Chinese palmistry, this is found in the area of the mounts of Saturn and Apollo. Its preferred color is red. As one's eye becomes trained, one will detect slight variations of color tones on the palm. These shadings will run from light colors, that indicate a white covering, to reds and darker colors such as greens and blacks. When observing the hand for favorable upcoming seasons, one looks for these hints of color variation.

Summit: Refers to the prominence found on the curve of creativity or curve of strength. If found on lower Luna, the person's strength is predominantly physical. On higher Luna, the swelling indicates a good balance between physical and moral strength, indicating gifts of endurance and authority. If found on upper Mars, it indicates remarkable strength of character but a lack of physical stamina, restricting endurance under pressure. If the swelling is above upper Mars, the subject's energy may be all in the head: all talk and no walk.

Sun: This term refers to the Apollo finger, mount, and line, and the area also known as Vulcan.

Sydney line: This refers, in medicine, to an elongated proximal (medial?) transverse crease that reaches from the thenar, first interdigital area edge to the edge of the hypothenar area. As pictured in an article by Seltzer and others, "Dermatoglyphics in the Identification of Women Either With or at Risk of Breast Cancer," *Am. J. Med. Gen.* 37:482, p. 483 (1990), it is a head line that reaches over to the edge of the percussion. It may become one of several significant hand signs in diagnosis of some forms of

senile dementia of the Alzheimer's disease type and in Down's syndrome.

Tassels: These are frayed ends of major lines, indicating the energy reflected by these lines dissipates about the time of the tassels. On the head line it may indicate a lack of calcium fluoride, potassium, and/or just plain worries.

Teaching marks: Squares found on the mount of Jupiter are often referred to as marks of a good teacher or manager. See also *managing marks.* This also refers to a line leading to the inside of the Mercury finger.

Temples: A special sign formed by several lines indicating eminence and/or wealth.

Texture: Refers to skin texture, such as soft, delicate, rough, scaly, coarse, damp, etc.

Thumb: The seat of willpower, logic, and desire.

Travel lines: Transverse lines across the percussion are generally considered travel lines. These show the desire to travel, and if one places the globe between the wrist and the area opposite the start of the head line and parallel to the heart line, the travel lines can indicate in what latitudes the subject desires to go. Actual travel may be indicated from downward angled lines emanating from the heart line.

Tree: This refers to two or more rising branches from a vertical palmar line. Could be harbingers of success as rising lines are generally considered favorably.

Triadius: Misspelling of *triradius* found in some palm books.

Triangle, large: This is a configuration composed of the head, life, and mercury lines; or in the absence of Mercury line, Apollo line; or in the absence of both, the fate line. Some believe it reveals information on temperament, intellect, and application of knowledge.

Triangles: Where these fall on mounts, they indicate exceptional talent or brilliance. If found between the head and heart lines, it is supposed to have the same significance as a mystic cross. On lines, they could indicate nasty problems, such as periods of intense frustration and feelings of confinement.

Trident on Apollo: Subject will always find the money he needs, but often at the last moment. This is formed by three lines in the shape of a fork at the top (distal) end of the Apollo line.

Tridents: A mark of good fortune when found on the end of the head, heart, and life lines.

Triradius: This designates a point where three ridge systems meet. This dermatoglyphic characteristic describes a point where three ridge systems fuse. Where three ridge systems adjoin but do not fuse, it describes the triangular area between them, in which case the point is in the center of the triangular area.

Ulnar: Refers to a nerve that feeds the little finger and part of the ring finger as well as the medial side of the hand. Thus, the ulnar side is the medial side or the side with the percussion, the little finger side of the hand. The ulna is the name of the bone in the forearm on that same side.

Ulnar loop: See also *loop of nature*. In medicine, this is a loop with ridge lines that start from the direction of the ulnar (little finger) side of the hand, and the curvature faces in a general distal and/or medial direction (toward the nails or more toward the thumb side of the hand).

Uneven arc: This arc forms an irregular line. The subject may not be very objective or self-confident, but he or she will stand against the tide.

Union, lines of: See *marriage line*.

Upper Mars: This is found on the ulna (medial) side of the hand below the mount of Mercury (just below the heart line) and above the mount of the Moon. It is associated with the qualities of defense, stubbornness, fortitude, passive resistance, resistance to pain and discomfort, courage, and moral fiber.

Uranus: A name sometimes given to the mount of Apollo. Also the name of a mount that sometimes appears in the middle portion of the palm, indicating something of an advanced metaphysical person with perhaps some special psychic insight. Also the name sometimes given to the line of intuition when it is a full, unbroken crescent.

Vanity loop: See *loop of vanity*.

Venus: The mount at the base of the thumb over the third, proximal phalange of the thumb. It is associated with the powers of emotions, feelings, and raw energies of vitality, virility, and sexuality, and qualities of sensuality, warmth, passion, desire, love, hatred, sympathy, euphony, harmony, and grace. The name has been given by one writer to the ring (Apollo) finger.

Via lascivia: Some refer to this as the line of poison, allergy, or addiction. Others may say it depicts excesses of sensuality, eroticism, or perversion. Two different lines have been identified with the title. Newcomer-Bramblett refers to the erotic nature of the line and describes it as running from upper Luna or upper Mars to an area between Luna and Venus after passing through the plain of Mars. This might easily be mistaken for a liver or health line. Fenton and Wright describe the more commonly recognized form as being a line that runs from Luna toward Venus, and they associate it with poison, sensitivity to drugs, and food allergies. It may also be associated with addictions. It could also be confused with a travel line or another health line.

Voyage lines: See *travel lines*.

Watch glass nails: See *hippocratic nails*.

Widowhood line: See *spinster line.*

Winter: In traditional Chinese palmistry, this refers to the area of Neptune on the palm just above the wrist. Its color is black. As one's eye becomes trained, one will detect slight variations of color tones on the palm. These shadings will run from light colors, that indicate a white covering, to reds and darker colors such as greens and blacks. When observing the hand for favorable upcoming seasons, one looks for these hints of color variation.

Worry lines: Horizontal lines across the mount of Venus, of significance to the subject only when they reach the life line.

Wrist wrinkles: See *rascette.*

X: Considered a favorable line marking if there is no horizontal line to impede its forces.

Yang: This refers to the right side and is considered as reflecting the male principles and characteristics. The yang hand (right) is connected through the nervous system to the left side of the brain.

Yin: This refers to the left side and is considered as reflecting the female principles and characteristics. The yin hand (left) is connected through the nervous system to the right side of the brain.

Zones: This is another term to refer to an area of the hand. The zone of thenar eminence is generally the mount of Venus and part of Neptune. The zone of hypothenar eminence is the opposite part of the hand, the mounts of Luna and Pluto and some Neptune. The zone of the superior transverse line generally includes the mounts of Apollo, Mercury, and upper Mars. The zone of the median transverse line (head line) generally includes the mounts of Jupiter, Saturn, and lower Mars. Parts of the plain of Mars can be in each zone.

BIBLIOGRAPHY

I have used or had available the following books for the preparation of this publication. I believe the material in this book will serve well enough for a reading list as I have tried to give credit to each author for his or her ideas as expressed in this book. Please refer to the endnotes. I regret and apologize for any errors I may have made.

Abayakoon, Cyrus D. F. **Astro-Palmistry: Signs and Seals of the Hand.** New York: ASI Publishers, 1975.

Altman, Nathaniel. **The Palmistry Workbook.** Wellingborough, Northamptonshire: Aquarian Press, 1984.

——. **Sexual Palmistry.** Wellingborough, Northamptonshire: Aquarian Press, 1986.

Altman, Nathaniel, and Andrew Fitzherbert. **Career, Success and Self Fulfillment: How Scientific Hand-reading Can Change Your Life.** Wellingborough, Northamptonshire: Aquarian Press, 1988.

Andreasen, Nancy C., M.D., Ph.D. **The Broken Brain: The Biological Revolution in Psychiatry.** New York: Harper & Row, 1984.

Asano, Hachiro. **Hands: The Complete Book of Palmistry.** Tokyo and New York: Japan Publications, Inc., 1985.

Ayer, V. A. K. **Palmistry for Pleasure and Profit.** Bombay: Taraporevala Sons, 1962.

——. **Sariraka Shastra: Indian Science of Palmistry (the Kartikeyan System),** 2nd ed. Bombay: D. B. Taraporevala Sons, 1965.

Bagga, Amrita. **Dermatoglyphics of Schizophrenics.** New Delhi: Mittal Publications, 1989.

Barsley, Michael. **Left Handed People.** Originally published as **The Other Hand.** North Hollywood, Ca.: Wilshire Book Co., 1979.

Bashir, Mir. **Palmistry: A Pocket Guide to the Lines in Your Hand; How They Reveal Your Past — and Your Future.** New York: Dell, 1968.

Battley, Harry. **Single Finger Prints.** London: His Majesty's Stationery Office, 1930.

Behari, Bepin. **Myths and Symbols of Vedic Astrology.** Passage Press of Moroson Publishing, Salt Lake City: 1990.

Benham, William G. **The Benham Book of Palmistry.** Preface by Rita Robinson. A reprint of **The Laws of Scientific Hand Reading.** North Hollywood, Ca.: Newcastle Metaphysical Classic, 1988.

——. **How to Choose Vocations from the Hand.** New Delhi: Sagar Publications, 1983.

——. **The Laws of Scientific Hand Reading.** Preface by Rita Robinson. North Hollywood, Ca.: A Newcastle Metaphysical Classic, 1988.

Berry, Theodore J., M.D., F.A.C.P. **The Hand as a Mirror of Systemic Disease.** Philadelphia: F. A. Davis Company, 1963.

Biccum, Gerald E. **Handology: How to Unlock the Hidden Secrets of Your Life.** Hillsborough, Ore.: Beyond Words Publishing, Inc., 1989.

Brandon-Jones, David. **Practical Palmistry.** Reno: CRCS Publications, 1986.

Brenner, Elizabeth. **The Hand Book.** Berkeley: Celestial Arts, 1980.

——. **Hand in Hand.** Milbrae, Ca.: Celestial Arts, 1981.

Bright, J. S. **The Dictionary of Palmistry,** 6th ed. Bombay: Jaico Publishing House, 1984.

Broekman, Marcel. **The Complete Encyclopedia of Practical Palmistry.** Englewood Cliffs, N.J.: Prentice-Hall, 1972.

Cheiro (Count Louis Hamon). **The Language of the Hand.** New York: Prentice-Hall, 1987.

——. **Palmistry for All.** New York: G. P. Putnam's Sons, 1916.

——. **You and Your Hand.** Revised by Louise Owen. New York: Berkley, 1971.

Clanchy, M. T. **From Memory to Written Record, England, 1066–1307.** Harvard University Press, 1979.

Compton, Vera. **Palmistry for Everyman.** Westport, Conn.: Associated Booksellers, 1956.

Costavile, Maria. **How to Read Palms.** New York: Crescent Books, 1988.

Damasio, Antonio R., M.D., **Descartes' Error, Emotion, Reason and the Human Brain**, New York: G. P. Putnam's Sons, 1994.

Davies, Rodney. **Fortune-Telling by Palmistry: A Practical Guide to the Art of Hand Analysis.** Wellingborough, Northamptonshire: Aquarian Press, 1987.

Domin, Linda. **PalmaScope: The Instant Palm Reader.** St. Paul: Llewellyn, 1989.

Dukes, Terence. **Chinese Hand Analysis.** York Beach, Maine: Samuel Weiser, 1987.

Eckhardt, Linnea. **Hands of Time.** Denver: Mission Press Research & Development, 1990.

Fairchild, Dennis. **The Handbook of Humanistic Palmistry.** Ferndale, Mich.: Thumbs Up Productions, 1980.

Fasulis, Mary Loison. **How to Know and Choose Your Men Through Palmistry.** New York: Warner Books, 1984.

Fenton, Sasha. **The Fortune-Teller's Workbook: A Practical Introduction to the World of Divination.** Wellingborough, Northamptonshire: Aquarian Press, 1988.

Fenton, Sasha, and Malcom Wright. **The Living Hand.** Wellingborough, Northamptonshire: Aquarian Press, 1986.

Fitzherbert, Andrew. **Hand Psychology.** London: Angus & Robertson, 1986.

——. **The Palmist's Companion: A History and Bibliography of Palmistry.** Metuchen, N.J.: Scarecrow Press, 1992.

Friedman, Alan F., James T. Webb, and Richard Lewak. **Psychological Assessment with the MMPI.** Hilsdale, N.J.: Lawrence Erlbaum Associates, 1989.

Frith, Henry. **Palmistry Secrets Revealed.** Edited by John Malcolm. North Hollywood, Ca.: Wilshire Book Co., 1952.

Gardini, Maria. **The Secrets of the Hand.** Translated by Judith Spencer. New York: Macmillan, 1985.

Gettings, Fred. **The Book of Palmistry.** Triune Books, London, 1974.

——. **The Hand and the Horoscope.** London: Triune Books, 1973.

——. **Palmistry Made Easy.** North Hollywood, Ca.: Wilshire Book Co., 1973.

Gibson, Litzka Raymond. **How to Read Palms** (revised edition). Hollywood, Fl.: Fell Publishers, 1989.

Grady, Yvette. **Hand-Picked Men.** New York: Hippocrene Books, 1989.

Grendahl, Spencer. **Romance on Your Hands: Palmistry for Lovers.** Simon & Schuster, 1990.

Haft-Pomrock, Yale. **Hands, Aspects of Opposition and Complementarity in Archetypal Palmistry.** Switzerland: Daimon Verlag, 1992.

Hansen, Darlene. **Secrets of the Palm.** San Diego: ACS Publications, Inc., 1985.

Hilarion. **Body Signs.** Ontario: Marcus Books, 1982.

Hipskind, Judith. **The New Palmistry.** St. Paul: Llewellyn, 1994.

——. **Palmistry: The Whole View.** 2nd enlarged ed. St. Paul: Llewellyn, 1983.

Ho, Kwok Man, Martin Palmer, and Joanne O'Brien. **Lines of Destiny: How to Read Faces and Hands the Chinese Way.** London: Rider & Co., 1986.

Hoffman, Elizabeth P. **Palm Reading Made Easy.** New York: Simon & Schuster, 1971.

Hoffman, Enid. **Hands: A Complete Guide to Palmistry.** Gloucester, Mass.: Para Research, Inc., 1985.

Hutchinson, Beryl. **Your Life in Your Hands.** London: Sphere Books, 1969.

Jaegers, Beverly. **Beyond Palmistry: The Art and Science of Modern Hand Analysis.** New York: Berkley Books, 1992.

Jaegers, Bevy C. **Hand Analysis Fingerprints and Skin Patterns — Dermatoglyphics.** St. Louis: Aries Productions, 1974.

Jaquin, Noel. **The Hand Speaks: Your Health, Your Sex, Your Life.** New Delhi: Sagar Publications, 1973.

——. **The Human Hand.** Published in India as **Practical Palmistry.** Bombay: D. B. Taraporevala Sons & Co. Private Ltd., 1964.

——. **Practical Palmistry.** Originally published as **The Human Hand.** Bombay: D. B. Taraporevala, 1964.

——. **The Signature of Time.** London: Faber & Faber, 1940.

Judson, Horace Freeland. **The Eighth Day of Creation: The Makers of the Revolution in Biology.** New York: Simon & Schuster, 1980.

King, Francis. **Palmistry: Your Fate and Fortune in Your Hand.** New York: Crown, 1987.

Kuhne, Frederick. **The Finger Print Instructor.** New York: Nunn & Co., 1917.

Laffan, M. N. **Handreading.** New York: Kegan Paul, Trench Trubner, 1931.

Larson, J. A. **Single Fingerprint System.** New York: D. Appleton, 1924.

Lawrance, Myrah. **Hand Analysis.** West Nyack, N.Y.: Parker, 1967.

Lehman, Leona. **The Key to Palmistry.** N.Y.: Bell Publishing, 1959.

Levine, Roz. **Palmistry: How to Chart the Lines of Your Destiny.** Simon & Schuster, 1992.

Logan, Jo. **The Prediction Book of Palmistry.** Poole, Dorset, England: Javelin Books, 1985.

Loye, David. **The Sphinx and the Rainbow: Brain, Mind and Future Vision.** Boulder: Shambhala, 1983.

Luxon, Bettina, and Jill Goolden. **Your Hand: Simple Palmistry for Everyone.** New York: Crown, 1983.

MacKenzie, Nancy. **Palmistry for Women.** Warner, 1973.

Marieb, Elain N., R.N., Ph.D. **Human Anatomy and Physiology.** The Benjamine/Cummings Publishing Company, 1989.

Martini. **Palmistry at a Glance.** Baltimore: I & M Ottenheimer, 1953.

Mavalwala, Jamshed, ed. **Dermatoglyphics: An International Perspective.** The Hague: Moulton Publishers, 1978.

Millimaki, Robert H. **Fingerprint Detective.** Philadelphia: Lippincott Company, 1973.

Morgan, Jean-Michel. **Palmistry: The Art of Reading Hands.** Translated by David Macrae. Barcelona: Ariane Books, 1975.

Mowrey, Daniel B., Ph.D. **The Scientific Validation of Herbal Medicine.** Cormorant Books, 1986.

Mumford, Ethel Watts. **Hand-Reading Today.** New York: Frederick A. Stokes Company, 1925.

Napier, John. **Hands.** Not a palmistry book but a scientific book on hands. New York: Pantheon Books, 1980.

Newcomer-Bramblett, Esther. **Reading Hands for Pleasure or Profit.** Austin, Texas: Woods Publications, 1982.

Niblo. **The Complete Palmist.** North Hollywood, Ca.: Newcastle Publishing, 1982.

Ockene, Robert M., ed. **Cheiro's Complete Palmistry, from the Words of Count Louis Hamon.** New Hyde Park, New York: University Books, 1968.

Oldfield, Harry, and Roger Coghill. **The Dark Side of the Brain: Major Discoveries in the Use of Kirlian Photography and Electrocrystal Therapy.** Longmead, Shaftesbury, Dorset, U.K.: Element Books, Ltd., 1988.

Powell, Jemma. **The Stars in Your Hand.** New York: Macfadden-Bartell, 1971.

Psychos. **The Mystery of Your Palm.** Philadelphia: David McKay.

Raymond, Pearl L. **Palmistry Explained.** New York: Vista House, 1958.

Reid, Lori. **The Female Hand: Palmistry for Today's Woman. Wellingborough, Northamptonshire: 1986.

Reid, Lori. Family Matters, Palmistry. London: Artillery House, 1990.

Rem, Henri. What Your Hand Reveals. New York: E. P. Dutton, 1922.

Renald, Joseph. Hands of Destiny: Your Life's Fate in the Lines of Your Palm. New York: Greenberg, 1931.

Robinson, A. The Graven Palm. Herbert Jenkins Ltd., 1924.

Robinson, Rita. The Palm: A Guide to Your Hidden Potential. Van Nuys, Ca.: Newcastle Original, 1988.

Saint-Germain, Comte C. de (Edgar de Valcourt-Vermont). Practical Palmistry: Hand Reading Simplified. Mokelumne Hill, Ca.: Health Research, 1970.

——. The Practice of Palmistry for Professional Purposes. London: Newcastle Publishing, 1973.

Schaumann, Blanka, and Milton Alter. Dermatoglyphics in Medical Disorders. New York: Springer-Verlag, 1976.

Scheimann, Eugene, M.D. The Doctor's Guide to Better Health Through Palmistry. New York: Parker Publishing, 1969.

Scheimann, Eugene, M.D., and Nathaniel Altman. Medical Palmistry: A Doctor's Guide to Better Health Through Hand Analysis. Wellingborough, Northamptonshire: Aquarian Press, 1989.

Siedel, Hanry M., M.D.; Jane W. Ball, R.N., C.P.N.P., Dr. P.H.; Joyce E. Dains, R.N., Dr. P.H.; G. William Benedict, M.D., Ph.D. Mosby's Guide to Physical Examination. Illustrations by George J. Wassilchenko. St. Louis: C.V. Mosby, 1987.

Sen, K. C. Hast Samudrika Shasta: The Science of Hand-Reading Simplified. Bombay: Taraporevala Sons, 1960.

Shepherd, Gordon M., M.D., D.Phil. Neurobiology, 2nd ed. Oxford University Press, 1988.

Sheridan, Jo. What Your Hands Reveal. New York: Crown, 1963.

Sorell, Walter. The Story of the Human Hand. Bobbs-Merrill, 1967.

Spier, Julius. The Hands of Children. New Delhi: Routledge & Kegan Paul, 1955.

Spong, John Shelby. Rescuing the Bible from Fundamentalism. San Francisco: HarperCollins Publishers, 1991.

Sprong, Edo. Hand Analysis: The Diagnostic Method. New York: Sterling, 1991.

Squire, Elizabeth Daniels. The New Fortune in Your Hand. New York: Fleet Press, 1960.

——. Palmistry Made Practical: Your Fortune in Your Hands. North Hollywood, Ca.: Wilshire Book Co., 1979.

Sussan, Nancy Frederick. Palmistry: All Lines Lead to Love. New York: Lynx Books, 1988.

Tabori, Paul. The Book of the Hand: A Compendium of Fact and Legend Since the Dawn of History. Philadelphia: Chilton, 1962.

Talbot, Michael. The Holographic Universe. New York: HarperCollins Publishers, 1991.

Thomson, Peggy. On Reading Palms. Illustrated by Dale Payson. Prentice-Hall, 1974.

United States Department of Justice, Federal Bureau of Investigation. The Science of Fingerprints: Classifications and Uses (Rev. 12–84) U.S.G.P.O.

Van Alen, Rita. You and Your Hand. New York: Greystone Press, 1948.

Warren-Davis, Dylan. The Hand Reveals. Rockport, Mass.: Element Books, 1993.

Webster, Richard. Revealing Hands: How to Read Palms. St. Paul: Llewellyn, 1994.

White, Carol Hellings. Holding Hands: The Complete Guide to Palmistry. G. P. Putnam's Sons, 1980.

Wilson, Joyce. The Complete Book of Palmistry. New York: Bantam Books, 1985.

Wolff, Charlotte. The Human Hand. New York: Alfred A. Knopf, 1943.

——. Studies in Handreading. Preface by Aldous Huxley. New York: Alfred A. Knopf, 1937.

Yaschpaule. Your Destiny and Scientific Hand Analysis. Petaling Jaya, Selangor, Malaysia: Heinemann Educational Books, 1982.

INDEX